QUESTIONING AND DISCUSSION

A Multidisciplinary Study

edited by

J.T. Dillon

ABLEX PUBLISHING CORPORATION
NORWOOD, NEW JERSEY

Printed in the United States of America.

Library of Congress Cataloging-in-Publication Data

Questioning and discussion: a multidisciplinary study / edited by
　J.T. Dillon.
　　p.　cm.
　Bibliography: p.
　Includes indexes.
　ISBN 0-89391-442-8
　ISBN 0-89391-493-2 (ppk)
　　1. Questioning. 2. Discussion. 3. Interdisciplinary approach in
education. I. Dillon, J.T.
　LB1027.44Q46　1988
　371.3'7—dc 19
　　　　　　　　　　　　　　　　　　　　　　　　　　　87-33355
　　　　　　　　　　　　　　　　　　　　　　　　　　　CIP

Ablex Publishing Corporation
355 Chestnut St.
Norwood, NJ 07648

Contents

CHAPTER I

A Multidisciplinary Venture Into Questioning and Discussion

J.T. Dillon

School of Education
University of California
Riverside, CA. 92521

The study that ended in this book began in a footnote. The final note of an article on "the multidisciplinary study of questioning" (Dillon, 1982) invited interested readers to write to the author. Two ventures resulted. One is a multidisciplinary journal on questioning, *QUESTIONING EXCHANGE* (published by Taylor & Francis). The other is the multidisciplinary research project reported in this book.

This project endeavors to enhance the multidisciplinary pursuit of questioning and discussion. Accordingly this chapter introduces the content of the book and the character of the study.

CONTENT OF THE BOOK

The book reports a multidisciplinary study of questioning and discussion in classrooms. Scholars from divergent perspectives here join in analysis over the same classroom transcripts.

The chapters are grouped into two parts according to broad analytic perspective: disciplinary and pedagogical. Each part has six chapters of analysis followed by a chapter reviewing all six. Each chapter analyzes the same transcripts in a different way, using various concepts, methods, and findings.

In Part I, scholars analyze the classroom transcripts from various disciplinary perspectives. These are, in order of chapters: philosophy, sociolinguistics, social psychology, logic, cognitive-developmental

1

psychology, and organizational psychology. The next chapter reviews these six analyses, from a broad disciplinary perspective—e.g., implications for understanding and studying questioning and discussion.

In Part II, classroom researchers analyze the transcripts from various pedagogical perspectives, concentrating on certain features of practice. These are, in order of chapters: the types of discussions and questions used in the classrooms; questions and wait time in the interactions; questions and responses; questions and arguments; group processes; and questioning and student initiative. A final chapter reviews these six analyses, from a broad pedagogical perspective—e.g., implications for teaching and teacher training in questioning and discussion.

The division of chapters is a contrivance, reflecting in part the plan of study that led to this book. The substance is not divided. All the chapters do the same generic thing. All authors, whether disciplinary or pedagogical, are concerned with practice and understanding. Furthermore, the authors all know one another and each other's analysis of the transcripts. They have not written discrete chapters in isolation, to be gathered only in this book. They have twice rewritten consciously interrelated chapters after mutual exchanges and discussion of one another's perspectives. Above all they are united on a common topic and common issues, moreover on a single subject-matter in common.

From start to finish the book has one and the same concrete subject matter, a set of five transcripts from secondary classrooms. The transcripts are reproduced in the Appendix for ready reference. (Originally they were produced for another study reported in Dillon, 1981.) Since it is the business of each chapter to analyze these transcripts, readers can use the Appendix to follow the text—referring to the classroom and the specific exchange being described, understanding and comparing the different analyses in various chapters, and conducting their own analysis if desired.

The convention for referring to these transcripts is to cite the teacher's initials and the utterance number. For example, the 19th through 22nd exchanges in teacher HK's class is cited as HK, 19–22. Authors also refer to the classes by the topic under discussion, as "in the history discussion" or "in MK's discussion on smoking." Thus a shorthand way to keep the classes in mind is to know the topic plus the teacher. These and other classroom characteristics such as class size are conveniently summarized in Table 1 in the Appendix. By contrast, the characteristics of *questioning and discussion* in these classrooms are described in each chapter.

On these accounts, readers can start anywhere in the book and make good sense of it. They can continue here and there in any order, following their interests and pursuing the interrelations among chapters. One convenient approach is to start with the two short chapters (8 and 15) that summarize and review the twelve analyses; or the analyses may be read first and the reviews thereafter as a way to recollect and compare the analyses.

At some point readers will find it useful, probably necessary, to read the transcripts in the Appendix. One approach is to concentrate on one, or one at a time, selected classroom of particular interest; for example, reading the transcript until familiar with that class and then perusing the diverse analyses of that one discussion.

In general, readers will find that the five discussions are recognizably distinct and that the twelve analyses render this distinction in mutually complementary ways. This suggests one systematic use of the book: to collocate the diverse features that individually and severally characterize each of the classrooms, each feature displayed differently in each of the five classes. The result is a matrix for analyzing any instance of discussion and for evaluating its practice.

This systematic use makes these divergent perspectives, their differing concepts, methods, and findings into a useful whole. The whole is an encompassing conception of classroom questioning and discussion. Its use is to enhance understanding and practice. That is a multidisciplinary approach. Readers may easily take this approach to the book because the authors have arduously taken that approach to the study.

CHARACTER OF THE STUDY

The study took a multidisciplinary approach in view of enhancing, not only questioning and discussion, but also the methodology of multidisciplinary research. In that respect it was planned from the start as a venture, a trial, something of an experiment. Everyone may adjudge the public results in this book. A description of the study, together with commentary on selected features, will reveal the background for understanding the book and also perhaps some of the foreground for undertaking other multidisciplinary ventures.

After a preliminary phase lasting one year, the study proceeded over a period of four years through a series of planned phases eventuating in this book. Along the way the researchers produced three versions of their analyses, continually receiving written evaluations, and twice meeting as a group to discuss their divergent perspectives over the common subject matter.

Preliminaries

The project started one year before the researchers actually began to do their first analysis of the transcripts. The preliminaries began with conceiving and announcing the project, as noted. They continued with the usual activities of planning and scheduling; defining the common subject matter and generic issues; consulting the methodological literature on inter- or multidisciplinarity; examining the publications of potential participants; selecting and inviting participants; and producing the materials for analysis. The final preliminary was to distribute the materials so that participants could begin to analyze them.

Amidst all of these, the process of selecting participants deserves comment. The criteria were *interest as a person* as well as *competence as a scholar*, so that participants would give promise of becoming congenial colleagues in a collaborative endeavor that, being in addition a multidisciplinary one, promised to strain collaboration. An overall criterion was *diversity of perspective*. Efforts failed to engage individuals from certain desired perspectives such as anthropology and curriculum theory. No effort at all was made to solicit "big names" for the project, nor to exclude little-known researchers. As a result the roster of participants numbers less-established scholars as well as prominent ones, female as well as male colleagues, and overseas as well as American researchers— each coming from a different tradition of theory, research, and practice.

The final roster was established before the invitations were issued, through a long process of individual negotiations with potential participants. At that point all participants received formal invitations simultaneously. The invitation included a chart showing who the other participants were, which perspective they represented, and how they were grouped for study, as well as including the schedule of phases and activities for the whole span of the project. In that way everyone could accept formally in fair knowledge of the commitment to actual collaborators and mutual roles.

Once everyone had accepted and all acceptances were announced, the project proceeded to its first substantive phase—the initial analysis of the transcripts.

Analysis

Each from his/her own perspective, participants analyzed the same concrete subject-matter, the set of five classroom transcripts. Then they exchanged their papers through the mail.

At the start of this phase, all participants received in a simultaneous mailing a package of identical materials for analysis: audiotapes and transcripts of the five classrooms, plus two tables of data describing the classrooms. Three generic issues were posed for all to address in analyzing this common subject matter:

1. How shall we *conceive* of these conversations, and how do we *describe* them?
2. What part do questions and questioning play?
3. What can we learn from these about educative processes?

Over the next months, each participant proceeded to analyze these transcripts, following his/her interests and customary ways of doing research—perspective, concepts, methods, data, format and so forth.

On a set date a year later, participants exchanged their papers through the mail. The simultaneous exchange brought to each researcher a dozen other analyses of the very same thing. These were not merely twelve different analyses. They were analyses from twelve divergent perspectives, each differing from the individual's own.

Once everyone had read everyone else's analysis, all were faced with appreciating and accommodating a dozen different perspectives over one and the same thing.

Revision

Each participant undertook to revise his/her analysis in light of the analyses contributed by others in the project, and in response to numerous written critiques or evaluations. Then all again exchanged papers on a set date.

The task of revising was manifold. Each paper could well be revised in its own right, as always is the case. And, as is usually the case in a collaborative endeavor, each paper could well be revised in light of the others. But in addition, this was a multidisciplinary enterprise. Each paper had to be revised to take into account not only a dozen other papers but also a dozen divergent perspectives. Moreover, the adjustments were mutual. Lastly, the subject matter for analysis was not general; authors did not talk about anything they chose to under some vague theme. The subject and the discourse was specific and concrete—*these* five transcripts in common. Each researcher was constrained to face multiple unfamiliar concepts, methods, data, and conclusions about the very same thing that he or she had just analyzed in detail.

To help everyone with this manifold revision, a comprehensive process of evaluation was provided at this and subsequent stages by "external" and "internal" reviewers. In the planning phase, referees had been engaged to contribute, anonymously, a series of nine distinct evaluations. (They too had received the classroom transcripts.) Written critiques were supplied for the individual papers, for the sets of papers (disciplinary and pedagogical) and for the whole collection of papers. Each paper, whether in the disciplinary or pedagogical set, was evaluated both by a disciplinary scholar and by a classroom researcher. Each evaluation assessed the paper both as an individual and as a member of its set, suggesting improvements for the paper in its own right and in light of the others. To enhance the mutuality of revision, each participant received not only the several evaluations of his/her own paper but also the various evaluations of the other papers in the set and the evaluations of the sets of papers.

Internal reviewers supplied still further evaluation. The project director sent written critiques to each participant (but not copies to others) as each paper was received at each stage. The authors themselves contributed written evaluations of the various papers, circulating critiques among themselves. Finally, some participants met to evaluate their papers as a group.

The character of these evaluations deserves comment, for few were general or brief. Whatever the norm in academic exchanges, these critiques were detailed, specific, and long—up to five and six pages of single-spaced type for a single paper, not to mention longer commentary on a set of papers. These naturally entailed further exchanges as well as revision of the paper. As for the anonymous reviews, authors were not expected to change their paper as suggested by each and every point of each reviewer. Rather, the assignment was to take these points into account, addressing them in some way. Two broad ways were indicated. One was to rewrite accordingly. The other was to append to the revised manuscript a discussion of those points not incorporated in the revised text. When again the papers were exchanged, again they were distributed as before to the reviewers.

Conference

Then for three days the whole group of researchers foregathered in closed conference to discuss their perspectives. No papers were presented, no lectures given. Papers had already been twice exchanged, read, and commented on.

The conference was held in a wooded retreat called Wingspread, generously provided by The Johnson Foundation. Participants met daily in several plenary sessions interspersed with small-group sessions. A set of issues would first be identified in a plenary session; next, small groups would discuss different issues or all groups the same issue; then the results would be discussed in a plenary session.

Participants also met in other ways thought critical to a collaborative endeavor that was additionally a multidisciplinary one. The schedule provided for meals and refreshments in common, and times for strolling and sitting in various groupings. The conference itself began with hospitality, dinner, and prolonged social hour. All of that was planned on the view that people had to come to know one another, precisely in order to appreciate and then to discuss and to accommodate their divergent perspectives as a group. In another kind of conference, these social affairs are niceties; they may come later, or not. In a multidisciplinary conference they are necessities. They must come first and they must plan to involve the whole group as well as willing pairs. The proof is seen in the process of discussion that follows, and in the fruits that the discussion yields.

On that point two earlier moves proved useful. One was to distribute near the start of the project a collection of autobiographies written by each participant according to a common outline or set of topics—including nonacademic aspects of the *curriculum vitae*. As a result, affinities were discovered and interests or curiosity piqued. Long before the conference, participants had engaged in other exchanges over other matters apart from papers and critiques; while papers and critiques were exchanged with enhanced receptivity. No one wanted to miss this conference where personalities and papers would join in discussion. There the collegial process nicely ensued as participants found themselves attending to one another in a new effort to appreciate divergent understandings and a new willingness to re-form their own twice-analyzed and publicized position. All of that proved in addition the earlier criterion of selection, for these interesting persons and competent scholars had now become congenial colleagues.

Symposium

Next the participants proceeded to form a public symposium at an annual meeting of the American Educational Research Association. There they presented their analyses in three two-hour sessions, one session each for the disciplinary, pedagogical, and methodological perspectives (which do not figure in the book). Each presenter spoke only for ten minutes, so as together to allow for a full hour's discussion with the audience in each session. Also to facilitate discussion, the audience was supplied with a pamphlet outlining the symposium as a whole, describing the classrooms involved, and excerpting the transcripts being analyzed by the presenters.

Evaluation in this phase of the project was contributed by the audience's remarks and through the prior process of applying for a place on the Association's program. Three anonymous reviewers from AERA provided written evaluations of the proposed symposium, and various officials of the Association passed on the proposal at successive levels. Lastly, the participants joined over dinner afterwards to share their evaluations.

Revision

Yet again the participants revised their papers, now taking into account the fruits of the conference and the symposium. This third version was also written in view of composing a book. For a third time the papers were exchanged on a set date.

Publication

In the normal process of publication, the papers were reviewed both in house and externally, then edited as chapters. The public product of the study is this book.

The book counts 20 authors but the study numbered many more participants. The following colleagues also count as participants, whether as analysts or as reviewers at various stages: *John Caputo* (Chaffey College, CA); *August Flammer* (Bern); *Judith Green* (Ohio State); *Ulf Lundgren* (Lund); *Dennis O'Brien* (Rochester); *Hugh Petrie* (SUNY, Buffalo); *William Reid* (Birmingham, England); and *Nick Smith* (Syracuse). Conversely, two of the authors are also counted among these "other" participants apart from their writing a chapter: *William Wilen* (chapter 8) and *William Knitter* (chapter 15) earlier served in addition as anonymous reviewers. Furthermore, Knitter, O'Brien and Smith also presented papers at the AERA symposium, in the third "methodological perspectives" session that reflected the third part of the research project itself while not forming a third part of this book.

That serves only to acknowledge those colleagues who figured as participants without also figuring as authors here. People other than participants also made various contributions to the project, while various participants also made other contributions.

Other features

Those researchers who are pondering a multidisciplinary venture might be encouraged to learn that no grant and no institution funded this research project. People did it by themselves, as it were.

Indeed, in certain cases participants had to work on the project outside of the appointed place, time, and task of their employment, much as a personal hobby. In other cases, some participants quietly covered out of their pocket certain expenses of colleagues, while others personally bore certain project expenses. In general, each participant found ways to support his/her research and other participation through, for example, the normal support services provided by a University. As noted, The Johnson Foundation generously hosted the whole group during its conference at Wingspread. Nonetheless, participants had to find ways of getting there and housing themselves. All of that serves to indicate the commitment that participants felt towards the collaborative endeavor.

It also reveals the importance of continually providing for social and interpersonal contacts among participants. As a result, for example, the people as well as the work are found to be engaging. Further it shows the importance of the double criterion that potential participants be interesting persons *as well as* competent scholars— neither without the other. To collaborate with people who see things in much the same way is one thing. A multidisciplinary endeavor can strain collaboration. People must first lean to appreciate multiple divergent perspectives, then bend to accommodate; they adjust their perspective, not just change a few words in their paper. Various nonacademic ways of fostering collegiality throughout a project prove critical to a multidisciplinary endeavor.

Maintaining continual contact also helps. In this project there were more than two dozen participants from various countries as well as different disciplines, working their way together through a number of phases over a few years' time. Keeping everyone together and on the move entailed sending to the group 30 periodic circular letters, and writing 300 letters to individual participants. As a way of enhancing group cohesiveness, some of the circular letters would give news of various participants, their activities and thoughts; in that way parts of individual exchanges became a group possession and people got to hear of others. Nonetheless, collegiality on all sides is difficult of arrangement, and hard for everyone to adhere to through it all.

Group cohesion and movement is also facilitated by mailing various group documents. In addition to the package of materials for analysis (the transcripts, tapes, and tables), these included the simultaneous invitation; a collection of biographies of participants; frequently mailed schedules of phases and activities over the whole project; charts of participant roles and categories, also frequently sent; a directory of names and addresses of participants, sent at every step; suggestions for agenda and procedures for the conference; the formal proposal for the AERA symposium; the pamphlet to use in the AERA sessions; the prospectus for the book; and the various reviews of the papers. Two manuscripts were also mailed as a general contribution to the group endeavor: one an analysis of the transcripts; the other a review on questioning and discussion, showing how the previous work of various participants contributed to a grander scheme. Both papers were appropriately published elsewhere (Dillon, 1984, 1985). The key group documents were the papers themselves, mailed by participants in successive versions to everyone at once.

Finally, three helpful publications on interdisciplinary methodology were mailed for group instruction. These were an article on the epistemology of interdisciplinary inquiry (Petrie, 1976); a chapter on the development of an interdisciplinary research project in forestry (Baermark & Wallen, 1980); and the preface to a special journal issue on literacy, detailing how authors and editors worked to develop a multidisciplinary perspective on that topic (Glasman, Koff, & Spiers, 1984). Some instructive points from the two earlier sources had been taken as good advice while planning this project. The three sources were mailed to participants at apt times, *after* their first analysis, as a way to offer instruction and encouragement in the ongoing endeavor. These sources are also commended to future endeavors in multidisciplinary research.

CONCLUSION

This venture brought divergent perspectives to bear on a single subject matter and common issues, in an effort to enhance the understanding and practice of questioning and discussion. The effort also bore on the methodology of multidisciplinary research. These are two activities deserving of a try.

Discussion and multidisciplinarity are much esteemed processes that are little understood and practiced, not alone in education. The instances studied here are taken from education, but the processes might well reach to good effect across fields and throughout society. Here is one venture to advance the multidisciplinary pursuit of questioning and discussion.

ACKNOWLEDGEMENT

Preparation of this chapter was supported in part by an intramural grant from the Academic Senate of the University of California, Riverside, CA.

REFERENCES

Baermark, J. & Wallen, G. (1980). The development of an interdisciplinary project. In K. Knorr, R. Krohn, & R. Whitley (eds.), *The social process of scientific investigation.* Dordrecht, Holland: Reidel, 221–235.

Dillon, J.T. (1981). Duration of response to teacher questions and statements. *Contemporary Educational Psychology, 6,* 1–11.

Dillon, J.T. (1982). The multidisciplinary study of questioning. *Journal of Educational Psychology, 74,* 147–165.

Dillon, J.T. (1984). Research on questioning and discussion. *Educational Leadership, 42* (3), 50–56.

Dillon, J.T. (1985). Using questions to foil discussion. *Teaching and Teacher Education, 1,* 109–121.

Glasman, N., Koff, R., & Spiers, H. (1984). Preface. *Review of Educational Research, 54,* 461–471.

Petrie, H. (1976). Do you see what I see? The epistemology of interdisciplinary inquiry. *Educational Researcher, 5* (2), 9–15.

PART I

DISCIPLINARY PERSPECTIVES

CHAPTER 2

A Philosophical Analysis of Discussion

David Bridges

Homerton College
University of Cambridge
Cambridge, England CB2 2PH

DISCUSSION AND THE DEVELOPMENT OF UNDERSTANDING

This chapter sets out to offer some *qualitative* criteria by reference to which one might judge whether a classroom discussion had been a good one—and then to apply them to the five examples of classroom discussion offered in James Dillon's transcripts (Appendix). But how can we establish such qualitative criteria, how can we decide what is a 'good' discussion, in a non-arbitrary way? The approach I adopt here is to derive criteria for a good discussion from an analysis of the central purpose or purposes of discussion. The analysis forshortens argument rooted in theory of knowledge and social philosophy which I have developed more fully elsewhere (Bridges, 1979). Though it is Aristotelian in style, I believe the qualified way in which it is expressed avoids some of the problems which confront Aristotle's own naturalistic/teleological approach.

So, why do we engage in discussion and, more specifically, why do we promote it in the educative setting of a classroom? What is its point or purpose? As a number of correspondents have warned me during the course of my preparation of this paper[1] I must beware of being over-prescriptive as to what *the* purpose or purposes of

---

[1] My acknowledgements are due in particular to Frederick Lighthall for this warning. I hope my attempt to deal with it is not over-laboured.

discussion are. Plainly, discussion provides a whole range of opportunities for the development of understanding, skills, attitudes and personal and social values which one might hold to be educationally significant (Bridges, 1979, chaps. 2 & 3). Teachers may perfectly intelligibly therefore promote discussion in the classroom primarily for the purpose of extending their pupils' articulacy of language,[2] their understanding of each other, their sensitivity to others' concerns in the negotiation of policy, their appreciation of democratic values and processes, etc. At any one time the activity may be guided by one or more of these purposes (or other more personal and idiosyncratic intentions). It follows that one might similarly evaluate a discussion at any one time in terms of its effectiveness or otherwise in promoting these kinds of developments. They provide criteria by reference to which one can judge the quality of the work of the group. However, there is one set of purposes which seem to me to occupy a special place in any discussion. One cannot simply "discuss" or "have a discussion." Discussion is always discussion of, about or on *something*. There is always a subject, question, matter or issue which is 'under discussion.' That the activity falls apart if there is not something which the group recognises as the subject of the discussion is a matter of logical necessity as well as (comfortingly) practical experience.

Groups of people talking about something may of course stand in different relationships with their subject matter as to each other. Some will treat it playfully for entertainment and amusement as in certain kinds of conversation. Some will have a concern to convert members of a group to a particular opinion on the matter under discussion as in certain kinds of debate, argument or proselytizing. Some will be trying to come to a judgement or decision about what ought to be done on the matter before them—as in certain kinds of committee or planning meetings. Some will simply be trying to understand better the matter which is the object of their attention (perhaps as a preliminary to the decision making already referred to). There are other possible relationships, but these will do for the present purpose.

Now it seems to me that it is this last kind of relationship which has special educational significance. Education ought to have rather more to do with the development of understanding than with either amusement or conversation—and in so far as it is concerned with

---

[2] c.f. the Woods' contribution to this collection which reports work which is centrally concerned with the extent to which a child is able and enabled to be "forthcoming and loquacious."

decision making this too in an educative setting ought to demand enlarged understanding.

Further I think that discussion is *usefully* distinguished from conversation, from debate from argument and a number of other forms of group talk by reference to, among other things, concern with the development of knowledge, understanding or judgement among those taking part.

I have presented briefly here some arguments in support of these preferences—the first explicitly evaluative in educational terms the second a matter of conceptual clarity. However readers of this paper do not have to accept either position in order to proceed, though those with some sympathy for them may well proceed with greater optimism or enthusiasm! Faced, as we in this collective endeavor have been, by a number of classroom episodes in which teachers were handling groups of youngsters talking—i.e. episodes in which group talk was deliberately promoted in an educational setting— one of the questions we might reasonably ask ourselves is "what evidence is there here of a concern for the development of the understanding of those participating in the session?" This is not to presuppose that such development was the conscious or unconscious intent of any member of any of the groups—we don't know from the evidence supplied what their purposes were. Nor is it to presuppose that it is the only quality that one might look for in group talk in general or those episodes in particular. There are plainly others.

So my weak rationale is: here is a question which we might ask and I happen to be interested in asking it. My stronger argument is: here is a question which is always of central relevance in evaluating group talk in an educational setting and more especially anything which is offered as an example of discussion.

QUALITY IN UNDERSTANDING

My central question is then "what evidence is there here (i.e. in the transcripts) of a concern for the development of the understanding of those participating in the session?" But what is actually meant by 'the development of understanding' requires some explanation. In particular I want to distinguish between developments which have to do with the enrichment of understanding and those to do with its refinement.

I include under the notion of the *enrichment* of an individual's understanding: fuller elaboration, formulation or awareness of one's own thinking which comes from reflection, self-examination and perhaps even the requirement to articulate one's ideas to others. ("How can I know what I think until I hear what I say?" asked E.M. Forster); and the fuller awareness and appreciation of other people's ideas—especially those which offer different perspectives to one's own. I include under the notion of the *refinement* of understanding a number of developments which have to do with making that understanding more precise, more rational and, where applicable, more correct: clarity of understanding, the more precise perception of the relationship between ideas; a concern for and appreciation of the reasons, evidence and arguments supporting or contradicting opinion; the elimination of logical inconsistency and contradiction in one's thinking and the development of coherence and consecutiveness—ingredients perhaps of what Richard Peters (1966) referred to as 'the impersonal normative order or value system' represented by developed systems of human thought.

Let me set out my stall in bald terms. I want to claim that classroom discussion might reasonably be expected to serve one or more of the functions of enrichment or refinement of understanding set out above.³ Whether or not this is intended, these functions can serve as criteria against which a certain kind of quality or success of the discussion can be judged. One can ask "To what extent do participants develop a fuller awareness and appreciation of others' ideas?" "To what extent do participants develop a concern for or appreciation of the reasons, evidence and argument relating to the matter under discussion?" etc.⁴

This then is the framework of expectation which I want to apply to James Dillon's transcripts. In this case of course we have no very

---

³ It is relevant to consider to what extent the same discussion can logically or psychologically serve both purposes simultaneously. John Elliott (1973) has employed a distinction between what he called "reflective" and "argumentative" discussion which has some similarity with the distinctions I am observing here. According to Elliott, argumentative discussion presupposes, and therefore can only apply, where there is some consensus upon the procedures by which judgements can be verified or falsified. Reflective discussion, by contrast, seeks understanding of among other things the variety of standards and criteria which people apply in their defense and criticism of judgements. In my search for evidence of a concern for the "refinement" of understanding in discussions in the transcripts I have not however assumed a consensus upon what rational demands or criteria are applicable—I have merely sought evidence of people applying *some* such demands or criteria in discussion.

⁴ c.f. Thomas Russell's chapter on questions and authority for arguments in this collection. The second question which I pose here invites a search for evidence in the transcripts of the kind that Russell takes as an indication that the teacher is concerned to establish an opinion on the basis of "rational" rather than "traditional" authority.

direct means of knowing what were the outcomes of the classroom episodes in question. We have only a rather partial form of evidence of what went on during the lessons which were recorded. This being the case, I propose to consider what evidence we have in the transcripts of a *concern* for any of the qualities of discussion I have indicated—exhibited by either the teacher or the students. What evidence can we find of:

1. *reflectiveness*—a concern that students should be thoughtful, reflective, and searching in their self-awareness;
2. *responsiveness*—a concern that students are sensitive, appreciative, and open-minded in response to the opinions of others;
3. *diversity*—a concern that an appropriate variety of perspective is made available to the group;
4. *clarity*—a concern for clarity and precision in the expression of meaning;
5. *evidence*—a concern for reasons, evidence and argument;
6. *consistency*—a concern for coherence, consistency and consecutiveness in thought and argument?

THE TEACHERS' CONCERN TO DEVELOP QUALITY OF UNDERSTANDING THROUGH DISCUSSION

What I propose to consider first is what indications there are in the transcripts of *teachers* demonstrating a concern for quality of understanding through their management of the discussions. To this end I shall focus on the kind of interventions which teachers make in the discussion and to what extent they demand, invite, call for, reinforce, draw attention to, or show concern for reflectiveness, responsiveness, diversity, clarity, evidence, or consistency in students' discussion.

In asking these questions I am not of course particularly concerned with offering judgement on the classes in question. I hope rather that the analysis will help to illustrate the kind of qualities which we might, and if I am right we should, look for in group discussion.

MK's class discussion of senior smoking privileges (see Appendix) is perhaps a useful place to start. For MK has a series of interventions which appear to be encouraging, by example as much as anything else, attentive and respectful listening, a certain amount of reflectiveness, and some diversity of opinion—in other words the kind of qualities which I have associated with the enrichment of understanding. Let me offer a brief commentary on the ten teacher interventions (MK 3a–12a) which seem to me to be revealing of this concern. I shall pick out simply what appear to be the significant phrases.

3a   Like what, say? (He calls for an example)

4a   Let me ask you something . . . (In his manner here as elsewhere he indicates real interest in what his students have to say.)

5a   No, I didn't ask that . . . (He demands close attention to what precisely was being asked.)

6a   You know, the way I understand the problem is—and correct me if I'm wrong . . . (He wants to offer a definition of the problem but shows sensitivity to the danger of imposing his own definition on the group. The invitation in this case sounds genuine though we don't really know whether the group would in practice feel able to challenge the definition.)

7a   Well, what if they said . . .

8a   Well, what if they say . . .
(He invites hypothetical thinking about alternative scenarios).

9a   O.K. I can understand that
(He shows himself as—and perhaps thereby encourages others to be—an open-minded and receptive listener.)

10a   What do the people—the rest of the seniors in here who don't smoke—what do you say to Joe? . . .
(He invites other opinions.)

11a   Does anybody else have anything to say to Joe and to Mark . . .
(Again opening it up.)

12a   Well, you—let me respond to that . . .
I hear a senior class saying . . .
(Expresses—cf. 4a above—a close and serious attention to what he believes his class is trying to communicate.)

In the next sequence of questions (MK 14a–17a) the teacher tries hard, but without much success, to get the group to consider what would be a more specifically Christian approach to the situation. But if it is sensitive attention to each others' ideas that he wishes to encourage, he gets his reward in the penultimate extract (MK 19a) when a student reflects:

I remember something you said Larry (Larry = Teacher), a while ago—I think it was right at the beginning of class . . .

MK's contributions to the discussion show some evidence of concern for sensitive listening, concern to allow a diversity of viewpoint to be expressed and, minimally, some concern to encourage thoughtfulness. What is almost entirely missing however from the teacher's intervention is any evident concern for the refinement of his students' thinking—any pressing demand for reasons, evidence or argument, any harsh tests of the consistency with which they could defend the principles embodied in their statements, any expectation that their meaning may be subject to serious analysis. But then the episode begins (MK la) with the invitation, "Does anybody have any strong feelings about . . . what happened . . . ?" Does this deliberately indicate a temporary suspension of the demands of rational argument in deference to the expression (rational or otherwise) of feeling?

I would guess that many teachers would take the view that if they are to get youngsters talking at all in class they do indeed have to suspend many of the demands of rational argument. No doubt there is something of a developmental process which has to be worked out here—one cannot expect everything at once. Nevertheless we are here reading a transcript of a discussion among a group of 17–18 year olds. If it is still too early to introduce into the process of discussion at this stage the demands of *rational* argument, one must begin to question what has happened before.

If my reading of the text is correct, MK does show some kind of concern for developing the quality of discussion and understanding of his class. I find no evidence of this concern in the transcript of SN's class discussion of sex in homelife (Appendix). The teacher's interventions here mainly take the form of echoing or rephrasing (to no great advantage) what someone has just said. Variations on the phrase "So you're saying . . . "occur six times (SN 3a, 10a, 15a, 18a, 21a, 27a).

The group does share something of its experience, though, despite the teacher's attempts to be pretty relaxed about the whole topic, the students sound uncomfortable and they rarely (cf. the following discussion in WB's class) expand about their experience. I find myself wondering (though we simply don't have the data here to answer the question) whether an informal chat among members of the class without the presence of the teacher might not have contributed more to their understanding.

I recognize however that in applying my rather demanding criterion of quality to this discussion (not only to this but perhaps especially so) I may be looking for too much too soon. I can readily accept (as both Lighthall and Dillon have suggested in correspondence) that SN has more limited objectives in this extract, at this stage and in the context of discussing emotionally sensitive issues. It may well represent a considerable achievement in this classroom simply to elicit some kind of testimony on these issues from so many pupils. The *improvement* of the quality of thought and understanding can come later. The teacher is not necessarily unconcerned with these qualities, merely concerned at this stage with some necessary preliminaries to their development. This seems to me to be a perfectly plausible interpretation. It is perfectly compatible with my observation of the lack of evidence, in the extract we have been offered, of a concern for the development of understanding *in the terms which I have defined*. If this judgement is correct it probably constitutes more a measure of the limitation of the evidence or (again) the inadequacy of SN's students' earlier schooling rather than any criticism of the teacher himself.

WB's class on parent–child relations (Appendix) stands out from among the other transcripts most obviously because of the length of time for which contributors (both teacher and students) talk— and this in the largest class in the sample. But it is also distinctive for the consistency with which the teacher appears to show a concern for the quality of thought and discussion which is going on.[5] Let me offer a commentary on again what I see as the significant aspects of the teacher's intervention:

1a   I don't think they're totally incompatible, the things you're saying. I just think there are two different ways of looking at them . . . (He then offers his version of what was being said). Does that fit, do you think? . . .
(The teacher shows that he is thinking about previous student statements and trying to relate them to each other—and ends with an invitation to anyone to contradict his gloss. Note however that he seeks consensus from student opinion rather than exploiting a potential opportunity for diversity.)

2a   . . . Why do you think that's important, or necessary, now?
(A relatively rare instance in the transcripts of what appears to be an open-ended search for reasons—which the student does make a serious attempt to provide.)

3a   . . . I think that's, you know, a really clear analysis . . .
(He explicitly picks out and reinforces the fact that the student has given an explanation to support the opinion.)

5a   O.K., good. That's a really good illustration there.
(Again encouragement to a contribution which this time helps to make a point by illustration).

---

[5] I shall not be attempting on the basis of our very limited evidence to discover what are the actual *effects* of this concern except by asking whether there are any echoes of the same concern in students' own contributions, though I am entirely of a mind with Lighthall (this volume) who has suggested this *is* an important question to ask.

6a   How do you mean?
      (He seeks clarification).
7a, 8a, 9a, 10a
      (He enters more substantively into the discussion with questions
      and his own statements.
END All right. I think this is really a good illustration . . .
      (Again cf. 5a reinforcement of the elaboration of a point through
      illustration.)

The number of instances I can point to here are few and the
evidence of transcript (as I shall go on to explain in more detail)
is always ambivalent, but we seem to have an example here of a
teacher who is deliberately and explicitly cultivating certain qualities.
The length of comment he elicits and allows may be an indicator
of the relatively thoughtful and reflective nature of the discussion.
He encourages the elaboration of points through examples; he seeks
clarification of meaning and presses for reasons or argument to
support a case. It is perhaps modest enough achievement and we
have the evidence of a very few contributions from a class of 41—
but it illustrates I think a teacher's concern with both the enrichment
and refinement of thought and discussion.

HK's session on the American Revolution (Appendix) has the
appearance of a concern for quality in the sense of the refinement
of student's thought. 5a, 6a, and 7a all press students to make clear
the *distinction* between two statements; 1a, 8a, 10a, and 11a press
for *explanation* of Washington's success; 9a points out a possible
contradiction between what a pupil said at one stage and what he
said at another; 27a, 28a, 29a, 33a, and 35a called for *definition* or
clarification of what one of the pupils meant when he talked about
"aid" from America's allies.[6]

All splendid evidence of demand for clarity, precision, argument,
and consistency? Perhaps—but perhaps not. The way I interpret the
piece (and it *is* an interpretation) the teacher is quite clear from
the beginning what factual points of history he wants to elicit from
the class and reinforce. As far as I can judge the class is engaged
in the ancient game of trying to work out what it is that teacher is
trying to get you to say.[7] You know that it relates to something that
you are supposed to have read or something that he said last lesson
but you've somehow got to put it into the words he's looking for
or he won't be satisfied.

---

[6] c.f. C.J.B. Macmillan's interpretation of this discussion in his chapter in this
volume. Thus far Macmillan and I agree, I think, but we go on to diverge both in
evaluation and interpretation of the events of this lesson.

[7] cf. Thomas Roby's "quiz show" in his chapter in this volume.

Thus the first part of the transcript (HK 1a–21a) shows the teacher attempting to piece together an answer to the question about Washington's success as a military leader. He gets a number of the ingredients but in the end has to present himself (21a) a full statement embodying the key, "He never permits what little army they had to be destroyed."

The next teaching point is actually prompted by a student's intervention but it nevertheless becomes something the teacher needs to emphasize (in 24a)—that the army broke up periodically as its men went home to farm.

But there is another ingredient of Washington's success he wants to bring out—the question of aid. But what sort of aid? He gets a lot of different responses before we reach (36b) the answer he was apparently looking for—"money"—and so (37a) he elaborates on this theme.

Soon after this we enter a phase of the class which has something to do with the importance of propaganda, disreputable tactics and/ or breaking the conventions of warfare. I'm not sure what he's after here because the transcript ends in midstream but I'd bet that just around the corner we will find out.

Now all this may be unfair. We would need to ask the students in the class for their account of what was going on if we really wanted to confirm or contradict my interpretation. What I am suggesting however is that we have an illustration here of what is sometimes referred to as the 'guessing game' in which students have to use a variety of clues provided by the teacher's questions (and along with this, typically, a whole battery of nonverbal clues) to give them indications of what it is that he has in his mind. Fairly rapidly in these circumstances the understanding which is cultivated is an understanding not so much of history but of that area of study in which school children develop a rarely equaled or acknowledged expertise—the mentality of teachers.

PR's class on the multiple personality of Eve White/Black/Jane (Appendix) is one that I find is even more difficult to interpret. It begins with a good deal of recall of the story of the character in question and then returns (10a) to the question of how this person might be helped. The teacher's questions which follow (15a–23a) seem to be encouraging evaluation, analysis reference to evidence, explanation. The teacher's summary (26a) seems to respect the accounts provided by the students and to grow out of them. Then (27a) the teacher invites a different 'model' or analytic approach: ". . . You're working—we're working on one model now aren't we . . . I wonder if there are others."

The teacher appears then to have a concern for thought and analysis and/or the application of previously taught or read ideas. However the ideas themselves, as expressed by the class, seem to be dangerously oversimplified and barely understood—to the extent that they inhibit rather than support any aspiration towards the cultivation of real understanding on the topic under discussion. In short, though the teacher's questions suggest that he has a concern to develop quality of understanding the conceptual apparatus which the students are required to use seems to me to stand in its way.

THE STUDENTS' CONCERN FOR QUALITY IN DISCUSSION

I have focused so far on the evidence provided by the teachers' contributions to the discussion of their concern for quality of understanding of one kind or another. But one criterion of success in cultivating discussion in the classroom must be the increasing commitment of students to the same qualities to the extent that they not only respond to the teacher's demands for certain qualities in discussion but themselves make those same demands on each other (and indeed on the teacher). Thus we might hope to find examples of students pressing for clarification ("Can you explain what that means"); evidence ("How do you know?"); sensitivity to the contributions of other members of the group ("I think what Carol said was really important"); consistency ("But how does that fit with what you were saying earlier?"), etc. What evidence of this sort of behavior can we find among student responses?

In practice I think we have very few examples. The only discussion in which there was any real challenge offered to expressed opinions—or indeed any real disagreement at all (?)—was in MK's class on senior smoking privileges. One student points out an apparent inconsistency: "Then why do they let the teachers smoke?" (MK 2b) And another asks a student contributor for clarification: "In taking them away, you mean?" (MK 3c). There are one or two examples in the transcripts of students seeking clarification of the teacher's question—(MK 8b). "What's the difference?" (SN 5c). "Are you talking about when we were kids?" But would I be right in observing that, this apart, there is *no* evidence in the transcripts that these students are themselves taking responsibility for cultivating quality of argument in their discussion?

In fact the problem—if that is what it is—goes further. The students have in practice very little share in the management of the discussion at all. The agenda, the issues raised, the questions asked are almost exclusively in the hands of the teacher. The questions people ask in a discussion are not the only means by which the agenda for that discussion is shaped but they nevertheless provide a rough and ready indication of who is calling the tune. As the Woods argue in their contribution to this volume, "children do not ask questions because they are inhibited from taking control of the teacher. After all, he who questions dictates how his listener will spend the next few cognitive moments as well as what they will say." A comparison of the number of questions asked in each case by the teacher and the students is quite revealing:

	HK	MK	PR	SN	WB	Total	Ratio
Teacher Questions	59	16	20	15	6	116	5.8
Student Questions	3	9	4	3	1	20	1

Only in the case of MK's class did students play anthing like a significant part in shaping the focus of discussion with, for example, questions thrown out for anyone to pick up: "Why can't you just smoke cigarettes in this school?" (MK 1f) and, almost uniquely in the transcripts, a question addressed by one student to another "Barb, what do you think of narcs?" If students are given so little sense of 'ownership' of the discussion, it will not be surprising if they do not develop much sense of responsibility for its quality.

CONCLUSION

I offer my analysis or, better, my interpretation of the transcripts with considerable misgivings. Three reservations in particular are perhaps worth noting because they relate closely to some of the other contributions to this volume.

First, I am acutely conscious of the limitations of transcript material as evidence—especially where one is trying to read it for clues as to the hopes, aspirations, or intentions of those whose words only (and then not all of them) are recorded. In this respect I share, with Frederick Lighthall in particular (this volume), some concern about our need to "de-contextualize" data. In particular—since it has been people's concerns, intentions and purposes (i.e. mental phenomena) with which I have been primarily concerned—I feel the absence of the kind of data which I might have been able to collect from interviews with the teachers and students concerned, through asking *them* to interpret for me what was going on. "Why

did you ask this question here?" I might have asked the teacher—
and then of the students "Why do you think the teacher asked that
question? How did you interpret it? What effect did it have on you?"
Given this kind of evidence *some* of the ambiguity in the transcript
might have been resolved, though different kinds of ambivalence
would no doubt have been introduced—but I might have been more
sensitive to the realities of the classroom as perceived by those who
were actually party to the discussion in question, and we would
have had the opportunity at least to negotiate the terms of my
analysis and evaluation.

In the absence of this opportunity I have perhaps used the transcripts to illustrate and explain the kind of evaluative framework
which I have argued might be applied to classroom discussion rather
more than I have used the evaluative framework to illuminate
Dillon's transcripts. (In this I believe I have good company.)

Secondly, I have experienced over the years increasing ethical,
professional and methodological anxieties about the kind of research
which makes the teacher the passive object of a study rather than
that which engages and supports the teacher as a researcher in his
or her own classroom. I have in mind the example of the British
Schools Council/Nuffield Humanities Curriculum Project, the U.G.C.
Project on Small Group Teaching in Higher Education, and the Ford
Teaching Project with which I have been associated. Within our
own group in this volume Eileen Francis' Discussion Development
Group and Todd Kelley seem to be closest to the spirit of research
which, in terms of the status it accords to teachers' own perceptions
and the responsiveness and intimacy of the relationship between
research and practice, has the potential for the kind of professional
enhancement which I would seek to cultivate.

My third reservation about my analysis is that it fails to provide
a developmental perspective. To Eileen Francis (this volume) the
kind of criteria I have applied look simply overambitious. She has
pointed out, quite properly, that before we get oversophisticated
about the quality of children's talk in discussion, we must at least
secure some quantity—we must get them talking (and listening). It
must be possible further to refine this elementary developmental
perspective. I am sure that the new Piagetian approach that Irving
Sigel (this volume) brings to our collaboration has enormous potential.

Notwithstanding these reservations, I hope my commentary will
serve to highlight certain principles and general observations which
I can perhaps best serve by expressing finally in their baldest and
most readily contradicted form:

1. that we ought in arranging discussion classes in school to have a concern with the quality of thought and understanding which is being cultivated;
2. that central to this cultivation of quality is a concern for the *enrichment* of understanding through the development of reflectiveness, responsiveness and diversity of perspective in discussion; and a concern for the *refinement* of understanding through the demand for clarity, evidence and consistency in argument;
3. that the transcripts reveal uneven but on the whole rather little evidence of teachers' commitment to these concerns and negligible evidence that students are actively supporting them in their contributions to the groups.

I suspect that this last observation has all sorts of implications for the earlier development of students' experience in group discussion; the size of the groups which teachers are trying to involve in discussion; the kind of subject matter which lends itself to discussion and the development in teachers (including experienced teachers) of skills in discussion leadership. But there will be those closer to the classrooms depicted in the transcripts than I am who can more sensitively explore these implications if—and only if—they are persuaded of the rightness of the principles and the correctness of the interpretation I have offered.

REFERENCES

Bridges, D. (1979). *Education, Democracy, and Discussion*, Slough, U.K.: Nelson. [Now only available from David Bridges, Homerton College, Cambridge, England.]

Elliot, J. (1973). Neutrality, rationality, and the role of the teacher, *Proceedings of the Philosophy of Education Society of Great Britain*, Vol. VII, No. 1, Oxford: Basil Blackwell.

Peters, R.S. (1966). *Ethics and Education*, London: Allen and Unwin.

CHAPTER 3

A Sociolinguistic Analysis of Discussion

Mary Thomas Farrar

*Frontier College,
130 Clergy St. E.
Kingston, Ontario, Canada*

Over the past twenty years, sociolinguistic analysis of classroom discourse has become an increasingly respected method for gaining insight into classroom life. The field is varied: approaches have been developed from a number of disciplines including philosophy, linguistics, sociology, psycholinguistics, and anthropology, combining ideas from these fields with ethnographic techniques to develop some understanding of the effects of social contexts on the verbal interactions of the classroom. The basic purpose of sociolinguistic studies has been to show how reality is constructed through social interactions.

In this sociolinguistic study of the Dillon transcripts (see Appendix), two analyses were conducted. The first was a very detailed qualitative analysis of the data that combined examination of paralinguistic features with three perspectives. A *speech act analysis* served to identify certain linguistic features of a given utterance as well as offer some account of speaker intention. A *conversation analysis* examined the position of the utterance in the discourse, its relation to prior and subsequent turns at talk and the manner in which an utterance was understood by the hearer. The third form of analysis, termed the *interactional analysis*, combined researcher conceptions with the results from the two earlier methods in an effort to interpret the transcripts more intelligibly and usefully. (For the underlying assumptions, strengths and limitations of each of these approaches and the rationale for combining them, see Farrar, 1981; 1984.)

The second was a more quantitative analysis. Here, the relative frequencies of various verbal interactional patterns, the use of topic control and other conversational management factors were tabulated and compared. See Table 1.

The results of these two kinds of microanalysis revealed three distinct models of discussion: discussion as course-covering, discussion as integrating, and discussion as expressing. Each model was then examined and compared with the others in four respects: (1) *centeredness* (subject-centered or student-centered talk); (2) *topic control* (tight, intermediate, or loose); (3) predominant use of certain verbal *interactional patterns;* and (4) *characteristics* (talk about text-based facts and explanations or feelings and opinions; features such as deliberative thinking, backtracking, etc.). Each lesson was then coded both ideally according to Roby's (this volume) formulations, and actually according to how microanalysis of the data suggested.

It was concluded that it is useful to conceptualize discussion in three models. The three models provide a framework for examining and differentiating among alternate modes of classroom interaction. Although no tight one-to-one match between each model and one specific verbal interactional pattern was discovered, there did seem to be a strong connection between each model and the predominant use of a small range of verbal interactional forms.

Following a description of the transcript conventions used, each of the five transcripts is examined in turn. First a sample qualitative analysis is presented. This is followed in each case by the quantitative analysis. Finally, in the summary, the analyses are compared and the implications for education discussed.

TRANSCRIPT CONVENTIONS

The transcript segments analyzed were coded originally by J.T. Dillon for the purpose of comparing relative frequency of teacher questions and teacher statements, percentages of higher and lower cognitive utterances, and gender differences in contribution frequency. Because the data were collected and numbered for these purposes, certain coding and transcription difficulties became apparent when a qualitative analysis of the same material was to be conducted. First, teacher turns coded as 1a, 2a, etc. were identified simply as questions or statements. This terminology was retained though more specific terminology is more revealing. Specific terms, however,

Table 1. Three Models of Discussion

Model of Discussion	Discussion as Course Covering	Discussion as Integrating		Discussion as Expressing
Centeredness	Subject-Centered	Integration of Subject-Centered and Student-Centered		Student-Centered
Focus	Explicating facts and explanations	(Predominantly subject-centered) Integrating facts and explanations with reflection based on theory and experience	(Predominantly student-centered) Integrating expressions of feelings, opinions and observations into some structural framework.	Expressing
Topic Control	Tight	Intermediate		Loose
Predominant Verbal Interactional Patterns	Teacher controlled questioning sequences	Statement/comment patterns Long teacher turns including positive evaluation moves, integrating statements and/or questions and possibly suggestions re future talk		Non-directive reflective statements Student/student exchanges
Characteristics	Searching for text-based facts and explanations	Deliberative thinking including backtracking, reviewing, revising, comparing, contrasting Critical reflection Responsiveness Using evidence and argument to support positions Articulating		Expressing feelings, opinions and observations Making unexamined generalizations Ideosyncratic sallies

(continued)

Table 1. (Continued)

Model of Discussion	Discussion as Course-Covering	Discussion as Integrating		Discussion as Expressing	
Roby Coding of 5 Lesson Types	Recitation	Problematic	Dialectic	Permissive Discussion	Bull session
Coding of the 5 Analysed Lessons	Recitation (HK)	Partial problematic (PR)	Partial dialectic (WB)	Permissive discussion (SN)	Bull session (MK)

seemed unnecessarily technical for the present project because the simpler vocabulary is in keeping with that of the other researchers on the project and, though more general in nature, is sufficient to convey the nature of the utterance. Overlaps are marked by square brackets. A slash indicates a pause of less than ½ second as timed with a stopwatch while dots indicate a pause of ½ second. Periods have been eliminated for purposes of clarity. Rising and falling intonation have been marked with rising and falling arrows respectively and stressed words have been underlined.

HK (THE RECITATION LESSON)

General Description of the Lesson

This is a recitation lesson dominated and controlled by the teacher question. According to Good (1983), a recitation lesson is a "traditional learning exercise and teaching procedure in which students repeat orally or explain material learned by individual study or previously presented by the teacher and in response to questions raised by the teacher." To use Roby's (this volume) terminology, it is a "quiz show". Students are being asked to recall previously studied facts and state explanations. The style is demanding and probing, not praising or supportive. The teacher uses questions to cover course content—to introduce topics and to request clarification. The subject matter is cognitive rather than affective. Previously studied facts and explanations for those facts are sought. For this teacher, discussion seems to be the joint achievement by student and teacher (through teacher questions and student responses) of text-relevant facts and explanations. In short, the model evident here is discussion as course-covering.

Paralinguistic Cues

The teacher's voice is high-pitched. The pace is fast. (There are 64 exchanges in the 10-minute segment.) Sometimes the teacher questions contain pauses and hesitations, at other times not. Pragmatic particles like "you know" do not occur commonly. There are variations in intonation and stress. The teacher's voice is not monotonous. The tone seems agitated, aggressive and businesslike for the most part though there is a curious tone change when the teacher is responding to student questions. Here the voice is low-pitched and the tone seems quieter and more intimate.

Qualitative Analysis

The first four exchanges were chosen for the sample analysis as they seemed to typify this lesson. They are as follows:

1a: What . . . ah . . . I want to go to another question about his/ military capabilities What was it/that made him/militarily successful? What <u>was</u> it about his <u>strategy</u>⌊/that enabled him to be successful? . . .⌊ Howard ↑

1b: He didn't fight straight out like the British/⌊

S: No he didn't

1b: He fought behind/brick walls, trees and stuff like that

2a: Did you read/anywhere in the book/where his army . . . was destroyed? ⌊

2b: No

3a: That <u>his</u> army/was destroyed ⌊

S No (—?—)

3a: Did you see that anywhere?

S: Uh Uh (—?—)

3a: That Washington's army was destroyed? ↑

3b: Not completely ⌊

4a: Not completely?

S: (—?—)

4a: Tony? ↑

4b: They were <u>outsmarted</u>, but not <u>destroyed</u> ⌊

THE FIRST EXCHANGE

Speech Act Analysis

In the first exchange, the teacher's first move (in 1a) is a statement identifying the teacher's intention to investigate a new topic. The two succeeding moves within the teacher's first turn are questions; they appear to be asking for student responses. These are then followed by a nomination which calls upon one student to respond. The student provides an apt response, stating Washington's strategy.

Conversation Analysis

Conversation analysis reveals that no space was provided for a response following either the initial statement or the first question. Consequently, both of these moves appear to serve as means of introducing the topic rather than actually asking a question intended to receive a response. In contrast, the third question is followed by a pause of one second indicating that a response is being sought.

This indication that the next turn at talk is to be taken by a student is further punctuated by the nomination.

Interactional Analysis

Why might the teacher use such a strategy? It would seem reasonable to suggest that through using a four move turn such as the above, the teacher allows the students time to reflect on the new topic at the same time as he avoids embarrassing silences and maintains control of the talk.

EXCHANGES NOS. 2, 3 AND 4

Speech Act Analysis

In the second exchange, the teacher asks a yes/no question. Based on speech act theory, an acceptable response to this presumably direct "Did you read anywhere—?" question should be "yes" or "no." A student responds "no." In the third exchange, the teacher rephrases the question of exchange 2. Again, some students respond with "no" and "uh-uh." Then a third student replies "not completely." The teacher question in exchange 4 repeats the student response "not completely." Rising intonation signals its function as a question as does the subsequent nomination "Tony." This question receives an acceptable response. Speech act analysis is revealing here as a means of explaining why the responses of "no" and "uh-uh" weren't accepted when, presumably, they should have been. By looking at the accepted response of "not completely," one can figure out retrospectively, that the teacher's use of the yes/no question in exchange 2 was indirect and conventional much in the way that one might ask "Can you pass the salt?" expecting not a "yes" or a "no" but an action. Here, the teacher seems to have been asking the explicit ("Did you read anywhere—?") yes/no question as a conventional means of implying the implicit question "What happened to the army when it fought?" But the students answer the explicit question instead.

Conversation Analysis

Typically, in much ordinary conversation, a yes/no question is asked as a presequence as in A1/A2 in the following:

A1:   Are you busy tonight?
A2:   No.
B1:   Would you like to go out?
B2:   Sure.

In the lesson example, following the presequence question "Did you read anywhere—?", the next question the teacher might have asked if a response of "not completely" had not been forthcoming (3b) might have been "If his army wasn't destroyed, what happened when it fought?"

Because the pattern of presequence followed by main question is so common, it has become an accepted convention to merely ask a presequence yes/no question, thereby implying the subsequent question. Some of the students may not have recognized this as evidenced by their "no" responses. Or, they may have recognized it but chosen to answer the explicit question for another reason. (e.g., the implied question may have been too difficult to figure out and/or to answer.) The respondent in 3b, however, has understood that another question was implied as indicated by his response of more than a simple "yes" or "no."

In exchange 4, the teacher repeats the student's prior acceptable response with questioning intonation and then nominates Tony. In this way, the response becomes the subsequent teacher question. The teacher's repetition of "not completely" with rising intonation and the subsequent nomination act as a signal for Tony to elaborate on the meaning of the prior eliptical (incomplete) response and to answer more fully the previous implied question.

Interactional Analysis

Why would the teacher use the ambiguous "Did you read any-where—?"form? It would seem reasonable to suggest here that this ambiguous indirect form is conventionally polite or face-saving. Students are ostensibly being offered the option of answering either the easier explicit yes/no question or the more difficult implicit question. But here instead of really being given such an option, the conventional form is being used with the expectation that students will respond to the implicit question just as one is expected to pass the salt in the example discussed above. Because of the inherent ambiguity in the question form, however, some confusion seems to have resulted. Some students answer the explicit question and the answers are not accepted. Through this technique then, the teacher gives the appearance of being polite and of offering face-saving options while simultaneously demanding more difficult responses.

Another issue is why the teacher might have repeated the student response (3b) in exchange 4. A number of reasons seem acceptable. First, it saves time if the teacher does not have to explicate the implied question. Second, it signals the class that the response "not completely" is on the right track. Third, it probes. The student's response is tacitly positively evaluated in that the teacher's question has moved to new ground while it is also tacitly partially negatively evaluated because it has been deemed insufficient. (cf. Griffin & Humphrey, 1978). Combined positive and negative evaluation such as this could be read as probing and challenging teaching. If such behaviour encourages the student to respond more appropriately, then instruction is facilitated. (It should also be noted in passing, however, that in some settings, some students might find such questioning intimidating. If this were true, instruction would not be facilitated.)

Quantitative Analysis

Predominant Exchange Patterns. The teacher question dominates. Almost all the exchanges consist of one of the following questioning patterns: question/answer, question, question/answer, question/answer/feedback—though sometimes question, nomination/answer, statement, question/answer or a combination of the above are used as in the first exchange where the pattern is question, question, nomination/answer.

Indirect questions (e.g., "Did you read anywhere- - -?") occur in approximately 1/4 (15/64) of the exchanges. This is a conventional device, ostensibly providing students with the face-saving option of having to respond to the explicit question only.

There are a couple of occasions where student questions are directed to the teacher; one is a single question, the other a series of questions and responses.

There is only one occasion where a student comment is based on a prior student comment.

Evaluation

Explicit evaluation is not common. Explicit positive evaluation occurs only seven times in the 64 exchanges.

The most common evaluation form is combined tacit positive and tacit negative evaluation as in, for example, clarification requests (where it is suggested that the response was partially correct but not complete). This type of evaluation is in 14 of the 64 exchanges.

Tacit positive evaluation alone (in the form of a prior student response repeated with falling (accepting?) intonation occurs only four times.

Topic Control

The teacher keeps tight control of the topic mostly by soliciting information in teacher/student question/answer sequences.

He introduces all the topics and is in charge of all topic shifts with the exception of the two occasions of student questions.

To focus topic, he uses question repeats or prior student responses with questioning intonation (clarification requests), rephrasings, and successive questions in one turn.

Typically, a series of exchanges on a topic is followed by a teacher turn that summarizes and consolidates.

The teacher takes a long turn (a) following a series of unsuccessful exchanges and (b) following student questions. These long turns tend to consolidate topic and reestablish teacher control.

In general, it appears that the teacher introduces topics in accordance with a preplanned agenda. The topics so introduced are not contingent, i.e., precipitated by and incorporating prior student comments. However, once a topic is underway, questioning tends to be based on prior student comments as students are requested to clarify and give reasons.

Teacher turns are liberally scattered with connectives like "well" and "so" that mark the connection between prior student comment and subsequent teacher question.

Topic completion is marked by a teacher turn where what has been stated is summarized.

Other Conversational Management Factors

The teacher talks most of the time (59% as coded in the Dillon analysis) and almost all the turns are teacher–student.

He ensures that the class is quiet, that only one person talks at a time.

Student questions and interruptions are rare.

The teacher does not contribute his own personal opinions or feelings or suggest solutions to a problem.

Students are addressed by first name, though formal address ("Miss Edwards") is used on one occasion.

There is no slang, joking or teasing.

There is no backchannel support (e.g., "um hmm").

There is no instance of the teacher talk occurring in the background.

PR (THE PARTIAL PROBLEMATIC LESSON)

General Description of the Lesson

The major focus of this lesson is on explicating a variety of explanatory models, although repeating and explaining previously learned material occurs initially. It is difficult to classify because it seems to have two styles: a fact gathering recitation style and a more intimate probing for explanations style. Roby (this volume) has classed this as a "problematic discussion" because there are apparently many possible explanations for the problem being discussed. At the same time, however, this lesson is not problematic because the acceptable possible solutions seem to be predetermined by the teacher's agenda—the course. In the end, two explanatory models are found (as opposed to the simpler explanations sought to describe events in the recitation lesson), but the lesson as a whole is still fairly strongly dominated by teacher question and topic control. In the first part of the lesson segment, the style is demanding and probing, not praising and supportive. In the second half of the lesson segment, however, a different manner becomes evident, one that seems to convey a joint groping on the part of teacher and student for the explanatory models. Here, particularly in the last five exchanges, both teacher and student turns are longer and the tone is more intimate.

In order to accommodate both styles, the lesson might be described as "guided discussion" following Good (1983): "a method of teaching by which students develop an understanding of the subject matter through discussion of pertinent points related to that subject." This definition is, however, too general to be useful. It seems better to suggest that two verbal interactional styles exist side by side: one, a question/answer style geared to explicate facts, the other more of a statement/comment style geared to eventuate in integrated explanations. The subject matter remains cognitive rather than affective. Once again, the interaction seems to fit a course-covering model. There is a very important distinction, however, between course covering here and in the case of HK (The Recitation Lesson). Whereas the course in the recitation lesson consisted of recalled information and relatively simple explanations, here it seems to consist predominantly of attempts to solve problems and integrate explanations that are thought out in class. In both cases, the teacher seems to have an agenda and part of a course seems to be covered. Therefore, in both cases, discussion can be conceived of as the joint achievement by teacher and student of text-centered facts and explanations though in one case the facts and explanations are actually in the text and in the second case though related, they may not actually be contained in the text. Because of these differences, the lesson has been coded as partial problematic rather than recitation.

Paralinguistic Cues

The teacher's voice is rather high-pitched. The pace seems fairly hurried (There are 28 exchanges in the 10-minute segment). Generally, there are few pauses and repairs. The phrasing is economical and probing. (Pragmatic particles like "you know" occur in his more intimate style.) Most teacher questions are uttered with the falling intonation characteristic of statements. The voice is expressive with changing intonation and word stress patterns. Key words are stressed. The tone seems aggressive, demanding and businesslike and even almost angry sometimes. A sense of urgency is transmitted during the parts of the lesson devoted to recalling facts. There is a marked change in tone and in general verbal style, however, when the teacher and students are working out the explanatory models. Here, the teacher's lower, more intimate, softer tone is accompanied by a number of hesitations, repairs and pragmatic particles.

Qualitative Analysis

The sample analysis here is of exchange Nos. 20–23.

20a: OK/Come on/find it Mike ↓
20b: You'd probably expect to find problems she had at home/you know like mistreatment from her parents
21a: How would/How would that
21b: 'cause ah/that can set up like/insecurity/and she might look for/ ah something else that's inside herself to compensate for that/ so she developed a new personality/you know ↑ . . .
T: OK Ah Darryl ↑
21c: like getting back to the childhood thing (—?—) like see who her idols were?/See where the person had her idols . . .
22a: OK but how would that/if you found out who her heroes/or her idols were/what would that have to do with splitting off into two personalities? Aaah Terrance ↓
22b: Would you/want to try and be like your idol? If/if you you know

if they were/if you idolize someone/you will/more or less want to be like them to a certain point/then like ah/ah if she had ah/an auntie that was shot/ and you know/she admired her for the way she was maybe she'd be shot down as long as she's like her auntie She'll go home and see that her mother's ah you know/a nice housewife/She'd want to be like that/And/go for reality and /(—?—) her friends (—?—) something like that

23a: We all experience what you just said . . . How come . . . ah so it . . . don't we?

S: Yeah

23a: How come she wound up in such a/such a/a (branch?)?

23b: Well would it have been some kind of/ah restrictions in her background that ah/wouldn't allow her to do that/such as her parents not letting her do something/to the point that/she reacted a lot/like ah . . .

24a: Did you see the movie?

24b: No

THE FIVE EXCHANGES

Speech Act Analysis

In exchange 20, the teacher exhorts the students to find out what might have happened in Eve's background to have caused her split personality and then nominates one student, Mike, to respond. Mike responds. In exchange 21, the teacher probes Mike to elaborate his response. Mike responds further. The teacher accepts his response (OK) and then nominates another student, Darryl. Darryl also answers the teacher's question (21a). Again, the teacher accepts (OK) and probes for further elaboration and then nominates Terrance. Terrance responds. In 23a, the teacher makes a statement commenting on Terrance's response, begins a new question, but then interrupts his own question to check for student agreement. Having achieved student agreement, the teacher continues to probe "How come—?" A student responds in 23b. Then, in 24a, the teacher shifts the topic to ask whether the student respondent of 23b had seen the movie. The question receives a negative response.

Conversation Analysis

Conversation analysis offers some insight into the mechanics of this probing style. First, the teacher exhorts the students in a clear imperative to "Find it." Then following Mike's attempt in 20b, he begins a probe "How would/how would that." This probe could be seen as simultaneously accepting the prior response (tacit positive evaluation) and asking for more, thereby indicating that the prior response was insufficient (tacit negative evaluation). Utterance 21a could also be described, however, as an "evaluation withhold" because it indicates that evaluation is being withheld pending the student's explanation. Following the 21b response, the teacher again can be seen as combining positive and negative evaluation, this time explicit positive and tacit negative evaluation, because the response (OK) is accepted but then Darryl is nominated. The nomination of Darryl indicates that the subject is not closed, that more remains to be said and therefore that Mike's response, although partially acceptable, was nonetheless incomplete. In the teacher turn 22a, Darryl's response is treated again in a manner that can be seen as combining positive and negative evaluation. It is first accepted with an OK indicating positive evaluation. But then a subsequent probe and nomination indicate tacit negative evaluation. This too, could be called an evaluation withhold pending student explanation. Following the student's response, the teacher's subsequent evaluation comment "We all experience what you just said" and (following the check for agreement) the probe "How come—?" both act as tacit negative evaluation. Undaunted, however, one student responds in 23b with a response that receives an evaluation withhold, a sidesequence question that will need to be answered before evaluation will be forthcoming.

INTERACTIONAL ANALYSIS

Why might the teacher choose this probing aggressive style of questioning? First, and most importantly, it seems to work. The students seem to be successfully pushed into wrestling with the problem of Eve's split personality. For some students, this aggressive style might seem overwhelming. They might feel intimidated rather than challenged. However, the students who respond in this lesson seem comfortable about trying. Further, it may be that students are capable of and possibly enjoy handling the ambiguity of an evaluation withhold or see the combined positive and negative evaluation as a challenge, as a stimulus for thought.

One curious thing about this lesson was the fact that two verbal interactional patterns seemed to be used. The first was the more probing aggressive style described above. The second was a more intimate, groping style evident in the segment that follows. Exchange Nos. 25–26 exemplify the second style.

24a: Did you see the movie? ↑
24b: No
25a: No . . . OK↑/ah/something like that is suggested in the movie/ that the trauma/was so great . . . that it caused the creation of a new personality ↓ . . . Ah Duane↓
25b: Yeh/It could be that ah/you like/like you want to do something like that you know/go/go with the stronger personality Thinking about it (whether to do it or not) a person you know like is reading a lot of books and stuff like that (He's going to say) "I want to be just like ah/I want to be just like her (—?—)
26a: OK I think you'd have to put that together with trauma/you know that kind of idea that you/that several of you have expressed/put that together with trauma In other words/if you try to imitate/imitate as a little child/your/idols/and you were severely punished for it/this is just one general example/then/ah/ for whatever reasons/you might be forced/to split in two . . . I think that's the only way I can put it together It's been a long time since I read that Aaah Yvonne↓. .
26b: OK um (—?—) OK Isn't it true that/whatever/your/your OK whatever your conscious mind turns out/you subconscious reacts don't it/ Right now say she's saying to herself . . . ahm she's getting in her mind that/she wants to be just like that lady and/ her her subconscious mind's gonna pick up on that and react on that/and she's gonna start acting like a certain person/doing the same kind of things that certain person do/ahm you know She's gonna pick up that personality act that person . . .

THE TWO EXCHANGES (25 AND 26)

Speech Act Analysis

In exchange 25, the teacher refers back to a prior student response in exchange 23 where the student had been discussing Eve's background and then the teacher nominates Duane. Duane's turn is a comment elaborating the teacher statement. Teacher turn 26a is a long integrating turn where he pulls together the notions that have been suggested previously about idols with the notion of trauma. Here, the teacher makes explicit what the idol model is. This is followed by a student comment in 26b elaborating on the notion of imitation the teacher suggested in 25a.

Conversation Analysis

Conversation analysis is somewhat revealing here when one tries to examine further the relations between prior and next turns. Exchanges 25 and 26 seem to be codeable as statement/comment adjacency pairs. A problem with this coding, however, is that it should be based on the relevance between statement and comment. In exchange 25, the student comment does seem to be based on and conditionally relevant to the teacher statement. In exchange 26, however, the teacher presents a rather complex idea—the integration of imitation and trauma—and explicates the idol model. The student comment in 26b, however, is not a comment on the teacher statement of 26a. The student does not discuss the idol model. Instead, the student comment is a further comment on the teacher statement in 25a. In short, the statement/comment form is there, only the comment is not really relevant to the statement as far as the specific topic is concerned.

Interactional Analysis

This demonstrates an interesting feature of exchanges that take the form of statement/comment. Just as in the question/answer format where a student may be responding not to an explicit question but to an implicit question asked a few turns back, so in the statement/comment format, the comment may not be actually specifically topic relevant. This lack of cohesion may indicate a problem associated with speed of thought—a student thinks of a response or a comment a certain time after the initiating question or statement has occurred and in the meantime given the speed of typical exchanges, a new topic may already have been introduced.

Quantitative Analysis

Predominant Exchange Patterns

The teacher question/student answer is the most common exchange pattern, occurring in 10 of the 28 exchanges. Another relatively common form is the teacher statement followed by a teacher question which then receives a response. This occurs in seven of the 28 exchanges. A third common form is the teacher statement/student response. This occurs in eight of the 28 exchanges.

Indirect questions are not common. Questions and commands are direct.

There are three student questions to the teacher. Two of these receive a number of student responses.

Although students talk at the same time on several occasions, these seem to be simultaneous attempts to answer the teacher question, rather than comments on one another's contributions.

Evaluation

The most common forms of evaluation are the combined tacit positive and tacit negative evaluation where the teacher probes for justification of a student response without first stating that the response is either acceptable or not, and the evaluation withhold. These occur in 10 of the 28 exchanges. Tacit positive evaluation occurs six times and tacit negative evaluation seven times. Explicit positive evaluation moves occur five times.

Topic Control

Most of the time, the teacher keeps tight control of the topic by soliciting information in teacher-directed question/answer sequences.

He introduces all the topics and is in charge of topic shifts.

To focus the topic, he uses short clear questions, statements and commands as well as longer turns involving longer statements combined with questions. He may also (a) repeat a response and immediately ask another question, (b) repeat his prior question, (c) ask a clarifying question, (d) take a long summarizing turn, (e) talk loudly in combination with question repetition, (f) ask a student to elaborate, and (g) restate a prior student comment.

After a series of nine exchanges that clarify the facts, a series of eight exchanges that deal with how Eve's problem might be solved and a series of six exchanges discussing Eve's childhood, the remaining five exchanges are used to consolidate and integrate, pulling together what has been stated or suggested previously in the form of explanatory models.

The teacher turns are longer on average in these last five exchanges, integrating prior student comments.

Major topic shifts are related to prior student comment in two cases whereas they seem to be related to the teacher's agenda on the three other occasions.

Connectives like "Well" and "so" and "now" are not common, occurring only three times in the 28 exchanges.

Generally, student comments are related to prior teacher questions or statements rather than to other student utterances.

Other Conversational Management Factors

The teacher talks 36% of the time but teacher/student turns are a relatively high 78% (as coded in the Dillon analysis).

Some background noise is tolerated. When the teacher is vague about the facts in the first few exchanges there is a considerable amount of overlapping student comment. Generally the teacher throws out a question, waits a bit and then nominates. Quite often, a number of students start to respond but the teacher eliminates the noise by focusing the topic.

Although simultaneous student attempts to respond seem to be encouraged, the teacher is quick to eliminate the noise. Student questions and interruptions are not encouraged.

The teacher does not contribute his own perceptions and experiences or offer suggestions as to how problems might be solved though he does identify the idol and conflict models.

Slang occurs on one occasion but the resulting noise is squashed. There is no joking or teasing.

There is no instance of teacher talk occurring in the background.

WB (THE PARTIAL DIALECTIC LESSON)

General Description of the Lesson

This lesson has been coded by Roby (this volume) as an example of a "dialectical discussion" where opposing views are brought to bear. The most striking feature of this lesson segment is that teacher turns are long and include both questions and statements. In addition, all teacher turns are contingent on prior student turns and they all tend to summarize or draw conclusions or to point to similarities and differences—in short to integrate and elaborate on prior student comment. There is also a lot of praise and support of student comments. The subject matter is affective rather than cognitive. Personal experience and real life problems are addressed. Discussion here can be conceived of in two ways simultaneously: first, as expressing relevant feelings, observations and opinions and second, as integrating and elaborating these explicated feelings and opinions into some coherent form—in this case, the dialectically opposed frameworks of parental authority then and now. Because it can be conceived of in these two ways simultaneously, it has been coded as a partial dialectic lesson.

Paralinguistic Cues

The teacher's voice is medium-pitched. The pace seems a little slow. There are only 10 exchanges. Both teacher and student turns contain hesitations and attempts to clarify ideas and pragmatic particles like "you know" and "like." The intonation of both teacher and student turns is falling, characteristic of statements.

Qualitative Analysis

The sample analyzed here is exchanges 8 and 9 and the first part of exchange 10.

8a: All right/How/how do you maintain the respect?/ Ahm Steve was you know that's another problem/ Ahm is there a way to really ask for/the reasons and that sort of thing without being disrespectful?↑/And where your parents can really maintain their/ their decision as your parents/without without/without having to/say Well I said so/that's gotta be the way it is?↓ Do you want to talk about that?

8b: You don't really lose no respect for them/by questioning them/ if they tell you to do something you could ask them why you want to do it/and they'll tell you But if they still want you to do it/you still gotta do it no matter what /No matter what the reasons/if they tell you to do it you gotta do it

9a: So in the end/the respect might come from/ahm accepting their wisdom whether you ahm understand it or not, huh?↑

9b: My parents will say (—?—)
(laughter)

10a: OK ↓ And yet/you know/ as Regina was saying in the past it did tend to be more like that↓/that/parents were considered/ kinda/total authorities and/and/I mean it seemed like it wasn't/ a completely/impossible situation/you know for people to live like that/for you know long times/Ah and yet for us/it just doesn't seem quite right↓/if/if you don't/have at least the opportunity to hear the reasons why/ (—?—)

10b: (—?—)

T: (OK ∧. . . . Chris ↑

10c: (—?—) our family has respect/and all that kind of thing Ahm when my parents ask us to do something like housework/ahm there's no question because you know housework has to be done/And ah/so if it does come to questioning why do they do things/they do (you're free?—?—BELL—) Both my parents they

didn't have ah/you know/when they were children they didn't
have the/strict parents you have to do this/that's it My mother
was in the hospital all her life My father was in an orphanage/
They never had/you know the strict parents So when it came
to us/we were just like/they/treated us as little people (—?—)
I dunno There was always respect/And yet whenever we wanted
it (—?—) you know they like to hear/what we didn't understand

T: OK Good⌋ Tommy ↑

THE FIRST EXCHANGE

Speech Act Analysis

This exchange begins with a teacher turn containing a number of
moves. It begins with an accept of a prior student move. Then there
is a question followed by a statement followed by another question
and an elaborating continuation of the second question. Finally,
there is a third question where the teacher asks whether or not the
student would like to address the issues raised.

Conversation Analysis

Conversation analysis reveals that neither the first question, nor the
second nor the elaboration constitute first pair parts of any adjacency
pair because no response is forthcoming and because no space is
provided following these moves in which a response might occur.
It is equally true, however, that no space is provided following the
final question which does in fact receive a reply. Perhaps then, it
is necessary to examine other features to see what might indicate
that a student response is in order. The teacher's first question "How
do you maintain that respect?", the subsequent statement "Ahm
Steve, you know that's another problem" relate back to the prior
student turn and appear to serve more as comments on the content
of the prior turn than as questions demanding responses. The wording and the placement of the subsequent question asked with rising
intonation "Ahm Is there a way to really ask for/the reasons and
that sort of thing without being disrespectful?" would seem on the
contrary to indicate that it is intended to receive a response as
would the wording and the placement of the elaboration that follows.
It may simply be that when no students seem to be forthcoming
(as indicated perhaps by some nonverbal means not visible on
audiotape such as lowered eyes) the teacher continues questioning

to clarify the topic, to avoid embarrassing silences and to allow the student a little time to think before speaking.

As discussed previously in the analysis of HK, the teacher in the recitation lesson about George Washington appears to have used a similar strategy. And yet though one could say both teachers use a strategy of repeated clarifying questions in a turn, the tone in the two examples is qualitatively different. Why? The most important difference between the two has to do with the relation of teacher turn to prior student turn. In the recitation example, the teacher questions do not build on prior student responses. They come from the teacher's agenda. In the dialectic example, however, the teacher questions and statements are based on the prior response and seem to be an attempt to clarify issues raised by that student. In the recitation example, the questions are short and concise and ask for answers the teacher already knows. In the dialectic example, a number of different responses would be appropriate and there are no right or wrong answers, just statements of personal opinion. Further, in the recitation example, the second elaborative question does not elaborate extensively. In effect, it adds the one focus "strategy." In the dialectic interaction, the elaboration is much more extensive and offers a variety of focuses for subsequent discussion. These differences may account in part for why the response in the recitation exchange is a short factual explanation whereas the response in the dialectic setting is more elaborated. The above comparison points to the danger of suggesting that the use of certain strategies is good or bad or is responsible for causing answers to take one specific form or another. It is not sufficient to look at the effects of specific strategies in isolation from other important contextual features that may also have a bearing on the quality of the response elicited.

Interactional Analysis

Why might the teacher use this technique? First, it is clearly encouraging or conciliatory behavior on the part of the teacher toward the student to allow the topic focus to be based on student contributions, here specifically on the notion of respect. Second, this is the only exchange in the interview where the teacher asks a series of questions. As Dillon has pointed out, question turns are only 40% of this teacher's exchanges. It would appear then, following the question "Is there a way to ask for/the reasons and that sort of thing without being disrespectful?" both the subsequent elaboration ending in falling intonation and containing a number of hesitations as well as the subsequent low key question "Do you want to talk about that?" may function as mitigating devices that serve to diminish the demanding nature of the prior question.

EXCHANGES NOS. 9 AND 10

Speech Act Analysis

Exchange 9 begins with a statement plus tag question checking for agreement. It receives a response that elaborates more than the agreement required. Exchange 10 begins with a teacher accept move of "OK" and then continues with a statement comparing past and present conceptions of parenthood. Following an indecipherable student response in 10b, the teacher accepts it (OK) and then nominates Chris. In 10c, Chris utters a fairly lengthy reply discussing how her parents treat her with respect. Following her response, the teacher accepts it with "OK Good" and then nominates the next student, Tommy. Tommy's turn is also followed by an accept of "OK" and a nomination of Regina. Both Tommy and Regina's turns have not been included in the sample.

Conversation Analysis

Exchange 9 is a question/answer adjacency pair although the question indicated by the tag "huh" is so low key that the exchange could almost as easily be characterized as a statement/comment adjacency pair. In exchange 10, the teacher's turn begins with an accept "OK" of the prior student comment concluding exchange 9. Then the teacher makes a long statement presumably relating the prior student's remark with the response in exchange 2 of Regina who discussed generational differences. The teacher embellishes on what Regina had said by adding that while parents used to be considered total authorities, people lived with that, though for us it doesn't seem right. His long statement is marked by a number of hesitations and pragmatic particles such as "you know" and "I mean." Following an indecipherable student response in 10b, the teacher accepts it and nominates Chris. Chris' turn in 10c is long and elaborate stating that her family has respect, if asked to do housework they do it because it has to get done, that her parents had deprived backgrounds with no strict parents of their own and hence they treat their children as little people but they are willing to listen. Like the teacher's turn in 10a, this turn also has a style punctuated by hesitations and "you know"s. This exchange is difficult to code in adjacency pairs because of the lack of 10b but it is interesting to note that the quality or style of response 10c is very like the quality of the teacher turn in 10a.

Interactional Analysis

Ostman (1981) has noted that when one person begins to use pragmatic particles like "you know," they tend also to be scattered through neighboring turns. It would seem here that the teacher's introduction of "you know"s and hesitations in 10a may have had a part in the student in 10c phrasing her turn as a series of statements also using "you know" a number of times. It is true also, however, that "you know"s are more likely to be included in longer turns where some kind of check that the message is getting through might seem necessary. In any case, this style of communication seems very relaxed and conducive to elaborating on personal experiences.

Quantitative Analysis

Predominant Exchange Patterns. Teacher turns take a variety of forms:

1. a series of statements, a check and a nomination (1)
2. an evaluation, a statement, a question, a statement, a question (2)
3. an evaluation and a question (3)
4. a response to a student question (4)
5. an evaluation comment and a nomination (5)
6. a short clarification request (6)
7. a question, a statement, a question, an elaborative statement and a question, (8)
8. a tag question (9)
9. a series of statements (10)

Questions tend to be related to prior student comments and integrate or clarify or elaborate what was said. They ask for opinion, not facts. Questions are modulated by being interspersed with statements.

Evaluation

Evaluation is not of the correctness of the response. Instead it seems to be more a comment on the appropriateness of the response and how it contributes to the discussion.

Topic Control

The teacher directs flow rather than solicits.

The teacher keeps relatively tight control of the topic.

Topics are not so much introduced as refocused from prior student comments using connectives like "so" and "and yet."

There are no open-ended questions. The teacher/student sequencing is tight. On one occasion, repeated questions are used to focus the topic (8).

Teacher turns are not direct, challenging, probing questions. The questions, when they occur, are modulated in a number of ways: (a) by tags (e.g., "do you think?"), (b) by being preceded by reflective clarifying statements and/or positive evaluation moves and/or expressions of personal opinion, (c) by questions being followed by elaboration of their content and invitations like "Do you want to talk about that?"

This teacher uses summarizing statements. Unlike the other teachers, however, they are short and common, occuring in six of the 10 turns.

The turns at talk are long.

Both teacher and student turns are contingent on (i.e., precipitated by and incorporating) prior turns. But because the teacher turn typically contains comments integrating prior student comments, subsequent student comments tend to be directed to prior student remarks as mediated by the teacher's integrative comments.

Other Conversational Management Factors

The teacher talks 33% of the time but, if one counts teacher nominations as teacher turns then 100% of the turns are teacher–student turns.

There is no noise and rarely simultaneous talk.

Student interruption is not encouraged. In one case it is preempted by the teacher question. In one case, a teacher response follows.

Frequent nominations and evaluations discourage student–student talk. Student comments tend to be addressed to teacher remarks although the teacher remarks incorporate prior student expressed opinions.

The teacher expresses his own personal opinions but not his experiences.

Students are called by first names.

There is no slang, joking or teasing.

Backchannel support is used on occasion (e.g., "um hmm") to encourage a student to continue responding.

There is no fading into the background with this teacher's comments. He never makes a bid to speak that is disregarded.

SN (THE PERMISSIVE DISCUSSION)

General Description of the Lesson

Roby (this volume) has classified this as a "permissive discussion" because taboo subject matter is addressed and students are encouraged to contribute observations, feelings and opinions. The predominant interactional feature of this lesson is the teacher's use of short reflective statements instead of questions. In order to reflect the importance of student contribution and topic direction, a new coding scheme was necessitated: (student)statement/ (teacher)comment/(student)comment. This is markedly different from the typical question/answer/feedback format of the classroom. The teacher's interactional style in this lesson is supportive rather than demanding. The subject matter is affective rather than cognitive. It is centered around personal experience. Because the teacher's role is one of facilitating student contributions, of getting students to express their observations, feelings and opinions, the model here is discussion as expressing.

Paralinguistic Cues

The teacher's voice is medium pitched. The pace does not seem hurried. (There are 29 exchanges in the 10-minute lesson.) There are pauses between and within teacher turns but little use of pragmatic particles. The majority of the teacher comments have falling intonation contours. Though there is not a lot of changing intonation, the talk is not monotonous. The tone is quiet and relaxed.

Qualitative Analysis

The sample analyzed here is of exchange Nos. 14–17.

14a: You all do this together: ↓

14b: Yeah My mother and father and all the rest of us And just like
        he said "control"/In a way I understand because you have to
        . . . specialize what you mean You can't use slang you know
T: Yeah
14b: like/vulgar language
T: Or street language
14b: You can't use that But you can express "What do you mean?
        What is this?" . . .
15a: So there is a time you're saying for questions and answers?⌊
        . . .
15b: Um Hm
16a: Um you seem to feel good about that . . .
16b: In a way yes 'cause (—?—)
T: Larry
16c: That's . . . something like that I think is/is good too because
        it / makes for more openness . . . Members of the family can
        talk in a/sense you know . . .
17a: Helps to tie it up . . .
(Cough and laughter from the class)
17a: (—?—)
S: (—?—)
17a: Ah John ↑
17b: (—?—) Ahm . . . my parents talked
T: Talk louder
17b: They talked to me about this/you know they'd discuss about sex
        and all that. But/I/feel/like ahm/a lot of times I feel uncom-
        fortable talking about sex I know that (—?—)
(laughter from the class)

THE FIRST TWO EXCHANGES

Speech Act Analysis

In 14, the teacher makes a statement clarifying whether or not the
student asked discusses sex with all her family members together,
a clarification based on a prior student response. The statement asks
for agreement or disagreement. In her response (14b), however, the
student agrees "Yeah" and then begins to elaborate on what happens
in the family discussions. The teacher overlaps this response with
"Yeah" on one occasion and adds a clarifying statement "Or street
language" on another. Following the teacher's clarifying statement,
the student continues with two further clarifying statements com-
pleting the response coded as 14b. In turn 16, the teacher makes
another statement, echoing the students responses in 14b and 13c
and again the student agrees.

Conversation Analysis

As has been discussed previously in analysis of prior segments, yes/no questions often serve as presequences to more complex questions and as a result, the very asking of a yes/no question may imply a more complex question. In this case, however, the accepting and simultaneously clarifying statement which also requires a response of "yes" or "no" as an indication of agreement or disagreement also receives an elaborated response as though the statement may also have carried some implicit meaning. If one looks at the content of the elaborated response, however, one can see that it relates back to the content of exchanges 7, 8, 9, and 10, where one student states that talk about sex was controlled and a discussion of control ensues. Hence, instead of a teacher's statement in 14 acting either as a presequence or as having some implicit meaning, it might be more reasonable to suggest that the student in possession of a turn at talk has some other comments relevant to the general discussion that she wishes to add and that given she has the floor, it would be an appropriate time to do so. The student does not take up a similar opportunity in turn 15, however. The teacher's turn 15a is also interesting because of the simultaneous functions it appears to serve. First, it might appear to function as an evaluative feedback comment on the prior student response because it accepts and because it occurs in the evaluation slot. However, because it is a reflective comment, not containing any overt teacher evaluation such as "Good," it seems simultaneously, albeit retrospectively, to turn the prior student utterance into a statement rather than a response, and treat it as a first pair part of a statement/comment adjacency pair which then receives a student evaluation move in the form of an agreement.

Interactional Analysis

The salient question to be asked here is why the teacher makes use of reflective or echoic statements in his turn at talk and why he uses the backchannel supports of "Yeah" and "Or street language" during the student's turn to respond. It would appear that the reflective statement like the implicit question is a polite or face-saving device the teacher uses to encourage student comment. Part of the reason why it may function to encourage student comment is because of the accepting or tacit positive evaluation that occurs simultaneously when an echoic statement is uttered. It could be suggested further that the use of the reflective or echoic statement is even more polite or even less face-threatening than the implicit question because it asks only for agreement or disagreement, nothing more, while it simultaneously accepts what has been said. Backchannel supports are in keeping with this supportive style of using reflective statements rather than questions.

THE SECOND TWO EXCHANGES

Speech Act Analysis

In exchange 16, the teacher begins with a statement saying "You seem to feel good about that." This statement again requires simply a "yes" or "no" response. Again, however, it receives a more elaborated answer. Following the response, the teacher nominates another student who makes two statements expressing his opinion about family discussions about sex. Then in exchange 17, the teacher makes another statement addressing the content of the prior student response. Following a cough and then some laughter and some indecipherable teacher and student comments, the teacher nominates another student "John". John's turn (17b) is interrupted by a teacher exhortation to "talk louder." Then John continues with a factual statement followed by a statement describing his feelings and a third indecipherable remark. Student laughter ensues.

Conversation Analysis

The teacher's comment in 16a addressing how the student feels receives an elaborated response although only a simple "yes" or "no" is required. As in prior cases discussed, it could be argued that this yes/no statement accepting and enquiring into the student's feelings is a presequence to be followed by a "why?" question. Or, it could be seen as a sort of implied statement given that the student responds as if some elaboration was required. It is indeed curious that echoic statements seem to have this effect. Following the nomination, Larry's response (16c) seems to function as an evaluative comment on the prior student responses in 14b, 15b, and 16b. This response contains a number of pauses and is followed by a 4 second pause before the teacher makes a further accepting and clarifying comment in 17a. Because this comment accepts, it can be seen simultaneously as tacitly positively evaluating. Again, as in the case of the teacher comment in 15a, this comment seems to function simultaneously though retrospectively as the second part of a statement/comment pair, initiated by the student in 16b. It is followed by a cough, laughter, and indecipherable comments from students and teacher. Conversation analysis of the rest of exchange 17 reveals no more than the speech act analysis.

Interactional Analysis

The teacher's use of echoic reflective statements could be seen as a skillful device for abdicating control of topic while still remaining in control.

Quantitative Analysis

Predominant Exchange Patterns. A new coding scheme was necessary here to convey the importance of the student contributions and the manner in which they directed the topic. The most common exchange pattern has been coded in the unusual form of (student) statement/(teacher) comment/(student) comment. Typically, these exchanges were initiated by a teacher reflective statement of some sort. They occur in 13 of the 29 exchanges. Typical question/answer exchanges occur in nine of the exchanges while teacher statement/ student comment exchanges occur four times. There are two exchanges where students ask questions for the teacher and one exchange where one student asks another a question.

Evaluation

There seems to be no real evaluation of content. Teacher comments like "O.K." seem instead to be acknowledgements rather then evaluations of student contributions. There are seven explicit teacher acknowledgements of student comments and 10 similar student acknowledgements of student comments (e.g., "Right." "Yeah"). The small number of explicit teacher acknowledgements, however, does not really convey the positive feeling of this lesson because the teacher comments following student statements act as tacit acknowledgements. Even the clarification requests assume a different flavour here because instead of partially positively and partially negatively evaluating the content of a response, they seem to be tacit positive evaluations where the teacher is simply asking for further information which may then be acknowledged further.

Topic Control

This teacher does not keep tight control over the topic.

He introduces the topic prior to the beginning of the taped excerpt and on one occasion responds to a student question about what the topic was by outlining it as nudity, talk about sex, and physical affection.

Students are encouraged to take control of the topic, to elaborate according to their own personal experiences and observations. On one occasion, the topic is focused by the teacher picking up on a student introduced topic and formulating a couple of questions from it. On another occasion, after a pause, he tries to reintroduce a topic by simply stating "What about affection?" On yet another occasion, he remembers a prior student remark and asks for agreement or disagreement. When the teacher tries to move the discussion from "talk about sex" to nudity and physical affection, he does so without much success. The conversation shifts for only one or two exchanges. Mostly, he offers reflective statements and some clarifying questions.

There is very little consolidation and summarization. After a number of exchanges, the teacher simply says "Let's go on to the last topic." Although topics are addressed, no conclusions are reached.

New topics are introduced when the conversation seems to fail (when a pause of three seconds occurred.)

Student comments seem to be successive responses to a teacher utterance rather than really contingent on one another.

Other Conversational Management Factors

This teacher talks 22% of the time though the percentage of teacher/student turns is higher (58% according to Dillon's original analysis).

Only one person talks at a time typically. The reflective statements tend to be directed to one person.

Student interruptions ($3\times$) and student comments on one another's contributions ($1\times$) are rare, as are student questions to the teacher ($2\times$).

The teacher contributes his own personal perceptions and experiences. No suggestions are made toward the solving of a problem—a problem is not really being discussed.

The teacher addresses students by their first names.

There is no slang. Joking and teasing are not common.

Backchannel comments are not common though the reflective comments have the same effect.

MK (THE BULL SESSION)

General Description of the Lesson

Roby has classed this as a "bull session", where participants throw out unexamined opinions, empty generalizations, clichés, and idiosyncratic sallies and where the right answers are unexamined right opinions. The predominant feature of this lesson is the amount of student–student interaction, particularly the amount of student evaluation. The teacher does not seem to be strongly in charge. Clearly, students are encouraged to question, challenge, and evaluate one another's contributions. The subject matter is affective rather than cognitive. Students are contributing their feelings and opinions about smoking rights. As in the case of SN (The permissive discussion lesson), the model of discussion seems to be expressing observations, feelings and opinions. Again, the teacher's role seems to be one of facilitating student contributions–only here (vs. SN) the teacher seems to want to do it as an equal without the authority of higher status (i.e. without being in charge of most of the exchanges.)

Paralinguistic Cues

The teacher's voice is medium-pitched. The teacher's pace seems neither noticeably fast nor slow (There are 19 coded exchanges according to Dillon's classification scheme, though this number is misleading because of the amount of student/student interaction that is not coded as separate exchanges.) Teacher turns typically contain hesitations, though pauses between turns are rare. Pauses following teacher questions 1½–2 second pauses) occur only three times. Similarly, there are only three occasions where pauses (½ second) occur after student contributions. When the teacher takes a long turn, it includes a number of pragmatic particles such as "you know" and "well". The majority of teacher questions and comments have falling intonation. The voice is expressive with changing intonation and word stress patterns. The tone seems somewhat agitated and excited.

Qualitative Analysis

The sample analyzed here is what was coded in the Dillon analysis as the first two exchanges. They are as follows: (Note: There is background noise of students talking throughout the first exchange except at 1d and 1j)

1a: OK Does anybody have/anybody have any feelings [about it ↓

S: [(—?—) on tape

1a: Alright Don't worry about the tape ↓ Does anybody have any/ does anybody have any strong feelings about that/about what happened about the seniors/having their privileges taken away? ↓

1b: I think (—?—)

S: S:Yeh (—?—)

S: Seniors should do what they want

Ss: laughter and noise

1c: Seniors should do what they want [Seniors keep walking off

T: [OK John

1d: If the seniors can't handle it/the juniors will handle it

1e: Oh (—?—) Why can't you smoke? (—?—either)

1f: Why can't you just smoke cigarettes at this school?

1g: Cause it's illegal

1h: Why?

1i: Cause you're a minor

S: Wah

1j: Cause like at Loyola . . . and Loyola is just as strict as this school [you can't um seniors can smoke there

S: [Yeh

1k: Yeh but they probably got a whole lounge

1i: I don't see why just because of what a few kids did the rest of us have to suffer

1l: It's not fair

T: (—/—) environment (—?—) doesn't it?

1m: Yeh just because it's (—?—) problem doesn't mean (—?—) this neighborhood

T: (—?—)

1n: What if you're 18

(Note: There is background noise of students talking throughout the second exchange until the teacher says "Now say that again" following the first part of turn 2c.)

2a: Still can't The reason/the reason we say that if you're 18/is/ because ah if we let/people/who/are/going to school here it'd be kind of a/two-faced/let people who are 18 smoke in front of people who are not 18 and they [smoke

2b: [Then why do they let the teachers smoke?

T: You know personally what I think well

2c: I think the teachers are justified and it's something the seniors have to decide amongst themselves

T: Now say that again

2c: The teachers are justified and it's something the seniors have to decide amongst themselves

THE FIRST EXCHANGE (PARTS 1A-1D)

Speech Act Analysis

In the first exchange, the teacher begins by asking "Does anybody have any feelings—?" and after an aside assuring students they need not worry about the tape, he rephrases his question. An adequate response to this question should be a number of "yes" or "no" responses from students but in addition it receives a series of student comments, related student questions and both teacher and student responses. Following what is coded as 1c, the teacher accepts 1c and then nominates a student who responds subsequently.

Conversation Analysis

Conversation analysis is revealing here as it was in the analysis of HK (the recitation lesson) because retrospectively the teacher's "Does anybody—?" question can be seen as a presequence, one that would typically be followed by a question like "What are your feelings on this subject?" But, because the subsequent question is predictable, the "Does anybody—?" question is read as implying the subsequent question. In fact, as far as can be deciphered, the question receives only one "yeh" response to the explicit question (and even this may be a response to a prior student comment 1b, "I think —?—") Three other responses, 1b, 1c, and 1d answer the implied question.

Interactional Analysis

Typically, a "does anybody" question is not recommended in teachers' colleges because it is seen as an invitation to chaos. Because it invites many students to respond simultaneously, it is seen as threatening to teacher control. This transcript segment, however, shows that such questions can also be seen as stimulating because the question does seem to elicit some worthwhile interaction. Students immediately begin discussing the issue and arguing pros and cons with one another.

THE FIRST EXCHANGE (PARTS 1E-1N)

Speech Act Analysis

The student move 1e is an unanswered question. Student moves 1f and 1g constitute a question and its response. The moves 1h, 1j, and the subsequent student utterence "Wah" are a student question/ answer/evaluation sequence. Next, there is a student statement 1j overlapped partially by a student evaluation "yeh" and another student evaluation move and an explanation. These statement/evaluation sequences are then followed by 1l and 1m, position statements that receive some comment from both students and teacher although it is difficult to decipher with all the background noise. Finally, 1n is a student question that receives a response in what has been coded as the second exchange. Clearly, what has been coded as one exchange is better seen as a series of exchanges where students raise questions, respond to one another, and make position statements about the issue of seniors' smoking privileges.

Conversation Analysis

Utterances 1e–1n are in the main student question/answer, question/ answer/evaluation and statement/comment sequences centered around the topic of senior smoking privileges. Students here, when they are talking with one another, use a question/answer format twice and a statement/comment format three times. (In other analyses of student/student discourse, I have observed that the statement/ comment format seems to occur more commonly than the question/ answer format.) The teacher does not control the interaction tightly through teacher directed question/answer sequences. His talk occurs more as part of the class, as though he is one of the students agreeing or disagreeing with another perhaps as part of a small subgroup that is discussing a particular aspect of the problem.

Interactional Analysis

Student exchanges of the statement/comment type might be seen as less demanding and hence more polite than question/answer sequences. They invite rather than demand a response. Because they diminish rather than enhance status differences, they may be a more appropriate form for peer interaction. This teacher in this exchange uses four strategies that could be seen as encouraging peer interaction. First, he makes his comments fit in like those of a student (e.g., between 1l and 1m). Second, he uses statements and tags rather than asking questions (e.g., between 1l and 1m). Third, he makes his questions sound like statements inviting comments (e.g., "Does anybody . . .?" in 1a). Fourth, he asks students to repeat comments that he evidently considers worth listening to.

THE SECOND EXCHANGE

Speech Act Analysis

Again what has been coded for other purposes as one exchange is actually better coded as a number of smaller exchanges. The first teacher utterance is actually a response to a prior student question (2a) followed by a teacher explanation. In 2b, a student asks a question to which the teacher begins to reply. However, his attempt to reply is interrupted by a student statement (2c). The teacher then asks the student to repeat his statement which the student does along with an elaboration.

Conversation Analysis

What is unusual in this series of utterances in a school setting is the occurrence of a student question that receives a teacher's attempted response and where the teacher's attempted response is interrupted and his turn taken over by the student.

Interactional Analysis

Why might the teacher allow this? I would suggest that this is yet another strategy for encouraging peer interaction and consequently student expression because by allowing student interruptions, the teacher demonstrates diminished teacher control and confirms a diminished status difference between student and teacher.

Quantitative Analysis

Predominant Exchange Patterns. There are teacher questions in 15 of the 19 exchanges (as originally coded). These questions are different from the recitation type because the teacher does not have access to the information (opinion) that is forthcoming. Three of the questions are open-ended (e.g. "Does anybody . . .?") inviting simultaneous response from a number of students. Following a number of simultaneous response attempts, the teacher then calls upon one of the students to repeat his response. Most unusual is the number of student-initiated exchanges (though they were not originally coded as such). Altogether, there were three (student) question/(student) answer/(student) evaluation exchanges, seven (student) statement, (student) comment pairs, five (student) question/(teacher) answer/(student) evaluation exchanges and six (student) statement/(teacher) comment exchanges.

Evaluation

The evaluation moves here, as in the case of SN (the permissive discussion) do not seem concerned with the correctness of the response. They are more acknowledgements than evaluations. Seven explicit evaluation/acknowledgement moves were noted. There were many more student evaluation moves (18) than teacher evaluation moves (e.g., "Yeah," "Right," "Get out of here," "Wah, Wah, Wah"). Contrary to the teacher evaluation moves, student evaluation moves agreed or disagreed strongly with prior student comments. These moves were about equally divided as to whether the evaluation was positive or negative.

Topic Control

This teacher does not keep tight control of the topic.

He introduces the topic initially as "Does anybody have any strong feelings about . . .?" and the talk ensues. On one occasion when the teacher tries to make a contribution, his turn at talk is interrupted and preempted by student turns. Topic is shifted once by the teacher when he attempts to get the students to relate the open talk to Christian behaviour.

To focus the topic, the teacher tends to ask one student to repeat his or her response that had occurred originally simultaneously along with a number of others. In addition, he asks and states his own views in longer turns. But for a large part of the lesson, students interact with one another without apparent guidance from the teacher.

There is no consolidation or summarization although the teacher does try once to clarify the problem being discussed (e.g., "You know, the way I understand the problem is . . ."). As a result the discussion doesn't seem to cover ground. No conclusions are reached.

Here the student turns relate to prior and subsequent student turns. They are not successive responses related predominantly to a teacher utterance. The teacher facilitates this by allowing so much student–student talk.

Other Conversational Factors

The teacher talks 34% of the time (according to the Dillon analysis) though less than one quarter of the turns are teacher/student turns.

Typically, there is a lot of overlap, simultaneous student talk, background noise, and calling out. (Students may be trying answers out on friends or in small groups without fear of negative evaluation.)

Student evaluations and interruptions are common.

The teacher contributes his own opinions, feelings and observations and suggestions toward the solving of a mutual problem.

Students and teacher address one another by first names.

Slang seems tolerated (e.g., "nic fit") but not common. Joking and teasing of students and teacher are accepted.

Backchannel comments are common.

On occasion, the teacher comments occur in the background as part of one or a number of simultaneously occurring small group discussions.

SUMMARY AND DISCUSSION

Two sociolinguistic analyses of the five lessons were conducted. Initially, considerable variation in the five teachers' verbal interactional styles was found and it was difficult to see similarities because of the differences.

The "quiz show" or "recitation" lesson (HK) was perhaps the easiest to analyse. Topic control was tight. The teacher used question/answer sequences predominantly to request recall of facts and explanations from previously studied material. Generally, topics were shifted by the teacher apparently according to some preplanned agenda. Hence, these shifts tended not to be contingent on (i.e. precipitated by and incorporating) prior student input.

The "partial problematic" lesson (PR) was more difficult. It was relabelled "partial problematic" rather than problematic for two reasons. First, part of the lesson was recitation, asking for recalled information while part of the lesson seemed to be a joint searching for explanations and explanatory models on the part of both teacher and students. In short, it seemed partly recitation and partly not recitation. Second, that part which was not recitation did not seem to be genuinely problematic because it did not contain episodes of critical reflection, backtracking, review or revision, comparing, for example, the pros and cons of the different explanatory models. The problem being discussed was not a perennial puzzler—a topic like "all men are created equal" where a variety of explanations and/or interpretations is possible and where there are no boundaries delineated by a course that need to be covered. Instead, it is what Roby (this volume) has termed a "particular puzzler"—a course-centered problem was being addressed: possible solutions and explanatory models for the three faces of Eve. This lesson was difficult to examine because it seemed to consist of two different verbal interactional styles related to two different models of discussion. One style contained three common verbal interactional forms: the question/answer, the statement, question/answer and the statement/comment. This was geared to explicating facts. The other was a statement/comment approach. It seemed geared toward the joint explication of more complex integrated explanations. Here both teacher and student turns were longer and more groping.

In both the recitation lesson and the first part of the partial problematic lesson, course-covering seemed to be a priority. Discussion here seemed to be the joint achievement by student and teacher of text-relevant facts and explanations. Where recall of previously learned facts and simple explanations were sought, questioning was predominant. In the latter part of the partial problematic lesson, discussion seemed to be integrating facts with possible explanations and explanatory models. The role of the teacher in both these lessons seemed to be one of guiding or controlling the joint teacher/student achievement of text-relevant facts and explanations. Sometimes these facts and explanations seemed to be given in the text (in the recitation lesson). At other times, they were not contained in the text, though clearly related to concepts contained in the text (in the latter part of the partial problematic lesson). These two lessons then revealed a model of discussion as subject-oriented course-covering. In the latter part of the partial problematic lesson, however, a different model of discussion was present as well: integrating (in this case, integrating facts with theoretical models). The product/process distinction may be made between these two approaches to subject matter. The recitation is concerned with products—facts and simple explanations. The latter part of the partial problematic lesson is concerned with process—with the process of integrating facts with more complex explanations.

In sum, teacher HK (the recitation lesson) retained tight control of the topic through utilizing tight question/answer sequences. The model of discussion was course-covering. Teacher PR (the partial problematic lesson) also retained tight control of the topic, typically through use of three forms: the question/answer, the statement, question/answer, and the statement/comment. These patterns, when used together, were associated with a model of discussion as course-covering. In the latter part of the PR lesson, however, where the statement/comment form was used almost exclusively and where control over the topic was not so tight, the model of discussion seemed to be integrating facts with alternative explanatory models.

It is really unfortunate that this example of a problematic lesson was not more consistently problematic. This lesson was instead somewhere between recitation and problematic.

A third lesson (SN) was coded by Roby as "informational discussion" because it dealt with taboo subject matter—sex. I preferred to relabel this as "permissive discussion." The term "informational" seemed confusing as discussions are all informational in some way. This was a lesson in a course on marriage and the topic for discussion was talk about sex, nudity, and expression of physical affection in the home. The lesson was most interesting because of the predominant use of the teacher reflective statement. The teacher seemed, in this way, to introduce an exchange that was dominated by the student. To reflect the importance of the student contribution, it was recorded as (student) statement/(teacher) comment/(student) comment. The teacher did not control the direction of topic flow in any strong way. The result of his use of the reflective statement was to allow students to take control of the direction of topic flow. The model of discussion here was expressing observations, feelings, and opinions. The role of the teacher was that of facilitator or almost of counselor helping students achieve those ends.

A fourth lesson (MK), coded as a "bull session" contained the greatest amount of student/student interaction of all the lessons and the widest variety of exchange patterns ranging from two-party to many-party. Again, the teacher did not guide the discussion in any strong way though the manner in which he abdicated control over the topic flow was different from that of SN (The permissive discussion). Here there were more student-initiated exchanges than teacher-initiated exchanges. And, there were almost twice as many student evaluation moves as teacher evaluation moves. Teacher questions were modulated in a number of ways such as being open-ended and including hesitations and rephrasings. The teacher was on first name basis with the students. Slang was acceptable. The teacher contributed his opinions as did the students. There was a lot of simultaneous talk and one time a student even interrupted and preempted the teacher turn! Student comments were based on one another's contributions. These features contributed to diminished status difference between teacher and students. Although there are certainly a number of differences between the verbal interactional patterns of this lesson and those of SN (the permissive discussion), the model of discussion here was the same—expressing feelings, observations, and opinions. Again, the role of the teacher was that of facilitator or counselor, helping students to achieve those ends.

Finally, there is a lesson (WB), coded by Roby as "dialectic" because opposing views are explicated. Here, the verbal interactional style was different again. Both teacher and student turns were long and few. Teacher turns typically consisted of combinations of moves such as an evaluation, a statement, a question, a statement and another question. In each turn, the teacher integrated prior student comments. Explicit positive evaluation was common. This teacher combined agenda (in this case, the dialectical framework) with student contributions. As in the case of PR (the partial problematic lesson) two models of discussion were evident here, though instead of existing side by side, they seemed to exist simultaneously: first expressing feelings, observations and opinions, and second, integrating and elaborating those expressed feelings, observations and opinions into some coherent form—in this case, the dialectically opposed frameworks of parental authority then and now. Unlike the case of PR (the partial problematic lesson), however, these dual models seemed evident in each exchange.

In sum, the lessons analyzed here can be described by three tacit models of discussion: discussion as course-covering, discussion as expressing, and discussion as integrating. (See Fig. 1.)

The two lessons that seemed to be based predominantly on a course-covering model where topic control was relatively tight were HK (the recitation lesson) and part of PR (the partial problematic lesson). In HK, the question/answer format was predominant. In PR, the question/answer and statement, question/answer and statement/comment forms were all used. In the latter part of the PR lesson, the statement/comment form was predominant, a form more associated with the expressing and integrating models. Two models were utilized in different parts of the PR lesson: the course-covering model and the integrating model.

The two lessons that seemed to be based purely on an expressing model of discussion were SN (the permissive discussion) and MK (the bull session). Though their verbal interactional patterns were different, i.e., teacher SN made predominant use of the reflective statement whereas teacher MK threw open the floor to a lot of student/student interaction, in both cases teacher control of the topic was minimal. And in both cases, student observations, feelings, and opinions were the focus of the lesson versus more academically or subject-oriented facts and explanations.

The third model, the integration model, was evident in part of teacher PR's lesson and also in part of teacher WB's style. Here, teacher turns were typically longer and often involved a positive evaluation move. Teacher WB's turns contained combinations of questions and statements integrating prior students' remarks in some way and some continuation indicating what might be addressed next were included in one turn at talk. In the integrating portion of teacher PR's lesson, statements rather than questions were used and the teacher utterances did not necessarily indicate possible future directions for talk. In both cases, student moves were long and the students expressed feelings and/or opinions and/or observations which were then integrated by the teacher. In teacher PR's integrating style, facts were integrated with possible explanatory models. In teacher WB's style, student expressed feelings, opinions, and observations were integrated into an overall framework.

Human verbal interaction is complex and an exercise such as this double-barrelled qualitative and quantitative examination of five different lessons draws attention to such complexity. Coding anything as an example of a group presents problems because of idiosyncratic and personal differences in verbal interactional patterns. Generalization becomes difficult. Sociolinguistic analysis of classroom discourse is valuable because it fleshes out important similarities and differences in verbal interactional patterns that more heavily statistical methods tend to pass over.

Although no necessary and exclusive one-to-one match between verbal interactional pattern and model of discussion was explicated, a strong relationship between models of discussion and certain kinds of verbal interaction has been demonstrated. If one acknowledges that each of the five transcripts is representative of a class of discussion, then some legitimate preliminary conclusions about the nature of classroom discussion are as follows: Broadly, the question/answer format seems to be associated with the subject matter-oriented course-covering model. Broadly, lack of strong topic control (as achieved here through teacher use of the reflective statement and/or the teacher deferring to a lot of student–student interaction) plus a focus on expression of feelings, observations, and opinions seems to be associated with the student-centered expressing model. Broadly, combinations of explicit positive evaluation moves and combinations of integrative questions and statements in single teacher turns at talk seem to be associated with the integrating model.

IMPLICATIONS FOR RESEARCH AND PRACTICE

Although these conclusions are useful as a preliminary step towards understanding the match between verbal interactional patterns and models of discussion, care must be taken not to gloss over important contextual features that could have a bearing, in future research, on the broad conclusions reached above. A number of cautions must be kept in mind.

First, the practice of coding teacher utterances as questions or statements without reference to other contextual features may be misleading at times. Such coding is based on the assumption that statements are more conciliatory than questions. However, both statements and questions can be either conciliatory or demanding depending on the context. Reflective statements may be conciliatory and encourage response in some contexts but this effect could be negated by paralinguistic features such as an angry tone of voice. Further, some statements such as negative evaluative statements may more typically inhibit than encourage response. Conversely, although questions may be demanding, they can also be modulated so as to appear conciliatory—by being indirect, for example. In addition, both questions and statements that are based on prior student contributions may seem more conciliatory than those that are not. Examination of context is necessary to try to determine some of these features.

Second, the practice of coding questions as either lower level or higher level is in need to examination. A number of problems persist: For example, questions may simultaneously ask a lower level question explicitly and a higher level question implicitly. Either/or coding schemes do not account for such occurrences. Neither do they address whether the lower or higher level question is addressing a topic of central or peripheral importance. Nor do they address whether the higher level question is concerned with integrating difficult academic concepts or whether it is on the level of asking what flavor of ice cream a student prefers. In addition, the problem of correspondence between level of question and level of response has not been investigated thoroughly enough. What contextual features contribute to the fact that there is only a 50% correspondence between level of question and level of response? Further, it has not been adequately understood that the same context may be addressed by using one higher level question or a series of lower level questions. So who is to say which is better? Similarly, the assumed correspondence between length of student response and its complexity is in need of further examination. It is certainly possible that some lengthy responses can be of recalled information only whereas a simple "yes" or "no" can require complex thought.

Another coding problem that needs to be addressed is the problem of reification. Methods of coding create preferred ways of seeing. Hence, certain important features in exchanges may go unnoticed. This problem became apparent in the analysis of teacher SN's lesson where a new coding scheme was required, one that stressed the importance of the student's contributions. One should always be prepared for these problems of reification and ready to alter or devise new coding schemes if the methods utilized seem to be inhibiting insight.

Finally, there is a danger in assuming that the use of a certain strategy will have a similar effect in all contexts. In these lessons, for example, both teacher HK and teacher WB made use of a strategy of repeating and refocusing questions in one teacher turn at talk but there were important qualitative differences in how this strategy was implemented and its results. In teacher HK's utterance, where there was no relation between the teacher's question and the prior student turn, the student response was inadequate, whereas in WB's turn, no right or wrong answer was being elicited, simply a statement of opinion, and the student elaboration was more extensive.

At this stage, research must be descriptive rather than prescriptive. We do not know enough as yet about teachers' verbal interactional patterns to be able to state with any certainty that one form of verbal interaction in the classroom is better than another. There are pros and cons to everything, including verbal interactional patterns and models of discussion. While some might deplore course-covering in tight question/answer sequences, finding it boring and uninstructive, others might find it useful, perhaps as a means of maintaining order and fulfilling what society seems to expect of schooling. While some might find uninhibited student expression of feelings a complete waste of time, others might find it beneficial both therapeutically and as an impetus to thought. Perhaps there is a place for all of these things in the life of the classroom, perhaps not. The point is we cannot make these judgments until we have a fuller idea of just what these verbal interactional patterns look like, how they are used, and what effects they have.

With regard to the match between models of discussion and teachers' predominant use of verbal interactional patterns and then the match between these and teachers' explicitly stated beliefs, again at this early stage of research, one can only speculate as to whether or not such knowledge might improve teaching practice. It is important that teachers understand their conscious beliefs and the relations between the models of discussion they espouse and their preferred verbal interactional patterns.

It may be that teachers are eclectic in their teaching, using alternative verbal interactional patterns based on alternative models in different contexts and even within a lesson. Or, it may be that they either alter curricula to suit their preferred verbal interactional patterns, or choose to teach subjects that accommodate use of their preferred verbal interactional patterns more easily. It may be that broader sociological features such as task, or subject matter or SES, for example, have a very strong influence on predominant use of one verbal interactional pattern rather than another. Further research is required to answer these questions. Sociolinguistic analysis of classroom discourse provides one useful tool for examining teachers' verbal interactional patterns and provides a solid base from which both teachers and researchers can try to determine the complex relationships among models of discussion, conscious beliefs about discussion, predominant use of certain verbal interactional patterns, and ultimately, other factors that influence instructional practice as well.

DIRECTIONS FOR FUTURE RESEARCH

Two suggestions. First, one most fruitful inquiry would be taping and analyzing "ideal" adult and/or classroom discussions, particularly where integrating is occurring—discussions that Roby (this volume) would class as either problematic or dialectic. At this point, we have a reasonably clear idea of what subject-centered recitation lessons are. In addition, the characteristics of student-centered expressive lessons seem fairly clear. Both problematic and dialectic lessons remain the most intriguing and possibly the most useful to know more about because they try to integrate subject matter with reflection and theory—product with process. These types of discussion promise to be more "educative" than either the predominantly subject-centered or the predominantly student-centered models.

A second useful inquiry would be to try to take a closer look at what Wood and Wood have referred to in their chapter (in this volume) as "contingency." Some initial work has been done in this area in a number of different fields, but it remains a very little understood area. If we can gain some clear picture of what ideal discussion really looks like [Bridges' (1979) work and Francis' (1986) work seems headed in this direction],and of the varieties of ways in which teachers and students can successfully build on one anothers' contributions, we would then have some basis for understanding what both students and teachers need to know to improve discussion in classrooms. It is premature to make value judgments concerning the overall value of one model of discussion over another. What we have, however, is a wonderfully exciting field for inquiry.

REFERENCES

Bridges, D. (1979). *Education, Democracy and Discussion.* Windsor, England: NFER.

Farrar, M.T. (1981). Defining and Examining Instruction: An Analysis of Discourse in a Literature Lesson. Unpublished Ph.D. Dissertation, University of Toronto.

Farrar, M.T. (1984). Four Models of Discourse Analysis: Assumptions, Strengths and Limitations. Paper Presented at the annual meeting of the American Educational Research Association, New Orleans, April.

Francis, E. (1986). *Learning to Discuss.* Edinburgh, Scotland: Moray House College of Education, Holyrood Road.

Good, C.V. (1983). *Dictionary of Education.* New York: McGraw-Hill, 1973.

Griffin, M. & Humphrey, F. (1978). Task and Talk. In R. Shuy & M. Griffin (Eds.) *The Study of Children's Functional Language in the Early Years.* Final report to the Carnegie Corporation of New York. Arlington, Va: Center for Applied Linguistics.

Ostman, J. (1981). *You Know: A Discourse-Functional Approach* Amsterdam: John Benjamins B.V.

CHAPTER 4

A Self-Attention Perspective on Discussion

Brian Mullen

Department of Psychology
Syracuse University
Syracuse, N.Y. 13210

> But this universal free education. . . . You can never reach the individual in so great a mass. This is the inherent defect in the free school system. Jesus himself chose only twelve apostles. . . . We have got to fight these people who call for cheap education. This idea of getting things cheap is the curse of our State.
>
> J.W. Bailey (The Raleigh News and Observer, 12/28/1900, p. 1)

As suggested by this educator at the turn of the century, submerging the individual student in the mass of a large class may be counterproductive to the basic goals of an educational system. This is consistent with recent research efforts in the social psychological self-attention theory. In this chapter, I will examine how the size of a class appears to affect the self-attention processes of the students in the class, and thereby the students' participation in classroom discussion.

SELF-ATTENTION THEORY

Self-attention theory (Carver, 1979; Carver & Scheier, 1981; Duval & Wicklund, 1972; Mullen, 1983) is concerned with self-regulation processes that occur as a result of becoming the figure of one's attentional focus. Manipulations of self-attention include the presence of an audience, a mirror, a videocamera, the tape-recorded sound of one's voice, or minority status in a group setting. Measurements of self-attention include Fenigstein, Scheier and Buss' (1975) Self-Consciousness Scale, the proportion of self-focused responses on Exner's (1973) Self-Focus Sentence Completion Blank, and proportionate use of first person singular pronouns (either in spontaneous speech, or on Wegner and Guiliano's (1980, 1983) Linguistic Implications Form).

Increased self-attention is inferred to begin a matching to standard process whereby the individual attempts to bring his or her behavior in line with whatever he or she takes to be the salient standard of behavior. Note that self-attention is not equivalent to popular conceptions of self-consciousness or embarrassment. Self-attention simply indicates attention toward or awareness of salient aspects of oneself. These other affectively negative states might be conceived in terms of self-attention in conjunction with low subjective probability of success (cf. Carver & Scheier, 1981).

Recent work in self-attention theory has examined the effect of the group on the individual (Diener, 1980; Duval & Siegal, 1978; Mullen, 1983, 1984, 1986a, 1986 b, 1987; Mullen & Chapman, 1987; Wegner & Schafer, 1978; Wicklund, 1980, 1982). This work reveals that members of a heterogeneous group become more self-attentive, and more concerned with standards of behavior, as the relative size of their subgroup decreases. This appears to be the result of a tendency for the smaller subgroup to become the figure of group members' attention (e.g., Coren, Porac, & Ward, 1979; Koffka, 1935; Kohler, 1947; Riley, 1958). Thus, individuals in the group will tend to focus upon the smaller subgroup as the figure of their attention. This leads members of the smaller subgroup to become more self-attentive and thereby more concerned with discrepancies between present states and salient standards. Conversely, this leads members of the larger subgroup to become less self-attentive (or deindividuated; cf. Diener, 1980; Festinger, Pepitone, & Newcomb et al., 1952) and thereby less concerned with matching to salient standards.

A numerical representation of this compositional effect of the group on the individual is the *Other–Total Ratio*. Consider a distinction between two subgroups in a heterogeneous group setting. The *self* subgroup refers to the individuals whose behavior is, for the moment, of primary interest to the researcher; alternatively, the *other* subgroup refers to the individuals whose behavior is, for the moment, not of primary interest to the researcher. The Other–Total Ratio is the ratio of the number of people in the Other subgroup to the sum of the number of people in the Other subgroup and the number of people in the Self subgroup. In other words:

Other–Total Ratio = other/(# other + # self)

Note that the Other–Total Ratio can be calculated for either of two subgroups in a heterogeneous group setting. Typically, however, one subgroup is generally of more research interest than the other.

Figure 1 illustrates the general application of this approach. This Other–Total Ratio has been demonstrated to be an accurate predictor of the effect of the group on the individual's level of self-attention (cf., Mullen, 1983, Study 1 and Study 2; Mullen & Peaugh, 1986). In addition, the Other–Total Ratio has been demonstrated to be an accurate predictor of the individual's attempts to match to standards of behavior. This perspective has successfully been applied to the prediction of conformity, prosocial behavior, social loafing and antisocial behavior (Mullen, 1983), participating in religious organizations (Mullen, 1984), stuttering in front of audiences of varying sizes (Mullen, 1985, 1986a), atrocity committed by members of lynch mobs (Mullen, 1986b), resource use in the commons dilemma (Mullen & Chapman, 1987), and participation in discussion by the President and his aides in the Executive Office Building (Mullen & Peaugh, 1986).

Thus, as the individual's Other–Total Ratio decreases, the individual becomes less self-attentive and less concerned with discrepancies between present behaviors and standards of appropriate behavior. As the individual's Other–Total Ratio increases, the individual becomes more self-attentive and more concerned with discrepancies between present behaviors and standards of appropriate behavior.

PARTICIPATION IN CLASSROOM SETTINGS

Consider the application of this perspective to classroom settings. As the number of students in the classroom increases relative to the number of teachers, a given student is likely to become less self-attentive, and thereby less likely to match to standards of "participating in classroom discussion;" as the number of students in the class decreases relative to the number of teachers, a given student is likely to become more self-attentive, and thereby more likely to match to standards of "participating in classroom discussion." This is consistent with Klitgaard's (1975) and Glass and Smith's (1979) reviews of the effects of class size on student achievement. These reviews observed student achievement to vary as a negatively decelerating function of class size.

General Overview:
Self-Attention Theory, Other–Total Ratio, and Effect of the Group on the Individual

Group	S S S S O	S S S O	S S O	S O	S O O	S O O O	S O O O O
Other–Total Ratio	1/5 = .20	1/4 = .25	1/3 = .33	1/2 = .50	2/3 = .67	3/4 = .75	4/5 = .80
Focus of S's Attention	O←						→S
Concern for Self-Regulation, Matching to Standards	Low←						→High

Figure 1. General application of the other–total ratio.

The purpose of the present analysis was to subject this line of inference to empirical examination. A sample of high school classroom discussions were analyzed to determine whether self-attention processes and discussion performance vary as a function of students' Other–Total Ratios.

PROCEDURE

The procedure for the collection of the 27 class discussion transcripts—five of which are in the Appendix—is discussed in detail elsewhere (e.g., Dillon, 1981, 1982). The Other–Total Ratios for the students in each of the 27 classes were calculated as specified above [i.e., Other–Total Ratio = # teachers/(# teachers + # students)].

Six variables were derived from the transcripts. These six variables can be considered in three categories: self-reference, discussion performance, and teacher behavior.

Self-reference

Philosophers (e.g., Johnstone, 1970) have given considerable discussion to the relationship between the use of first person pronouns and awareness of the self. For example, Johnstone (1970) proposed that, ". . . a person can refer to himself only when he is conscious of himself." (p. 51); and, ". . . the self is the ground of the use of the first-personal pronoun by a person." (p. 54). Consistent with this philosophical foundation, social psychologists have employed the individual's use of first person singular pronouns as an index of the individual's self-attention (e.g., Cooley, 1908; Davis & Brock, 1975; Mullen & Peaugh, 1985; Wegner & Guiliano, 1980, 1983). In the present analysis, the proportionate use of first person singular pronouns per student was derived for each class [i.e., (number of first person singular pronouns/total number of words spoken)/number of students]. It was predicted that this index of self-focused attention would vary as a function of the Other–Total Ratio, indicating an increase in self-attention as class size decreases.

Discussion performance

Three discussion performance measures were derived from these transcripts: the number of student turns taken per student, the number of student words spoken in discussion per student, and the number of student seconds spent talking per student. As a package, these measures of class discussion performance serve to capture the quantity of the students' participation in the class discussion. Note that no attempt is made here to gauge the quality of discussion participation.

Teacher behaviors

It is possible that the teachers' supportive or interactive behaviors could account for the relationships observed between the Other–Total Ratio and self-reference and discussion performance. In order to examine this possibility, two additional variables were coded from these transcriptions: the number of questions asked by the teacher, and the number of encouragements provided by the teacher (e.g., "That's good"; "Very nice"). Agreement between two independent coders exceeded 94% for these six variables (disagreements generally consisted of one of the coders missing one or two exemplars of a variable, and were resolved by locating and including the missed exemplars).

In order to determine whether students' self-attention processes and discussion performance vary as a function of group composition, the four dependent measures (use of first person singular pronouns, number of turns, number of seconds, number of words) were re-gressed upon the Other–Total Ratios derived for each class. In order to determine whether the supportive or interactive behaviors of the teacher are the operative variables, the four dependent measures were also regressed upon the number of teacher questions and the number of teacher encouragements.

RESULTS

Table 1 presents the results of these regression analyses. Visual inspection of these analyses reveals that the Other–Total Ratio does appear to accurately predict both the students' level of self-focused attention and the students' participation in the class discussion. Thus, students did seem to become more self-attentive, and to participate more in class discussion, as class size decreased (i.e., as the Other–Total Ratio increased). By contrast, if the number of teacher encouragements and the number of teacher questions have any effect at all, it is to undermine the students' level of self-attention and resultant participation. This latter finding, that teacher questions seem to impair student participation, is consistent with previous rsearch (cf., Dillon, 1985; Wood & Wood, 1983).

One way of summarizing these results is through the use of meta-analytic statistics, provided at the bottom of Table 1. Computational formulae for these meta-analytic techniques can be found in Mullen and Rosenthal (1985) and Rosenthal (1983). Regarding the Other–Total Ratio, there is a highly significant and powerful tendency for the Other–Total Ratio to predict students' self-attention and participation in classroom discussion. Consistent with current social psychological research in other behavioral domains (cited above), an increase in the students' Other–Total Ratio (i.e., a decrease in the number of students relative to the number of teachers) results in an increase in the students' self-attention, and an increase in attempts to match to standards of participating in classroom discussion.

Regarding teacher encouragements, there is a statistically significant, albeit weak, tendency for teacher encouragements to be as-

Table 1. Regression Analyses (Based on 27 Classroom Discussions)

		Other-Total Ratio	No. Teacher Encouragements	No. Teacher Questions
Self-reference	R	.5147	−.3367	−.0997
	R^2	.2650	.1133	.0099
	F(1,25)	9.011	3.196	0.251
	p	.0030	.9570	.6896
Turns taken	R	.6972	−.0070	.2229
	R^2	.4860	.00005	.0497
	F(1,25)	23.642	0.001	1.307
	p	.00005	.5138	.1320
Seconds talking	R	.7537	−.3192	−.3012
	R^2	.5680	.1019	.0907
	F(1,25)	32.874	2.836	2.493
	p	.00005	.9475	.9366
Words spoken	R	.7578	−.3759	−.3026
	R^2	.5743	.1413	.0916
	F(1,25)	33.730	4.112	2.520
	p	.00005	.9733	.9375
Meta-Analytic Summary Statistics				
Significance	Z	7.949279	2.653603	1.219863
	p	<.000000001	.0039176	.111258
	N(fs.05)	89.407836	6.408783	−1.800365
Effect size	$\bar{Z}$	.851153	−.270908	−.124241
	$\bar{R}$	.691671	−.264469	−.123605
	$\bar{R}^2$	.478409	.069944	.0152783
	$\bar{d}$	1.915423	−.548467	−.249121

sociated with reduced levels of self-attention and resultant participation. Finally, regarding teacher questions, there is a marginally
significant, weak tendency for teacher questions to be associated
with reduced self-attention and resultant participation.

Note two implications of these findings. First, the social psychological, self-attention theory approach to the effect of the group on
the individual provides a powerful means of characterizing the effects
of the relative size of the class on the students. This characterization
accomplishes both the description of these effects [similar to Glass
& Smith's (1979) review], and the explanation of these effects (in
terms of the current and testable self-attention theory). Second, this
social psychological, Other–Total Ratio approach revealed effects
which overshadowed the effects of the teacher's behaviors. The
Other–Total Ratio generated predictions of student behavior which
were substantively more powerful than those predictions provided
by the teachers' use of questions or encouragements.

Figure 2 depicts the relationship between the Other–Total Ratio
and self-reference; Figure 3 depicts the relationship between the
Other–Total Ratio and participation (the number of student turns
per student). The five classroom discussions chosen for focused
examination in this multidisciplinary study are highlighted in these
figures.

ALTERNATIVE INTERPRETATIONS

It is important to consider alternative possible interpretations of
these results. A common objection raised at first exposure to the
Other–Total Ratio is that this algorithm may be obscuring, rather
than capturing, the effect of the group on the individual. For example,
it could be that the observed effects are attributable to the number
of people in the self subgroup (in this instance, the number of
students), independent of the number of people in the other subgroup
(in this instance, the number of teachers). However, it is important
to recognize that the Other–Total Ratio is part of a current trend
in social psychological theorizing which attempts to describe the
demonstrably nonlinear effects of group size and composition on
the individual (cf. Latane, 1981; Tanford & Penrod, 1984). The
Other–Total Ratio is able to address the simultaneous effects of
variations in the number of others and the number of selves.

To illustrate, an alternative set of regression analyses were conducted, regressing the four dependent variables upon the mere
number of students in the class. These regression analyses produced

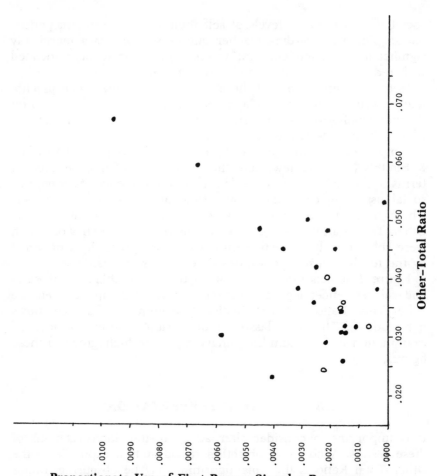

Proportionate Use of First Person Singular Pronouns

Figure 2.   Relationship between self-referencing and the other-total ratio.

a meta-analytic mean correlation coefficient of $\overline{R}$ = −.623738, and a corresponding coefficient of determination of $\overline{R}^2$ = .389049 (to be contrasted with the $\overline{R}$ = .691671 and the $\overline{R}^2$ = .478409, derived for the analyses using the Other–Total Ratio). Thus, the Other–Total Ratio does account for more of the dependent variables than the mere number of students.

Further, bear in mind that all of these group settings had the same number (one) in the other (teacher) subgroup. When the number of others is varied as well as the number of selves, the predictive accuracy of the Other–Total Ratio becomes even greater relative to the mere size of a given subgroup. For example, Mullen

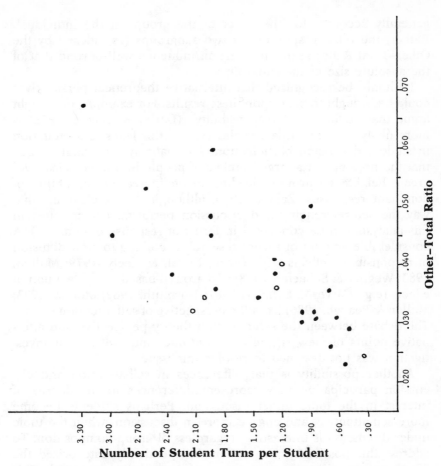

Figure 3.   Relationship between discussion participation and the other-total ratio.

(1984) provided an analysis of participation in religious groups as a function of group composition. Ten regression analyses (based on a total of 480 different religious congregations) examined the relationship between the congregation members' Other–Total Ratios [i.e., # ministers/(# ministers + # congregation members)] and various indices of congregation member participation in the religious groups. The meta-analytic combination of effect sizes produced an $\overline{R} = .602$ and $\overline{R}^2 = .362$. This was substantively higher than the results of predictions based upon the mere number of congregation members ($\overline{R} = -.326$, $\overline{R}^2 = .106$) and those based upon the mere number of ministers ($\overline{R} = .011$, $\overline{R}^2 = .0001$). Thus, it does not seem to be the case that the absolute size of one or the other subgroup generally accounts for the effect of the group on the individual. Rather, the relative sizes of the two subgroups (as indexed by the Other–Total Ratio) seems to exert an influence well beyond that of the absolute size of the subgroups.

It should be recognized that alternative theoretical perspectives could be brought to bear upon these results. For example, one might argue that "diffusion of responsibility" (Darley & Latane, 1968) is more likely to occur in larger classes, and this leads to a reduction in student discussion participation. Alternatively, one might argue that the presence of a large number of people in a larger class will create heightened arousal, leading to an increased probability of dominant responses (Zajonc, 1965; although it is unclear in what way the self-referencing and discussion performance measures in this analysis can be conceived in terms of response dominance). A considerable amount of recent research is coming to view diffusion of responsibility effects (e.g., Duval, Duval, & Neely, 1979; Mullen, 1983; Wegner & Schaefer, 1978) and arousal-based social facilitation effects (e.g., Carver & Scheier, 1981; Hormuth, 1982; Mullen, 1983; Mullen & Peaugh, 1986) from the perspective of self-attention theory. The debate between the self-attention theory perspective and alternative points of view is likely to continue, and the present investigation was not designed to resolve this issue.

Another possibility is that differences in self-attention and discussion participation may represent differences in the degree of interest in the topic under discussion. Perhaps students become more self-attentive, and engage more in discussion, when the topic under discussion is interesting, regardless of group composition. To address this possibility, two coders independently categorized the 27 classroom discussions in terms of topical interest level. This produced 11 high interest discussions (e.g., sexual behavior, abortion), nine medium interest discussions (e.g., deviate behavior, personality traits), and seven low interest discussions (e.g., early nationalism, allocation of monies). Agreement was obtained on 25 of the 27 discussions, and the two disagreements were resolved by discussion between the coders.

Table 2 presents the correlations between this topical interest variable and each of the variables described above. Note that topical interest did not vary as a function of group composition, and it did not predict any measure of student participation or either of the teacher's behaviors. The only significant relationship was between topical interest and self-reference, indicating that students did use proportionately more first person singular pronouns when discussing an interesting topic. In an additional regression analysis, proportionate use of first person singular pronouns was regressed upon topical interest; then, the remaining variability in first person pronoun usage was regressed upon the Other–Total Ratio. Even after removing the potential effects of topical interest, the Other–Total Ratio still provided substantial and powerful prediction of self-referencing behavior (partial regression coefficient R = .564, R^2 = .318, t(24) = 3.345, p = .001355). Thus, the present results cannot be attributed to differences between classes in the level of interest of the topics under discussion.

IMPLICATIONS AND CONCLUSIONS

These analyses reveal that student self-attention and discussion performance vary as a function of the students' Other–Total Ratio. This is consistent with the results of current research in the area of self-attention theory (cited above). A highly similar pattern of results has recently been obtained from an analysis of transcripts of discussions held in the Executive Office Building during the Watergate era. Therein, the proportionate use of first person singular pronouns and the rate of discussion participation, decreased as group sized increased (i.e., as the Other–Total Ratio decreased) for Richard M. Nixon, John Ehrlichman, and H.R. Haldeman (Mullen & Peaugh, 1985).

The most straightforward application of these findings would be to try to increase the number of teachers per classroom and/or to decrease the number of students per classroom. This is consistent with the conclusions of Klitgaard (1975) and Glass and Smith (1979). This is also consistent with the epigraph by Bailey, presented at the outset of this chapter.

Table 2. Relationships Between Discussion Topic Interest and Other Variables

Variable	R	p
Other–total ratio	−.032	.437
Self-reference	−.463	.007
Turns taken	−.136	.249
Words spoken	−.073	.358
Seconds talking	−.099	.312
Teacher encouragements	.196	.164
Teacher questions	.166	.205

Note: negative correlation indicates that the variable increased as topical interest increased.

It is recognized that this recommendation may be untenable for economic and practical reasons. However, there might be ways in which the foregoing perspective could be implemented while still utilizing existing resources and personnel. Nontraditional scheduling of high school classes (a vogue for the past decade in this country) might be turned to good advantage from a self-attention theory perspective. Consider, for example, a setting involving 75 students and three teachers. The traditional approach would be to establish three equal size classes with 25 students and one teacher per class [wherein the students' Other–Total Ratio would be $1/(1 + 25) = .0385$]. An alternative would be to variously break the students into one large lecture section with 50 students and one teacher [students' Other–Total Ratio is $1/(1 + 50) = .0196$] and one small discussion section with 25 students and two teachers [students' Other–Total Ratio is $2/(2 + 25) = .0741$]. This approach could utilize the same resources, while at the same time accomplishing a group context more likely to engender student self-attention and thereby individual participation in classroom discussion.

More generally, efforts on the part of teachers to enhance students' self-attention processes might be able to balance or outweigh the effects of class composition. Pointing to a student or using the second person pronouns (you, your, yours, yourself) are techniques by which self-attention might be increased (Roloff, 1984). In support of this line of reasoning, the teachers' use of second person pronouns was found to be a marginally significant predictor of students' self-reference [$R = .258$, $R^2 = .067$, $F(1,25) = 1.7876$, $p = .0966$].

However, this inference should be tempered with common sense. If a student has a low subjective probability of success regarding discussion performance (e.g., if the student is unfamiliar with the material under discussion), increasing the student's self-attention will not effectively enhance performance (cf. Carver & Scheier, 1981). Moreover, if a student happens to be prone to dysfunctional breakdowns of self-regulation processes, increasing the student's self-attention may actually be counterproductive [cf. Mullen's (1986a) treatment of the effects of audience size on verbal disfluencies in stutterers]. Nonetheless, these techniques might prove to be generally effective in counteracting the detrimental effects of group composition on students' participation in classroom discussion.

In closing, we should consider the implications of this analysis for educational research. These results suggest that the cognitively oriented, information-processing social psychological theories of the 1980's are relevant, and may be fruitfully applied, to educational research. The classroom is one of the most common and most influential group settings. It is therefore reasonable that researchers devoted to the general study of human social interaction and influence made some contribution to the study of events taking place in the classroom. This trend is evidenced in Feldman's (in press) upcoming text entitled Social Psychology Applied to Education. As these types of research efforts become more common, it will become harder and harder for social psychological research and educational research to resist mutual influence.

REFERENCES

Carver, C.S. (1979). A cybernetic model of self-attention processes. *Journal of Personality and Social Psychology, 37,* 1251–1281.

Carver, C.S. & Scheier, M.F. (1981). *Attention and Self-Regulation: A Control Theory Approach to Human Behavior.* New York: Springer-Verlag.

Cooley, C.H. (1908). A study of the early use of self-words by a child. *The Psychological Review, 15,* 339–357.

Coren, S., Porac, C., & Ward, L.M. (1979). *Sensation and Perception.* New York: Academic Press.

Darley, J.M. & Latane, B. (1968). Bystander intervention in emergencies: Diffusion of responsibility. *Journal of Personality and Social Psychology, 8,* 377–383.

Davis, D. & Brock, T.C. (1975). Use of first-person pronouns as a function of increased objective self-awareness and performance feedback. *Journal of Experimental Social Psychology, 14,* 381–388.

Diener, E. (1980). Deindividuation: The absence of self-awareness and self-regulation in group members. In P.B. Paulus (Ed.), *Psychology of Group Influence.* Hillsdale, NJ: Erlbaum.

Dillon, J. (1981). Duration of response to teacher questions and statements. *Contemporary Educational Psychology, 6,* 1–11.

Dillon, J. (1982). Male–female similarities in class participation. *Journal of Educational Research, 75,* 350–353.

Dillon, J. (1985). Using questions to foil discussion. *Teaching and Teacher Education, 1,* 109–121.

Duval, S., Duval, V.H., & Neely, R. (1979). Self-focus, felt responsibility, & helping behavior. *J. Personality & Social Psychology, 37,* 1769–1778.

Duval, S. & Siegal, K. (1978). Some determinants of objective self-awareness: Quantitative novelty. Paper presented at the meeting of the American Psychological Association, Toronto, Canada.

Duval, S. & Wicklund, R.A. (1972). *A Theory of Objective Self-Awareness.* New York: Academic Press.

Exner, J.E. (1973). The self-focus sentence completion blank: A study of egocentricity. *Journal of Personality Assessment, 37,* 437–455.

Feldman, R.S. (Ed.) (in press). *Social Psychology Applied to Education.* New York, NY: Cambridge University Press.

Fenigstein, A., Scheier, M.F., & Buss, A.H. (1975). Public and private self-consciousness: Assessment and theory. *Journal of Consulting and Clinical Psychology, 43,* 522–527.

Festinger, L., Pepitone, A., & Newcomb, T. (1952). Some consequences of deindividuation in a group. *Journal of Abnormal and Social Psychology, 47,* 382–389.

Fuchs, W. (1923). Experimentelle untersuchungen uber das simultane hintereinander auf derselben sehrichtung. *Zeitschraft fur Psychohogie, 91,* 145–235.

Glass, G. & Smith, M.L. (1979). Meta-analysis of research on the relationship of class size and achievement. *Educational Evaluation and Policy Analysis, 1,* 2–16.

Hormuth, S.E. (1982). Self-awareness and drive theory. *European Journal of Social Psychology, 12,* 31–45.

Johnstone, H.W. (1970). Persons and self-reference. *Journal of the British Society for Phenomenology, 1,* 46–54.

Kaufman, L. (1979). *Perception: The World Transformed.* New York: Oxford University Press.

Klitgaard, R. (1975). Going beyond the mean in educational evaluation. *Public Policy, 23,* 59–79.

Koffka, K. (1935). *Principles of Gestalt Psychology,* New York: Harcourt, Brace.

Kohler, W. (1947). *Gestalt Psychology,* New York, Mentor.

Latane, B. (1981). The psychology of social impact.*American Psychologist, 36,* 343–356.

Mullen, B. (1983). Operationalizing the effect of the group on the individual: A self-attention perspective. *Journal of Experimental Social Psychology, 19,* 295–322.

Mullen, B. (1984). Participation in religious groups as a function of group composition: A self-attention perspective. *Journal of Applied Social Psychology, 14,* 509–518.

Mullen, B. (1985). The effect of multiple subgroups on the individual: A self-attention perspective. Paper presented at the 1985 Annual meeting of the Eastern Psychological Association, Boston, MA.

Mullen, B. (1986a). Stuttering, audience size and the Other–Total Ratio: A self-attention perspective. *Journal of Applied Social Psychology, 16,* 141–151.

Mullen, B. (1986b). Atrocity as a function of lynch mob composition: A self-attention perspective. *Personality and Social Psychology Bulletin, 12,* 187–197.

Mullen, B. (1987). Self-Attention Theory. In B. Mullen, & G.R. Goethals (Eds.). *Theories of Group Behavior.* New York: Springer-Verlag.

Mullen, B. & Chapman, J.G. (1987). Resource use in the commons dilemma as a function of group composition: A self-attention perspective. Paper presented at the 1987 annual meeting of the Eastern Psychological Association, Arlington, VA.

Mullen, B. & Peaugh, S. (1986). Focus of Attention in the Executive Office Building: A self-attention perspective. Unpublished manuscript, Syracuse University, 1986.

Mullen, B. & Rosenthal, R. (1985). *BASIC Meta-Analysis: Procedures and Programs.* Hillsdale, NJ: Erlbaum.

Roloff, M. (1984). Verbal inductions of self-attention, and their effects on persuasion. Unpublished manuscript, Northwestern University.

Rosenthal, R., (Ed.) (1980). *Quantitative Assessment of Research Domains.* San Francisco, CA: Jossey-Bass.

Rosenthal, R. (1983). Assessing the statistical and social importance of the effects of psychotherapy. *Journal of Consulting and Clinical Psychology, 51,* 4–13.

Rush, G.P. (1937). Visual grouping in relation to age. *Archives of Psychology, 31.*

Tanford, S. & Penrod, S. (1984). Social Influence Model. *Psychological Bulletin, 95,* 189–225.

Wegner, D.M. & Guiliano, T. (1980). Arousal-induced attention to self. *Journal of Personality and Social Psychology, 38,* 719–726.

Wegner, D.M. & Guiliano, T. (1983). On sending artifact in search of artifact: Reply to McDonald, Harris and Maher. *Journal of Personality and Social Psychology, 44,* 290–293.

Wegner, D.M. & Schaefer, D. (1978). The concentration of responsibility: An objective self-awareness analysis of group size effects in helping situations. *Journal of Personality and Social Psychology, 36,* 147–155.

Wicklund, R.A. (1980). Group contact and self-focused attention. In P.B. Paulus (Ed.), *Psychology of Group Influence.* Hillsdale, NJ, Erlbaum.

Wicklund, R.A. (1982). How society uses self-awareness. In J. Suls (Ed.), *Psychological Perspectives on the Self (Vol. 1).* Hillsdale, NJ, Erlbaum.

Wood, H. & Wood, D. (1983). Questioning the preschool child. *Educational Review, 35,* 149–162.

Zujonc, R.B. (1965). Social facilitation. *Science, 149,* 269–274.

CHAPTER 5

An Erotetic Analysis of Teaching

C.J.B. Macmillan

Educational Foundations
Florida State University
Tallahassee, FL. 32306

In this chapter I shall try to summarize the features and uses of an "erotetic" concept of teaching, to show how it helps us understand what is happening in teaching, and to indicate what it does not (or *cannot*) do for research on teaching.[1] Along the way, I shall examine two of the episodes of teaching which provide the focus of our interdisciplinary discussion, HK's catechetical discussion of the American Revolutionary War, and MK's less structured treatment of student conduct (see Appendix).

THE EROTETIC CONCEPT OF TEACHING

The theoretical structure that I shall assume here is found in Macmillan and Garrison (1983), an "erotetic" conception of teaching; in the background is Hintikka (1982), who considers teaching as a dialogical game with rules and strategies that can almost be computed for effectiveness and expense.

The erotetic concept of teaching asserts this: when a teacher is teaching what he is doing is attempting to answer the students' questions about the subject matter. Not the questions that the stu-

---

[1] About terminology: "erotetic" is nothing more than a derivative of the Greek word for "question". I choose to use this term because it avoids some possible misinterpretations of labels like "question-based teaching," "question-answering teaching," and so forth. It also ties up with erotetic logic, a lively if not burgeoning area of formal logic. It is important to be able to tie in with logic, as I hope will become evident as I go along.

dents have actually asked, but rather those that the teacher thinks or assumes that they *should* ask, given their present state of knowledge about the subject matter under consideration. This conception of teaching has a great deal of power in helping us understand what is happening in teaching, for it not only gives a way of describing what is going on but also provides a rigorous set of criteria of completion for teaching: teaching is accurate and on the mark when the teacher provides complete answers for those questions, and when the questions are themselves the ones that the students indeed ought to be asking about the material. It also provides a way of diagnosing failures in teaching, but that will not be the major concern here.

A basic assumption of the erotetic conception of teaching is that at its most precise level of distinction, teaching necessarily involves what various authors have called "intellectual acts" (Komisar, 1967), "logical acts" (Green, 1971), or "lecting" (McClellan, 1976). Intellectual acts are exemplified by an open-ended list of verbs like "explain," "narrate," "prove," "demonstrate," and so forth, taken in their "auditor-directed" use. These are uses which gramatically require or logically entail an indirect object: one explains the situation *to* someone else. These acts, in turn, are logically analyzed as the answering of particular forms of questions; explanations answer *how* and *why* questions, narrations answer *what happened* questions, and so forth.[2]

What is most important about seeing teaching as an erotetic interaction is that the logical structure of the lesson can be shown clearly. It is an improvement upon attempts to see this structure as a version of *sentence* logic or propositional logic in that it sees the logical relations as *dynamic;* what is important is how a teacher's comments, or a lesson taken as a whole, is a response to the students' knowledge or state of mind regarding the subject matter. The logical structure is the structure of this interaction of teacher, student, and subject matter.

A more static propositional logic can show logical relations among propositions: contradiction, logical connectedness ("following") and so forth, but it cannot deal explicitly with how the propositions interact as part of an ongoing conversation.

A second important feature of the erotetic approach is that it provides a clear place for the psychological complexities of teacher–student–subject relationships. When these relations are seen

---

[2] For a more extensive discussion of the defense of this type of analysis, see Macmillan and Garrison (1983).

as primarily matters of "affect" or "psychological feeling," the intellectual content is too easily lost. The erotetic approach puts the intellectual content at the core of teaching, with other aspects considered as means to this end or as peripheral necessities for the intellectual acts.

It is necessary to make some comments about what this vision of teaching is *not* intended to do.

First, it is not intended to lay out a particular view of how teaching should be conducted. Should teachers ask specific questions, or lecture, or give a chance for undirected discussion? The erotetic conception of teaching will not—by itself—answer this question or any of the myriad like it.

Rather, what is asserted is that the correct way of describing teaching *logically* will involve the answering of student's questions about the relevant subject matter. The issue for planning and research would be what method is best for answering those particular questions, an issue that can only be settled by conceptual clarification and empirical investigation.

Second, it is not intended to say that the *teacher* must provide the answers to the questions. Whether the best way to get students to comprehend the answer to a question—or even to see that they have a question—is through a direct answer, is an open question itself. What is important is to see that the *logical* conditions for success in the acts of teaching are as if the students had asked the question—for the question determines the form of its answer. The form of the lesson may, however, be a different thing. The authority in this case is the authority of logic, supplemented by the teachers' knowledge of the material. (Note that this leaves out of the picture the notion of the policing authority of the teacher; that's an important question, but not the central one here.)

Again, empirical investigation is necessary here. Just what is the range of methods appropriate for coming up with an answer to a particular question? Much will depend upon factors other than the mere logic of the issue. But without the logic, that question cannot even be asked. The erotetic conception makes it possible to design empirical studies in a way that shows their relevance to the content of the lesson as it is related to teacher and student.

Third, it is not intended to provide lessons in manner, counseling, classroom management, or any of the other things that have to worry teachers. It is intended to provide the stable center around which all of these other things whirl.

The erotetic conception of teaching is intended to get at something like that essential aspect of a bridge party, the game. If we want to teach people how to teach, if we want to investigate the relations among teacher, student and subject matter as a unique kind of relationship, then we need something like this conception. Then we can begin to see how other things fit around the core; the interpersonal relations of teachers and students might be better organized than they are now if we were to study what led to the promotion of the interaction of the three elements of the situation; perhaps HK's questions (see HK's transcript in the Appendix, and the analysis herein) aren't the best way to get those questions about Washington's victories on the table, under discussion, answered for the students; perhaps the quibbling of the juniors and seniors about smoking (see MK's transcript in the Appendix) isn't the best way to organize a discussion around questions of the responsibilities of individuals to the institutions in which they find themselves. But can we get at those questions without some sense of what is going on *logically*, at the center of the interactions? Bridge parties might be better with a better brand of cheese—and our classrooms might be healthier with a better dressed teacher or with better breakfasts for the students. But let us not confuse the brand of cheese with the quality of bridge playing, or the teacher's hunger with the teacher's ability to put together a strategy for answering questions about the effects of multiple personalities.

TEACHERS' QUESTIONS: SOME LOGICAL PECULIARITIES

One way to get into an erotetic analysis of specific teaching episodes is to consider some important peculiarities of the use of questions in classrooms.

It has long been recognized that the questions teachers put to students are not governed by the same conditions as the usual or ordinary information seeking (IS) question. From an ordinary IS question, a listener is entitled to infer these (pragmatic?) conditions:

1. That the questioner does not know the answer to the question.
2. That he wants to know or find out the answer.
3. That he believes that there is an answer.
4. That he believes that his auditor can answer his question.

In addition, each form of question has a set of semantical and logical presuppositions; for a question like "Who lives in that house?" we can assume that the questioner

a. Believes that someone lives in that house.
b. Believes that it is a house (and not a stage-set, for example).
c. Believes that the form of the answer will include mention of one or more individuals who live in the house.

Teachers' questions share the latter group of presuppositions with ordinary IS questions, for these are foremal, in that the form of words makes no sense if they are not met. But they do not share the former group of presuppositions. In ordinary information seeking contexts, we would not be able to understand the person who asked "Who lives in that house?" knowing that it was Governor Bob Graham. [Assuming here, that we are driving on Adams Street in Tallahassee, Florida in 1984.] In a pedagogical context, however, it is expected that the teacher knows the answer to his own questions.

When Updike's teacher, Mark Prosser (Updike, 1959) responds to his own and a student's question "What does Macbeth's soliloquy mean?" by saying, "I don't know. I was hoping *you* would tell *me*," the students' response is amazement, or horror, or some such thing.

> But to [this class], ignorance in an instructor was as wrong as a hole in a roof. It was as if Mark had held forty strings pulling forty faces taut toward him and then had slashed the strings. Heads waggled, eyes dropped, voices buzzed. Some of the discipline problems, Like Peter Forrester [who had asked the question], smirked signals to one another. (Updike, 1959, p. 32)

A teacher's questions, then, are different. But teachers' questions have different purposes also. The form of two questions may be the same, but the pedagogical context changes the point and purpose of the questions.

If, with Hintikka (1976), we think of a question as consisting of an imperative operator (an "optative") and an (epistemic) "desideratum," the ordinary question, "Who lives in that house?" is translated as

Bring it about that I know who lives in that house.[3]

Teachers' questions differ from ordinary questions in having more complex optatives: the information that the teacher seeks—and that the students know that he seeks, since this is the nature of the pedagogical game—is not that requested in the ordinary question's

---

[3] It might be that the imperative operator (the "optative") should be "Tell me . . . , but this quickly brings us back to something like the same conditions; although more normal sounding than the awkward "Bring it about that I know . . ." it doesn't carry us so far so easily.

desideratum, but rather information of other types, usually about the students' knowledge. Some categorization is possible, based upon the point and purpose of the teacher's questions and upon the question's place in the interaction of teacher, student, and subject matter.

Two question types have the same optative, but differ according to their place in the pedagogical context; these are diagnostic and test questions. The operative is:

Bring it about that I know that you know . . .

As diagnostic questions, these provide the teacher with information upon which to base decisions about what questions should be asked by the student in order for the lesson to continue. Thus, if to a teacher's diagnostic question "Who lives in that house?" a student answers "The governor," the next question the student ought to ask is probably "Who is the governor?" The questions' order might be reversed: "Bob Graham." "And who is he?" The point is the same in terms of completeness of answers, given the background conditions of student knowledge and belief. The teacher uses the first question to see what the student's knowledge amounts to, in order to add to it or rearrange it.

The form of a test question is the same but its point is different; here the teacher is in the situation of determining the success of the student (and of the teacher, indirectly) in learning or comprehending the subject matter. The conditions of completeness put on such an answer would in all fairness have to be stated in advance (e.g., "Who lives in that house, and what is his governmental office?") or at least understood by teacher and student alike.

But there are other more interesting uses of questions by teachers and it is these that I want to explore by examining the HK transcript. I shall call these "pedagogical questions" for they are put to use in the lesson in order to further the study of the subject matter rather than (necessarily) to test or diagnose the students' states of mind.

The optative for pedagogical questions is closer to the ordinary than to that of the test or diagnostic question. Here it says something like

Bring it about that *we* know . . .

where *we* includes teachers and students; the questions, put by the teacher, are based upon presuppositions that he thinks the students should have in their subject matter (or, generally, cognitive) repertory. Pedagogical questions are one way that the teacher can make explicit the questions that the students ought to ask themselves.

If the erotetic conception of teaching has relevance to understanding what is happening in classrooms, pedagogical questioning can be seen as a strategy of teaching that differs from "mere" recitation or catechetical teaching. In the latter form, the optative practically leaves the normal question in the dust. It probably would be something like "Give the answer that you have memorized, so that I know that you can say it. . . ." The pedagogical question also differs from diagnostic and test questions in that it furthers the discussion without further inference or planning. It is part of the lesson rather than of the other tasks of teachers.

[As an aside, the effects of this kind of question strategically and psychologically need to be investigated. The former is my concern here, but the latter deserves some comment. (1) It might be that this strategy misses badly when the teacher has the wrong assumptions; students might be made to feel stupid as a result ("What does *that* have to do with me?"); this also could be considered part of the strategic cost of the move in the dialogue. (2) It could well be that such moves shut off thought rather than structuring it; it does strange things to the *discussion*, but it is debatable whether it necessarily harms the students' intellectual development.]

Pedagogical questions can be viewed as information ordering (IO) rather than information seeking, since their point is to bring order to information that the teacher assumes the students have in hand or in mind. A full treatment of IO questions will require attention to the relations between questions, deductive moves, and other ways of distributing and ordering information in pedagogical contexts. (See Hintikka, 1982 for some beginnings.)

HK'S LESSON ON WASHINGTON

It is easy to sneer at a teacher who asks a lot of questions, who carries on a class as a series of short interchanges focused around specific well-formed questions to which he thinks he has clear answers. HK is such a teacher (see Appendix); he almost might be considered catechetical in his procedures, for he asks questions in machine-gun style, one question and answer leading to another very rapidly.

But I want to look at this teaching episode in a different light; it is remarkably well-structured when one gets below the surface questions into the point of the lesson, which I shall interpret as itself only comprehensible if seen as an attempt to answer certain questions.

HK begins the class with a general question, "Why did the Colonies win the war?" [This comes at the beginning of the tape, not at our 10-minute segment in the Appendix.] He treats this as a question that the students ought to ask, not merely as a test or diagnostic question. He mentions that they will not have done research specifically on this question, showing that he intends them to think about what they have tried to find out in a new light. Why should they ask this question, though? One might assume that they know the following sorts of things:

1. The colonies were sparsely populated, widespread geographically, and relatively poor.
2. The mother country had many more soldiers and was relatively rich, with a well-developed political tradition.
3. New intellectual, political, and moral ground was being plowed here.

One would expect a small, poor country with little trained leadership, a volunteer militia, and so forth, to do badly against the rich, well-trained armies of England. There is a real question to be asked here, and it is one that the students ought to ask—whether they know it or not—once they have learned about the background. It serves as the focus for the whole class period.

Note that if all they know is that the colonies did in fact win, without the rest of the background about the social and economic conditions, there is little reason for them to raise this question. Indeed, there might have been no raising of it without HK's intercession. He does not make the background explicit as he asks the question, and his first raising of it is met with a long pause. The student whom he addresses seems not to see the relevance of the question; he finally suggests that it is because of the importance of their cause.

This general question sets the problem for the whole class period including our 10-minute segment (Appendix). Here we begin with a more specific question, "What was it about [Washington's] strategy that enabled him to be successful?" (HK, la).

Again, this is best viewed as a question put to the students as if it were the one that they ought to ask, i.e., as *their* question. It is an information ordering question, calling up the knowledge or information they have about Washington, but which has not previously been put to such pointed use.

HK's next question (2a), "Did you read anywhere in the book where his army was destroyed?", is even more interesting, for it brings in a counter-factual assumption: Washington's army could have been destroyed. What is most striking about this question is both that it seems inevitable once it is made explicit and that it carries the discussion so far. Like a geometer's auxiliary construction, this negatively answered question brings a new dimension to the discussion, one that enables Washington's success to be seen as a question of certain kinds of strategies that would not have been obvious without the question. Its inevitability is logical, however, for it is unlikely that the students, left to themselves, would have raised it. Here we see how the teacher's information ordering question focuses the discussion. [We also may have a criterion of genius in teaching here—the selection of the brilliant focusing question. That's a subject for much further research!]

After a question-and-answer exchange of 10 interchanges, leading to the conclusion by a student that Washington had to learn from his mistakes and did so (11b), HK raises a new question, again information ordering: "Well, did the colonies have a large army?" This change is open to criticism in its context. The student's answer at 11b had been incomplete; it was incomplete because unspecific; HK's follow-through should have asked for examples of his mistakes and how he learned from them. One might assume that the students know enough about the war to be able to think of examples; without them, they have only a very general understanding. Later, when HK does raise issues about specifics (at 27a), the problem seems much more trivial, "How can we define aid?" He rejects synonyms ("help," "assistance") in the search for examples, but he doesn't follow through on these questions either.

Note that this criticism is only possible if we see what is happening in this classroom as a joint attempt to answer certain questions completely and fully; the secondary question about Washington's success as a general fits neatly into the major question about why the colonies won. But turning from the specifics in order to get on with the discussion may hinder the flow of thought here. More on another example of this later.

I shall look at two episodes in the class more closely. The first (14a–22a) is concerned with the fact that the Colonial Army was all volunteer and the effects of that fact upon military leadership and strategy. The second (37a–40a) takes up the monetary aid from foreign countries.

The first passage begins with an apparently irrelevant question, "How did one get to be a member of the army? By way of the draft?" (14a) (This is not totally irrelevant, since 13b, one of the longest student responses in the lesson, talks about the individual colonies' militia being outnumbered.) HK changes the subject in order to stress the relationship between the volunteer army and the necessity of good leadership by the generals. He does it by another information ordering question, this time stating a presupposition that the students might believe: that the colonial army was staffed by draftees as a modern army is. The question has to be refused, and it is at 14b. Then a new presupposition takes its place: that men would volunteer for the national army as they might now volunteer for the U.S. Marines. HK raises this question, again as a series of information ordering questions about congress's role in the selection and reception of volunteers. He weasels an answer from the students finally at 20b: "[They volunteered in?] their colonies back home." This sets the stage for HK to summarize what has gone on so far: the American soldiers were volunteers in each colony, giving peculiar problems of leadership and strategy that (as the students had seen in earlier parts of the discussion) Washington had solved.

At this point a student asks a "real" (IS) question: "When did the draft begin?" and he points out the relevance of this to the leadership question (22b). HK picks up a subquestion about the soldiers coming and going rather than following through on the draft question or pushing deeper into the nature of leadership problems in volunteer armies. He has somewhere that he wants to move to—the first question of the class: "Why did the Colonies win?" which is asked again at 24a.

This passage is particularly important because it shows how the teacher can use questions not for diagnosis (although there is some of this in the interchange: What do these students know about this? Am I right in my assumptions? etc.,) but in order to arrange the information they have about the subject under discussion. One can criticize particular moves made by the teacher only if they are seen for what they are. The weaknesses are missed opportunities to make the material more cogent, to follow through to make sure that complete answers are presented. This logical type of critique should probably precede any other criticisms having to do with the nature of learning, psychological processes in the classroom, or whatever.

Similar points can be made about the passage at 37a–40a, concerned with forms of foreign aid. In a set of question-and-answer exchanges before this passage, it is determined that France and Spain provided men, material, and money; again, HK is ordering the information the students have gained through their reading, putting it into a new context. And again a student raises questions from the real world: ". . . after this is over, we have to repay them, right?" (37b) HK, a bit startled, gives partial answers here, putting off till later the discussion of this issue. This move opens the way to new questions when the discussion moves to the first years of the American Republic. He is up on the question, and he knows where it is going to take the discussion now if it is followed through on, so he puts it off with a promise. Here, there is a question that ought to be asked by the students, is asked now, and will provide a focus for a future discussion.

By the end of our 10-minute segment, the discussion has changed topics to the nature of rules in warfare; there are rules, we find; the Americans did not follow some of them, but there are others (perhaps) that they did follow. There is another missed opportunity here, for HK does not ask for the students or for himself what rules Washington *did* follow. The concern moves from strategic rules to the moral rules of war, and this distinction is not caught up adequately. Washington broke the rules of fighting, but one can make a case for his carefully following the moral rules, specifically those having to do with the treatment of civilian enemies and prisoners of war.

The discussion does not come back to this, perhaps, because HK thinks that Washington's leadership has been covered and that this is a feature of that aspect. There's a danger in "covering ground" and summarizing too soon. In shutting off apparent repetitions (as he does with earlier questions about leadership (at 24a) and foreign aid (at 41a), HK misses opportunities that could have deepened the students' knowledge of that period and their own understanding of the present situation in the world.

Is there anything general to be said about this discussion erotetically? We have here a surface manifestation of a question-asking teacher; to understand the logic of the lesson we have to look below the questions to see how they serve a pedagogical point. The questions he puts are not for *his* information seeking purposes, but rather for the students' understanding of the information they already possess. Ranging from a few diagnostic questions, through some general questions that they ought to ask, back and forth through specifics and generalities, HK finds ways of putting their present information into new contexts, giving it new importance for them. He asks their questions, and insofar as he hits them right, i.e., insofar as these really are their questions, HK moves them from a state of rather diffuse knowledge about the Revolutionary War into a state of much more highly structured knowledge; what they know is shown to be relevant to different types of issues. He also moves them back and forth from their knowledge—also diffuse—of modern war to the situation faced by the colonies. The moral points of the later parts of the discussion are not to be sneezed at in this context, for they make the humanity of the situation immediately relevant to their present experience of political and military involvement.

HK is no Socrates, but he is doing what Socrates does in the *Meno's* slave-boy episode: by questioning the students, he's helping them realize what they already know. Not a bad thing to do!

NO SMOKING: MK'S CHRISTIAN LIFE CLASS

MK's treatment of the seniors' loss of privileges is a different sort of episode. (Appendix) It is harder to find a structure here, in large part, I suspect, because he did not set out to have the class discuss this issue. Again, one must retreat to the beginning of the tape to get the point. As the lesson begins, MK notes that the topic for the day was to have been slightly different:

> Before we go on talking about the concept of being at home, feeling welcome, feeling like you belong somewhere, . . .

he wants to consider an incident that occurred the day before. He asks someone to explain to the others. Only a garbled version comes across, but it seems that a teacher went to a place outside the school where only seniors were permitted to gather; the teacher smelled marijuana; this presumably was reported to the principal; the seniors' privileges were rescinded, whereupon the seniors threatened to walk out of school.

At this point our segment begins. MK asks, "Does anybody have any strong feelings about . . . the seniors having their privileges taken away?" (MK, 1a).

We must ask what the pedagogical point of this question in this class is. There doesn't seem to be any reason for MK to believe that *no one* in this class has strong feelings about the incident. An information seeking question of this form would admit of such a possibility. The background would be something like, "Either someone has strong feelings or no one does." But MK knows that they do have strong feelings about it. His question serves the purpose of starting the discussion onto a manageable track. It is an information ordering question: "What are your feelings about this?" Note, however, that it is a different kind of information ordering from HK's.

The question is not "What do we know?" but "What do our feelings amount to?"

The question succeeds in starting something: 13 rapid-fire responses (1b–1n), garbled and heated talk among the students, not *giving* feelings ("I hate it," or "I love it") but expressing feelings along with attempts at clarification, questions about rules and rights and plain frustration at their lack of power in this area.

Note that this is a doubly unfocused question: first in that it is directed at "anybody" rather than any specific student; second, in that it does not limit the answer to a *particular* feeling. A focused question on this might be something like, "Barb, do you feel angry about this?" Such a question would narrow the range of response to a single yes or no. MK has more fish to fry, though.

The underlying question that he assumes they should be asking only comes up later: What is the Christian attitude to take in such a situation (14a–17a), where there are conflicts among parties, when punishment will be laid upon the innocent as well as the guilty? It's an interesting variation upon what was to have been the theme of the class: being part of a family, having a place. This *general* question provides the underlying logical structure of the lesson, around which the subordinate questions and proposals whirl.

It is not a carefully structured, planned-in-advance class like HK's history lesson, but the general question does provide the point to which MK and the students return.

I shall not trace out all the moves of this class. One final disclosure of the recurring theme, though: The discussion ends (beyond our excerpt) with this exchange:

> MK: It is possible that you could win by losing?
> S: What do you mean? (quietly)
> MK: I won't say any more about that. We'll talk about that a little later.

Perhaps MK had a hidden question or a message to get across here. The answer to the general question is to be found in "winning by losing." He puts the seeds of this idea forth as the ending—but not *concluding*—point of the lesson with a promise to return to it. They have, perhaps, reached a point in their discussion of the practicalities of Christian ethics where the question he thinks they ought to be asking is this more or less strategic point: how can one *win* and still remain true to Christian principles?

MK's lesson on smoking in the "back" comes back to the central questions of the class. It is one of those serendipitous episodes that teachers all too often miss. He turns this into an opportunity for making the central questions of Christian life come alive in a living example for his students. The logic is not as clear as in a more structured class; perhaps this is as it should be. For the questions of modern life and the place of Christian ethics in modern life are not as clearly approachable as issues of history, for example, or even more structured subjects like science and math.

CONCLUDING REMARKS

I hope that this tour through these two classes shows some of the force of the erotetic concept of teaching as an analytical tool. I find several useful and promising things in the approach.

First, we can see the *structure* of classroom discourse as given in the relations among the questions students ought to be asking, the answers the teacher provides or authorizes, and the continuation of the discussion of the subject under consideration.

Second, these features can be seen in the lessons even though the teachers themselves were not consciously aware of the logical structure viewed this way. That is, these teachers can be fruitfully described "erotetically" even though they did not plan it that way. This suggests that the claim that this *is* the logic of teaching is at least thus far defensible. Other analyses of teaching episodes that I have tried suggest the same, even where there is more "noise," where subsidiary activities take up more time in the classroom.

It does not appear that putting this theory onto the classroom descriptively does an injustice to the facts. But much more needs to be done before I'm willing to assert this unqualifiedly.

Third, there is promise for more research using this model. Some of this research will be empirical, in that it will address the issue of how best to uncover the "intellectual predicaments" that underlie those questions that ought to be asked. (See Macmillan & Garrison, 1983, for clarification but no answers.) Some will be logical analyses of subject matter with an eye to the question answering power of different forms of presentation. Others will be investigations into strategies and tactics, combining empirical and logical elements in ways that may be specific to particular subject matters and students.

One caution: To be able to do this kind of analysis, the investigator must be familiar with the subject matter. In order to assess HK's treatment of Washington's strategies and tactics, it was necessary for me to study up on the period by reading a biography of Washington and searching textbooks for discussions of his strategies. One cannot see missed opportunities without knowing what they might have been.

What seems most promising about this approach is the almost direct translation into practice; for the erotetic approach uses a literal, intentional) conception of teaching (not a metaphor), so that the findings of research are cast in the same language as that used by teachers themselves. If I am right about this, such an approach goes a long way toward bridging the gap between research and practice. The training and evaluation of teachers might take a new turn as well; and finally, teachers themselves might find new ways of answering all those questions. Would HK or MK have been able to focus their lessons more adequately had they thought of teaching in this way? We'll never know—but perhaps that kind of question can at least be raised now.

REFERENCES

Green, T.F. (1971). *The Activities of Teaching*. New York: McGraw-Hill.

Hintikka, J. (1976). The semantics of questions and the questions of semantics. *Acta Philosophica Fennica, 28*, 4.

Hintikka, J. (1982). A dialogical model of teaching. *Synthese, 51* (April), 39–59.

Komisar, B.P. (1967). Teaching: Act and enterprise. In C. J. B. Macmillan and T.W. Nelson (eds.), *Concepts of Teaching*. Chicago: Rand-McNally.

Macmillan, C.J.B. and Garrison, J.W. (1983). An erotetic concept of teaching. *Educational Theory, 33 (Summer/Fall)*, 157–166.

McClellan, J.E. (1976). *Philosophy of Education*. Englewood Cliffs, NJ: Prentice-Hall.

Updike, J. (1959). Tomorrow and tomorrow and so forth. In *The Same Door*, Greenwich, Connecticut: Fawcett, 28–37.

CHAPTER 6

A Cognitive Developmental
Approach to Questioning

Irving E. Sigel

Educational Testing Service
Princeton, New Jersey 08641

Todd D. Kelley

Shoreham-Wading River School District

The aim of this chapter is to discuss the role of questioning in a classroom context, with particular emphasis on the cyclical nature of the teacher–student dialogues. Embedded in this cyclical movement are questioning strategies which serve to propel the individual along a cognitive developmental trajectory, leading to new knowledge and understanding. Our argument is that the content of questioning strategies, their target, and the timing of their use coalesce to influence the course of cognitive change.

CONCEPTUAL FRAMEWORK

In this chapter we shall zero in on the role of a particular class of events which activates, maintains, and furthers cognitive growth and in which question asking plays an important role. But first let us provide some of the fundamental propositions upon which our case will rest. Following this discussion we shall construct a model and demonstrate its practical utility in elementary- and secondary-school classrooms.

One proposition that has guided the work on cognitive development is that development proceeds as an adaptation to the perturbation created by the mismatch between exogenous experiences and endogenous wishes, desires, interests, or states. The mismatch might be referred to as _discrepancy_ (Sigel & Cocking, 1979). Functionally, discrepancies are postulated as producing discrepant states which activate the individual to do something to recreate an equilibrated state (equilibrium). The actions required to recreate equilibrium take many forms, such as reorganizing one's perspective, which involves assimilating new knowledge or rejecting the validity of the new experience and hence expunging it as illegitimate. We proceed by identifying types of discrepancy and defining events which generate them. Then we shall proceed to demonstrate various ways of coping with discrepancies.

Types of discrepancy. The generic notion of discrepancy is that it is a mismatch of two or more events. "Three types of discrepancies can be identified: (1) *a mismatch between an internal state and an external event*," e.g., the individual wants to buy a new car and he/she does not have the funding; "(2) *a mismatch between two internal events*—an expectancy and an action are in conflict; and (3) *a mismatch between two external events*" (Sigel & Cocking, 1979, p. 216), e.g., when an individual is given two sets of orders to be executed at the same time.

The discrepancy construct is defined in terms of its formal properties. Discrepancies can also be identified in different content areas, which may require different modes of resolution. Cognitive discrepancies may involve logical mismatches, e.g., a child may be presented with a problem requiring logical inference, but he/she does not interpret the question as intended by the questioner; discrepancies may be in the affective domain, e.g., loving someone who does not reciprocate.

Sources of discrepancies. Discrepancies are intrinsic to living and they occur in planned or unplanned ways during the course of one's existence. The type of discrepancies that are of interest in this chapter are those planned by social agents, especially parents and teachers with their children. Through generating discrepancies in children, adults contribute to children's cognitive growth. Discrepancies are generated by distancing behaviors.

Distancing strategies refer to classes of behavior which create any of the type discrepancies described above, and which also serve a mediating function (see diagram).

The Distancing Hypothesis

Distancing behaviors can be characterized as to their form, function, and determinants. Each of these characteristics contributes to the

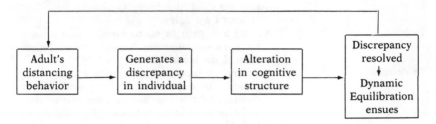

development of representational competence, the capability to represent social, physical, and personal realities, and the concurrent development of an understanding of the media of representation (pictures, verbalizations, and gestures). Distancing behaviors are actually stimulus situations for the child in that they:

> create temporal and/or spatial and/or psychological distance between self and object. "Distancing" is proposed as the concept to denote behaviors or events that separate the child cognitively from the immediate behavioral environment. The behaviors or events in question are those that require the child to attend to or react in terms of the nonpresent (future or past) or the nonpalpable (abstract language). (Sigel, 1970, pp. 111–112)

Although distancing stimuli (behaviors of others and events) can emanate from social *and* physical events, the focus in this chapter will be on verbal or gestural distancing behaviors, one subset of the general class "distancing stimuli," the other, manipulation of the physical and/or social environment. The hypothesis is as follows: Distancing strategies comprise a class of events which foster the development of representational thinking.

Forms of Distancing Behaviors

The distancing behaviors described in this chapter are verbal, which share characteristic features of verbal communication, for example, content (meaning) and syntactical structure.

Each distancing behavior is defined in terms of the "mental demand" presented to the receiver of the message (see Table 1). For example, a distancing behavior is labeled *inferring cause–effect* because the message for the receiver is to engage in inferential thinking to determine causal relationships. Perusal of the table will show the range of messages which demand representational and inferential thinking.

The form of the communicative strategy can be either declarative *or* interrogatory. In the declarative statement, the sender "tells" the

Table 1. Distancing Strategies[a]

To observe	Asking the child to examine to observe, e.g., "Look at what I am doing."
To label	Naming a singular object or event, e.g., naming a place, person, alternate. No elaboration. "What color is the block?" "Where is Joel?"
To describe	Providing elaborated information of a single instance. Descriptions are static; provide no dynamic relationships among elements, no use and functional characteristics. "What did the car look like?"
To sequence	Temporal ordering of events, as in a story or carrying out a task. Steps articulated; *last, next, afterwards, start, begin* are possible key words. "First we will look at the pictures, then we will make up a story." Teacher telling, "Your turn is after Paul's." "Are you next?" (sometimes confused with structuring, as in "Paul, it's your turn.")
To reproduce	Restructuring previous experiences, dynamic interaction of events, interdependence, functional. "How do you do that?"
To compare	Noting (describing or inferring) characteristics or properties.
(a) Describe similarities	Noting ostensive common characteristics (perceptual analysis) "Are those the same?"
(b) Describe differences	Noting ostensive differences among instances (perceptual analysis). "In what way are the truck and airplane different?"
(c) Infer similarities	Noting nonobservational commonalities (conceptual).
(d) Infer differences	Noting nonobservable differences (conceptual).
To propose alternatives	Offering different options, different ways of performing a task.
To combine	
(a) Symmetrical classifying	Recognizing the commonalities of a class of equivalent instances. "Why did you put those two together?"
(b) Asymmetrical classifying	Organizing instances in some sequential ordering— seeing the relationship as a continuum, seriation of any kind, comparative, where each instance is related to the previous one and the subsequent one, relative (big to small, more or less).
(1) Enumerating	Seriation: enumerating of numbers of things unalike; ordinal counting (1, 2, 3, 4, 5). "Count how many there are." "Is this tree bigger than that one?"
(c) Synthesizing	Reconstructing components into a unified whole; explicit pulling together; creating new form, sum of a number of discrete things.

[a] Each strategy is a "demand" for the child to engage in particular operations which are inherent in the structure of the statement. The "demand" quality is implicit in the strategy. The form of the strategy may vary (see Table 2). The singular examples listed here are illustrative and not to be construed as exhaustive.

receiver something, for example, "This is a pen (pointing to a pen)," or "The reason the rabbit went away is because the dog frightened him," a cause–effect statement.

Distancing strategies can also be interrogatories. A further distinction is made between questions which are for verification of messages already presented and questions which stimulate problem solving. The first type is the condition which could occur after a declarative statement has been made; for example, (a cause-effect statement), after reading a child a story the adult might say, "The reason the rabbit in the story ran away was that he was frightened." The child could then be asked, "Now why did the rabbit run away?" and the child could answer by reproducing part of the initial statement (e.g., "Because he was frightened").

On the other hand, question asking could take the form of an open-ended approach. Using the previous example, the adult might ask, "Why do you suppose the rabbit ran away?" The child reconstructs the encounter.

Another feature of a distancing strategy is the "temporal" aspect. The time frame may be the contemporaneous present, the past, or the future. Targeting any of these temporal phases activiates different schemas—the future (antipatory schema); the past (reconstructive schema), or the present (contemporaneous schema). Each schema employs different cognitive operations. Anticipation requires organization of experience in the context of prediction or expectation, in contrast to the past, which requires an organization of previous experience with no projections into the future. Contemporaneous schema constructions involve transformation of immediate experience into various symbolic modes.

The temporal aspect of distancing is a crucial dimension since it is the coping with time that instigates representational thought. To reproduce or to reconstruct the past or to plan for the future requires mental representations.

Functions of Distancing Behaviors

Although distancing behaviors share the basic characteristic of a cognitive separation between the individual and the immediate present, they are presumed to vary in the degree and the way they activate this separation. The demand characteristics are contained in the message *and* the form. The function of the message is defined by the behavior as listed in Table 2, but the significance of the linguistic form is not to be overlooked, since structures of statements serve to affect mentations.

Table 2. Structural Characteristics of Distancing Behaviors

Statement	Type	Declarative	Direct	Indirect	Intonation	Imperative
			Interrogatory			
Closed	convergent	The boy is upset because his dog ran away.	How did the boy feel when his dog ran away?	I wonder if the boy was sad when the dog ran away.	The dog ran away. The boy was sad.[a]	Tell me why the dog ran away.
Open	divergent	There are other ways the boy could feel when his dog ran away.	What can you tell me about the boy and his dog?	The dog ran away. I wonder how the boy feels.	The dog ran away and you said he is sad about it; he might have some other feelings.[a]	Tell me about the boy and the dog.[b]

[a] The interrogatory is reflected in the intonation.
[b] The difference between declaratives and imperatives is intonation as well as syntactic structure.

Declarative statements, which demand convergent responses, require passive listening, in contrast to inquiry, which demands active engagement; for example, "The dog's name is Gimcrack" versus "What is the dog's name?" or "Can you tell me anything about the dog?" A declarative distancing strategy does not require the child to employ the same mental operations as an inquiry. In the former, the child receives the message, may retain it, processes it, and may or may not have to demonstrate understanding of the message. The inquiry strategy makes specific requirements for the child to engage mentally to answer the question.

The demand characteristics of open-ended inquiry, in particular, function as *instigators*, *activators*, and *organizers* of mental operations. The only way the child can answer a question is to become *actively* engaged, producing those mental activities demanded by the inquiry.

Table 2 is a summary of the forms verbal distancing often takes when adults attempt to instigate thinking in children. The form, whether declarative, imperative, or one of the interrogatives, is effective to a greater or a lesser degree according to the open-endedness, so that requests for convergent responses ("Tell me the name of the dog") are less demanding in their reliance on representational thinking than are more open-ended discussion initiators ("Tell me more about the story.")

Functions of Questions

The structure of questions is conceptualized in terms of two additional categories: (1) the types of verbal response questions will elicit determined by their linguistic structure and (2) the psychological effects which questioning may elicit, especially affective states.

Beginning with the relationships between structure of the question and response, the linguistic structure generates "demands" that reduce the degrees of freedom of the respondent, not only in terms of content, but also in terms of cognitive demand. For example, asking a *why* question is intended to elicit an explanation, but also a justification. In effect, a *why* question asks for two levels of explanation—one in context and one in the psychic level, whereas a *how* question asks for a description of an event, but does not imply justification. Each question form: *what, where, why, when,* and *who,* engages a different mental process as well as different types of content. *When* is time oriented, *where* is location, and so on. Each interrogative arouses particular schema, e.g., time, place, person, etc. These interrogatives in themselves have cognitive implications and the responses are contingent on the developmental level of the respondent.

Respondent characteristics that must be considered include developmental level, intellectual level, verbal sophistication, context, and informational demands. For example, the same simple *time* question, "When did your mother bring you here?" will yield a different level of response from a five-, compared to a fifteen-year-old, the concept of time is differentially understood by the young child compared to the adolescent or the adult. This is not a vocabulary problem for the child, but a conceptual one.

The cognitive level of a child can be described in stage-like characteristics. Children's understanding varies according to their stage, moving from concrete to abstract (conceptual). Questions have to be geared to the appropriate level to be effective. For example, an 8-year-old student typically has some difficulty in understanding causal relations and so would not answer a question requiring inferential reasoning, compared to a 14-year-old who typically can think and reason in logically, deductive ways. Another example of differences in response as a function of developmental level is where a preschool child is asked to classify a number of familiar objects. The young child tends to use only one criteria, e.g., color, or form, or function, whereas the older child can combine two or more attributes to form the category.

In sum, each interrogative in and of itself generates a cognitive demand on a particular schema. The response of the child has to be evaluated in terms of the his/her developmental level. The child can only understand the question to the degree it is consistent with available cognitive schema, disturbed by the type of interrogative.

Comprehension of the interrogative interacts with the remaining content of the question. The child may not understand the meaning of *why*, but know something about elements of the message, or the child may know the meaning of *why*, *but* not have the knowledge necessary to answer the question. The test for the inquirer is to be able to use the child's response as a clue to his/her understanding.

Questions arouse affect. Every interrogative arouses affect from mild to intense. The tendency, however, in much of the discussion of questioning is to minimize or ignore the affective aspects, especially when they are not obvious. It is obvious that a student can be disturbed by the way a question is asked. We contend affect is intrinsic in any inquiry interaction however intense or mild and how apparent or not. Students may well mask feelings when asked questions. Difficult as it may be to identify such affective states, the inquirer *must* be sensitive and try to tune into the respondent's affective state. Chances are questions might be interpreted as hostile, disparaging, seductive or warm, friendly, supportive. Among the oft overlooked features of the inquiry process that foster the particular class of feelings are the intonation, the lexical structure of the question, the nonverbal cues (body language), and the timing of the question relative to other ongoing activities.

Questions may engender tension. Questions that probe, that go beyond the superficial information seeking, generate tension. Tension can vary in intensity and comfort level as a function of how the questions are asked. One inquirer may generate distress because of tone and frequency intent to criticize or to destroy. The benign interrogator would present the question with an honorable intent and with hope to clarify. Between these polarities exists a broad range of inquiry styles which activate various emotional states.

While various styles of interrogation serve different purposes, we would suppose that for education there is an optimal style that while generating discomfort, the intent of the inquirer is not suspect and the tension generated is not destructive but rather, is adequate to activate the child cognitively. This arousal may be broadly considered affective.

Questions are multi-level. Since questions have both a cognitive and affective quality, they are in effect multi-level stimuli. In some cases the term cognitive-affect complex may be in synchrony, i.e., the content of the question and affect arousal are equally moderate and appropriate or there can be asynchrony where either the cognitive or affective features may be emphasized. A question with a seemingly benign cognitive demand but intense negative affective tone may preclude an appropriate answer. Conversely, a question might pose a difficult cognitive demand but the affective arousal tone may be benign. An example of the former might be where the five-year-old is asked, in a sneering tone, to tell about a trip he/she made "So, where did your parents take you yesterday?" or in a benign tone, "Can you tell me what was wrong with your grandmother when you saw her yesterday?" The tone in this case may be benign but the type of information requested may be too complex for the child. Hence he/she may turn away and not answer. Thus, the inquirer should be sensitive to the cognitive–affective features of a question.

The impact of any of these questions is greater when the question is a follow-up one rather than an initial question. In two studies done on cognitive-type inquiry, it was found that the significant psychological effect of inquiry is the effect of the follow-up question (Rosner, 1978). The initial question by itself seems to be of less moment, perhaps because the discrepancy is not as intense. When a question is answered and followed by another question, it might suggest to the student that the initial response was unsatisfactory and therefore the need to provide a more satisfactory answer is required. If the inquiry goes on, then the student may get increasingly dissatisfied and frustrated, feeling he/she is always on the spot. Questions may inhibit learning rather than facilitate it because the intent of the inquirer is perceived as critical and non-accepting of the respondent's response. If the teacher answers a question with a question, the student wonders, "What did I say wrong?"

DISTANCING AND QUESTIONING STRATEGIES

To gain a broader perspective of the situation in which distancing behaviors are expressed, let us place the questioning strategy in a social context from an interactionist point of view.

Role of Adults in the Inquiry Process

Any observer of an adult–child interaction must be immediately struck with the obvious: the adult is larger, older, more experienced than the child, and as a consequence has power—power to control material and psychological resources. The powerful adult plays many roles in the child's life in the context of power. Not only does the adult control resources, the adult also judges when and how to dispense these resources. Distribution of material and psychological resources is at the discretion of the adult. The child's choices in this interaction are contingent upon what the adult allows the child to do. These structural and phenotypical actions describe the adult–child interactions in a "power" context, which is indigenous to any adult–child context.

From current research on parents' beliefs about children, for example, a variety of beliefs are found, ranging from beliefs that children learn through action on materials and exploring these materials, to beliefs that children learn through direct instruction (McGillicuddy-DeLisi, 1982; Sigel, 1985). The former beliefs may well be expressed in strategies that enable the child to be exploratory and to construct his/her own knowledge of the world through his/her own actions. In the latter case the child is the passive recipient of parental guidance. These are examples of how the parents expressed their power. The term *teacher* can be substituted for the term *parent*, since in every interpersonal situation with any adult and child, the adult is nominally the power agent.

The Role of Power and Affect

The "power" issue may appear tangential if one focuses solely on the linguistic rational discourse. However, if one shifts the focus to the psychodynamic aspects of human interaction, then two relevant interactive dimensions immediately come to mind in the "power" context. These are the *affective relationship including trust* and *the developmental level of the students.*

Affect is inherent in *every* interpersonal transaction and inquiry interactions are no exception. Irrespective of the individuals involved, posing a question to an individual "puts him/her on the spot" because there is a cognitive demand to respond. Irrespective of how the question is phrased, it "demands" *some* response. Questions, to be sure, can vary in degree of "threat" or provoking anxiety. There is a close connection between the power role and affect arousal.

Our contention, as previously stated, is that *every* question, no matter how psycholinguistically simple, can arouse affect. The particular affective response, of course, can vary. Questions posed by adults to children should be evaluated in the power context. For example, a teacher asking a child where he/she is going, or what his/her plans are, can be interpreted as intrusive and expression of power. An excellent example of this in the classroom is a teacher asking a child questions aimed at determining what the child knows or how he/she will go about solving a problem. Such questions, in effect, test the child's knowledge and challenge him/her to demonstrate competencies. There is probably an implicit right and wrong answer here. Thus, the child may well become anxious or feel threatened. Such interrogatory situations are one-sided; the adult being the interrogator, coming from a position of power. Evidence for the one-sided power relationship can be found in the discourse. Of course, some teachers encourage two-way questioning, as will parents. However, the fact that the *adult* allows this type of interaction is an indication of power.

The way the argument has been presented suggests that the *power* factor is a deterrent to developing productive inquiry interactions. This is not necessarily the case. It is the recognition of the power factor that is a necessary first step toward generating a positive, meaningful and fruitful interaction.

Affect arousal during an inquiry can be positive—the excitement, the thrill, the enjoyment of partaking in an interesting discussion, or problem solving, or problem defining. Or, affect can arouse feelings of threat, self, anxiety, a sense of powerlessness, and similar negative states. This may be particularly the case since the child may feel that he/she is being evaluated.

Affect is aroused not only by the inquiry but by the context in which the inquiry process takes place. Imagine a student being asked a question in a classroom setting and not knowing how to respond; or imagine a student struggling to articulate a problem solution, but not fast enough for either the teacher or fellow students.

Since inquiry can generate such a range of feelings, it behooves the teacher to be cognizant of how affect might influence student gains from inquiry.

The Role of Affect in the Distancing Model

The theory holds that cognitive demands made by the adult to the child encourage the child to separate self from the ongoing concrete present. Distancing behaviors serve to activate or generate schema that involve reconstruction of the past, anticipation of the future, or disengaging from the ongoing present.

Distancing cognitive demands also indirectly require the child to separate "self" from the teacher. The child is in a sense "pushed" away by the logic of questioning, and at the same time cognitively separating self. Imagine the following dialogue:

C: (painting with an easel) Every time I put my brush in the paint can and take it out it drips over the floor.
T: Can you think of any ways to stop the dripping?
C: (thinks to self—I want to paint my picture. Why is she bothering me?) No I can't.
T: What makes it drip?
C: I have too much paint on the brush.
T: What might you do to check that out?

What is happening in this interaction is that the child has a problem which is merely instrumental—a means to the end—painting. The child asks for help, but the teacher used this situation as a "learning to problem solve" situation. The teacher's goal and the child's goal are in direct conflict. The teacher is diverting the child, frustrating his/her painting activity. One can imagine the child leaving the scene or ignoring the teacher and continuing on his/her own way. In either event, the teacher has activated feelings that can intrude in the primary activity of the child. This example illustrates how the disregard for the child's affective status by the teacher can undo the educational opportunities in a situation.

Distancing strategies not only can generate a sense of frustration when the child is interrupted during a task, but can also create distress when the teacher "bombards" the child with questions. Rapid-fire pacing of cognitive demands may overwhelm the child, in a sense suffocating him/her. Not allowing the child sufficient time to think, to reflect about what is asked of him/her, can also create distress. Further, such pressure may contribute to the child's sense of being rejected since the adult is not sensitive to the child's state.

Overall, distancing strategies can be perceived by the child as an interactive mode that "pushes" him/her away from the adult. After all, "If the teacher cares about me," thinks the child, "why is he/she not helping me but always asking questions?"

In conclusion, the emphasis on the emotional aspects of inquiry should not be underestimated—it is a double-edged factor. On the one hand it can undo the very process it is intended to achieve; on the other hand, it can create excitement and exhilaration in the process of discovery. It is incumbent on the teacher to become sensitive to these affective components by tuning in to the child's total response, by pacing the inquiry, and by noting when to back off. We find that only by such sensitive responses on the part of the adult can the effort work.

STRUCTURAL AND MEANING CONSIDERATIONS

Form of the question is an important feature of the inquiry process because *how* a question is posed and when it is presented structure the response of the respondent. Questions constrain responses in part due to the directive terms used. Of course, use of introductory terms by teachers presupposes the child truly understands the meaning of the *wh* terms and so can follow the directions. That is to say the teacher may introduce a question with *why* assuming the child is aware that "why" questions require justifications or cause–effect answers. If the child fails to answer the question, is it because he/she does not understand the meaning of *why*, or that he/she does not know or does not have an answer? Question users must be made keenly aware of the issue of the relationships between the child's knowledge and the structure of the question. The search for connections between the complexities of language and consequent thinking that evolves from linguistic interactions will enhance our understanding of *what* there is about questioning that contributes to the development of thought—which is, of course, the basic goal of our collective endeavor.

In addition to the relevance of linguistic structural analysis, the role of meaning or interpretation of the question comes into play. The child has a meaning system, but whether or not it is shared with the adult is unknown. The activation of the child's meaning system will also depend on his/her development level. For communication to transpire, i.e., for mutual understanding of the message, there has to be *shared meaning*. If this is not the case, then the student will not be able to engage appropriately in the discourse. In fact, it is likely the student will not profit from such interaction. The requirement for positive inquiry interaction is that the questions be calibrated in terms of the respondent's status. Here we emphasize the meaning aspects which may not only be directly related to the development level of the student, but also to nondevelopmental factors such as educational background, knowledge base, language background, etc. The lack of comprehension then may be due to a number of discrepancies in meaning or interpretation of a message or question. The dictum, *define your terms in an argument,* although a cliche, has truth because of the potential miscommunication that can occur if the meanings of terms are not shared. For example, consider many abstract nouns as value, love, morality. Each has multiple meanings.

Meaning refers not only to cognitive aspects of an action or utterance, but also to the speaker's intention, e.g., the speaker can be trying to influence the student subtly, or to motivate him/her, or to get the student to become aware of his/her limited knowledge. Many times the question can serve different purposes in the context of the inquiry interaction. Each of these factors can play an important part in influencing the response and hence the inquirer must be alert to all these factors if the process is intended to promote thinking and learning.

In sum, inquiry, and the use of questions, are complex, involving cognitive, social, and emotional features. Since the intention of inquiry strategies is to enhance learning of the student, then it behooves the inquiring adult to be sensitized to these issues. As we shall see in our review of the Dillon tapes, many questions were asked by teachers. Did these questioning strategies help the student to increase his/her thinking skills or solve problems?

The conceptual framework describing distancing theory in general, and functions of questions in particular, forms a backdrop against which the practice of questioning can be derived. Three central propositions undergird our perspective: (1) cognitive growth central propositions undergird our perspective: (1) cognitive growth proceeds through assimilative–accommodative processes activated by discrepancies arising from internal and/or external violation of expectations; (2) by appropriate use of inquiry, distancing strategies can generate discrepancies which can further cognitive growth; and (3) targeting questions for particular cognitive processes can enhance change laterally (i.e., expanding one's skills) and vertically (i.e., contributing to movement from one cognitive stage to another).

This conceptualization, however, can be actualized if and when the inquiry process is skillfully executed. Let us outline some guidelines for "good" inquiry deriving some of the rules from the above conceptualization.

What does it take for good inquiry and was only evident in the tapes?: A good inquiry teacher should follow the following rules:

1. A question must be asked for a reason, be it for information, diagnosis, or to activate thinking.
2. A question must be the target, i.e., the sequence should have the object or purpose of the question in mind.
3. The question should be clear and appropriate to the developmental level of the child. This means the vocabulary level and the symbolic structure should contribute to clarity of the message.
4. The question should be calibrated to a discrepancy—neither too easy nor too hard to get the child to think.
5. The inquirer should listen to the response, both its manifest and its latent meaning.
6. The inquirer should make certain he/she understands the response.
7. The inquirer should be sure his/her questions move the discussion forward to an objective, *but* he/she should be aware when he/she has acquired the necessary information, i.e., know when to quit or shift to someone else.

We have presented our distancing model which we contend influences the course of representational thinking. In the next section, we will demonstrate how this model can be incorporated in teaching situations in two classroom settings—elementary and secondary levels.

THE SPIRAL LEARNING CYCLE:
A CONTEXTUAL GUIDE FOR THE USE OF
DISTANCING STRATEGIES

The patterns of teacher behavior which include the use of distancing strategies may be viewed within a cycle of three invariant phases: focus, explore, and restructure. Each phase consistently reappears in the cycle, but at a more developed state of knowledge and experience. We call the pattern the Spiral Learning Cycle (see Figure 1), which serves as a heuristic for immediate and long-term planning of the social and physical environment of the classroom, as well as conceptual framework for the analysis of classroom behavior.

The initial task of the teacher is to assess the experiential, cognitive, and emotional status (as discussed above) of the students relevant to a particular goal or objective. Methods that are used during the focus phase may include asking an open-ended question, or presenting a problem, or presenting a discrepant situation. Of these three, open-ended questions are best suited to initiate a major learning cycle because of the immediate information about students such types of questions arouse. The careful wording and presentation of this type of question has a psychological demand quality, in that it empowers students to select their own way to organize their relevant knowledge and/or experience.

Through the use of representations (answering the question), the students are engaged in internal distancing, i.e., transforming their experiences into a symbolic mode. This type of question also brings social-affective aspects into play in that the teacher as a source of power and authority empowers the students to provide their own unique personal type of response.

For example, when setting out to teach the concept of measurement to a class of kindergarten children, we would present our first question as: "What does it mean when we talk about the size of something?"

Our past interaction is reflected in the following excerpt.

DIALOGUE #1 (FOCUS)

TEACHER: What does it mean when we talk about the size of something?
BUDDY: Some things are big and some things are little.
MELISSA: You're big and we're little.
KEVIN: If something is from the floor to the ceiling then it is a real big building.

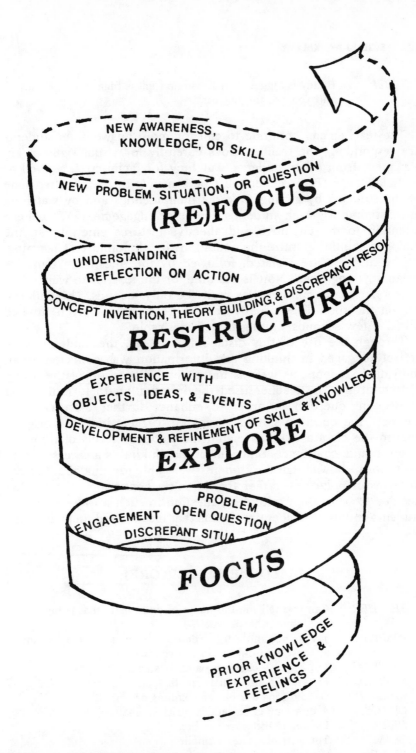

NEW AWARENESS,
KNOWLEDGE, OR SKILL

NEW PROBLEM, SITUATION, OR QUESTION

(RE)FOCUS

UNDERSTANDING
REFLECTION ON ACTION

CONCEPT INVENTION, THEORY BUILDING, & DISCREPANCY RESO

RESTRUCTURE

EXPERIENCE WITH
OBJECTS, IDEAS, & EVENTS

DEVELOPMENT & REFINEMENT OF SKILL & KNOWLEDG

EXPLORE

PROBLEM
OPEN QUESTION
ENGAGEMENT
DISCREPANT SITUA

FOCUS

PRIOR KNOWLEDGE
EXPERIENCE &
FEELINGS

Figure 1. The Spiral Learning Cycle©

GIBBI: Buddy is bigger than Kevin and Pat is bigger than Buddy
              and you are the biggest.

The teacher can continue to call for more answers. As students
are responding, the teacher looks carefully for visual signs of engagement from other students, watching for facial cues, as well as
body language. The teacher must be sensitive to the affective state
of the students by getting to know their feelings and by watching
and listening for each student's degree of engagement. We believe
attention to the cognitive and affective features emerging in the
dialogue should optimize the conditions for the children's learning.
    The answers are restated, followed by the question: "Can size
mean anything else?" Now is the time for the teacher to wait. What
seems like many minutes may really be only seconds. The children
are on the spot. They usually have more to give if given time to
think. A few seconds waiting time is desirable.
    Through the use of this distancing strategy, the students were
actively engaged in thinking and information was collected about
individual students, as well as the general dispositon of the group
(20 children). The teacher used the information to formulate the
subsequent question in order to enhance further discussion. In
addition, the question should be geared to meet both the original
goal in the class as well as match the students' levels of thinking,
interest, and experience. Since all of the children's answers, except
for Gibbi's, showed that the students were able to think about "size"
in terms of polarities, rather than along a continuum, the teacher
decided to word the exploration question in such a way so that the
students could list or identify objects that instantiated their thinking.

DIALOGUE #2 (EXPLORE)

TEACHER: Can you tell me the name of one object that is big and
               one object that is small?
JOSEPH: T.V. is big and a tape recorder is small. (He is looking
               at these two objects in the room.)
MELISSA: I'm big, my cabbage patch is small.
KEVIN: Flag is big, the bell is small.
CHRISTINE: Daddy lions are big and kittens are small.
CURTIS: A dinosaur is big and a pearl is small.
HEIDI: Flower is little, tree is big.
SEAN: Thirty is big, one is small.
BUDDY: School is bigger than a flower.

The teacher's second question was designed to provide the students with the experience of recalling or identifying objects which they class under the categories of big and small. It was also designed so that each child would have a knowledge of the objects which others stated, so that all students would come to know that a wide range of possibilities was available. For the teacher, the answers not only gave more concrete information about the student's interests (dinosaurs from Curtis and dolls from Melissa, for example), but they also indicated that some of the students were beginning to think about size in relativistic terms instead of just absolutes (Buddy's answer, for example). These realizations provided the basis for the restructuring problem which the teacher then presented.

DIALOGUE #3 (RESTRUCTURE)

TEACHER: Melissa said that she is big and her Cabbage Patch Kid is small. If she is big and her Cabbage Patch Kid is small, then what size is her dad? (wait)

GIBBI: She's bigger than Rachael (the doll's name) and her dad is bigger than her.

TEACHER: You seem to be saying that big is different than bigger and small is different than smaller. (Several children nod in the affirmative.)

By injecting a third object into Melissa's examples and asking how to fit in, a discrepancy was created. A need was created for a new idea (scheme) and for a new word or words. While the teacher created an appropriate *opportunity* for the students to redefine, restructure, or transform their thinking, he didn't impose his knowledge on the students. Instead, the idea was shared by students with each other as much or more than between the teacher and the students. It must also be remembered that the original goal was to teach the concept of measurement. It is with the previous experience and knowledge in mind that the teacher formulates a (re)focus question.

DIALOGUE #4 (REFOCUS)

TEACHER: If we talk about sizes being bigger and smaller, we need a way to find out how much smaller or how much bigger. What could we do to find out Melissa's size and her doll Rachael's size?

BUDDY: Measure.
TEACHER: How do you measure?
BUDDY: You can use a stick or something that tells you how big it is.
TIMMY: You can step on something and it tells you how much you weigh.
KEVIN: And the scale has a pole on it that tells you how tall you are.
TEACHER: Yes. Could we use these blocks (pointing to a pile of blocks) to measure Rachael? Let's see. (He lines up blocks next to the doll.) How many blocks long is Rachael? Help me count!
ALL: 1, 2, 3.
TEACHER: Rachael is three blocks long. Let's measure Melissa and see what her block size is. (All help to line up blocks)
TEACHER: Let's count the blocks together.
ALL: 1, 2, 3, 4, 5, 6, 7, 8.
TEACHER: Melissa's size is 8 blocks long. Since her dad isn't here, you can measure me because I think I am the same size as her dad.
            Everyone giggles as they line up the blocks next to the teacher.
            They count.
ALL: 1, 2, 3, 4, 5, 6, 7, 8, 9, 10, 11, 12, 13.
TEACHER: I'm 13 blocks long.
            I'll write the size of Rachael (3), Melissa (8), and me (13) on the board. Would you and your partner get some blocks and measure each other to find out your body size? Be sure to remember your size so you can write it down later. (Explore)

The independent activity which the students then became involved in, provided a chance for them to develop and refine a repertoire of experiences around the idea of measurement. During the activity, some of the children did not use uniform measuring practices (they measured around a body) and some used very long blocks so that the unit of measurement would not be uniform among all children. The activity behavior of these four students reflected their thinking and exploration of something new. It would be counterproductive to impose the "right way" on them. During the "reporting" time they will be asked to describe or show what they did so that they can understand their own behavior.

The "reporting time" is when everyone convenes after an activity. The students are asked to reconstruct what happened during the activity time. It is a time for the children to reflect on their own actions. A brief example is described below. The students are asked: "Would you please tell whose body length you measured and report what their block size was."

Some responses were:

KEVIN: "I measured Danny and he was 7 blocks long."
GABE: "Buddy was 8 blocks long."
P.J.: "Bryan was 4 blocks long."
MELISSA: "Clair is 9 blocks long."

The names are written on a large chart and each reporter is asked to write the number next to the name. After all the numbers are on the chart the last dialogue for this session begins.

DIALOGUE #5 (RESTRUCTURE)

TEACHER: Let's take a look at these numbers. Who is the biggest person?
GABE: Claire. She is 9.
TEACHER: Who is the smallest person?
SEAN: Bryan.
TEACHER: How do you know Bryan is the smallest?
SEAN: Because he is 4 long.
TEACHER: Bryan, would you please stand up. Does Bryan look the smallest?
ALL: No.
TEACHER: Buddy, would you lay down next to Bryan on the floor.
MELISSA: They're the same.
TEACHER: Why is Bryan's size number so much less than Gabe's?
BRYAN: I know why. Because this block (picks up 10-inch block) makes three of those (points to 5-inch block).
TEACHER: How could we find out if that is so?
BRYAN: . . . picks up a 5-inch block and puts it on the 10-inch block.
BRYAN: I mean two.
TEACHER: O.K. Did you use the larger blocks to get measured?
BRYAN: Yes.
TEACHER: You were 4 of these blocks long. Let's see what that means in shorter blocks. (Teacher places four long blocks on floor. Bryan helps to put short blocks on top.) Let's all count the blocks.
ALL: 1, 2, 3, 4, 5, 6, 7, 8.
TEACHER: What does this tell us about measuring? (Wait—long silence.)

> *BRYAN:*   We should all use the same size blocks.
> *BUDDY:*   It isn't fair if some people use long or shorts.
> *TEACHER:*   Yes, if we don't know what kind they are using, but if they tell us then we can still understand their size.

The reporting session is valuable because it gives the students information about the thoughts, activities, and knowledge of other students. It gives the teacher more information about students' information, perceptions, and misperceptions. It gives students a chance to practice communication skills. If the student is having trouble describing his/her behavior, more questions are asked which will aid in the description of the activity. Most importantly, it is part of a process which is directed toward students forming generalizations, theories, or new hypotheses.

What has been shown by the above dialogues is how distancing strategies are used in the context of classroom planning and behavior. The examples involved the content area of physical concepts. The strategies may be used in any content area and with any age or experience level. It may be instructive to also point out that it can be used effectively to teach students about their own cognitive processes. That is, questions which ask a group of students to reflect upon their group (behavioral) process as well as their individual (mental) process. The reflection on group behaviors may begin with questions like, "What did we do first?" After reconstructing the behaviors, a question may be asked which calls for a generalization, conclusion, or prediction. To promote thinking about thinking, there must be important meaningful content to reflect on.

We have tried to provide the basic contextual components of an approach which strives to give students the opportunity to develop their thinking processses while learning the information and skills that are necessary. The distancing model has been a guide in helping to determine what kinds of questions are best suited to promote particular thinking responses.

How and when, and most importantly, why, each of these expressions takes place are directly related to the mental development of each student, as well as the class as a whole. Through the purposeful, sensitive use of appropriate distancing strategies, students appear more self-confident in their ability to deal with life in the school setting.

What we learn from classroom dialogues is that the students learn, not only content, but also how to think reflectively, how to analyze, and how to synthesize the information dealt with. Taba puts the effort in perspective when she writes about inquiry and questioning, to wit *"to cultivate the type of mental processes which strengthen the capacity to transfer knowledge to new situations, the creative approaches to problem solving, and the methods of discovery and inventiveness"* (Taba, 1962, p. 275). The distancing model described in the foregoing section helps achieve the above objectives.

ANALYSIS OF DILLON TAPES

The transcripts we have elected to analyze include a discussion of a history lesson, a psychology lesson, and a school policy issue. Our analysis will be guided by the Spiral Learning Cycle Model which we have discussed previously, as well as the embedded distancing strategies, since it is these strategies which move the student through the cycle.

Analysis of HK

This excerpt opens with two questions where the teacher tries to focus the discussion on Washington as a successful military leader. The questions HK asks appear to be requests for reproducing familiar materials which are low-level distancing strategies. Each question is structured the same. The *focus* is double-barrelled, leaving the student with the choice to respond to the "success" aspect of the teacher's inquiry or to the issue of tactics. The student responds by describing how the American soldiers fought, *focusing* on neither the teacher's questions nor offering any new ideas of his/her own. The teacher continues to question, not getting involved in the student's question. HK proceeds to ask another reconstruction memory closed question on a seemingly tangential issue; namely, "What is happening to Washington's army?". There is no ostensive connection between either HK's initial inquiries and the student's answers. Hence we can conclude that the *focus* continues to be muddled. A new *focus* emerges briefly regarding the issue of Washington's army being outmaneuvered and destroyed. HK explores this issue briefly using a Level 2 question (see Table 1), i.e., "What is the difference between being outsmarted or destroyed in a military context?" The teacher does return to the issue of Washington's success, apparently in an attempt to review the lesson and obtain closure to move on to some other issue. However, students continued to *explore*, but the teacher shifted the *focus* again by pointing out that the student had contradicted himself. A new *focus* emerges which has to do with the nature of the colonial armies. There is some evidence of exploration here, but the teacher used closed recall questions with minimal cognitive demands to reconcile differences discussed previously, to present and to discuss alternatives, or to engage in any evaluation. Each of these is a reasonable option to engage the students to think about the assertions they and the teacher have been making about Washington's military prowess. *Exploration* follows on the topic of the army, and here again most questions were closed, engaging reconstructive memory. In fact, most questions dealing with the Continental Army were closed, and all the student had to do to answer them was to retrieve already acquired knowledge in contrast to the teacher using distancing strategies which would generate discrepancies which in turn would lead to the restructuring of the student's existing schema into new integrated knowledge.

In the course of the exploration phase, HK finally challenged students to transcend their textbook recitations to evaluate the meaning of their comments when he says, "What do you mean by that?" He asks for concrete examples of aid to the armies, but here again the students regurgitate what they already know. In this restricted context, using essentially low-level distancing strategies, the teacher proceeds to the end of the lesson. Not only does he move to the end of the lesson by using low-level strategies, but he also seems to move quickly, giving the students little "wait time".

In sum, HK does use a lot of questions, but they are low-level, giving the students little time to reflect on what is going on, both in the text and in the discussion. There is little evidence of thoughtful, evaluative questioning. Most of the questions also prevent the students from *exploring* and hence preclude moving on to *restructuring* their knowledge of the events under discussion. On the basis of this transcript, we would think this teacher is not very effective in helping his students develop analytic skills.

Let us turn now to PR who does move the students along by provocative inquiry strategies.

Analysis of PR

The lesson the students are working on is an analysis of the book "The Three Faces of Eve." Initially, the teacher structures the lesson, *focusing* on the immediate task for the class by asking, "How are we going to help her deal with the three personalities?" which reflects the theme of the book. The teacher, having focused the discussion, then moves quickly into the *exploration* phase which moves the discussion step by step to requests for inferences about various options proposed for helping Eve integrate the three personalities or so deal with the problem that she emerges as a whole person. Although the students' responses are short, the teacher persists in asking the students to explain or to justify their particular offerings. In addition, the teacher proceeds to offer counter-examples to any assertions made by the student. For example, in discussion of which personality was more dominant, the student says that Eve Black was more dominant. The teacher challenges the student by asking if Eve Black was not the more extrovert, kind of sleazy? It is concluded that in spite of the extroversion, Eve White the introvert is the more dominant. Rather than getting involved in disputing the issue further, the teacher *focuses* the discussion on the basic issue: how to help Eve achieve a single personality. The teacher brings the students back to the *exploratory* phase by asking them to describe what they might do to solve Eve's problem. Now the students are in the *exploration* phase, but at a high level; they are involved in anticipation, predicting and using imaginative processes to solve a problem. To accentuate the task before them, the teacher poses conflicts for the students by responding to a student's suggestion, for example, that two of the three personalities should be knocked out, instead of trying to integrate them. The teacher asks what the consequences of such a decision would be. Why not integrate them? Or to the suggestion of integrating the three personalities or even the teacher asking students to justify their point's consequences. In effect, the teacher asks the students to justify their points of view. The discussion has now entered a transitional phase moving from *exploration* to *restructuring*. What the students are being asked to do is to formulate hypotheses to be used in coming to terms with the problems. The cognitive processes involved in this *exploratory* phase are anticipation and predicting, each of which narrows the focus leading to a *restructuring* of their efforts. Now a new set of issues arises involving an analysis of the patient's background. Having restructured the problem, the new hypotheses serve as a new *focus* and the cycle repeats itself as the students begin to explore ways of examining their hypotheses.

The distancing strategies the teacher used in this excerpt tend to be at Level 3, e.g., seeking causal connections, seeking explanations, and seeking alternative plans to problem resolution. Each of these types of questions enhances the data base for the students, creating movement toward deciding a course of action.

The teacher does integrate the material as they proceed in the discussion, and in this way, brings the students' ideas together. The students, with the teacher's guiding questions, come to develop a point in the discussion that does not accept the final solution but asks if there are any alternatives to the ideas proposed. Although this shifts the *focus*, the teacher is staying within the parameters of the original problem; namely, coming to understand the dynamics of Eve and offering choices for ultimate solution to the multiple-personality problem.

The teacher moves the discussion along at an active pace, he seems to involve many of the students in the discussion. The teacher creates the environment wherein the students are encouraged to *focus* on issues, *explore* ideas, and come to *restructure* their thinking. What seems to contribute to this movement is the level of question-asking, which consistently makes strong cognitive demands on the student to generate ideas, either in the form of hypotheses or of explanations.

The contrast between HK and PR is striking. HK asks more low-level questions, which are tangential and not focused on the specific goal he sets out for himself, while PR moves directly to the goal which is set in the beginning. If one were to draw a tree diagram depicting the sequence of HK, the picture would reveal a series of branches moving away from a trunk with only slight reference to the trunk. Thus in the elaboration phase of the discussion, the questions move the students away from the central theme rather than toward coming to some understanding of the issue before them; namely, evaluation of Washington as a military leader. The lack of analysis of the issues is particularly evident in this except of HK in contrast to PR.

PR, on the other hand, by relatively direct associative recall questions (Level 1 and Level 2 questions) established a basis from which to move on to higher level questions involving hypotheses-generating thinking. In this way the discussion moves forward toward the goals set at the beginning of the lesson. Let us turn now to an analysis of the excerpt of teacher MK.

Analysis of MK

In this excerpt, the class is discussing a school policy on smoking. In contrast to the previous excerpts *focusing* on a strictly academic subject matter, this one involves policy questions which seem to elicit students' and the teacher's personal experiences and opinions. The teacher structures the situation in terms of students' opinions regarding school policy on smoking. In this episode students and teacher ask questions of the group and they tend to be Level 3 questions, e.g., alternatives to policy restriction on smoking. The content, as well as the *focus*, seems to foster a general discussion mode emphasizing feelings about the policy. As the session develops and the students proceed to argue the pros and cons of the policy which bans smoking from school grounds, they do begin to seek a solution. Reasons for the policy are brought up by students and the teacher, with the teacher *refocusing* the issue to explain why there is a ban on smoking. The students are encouraged by the generally apparent informality to voice their own opinions, offering alternatives such as restricted areas, etc., where smoking can be allowed. These alternatives are not elicited by the teacher, but by the student's own interest in the issue. The teacher in the *elaboration* brings his own experiences as a smoker and the students do the same. This *elaboration* is not directly aimed at coming up with suggestions for formulating policy, but rather, it seems to be a sharing of feelings with no clear-cut goal other than to ventilate. The discussion also involves suggestions for disciplining students who violate the policy. The students come up with their own solution that smoking is a personal responsibility, but there is no consensus decision regarding the issues before the group. A new focus, or at least a new aspect, of the general problem arises when the teacher asks, "What is the Christian response to smoking?" He poses this as a hypothetical situation. He asks open-ended questions to get students to elaborate on their attitudes and experiences. There is no *restructuring*.

What does this excerpt teach us? This is a lively discussion with minimal teacher leadership. The teacher is more like a participant in the discussion, sharing his own experiences on the same level as the students. The movement was consistent in the overall direction, and in a sense the students, with their own open-ended questions, moved the discussion forward.

Reflections on Excerpts

These three excerpts demonstrate variation among the teachers' individual styles of conducting a lesson. The differences were not only a function of teacher preferences and perhaps skills (note comparison between HK and PR), but a function of the subject matter under discussion. In the MK situation, on the other hand, the teacher did not serve as the expert or as the judge of the appropriateness of the students' comments. He was more like a referee.

What we believe is the contribution of our analysis of these tapes is the analytic approach we have taken. Using the Spiral Learning Cycle as the overarching framework helps define the structure in which the distancing strategies is embedded. These strategies reflect teachers' behaviors which propel the child from one phase of the cycle to another.

Our approach provides for a method by which to compare classroom teachers' interactions with their students because the categories are observable and inherent in classroom discussions. It seems to us that when a discussion moves along, the phases described in the Spiral Learning Cycle happen in the natural course of events. We are articulating the cycle to provide teachers with a system by which to analyze the flow of the discussion.[1]

The Spiral Learning Cycle concept provides an overarching approach that describes the teaching context, whereas the distancing strategies are the teacher behaviors which provide the movement both in direction and in the pace of the discussion.

SUMMARY AND CONCLUSIONS

Two major issues form the underpinnings of this essay: the first is the psychological significance of the inquiry process, particularly in the sense of questioning; the second has to do with the development of a conceptual framework to study the questioning approach.

In the discussion we have presented a theory describing the questioning approach, which we have referred to as distancing. However, we discovered that the questions used seem to alter the context in which the questions were asked. Kelley came up with the Spiral Learning Cycle concept, because as a classroom teacher, the cycle was evident in the movement in the class.

The Spiral Learning Cycle incorporates the distancing strategies. This is a total system since the Spiral Learning Cycle and the distancing strategies are inextricably linked. To be sure, the distancing strategy level can vary. The teacher decides what type of strategy to use. Some strategies will facilitate the discussion and move it from one phase to another, while other strategies preclude movement (note the strategies used by HK). The important point here is that it is the type of distancing strategy the teacher uses that is a key determinant of the direction of the discussion, and hence, of the Spiral Learning Cycle.

We believe the Spiral Learning Cycle–Distancing Strategy Model is valuable as a conceptual tool, and also as a practical analytic method to describe what goes on in a classroom. Conceptually, the

---

[1] Coding systems are already available for the distancing strategies. These systems have been used successfully by teachers and researchers.

Spiral Learning Cycle provides a developmental context in which cognitive movement occurs. It specifies the dynamics of change within that particular context. However, it also can reveal that no movement is occurring, and since movement implies learning, it becomes patently clear that the students are not assimilating nor accommodating to the new knowledge. The reason for this lack of movement can be determined by examining the distancing strategies the teacher uses. The Spiral Learning Cycle describes the movement phases and their distancing strategies inform us of the rationale of the movement. By demonstrating the system for young children and high school students, we have demonstrated that the system is applicable to a wide spectrum of classrooms. It seems to us that the cyclical movement in classroom discussions, while generally observable, has yet to be evaluated in terms of the long-term effects on the children's learning and retention of material. Just what is learned and how well the experience provides the children with both a substantive knowledge as well as skills in problem solving competence remains to be seen.

On the basis of informal classroom observations, and on the basis of the analysis of the Dillon tapes, we feel optimistic that the system we propose can serve the two purposes described in this chapter: a basis for conceptual analysis of classroom interaction and a heuristic one, a way of analyzing classroom interaction.

REFERENCES

McGillicuddy-DeLisi, A.V. (1982). The relationship between parents' beliefs about development and family constellation, socioeconomic status, and parents' teaching strategies. In L.M. Laosa & I.E. Sigel (Eds.), *Families as Learning Environments for Children* (pp. 261–299). New York: Plenum.

Piaget, J. (1950). *The Psychology of Intelligence*. London: Routledge & Kegan Paul.

Redfield, D.L. & Rousseau, E.W. (1981). A meta-analysis of experimental research on teacher questioning behavior. *Review of Educational Research, 51*(2), 237–245.

Rosner, F.C. (1978). An ecological study of teacher distancing behaviors as a function of program, context and time. *Dissertation Abstracts International, 39*, 760A, (University Microfilms, No. 7812235).

Sigel, I.E. (1970). The distancing hypothesis: A causal hypothesis for the acquisition of representational thought. In M.R. Jones (Ed.), *Miami Symposium on the Prediction of Behavior, 1968: Effect of Early Experiences* (pp. 99–118). Coral Gables, FL: University of Miami Press.

Sigel, I.E. (1985). A conceptual analysis of beliefs. In I.E. Sigel (Ed.), *Parental Belief Systems: The Psychological Consequences for Children* (pp. 345–371). Hillsdale, NJ: Erlbaum.

Sigel, I.E. & Cocking, R.R. (1979). Cognition and communication: A dialectic paradigm for development. In M. Lewis & L.A. Rosenblum (Eds.), *Interaction, Conversation, and the Development of Language* (pp. 207–226). New York: Wiley.

Sigel, I.E. & McGillicuddy-DeLisi, A.V. (1984). Parents as teachers of their children: A distancing behavior model. In A.D. Pelligrini & T.D. Yawkey (Eds.), *The Development of Oral and Written Language in Social Contexts* (pp. 71–92). Norwood, NJ: Ablex.

Taba, H. (1962). *Curriculum Development: Theory and Pratice.* New York: Harcourt, Brace and World.

ACKNOWLEDGMENT

Portions of this paper are taken from Sigel and Cocking (1979). Part of the research reported in this paper was supported by the National Institute of Child Health and Human Development Grant No. R01-HD10686 to Educational Testing Service, National Institute of Mental Health Grant No. R01-MH32301 to Educational Testing Service, and Bureau of Education of the Handicapped Grant No. G007902000 to Educational Testing Service.

CHAPTER 7

An Organization Watcher's View of Classroom Questioning and Discussion: Multiple Realities and Sequential Dependencies

Frederick F. Lighthall

*Department of Education and
Committee on Social and Organizational Psychology,
Department of Behavioral Sciences
University of Chicago
Chicago, IL. 60637*

PERSPECTIVES ON CLASSROOM INTERCHANGES FROM ORGANIZATINAL PSYCHOLOGY[1]

Suppose you believe, as I do, that interdisciplinary studies of social phenomena, such as educative exchanges in classrooms, are essential to combat the fractionated knowledge that now pervades the social sciences. What happens, then, if you see that the particular interdisciplinary project in which you embark, namely the one reported in this book, has been infected by the very disease it seeks to treat, namely, *fractionation in inquiry and knowledge?* What happens, in the terms I shall set forth below, is that you have a problem.

Let me begin to explain by quoting from the concluding paragraph of Hugh Petrie's (1976) useful paper, "Do you see what I see? The epistemology of interdisciplinary inquiry:"[2]

[1] I must express gratitude for helpful discussions of earlier versions of this paper to project colleagues, particularly David Bridges, Jim Dillon, Bill Knitter, and Tom Roby, but I also am much indebted to Larry Hedges and Tony Bryk for their close reading and discussions of an earlier draft.

[2] Hugh G. Petrie, (1976). *Journal of Aesthetic Education, 10,* 29–43.

With respect to epistemological considerations, I have urged that some mixes of disciplines require as a necessary condition for success that *the participants must learn the observational categories and meanings of key terms* of each other's discipline. This knowledge is then tacitly used in an interpretive way on the problems facing the group . . . Only *when you see what I see* does interdisciplinary work have a chance [p. 42, emphasis added].

Two Distinctions

I shall make two basic distinctions and apply two principles. These will set the stage for enabling you to see what I see in this project's common corpus of data. First, I must distinguish between *manifest* action or function and *latent* action or function. Second, I introduce distinctions among three "kinds" or views of reality: a single, "objective" reality, multiple realities, and shared reality.

Observation of people working together, and sometimes refusing to work together, in ongoing organizations leads one to appreciate the classical distinction between manifest and latent. Manifest is what people say, latent is what they are up to in the saying. Manifest is the printed agenda; latent, the hidden one. Manifest is action taken in solving problems; latent are the "problems" (a term whose special sense I take up below). Manifest is the question posed and the answer. Latent are the reasons for posing that question—the (conscious or unconscious) purposes behind it. One stumbles badly in either participating in or analyzing organizational action—or classroom questioning and discussion—if one fails to make this distinction. I will illustrate this presently.

The second distinction I wish to make is that between "thingy," point-at-able, "objective" reality, "out there," and the subjective reality that operates "in here." While it is useful to posit a single, lawful reality out there, a reality that includes us impersonally in it, one an omniscience knows from all points of view at once, it is essential that one not confuse that single, "objective" reality with the one to which humans respond. Humans are more creative than to respond merely to what is given: they insist on *making*, or as I prefer, *synthesizing* a world to which they respond. That synthesized, responded-to reality I call *operating reality*.

People do not respond directly to an outer world, to observable "stimuli," or to other people—or to classroom questions or statements. Rather, humans respond to accumulated constructions that are not merely cognitions or values or fears or hopes or judgments but are synthesized cognitions–valuings—fears–hopes–judgments. Percepts of the outer world and of other people *participate in* these constructions as parts, not wholes. The realities humans synthesize and respond to are different from one person to the next. Values and goals and imaginings are not visible but *they are parts of operating reality*—every bit as directing and blocking of human action as are hurricanes, cement walls, or bullets. An actor's subjective, synthetic constructions become crucial (not sufficient but necessary) data for understanding the functions or origins of an actor's actions.[3]

The concept of operating reality would be too diffuse to be very useful but for one fact: The most demanding, attention-getting *form* of operating reality—a form whose content can vary infinitely but whose *structure* is highly stable—turns out to be simple in its organization, powerful in its control over the individual's energies and thought, and, I would argue, universally present in persons across cultures.[4] This form of operating reality is one in which elements of the individual's thoughts, feelings, commitments, or perceptions become *incompatible* with one another. The form, that is, is that of a relationship between two opposing contents of operating reality, of minding. These incompatible conditions of operating reality I call *problems*. As a working assumption, problems and the problem-solving transformations of problems exert complete and ongoing control over the energies and thought of the person in whom the problems operate. All actions, inward in thought or outward in manifest behavior, are problem-solving actions. That is, whenever a person senses an incompatibility between two parts of his or her own operating reality—e.g., between two percepts, a percept and a concept, a percept and a goal, etc.—that incompatibility has preempting power to arrest that person's attention and to encumber that person's resources over other elements which do not form incompatible relations. The only operating reality that has greater power is an incompatibility of greater magnitude.[5] Actions

---

[3] The contents of operating reality (e.g., goals, emotions, attitudes) need not be conscious, but to invoke any unconscious content of operating reality in an explanation requires data sufficient to show the presence and influence of that element as unconscious. This implies gathering the kind of data ordinarily gathered by clinicians.

[4] While the *concept* of problem is distinctly Western, the psychological conditions and effects it refers to—incompatible elements of an individual's ongoing, (consciously and unconsciously) assembled world which impel the individual to act so as to reduce the incompatibility to tolerable proportions—are observable across cultures. Examples are easily found in the fairy tales of widely differing cultures.

[5] Festinger's (1957, p. 9–18) concept of dissonance is essentially similar to the meaning I intend for problem. March and Olsen's (1979, pp. 12–13) characterization

taken to reduce the incompatibilities to tolerable levels are problem-solving actions (irrespective of their effectiveness).

The variant of symbolic interactionism that I shall be drawing on, then, claims that we humans respond (1) pre-eminently to these synthesized incompatibilities I call problems, (2) to nothing but problems, (3) to problems in the particular hierarchy of salience in which they operate in us, and (4) to only our *own* problems.[6] It is precisely this fourth aspect, this individualistic and idiosyncratic nature of realities that poses the fundamental human dilemma of creating *shared* realities. The dilemma of being in largely separate worlds but creating shared worlds is a central dilemma, perhaps the central dilemma, of teaching. It was precisely that dilemma

---

of the "familiar conception" of the first part of what they call the "complete cycle of choice" captures the idea of problem nicely in terms of a "discrepancy" between a subjective "ought" and a perceived "is." Studies of dissonance and its reduction, however, (see Abelson, R.P., Aronson, E., McGuire, W.J., Newcomb, T.M., Rosenberg, M.J., and Tannenbaum, P.H., 1968, for scores of examples) focus on rearrangements of merely cognitive elements—beliefs, evaluations and the like—rather than actions to rearrange environmental conditions.

[6] Multiple reality theory differs from Blumer's (1969) symbolic interactionism in important regards. It shares with symbolic interactionism the general proposition that people respond to inner constructions, not directly to outer reality. But Blumer's inner "meaning" repeatedly emphasizes *interpretation* and de-emphasizes *commitments*. A typical assertion, for example, is this one: "We must recognize that the activity of human beings consists of meeting a flow of situations in which they have to act and that their action is built on the basis of what they note, how they assess and interpret what they note, and what kind of projected lines of action they map out." (p. 16) Commitments are buried here in the phrase, "in which they have to act," while situations, notations, assessments, and interpretations are brought into the foreground. What is noted, the manner and direction of assessment, and the very definition of situation, however, are already constrained by commitments of the kind we refer to by goals, wishes, values, and fears. The foregoing quote from Blumer, translated into multiple reality theory, would read: We must recognize that the activity of human beings is in response to incompatibilities they sense among the contents of their minding, minding which includes perceptions, previous conceptions, goals, values, emotions, assessments of opportunity and obligation and the like—responses designed to reduce the incompatibilities to tolerable levels.

A second difference from Blumer is that the categories of interpretation and of thought in general are not restricted, in multiple reality theory, to those offered and internalized through social interaction, as indicated by Blumer's (1969) second basic premise (p. 2). Indigenous generation of categories is prodigious—even, or especially, in autism, for example. While much minding is social and cultural in origin, much is local and situational. We must guard against both psychological reductionism and social–cultural reductionism.

Finally, multiple reality theory provides an explicit niche, as symbolic interactionism does not, for the "meanings," the operating reality, of the scientist–observer. The observer's reality provides information about causes of actors' action of which the actors often cannot be aware.

which Hugh Petrie ran into in his observations of academics struggling to cooperate on intellectual tasks and which led him to issue
the warning with which I opened this paper. If you are to see what
I see, you must conceive of people responding not to what just
happened in front of them, but rather to salient problems in operating
reality, incompatibilities or dissonances they sense in which that
something in front of them may participate centrally, tangentially,
or not at all.

Our use of language always suffers from an imperfect fit with our
reality—even with our most salient reality. Those who come closest
to forging a fit are called poets. The rest of us are caught in stumbling
prose. And so it is with teachers and students carrying on a classroom
discussion. The appearance of communication between them is
manifest; tarry long enough to glimpse the latent operating realities
and you often see the teacher's and student's worlds as traveling in
very different orbits even while they seem overtly to be in touch
with and responsive to one another.

Two Principles

The first principle I bring with me from the organizational context
is the part–whole principle or more accurately the principle of
superordinate–subordinate constraint. It says that a social structure,
say a relationship between two persons, that encompasses some
action, say a conversation between them, sets more potent and
continuing constraints on the action than the action sets on the
structure. Thus, the *relationship* between Peter and Paul, being of
longer duration and greater cumulative effect than an *interchange*
between them, sets more constraint on the content and process of
that interchange than the interchange sets on their relationship.
Similarly, problems set more constraints on actions than actions do
on problems. Group qualities—e.g., solidarity versus conflict, instrumental versus expressive orientation, even versus uneven distribution of power among members—constrain subgroup qualities
more strongly than the reverse. Similarly, ends constrain means
more than the reverse, and so on. If you want to understand X,
therefore, one necessary (not sufficient) move is to understand the
larger structure or process or function of which X is a part.

The second principle, the principle of indeterminacy, requires
more introduction. Observations of people struggling with their
multiple realities in organizations have led me to appreciate the
cumulativity or non-cumulativity of collective action over time. It
is a commonplace in organizational life that certain actions can be

undertaken *only after* other actions precede them. Action, thus, reveals one kind of *sequential dependency*, one that refers to the *opportunity* to undertake Z, given prior actions X and Y. There is a second kind, a sequential dependency having to do with *effects*.

As one studies organizational processes over time, one cannot help but be struck by those events within, between, and among persons *which transform or reverse earlier actions*. It is commonplace that today's action nullifies effects of yesterday's. For example, one may take the processes and outcome of a certain meeting to be creative and cumulative only to find that, as subsequent actions unfold, the decisions apparently made and directions apparently set in that meeting become radically transformed or reversed in a later meeting or at a different level in the organization. The reverse happens as well: "errors" become "corrected." But neither of these kinds of radical transformation is guaranteed. Sometimes the accomplishment at time t eventuates, at t + 10, in cumulative, effective fruition. Sometimes, too, the disastrous decision at t eventuates in cumulative, unmitigated destruction at t + 10. Thus, the *organizational effectiveness* of a segment of action at time t is a function, not of its properties at time t, but of how processes pick the action up later and carry it forward. More generally, the contribution that an organizational event or action makes to the organization at time t depends on processes which come after time t. To put the matter in manifest–latent terms, a segment of action at time t is manifest; many of its latent properties lie in the time interval between t and t + 10 or t + 20 or, in general, t + u, where u is the added amount of time required to complete the contemplated action—e.g., a unit of study, a course, a degree. I take up the problems of establishing boundaries to such units below.

Important to study, therefore, are not the short-term segments of action in isolation but these short-term actions together with the later processes which determine how the short-term segments of action are built upon or undermined; how the product of actions becomes processed cumulatively or blocked, using up energy but going nowhere.[7]

---

[7] To use the phrase "later processes" may be taken to imply that the earlier action segments are somehow unitary, separate from the later processes. I do not intend that implication. Action segments or "events" at time t are most usefully conceived as artificial slices from ongoing processes, not separated from the "later processes" except in time. The units frequently chosen by social scientists—e.g., "response," "utterance," "attribution," or "10-minute segment"—are assumed to be neutral. I am arguing that they are not, that they do unnecessary violence to the very subject matter being studied. These units of convenience are best thought of as short-term

I distinguish two kinds of sequential dependency, then. One, let us call it forward dependency or the dependency of opportunity, refers to a future action's dependence on the present: action X must be accomplished in order for us to be in a position to carry out action Y. The second kind of sequential dependency, let us call it backward dependency or the dependency of effects or of function, refers to the present action's function or participation in the future: we must wait upon Y later events in order to assess how X earlier actions contributed (not promised to contribute) to ongoing functioning.

This second kind, *sequential dependency of functional effects*, implies that if we wish to develop scientific study of education we must develop units of observation extensive enough in time and in complexity to inform us about an action's educational effects, effectiveness, and function as well as its immediate, focal characteristics. This implies for a project such as ours, focused on the educational effects of questioning and discussion, that 10-minute segments will be useful only to the extent that they inform us not only about some action, say an interchange between a teacher and a student, but also about how that action actually came to function educatively (i.e., its effects) in at least one of the participants' lives or thought. Even 10-minute segments of spelling bee or of rote recitation of arithmetic "facts" depend for their educational significance on what students *do* as a result that is different by virtue of having undergone the experience.

Implied by the foregoing is a *principle of indeterminacy* that can be now stated: The educational function, effects, or effectiveness of a segment of action at time t are indeterminate at time t; they become determinate only within and in reference to, functional units of action. The claim of indeterminacy rests on observations mentioned earlier that short segments of action depend for their educative contribution to the actors on actions *afterward*, actions that continue, build and strengthen, or that interrupt and undermine, the educative effects of those short segments of action.

In order to point up the problems of our interdisciplinary project's focus on classroom discussion of the kinds we have sampled, I shall present classroom data of a different kind. These data contrast with

---

solutions to *scientists'* problems, problems of fitting schedules of data-gathering into schedules of scientific study and of career evaluations and advancement, for example, rather than as stable units in the subject matter of social life itself. Put another way, these units come from the subculture of the scientist, not that of the persons being studied. As such, they conflict with the cultural units to which the actors have strong, if unspoken, commitment.

the project's five transcribed segments in one important respect: They address some of the latent realities behind the classroom discourse, realities to which one of the participants was responding but which were not captured in the classroom discussion itself.

AN EDUCATIONAL NARRATIVE AND AN ILLUSTRATIVE CLASSROOM INTERCHANGE

Here is a narrative, a true story adapted from Richard Jones (1968). First, the classroom interchange:

TEACHER: [of Billy's sixth grade class, introducing a new concept in mathematics]: And now can anyone tell me what infinity means?
[silence] What is infinity?
BILLY: [pause] Uh, I think it's like a box of Cream of Wheat.
TEACHER: Billy, don't be silly! (Jones, 1968, p. 72).

As it happened, Billy had been troublesome for his teacher—and for previous teachers. He had long had difficulty reading and made free use of what his teachers regarded as foul language. We come to know Billy's story through his psychotherapist, Jones:

> When Billy was two, his father . . . deserted the family, [went] off with another woman, married her, and started another family, without benefit of divorce. His devoutly Catholic family could find no better solution to their resulting fear and shame but to surround the man's memory with a dense wall of secrecy and dissimulation. Divorce could have meant excommunication . . .; notoriety could have meant prosecution for bigamy. The mother, . . . in her early twenties, had her own and the child's subsistence to think of, and therefore had to manage her humiliations in silence. For example, once when the school nurse asked Billy his father's occupation Billy said he would have to find out. This led to a crisis at home, and instructions that to future such questions he should say his father had died! (Jones, 1968, p. 73–74)
> Billy later recalled "that his mother used to put a bowl of Cream of Wheat before him as she left for work mornings," and, in Billy's words: "I'd sit there, kind of bored, all by myself, and make up . . . stories about things. Maybe I used to look at the man on the box when I was thinking of them" (Jones, 1968 p. 76). In his earlier play therapy, "Billy played out with his doctor imaginary version after imaginary version of what makes fathers leave families" (Jones, 1968, p. 74), including, most especially, versions in which the boy's character and behavior were the cause of the father's running off. Jones continues:

At the time of the Cream-of-Wheat-box episode, Billy and his mother
had made considerable progress. . . . I had been able to tell Billy
the sad but true story of his father, thus relieving him of some of the
more fantastic of his speculations. In fact, he had left his last session
consciously resolved to try harder in school, and he returned to relate
the Cream-of-Wheat-box interchange in tones that said: "See, it's too
late, Doc. I cried 'wolf' too often. Nobody will believe me now."
"Doc" had to do what the teacher would have been better equipped
to do: "Billy, *how* is infinity like a box of Cream of Wheat?" "Well,"
said Billy, "think of a box of Cream of Wheat. It shows a man holding
a box of Cream of Wheat. Right? And that box shows the same man
holding the same box. Right? And that box. . You can't see them all,
like you can't see infinity. You just know the're all there, going on
forever and ever" (Jones, 1968, p. 75–76).

Was Billy responding to his teacher's question? Manifestly, yes.
He told her his version of the concept of infinity. But by answering
he was doing far more, and far more important, than providing the
teacher with an answer. He was trying out a whole new way of
responding to school. And in doing this he was solving a problem.
On the one hand, he had come to realize that reading and textbooks
and homework assignments and cooperative participation in the
classroom could be terribly important for him. But on the other
hand, he also clearly saw that his present role and reputation, his
level of reading skill, and, yes, often his own spur-of-the-moment
feelings, blocked much of those school benefits from him. This new
goal of getting more out of school was incompatible with his perception of his relationship to his teacher, his current level of skill,
his accumulated habits. Something had to be done. But taking school
seriously and going along with *its* demands as allied with his own
was a whole new way of thinking, strange, unpredictable. With his
reading weaknesses, allying himself with serious learning purposes
made him vulnerable. Could he really afford to trust those people,
to try to be like them?

In Billy's reality, the question of importance was not the one
asked by his teacher. The central question for him was not about
infinity. The teacher's question was an occasion for Billy to try out
a contributory, cooperative mode of participating with a teacher.
And he put his heart into it.

So we have two kinds of data here, one about a manifest classroom
interchange, the other about what was going on in one of the
participants. That second kind of data, about the latent action,
showed the manifest action of Billy to have been impelled not merely
by the teacher's question but by the question together with a far

more important part of Billy's life, a larger unit of action of which his manifest answering was merely a contributing part. That larger unit of action was a unit of problem solving. While *linguistically* the teacher–pupil interchange can be taken as a unit, educationally and psychologically, i.e., functionally, that interchange excludes most of what was going on with the most important part of Billy's education—trying harder in school.

What was going on with Billy's teacher? Well, we don't have those data. But it is not outlandish to suspect that she was not responding merely to Billy's words about a Cream of Wheat box when she said, "Billy, don't be silly." After all, this teacher had been hearing Billy's foul mouth for some time and probably knew him by reputation even before he first stepped into her classroom. She was responding to his answer about a Cream of Wheat box *synthesized with* the cumulative reality Billy had already helped build up in her. In Piagetian terms, she assimilated his answer into already well structured schemata, schemata which said, in effect, "This kid is trouble and I better move quickly away from any bizarre comments he makes." The human responsiveness that was going on between her and Billy is not captured in the manifest data of the classroom interchange.

At another level of analysis, the level of teacher–pupil relationship, what was going on was a conflict. Billy was trying to change his relationship with the teacher to one more typical of his classmates' relationships with her. She, in contrast, was maintaining her stance of self-protection against this pupil whose mouth could not be trusted. The part–whole principle was operating here. The structure of their relationship exerted more constraint on this interchange than the reverse—greater stability (of the relationship) constrained lesser stability (of the interaction). The more stable phenomenon, the relationship, was excluded from the data of the manifest classroom interchange.

It should be clear now that I am mounting an argument against the use of data which capture merely the manifest. The data which Jones provides about Billy's problem solving—turning over a new leaf with his schoolwork and teacher—tell us the *function* of Billy's response to his teacher's question, that is, how his answering contributed to the larger project of solving his problem.

As illuminating as Jones' data are about this interchange, they include only one of two basic dimensions to action. They concentrate on antecedent operating realities—and even there only on the realities of one of the key participants. Jones' data excluded the second dimension, subsequent action—the action and processes after time

t. Well, not entirely: Billy's report of his own reaction to the interchange, made afterward to Jones, is included. But the problem-solving action remained unfinished at the time Jones' narrative broke off. Did Billy give up and go back to his old ways of participating in school? That is, was the educative impact of the interchange that he had, indeed, cried wolf too often, that he had made himself an iron cage that he now could not escape from? Or did he try again and find increasing success? Jones' narrative is simply incomplete with respect to the action undertaken by his focal subject, Billy. If Billy did persist, then the significance of his teacher's rejection of his remark, for example, fades to nothing; if he did not, then her rejection takes on substantial significance.

Without such subsequent data, the educativeness of this brief interchange is simply indeterminate. On its surface, it looks like Billy is making a wisecrack. Dig a little deeper and we see that the teacher becomes the villain, passing over a beautiful image of exactly what she was trying to impart to the kids. But stay a little longer, and we find, at least implied by Jones' data, that Billy has indeed learned an extremely important lesson from the interchange: Once you set yourself up in others' eyes as uncooperative and disruptive, not even your own change of heart, sincere good will, and positive contributions will be enough quickly, and may not be enough ever, to change yourself in their eyes. It is a lesson, indeed, that many leaders of nations have yet to learn.

Nonetheless, we are left with only part of the story of Billy's education here. Did he solve his problem effectively, or did he solve it by resorting to the old ways? Only following his problem-solving to the end of his school year with this teacher can we give an answer with respect to this particular teacher–student relation.

THE PROJECT'S CLASSROOM SEGMENTS AS DATA ABOUT THE MANIFEST

Let me turn now to two of the five transcribed classroom segments (Appendix) and comment on them from the foregoing perspectives. Because the transcriptions are so decontextualized, not only from the problems of their participants but also from the previous discussion of each respective class hour, I can only fill that vacuum by speculation. I shall try, through the medium of speculation, to make clear what a problem-solving analyst would look for and at.

HK's class: Washington's army. It is clear that HK has certain conclusions he wants to get across to his students. It is just as clear that he is committed in this class to avoid simple lecturing—but not to avoid long answers to his own questions (e.g., 21a, 24a). My view of what he is up to is solving the problem of having content to get across yet wanting to avoid the usual medium for doing so, readings and lectures. His solution is to generate a series of questions and probes which give successive cues about the "points," but which keep students guessing at, rather than merely listening to, his points.

Are the students learning anything about solving their problems? Do HK's questioning and occasional answers induce in some of the students any important problems about war or survival or George Washington—i.e., induce any important incompatibilities in the students' own realities, among their own commitments, thoughts, or feelings? The data needed to answer any of these questions would come from conversations with the students—including both the active students, the ones who show up in these transcripts, and the silent ones—about their recollections and speculations about what was going on in them when this or that was being said in the question-answering.

As to a longer time perspective, my organization-watcher's concern for cumulativity and non-cumulativity of effects makes me wonder whether HK's directed questioning—Tom Roby's (this volume) "quiz show" form of instruction—is so typically used by HK that it generates in the students a growing sense of being merely manipulated, of being forced to guess when they could be easily told, and therefore once again being induced into a game of decreasing interest to them. On the other hand, to the extent that students were active—and one flaw of these data is that they do not show the concentration or distribution of participation—the kids may learn more of a teacher's conclusions from this mode than from straight lecturing.

What is clear from these data is that questioning and answering can go on, apparently without limit, without evidence that problems are being either solved or induced, either for the teacher or the students, without ever entering into the content of the questions or answers—all left latent, behind the scenes. To study these data alone, then, is to study not merely an incomplete set of data. To study these data is to study an incomplete, indeterminant phenomenon: To exclude data which capture *some* whole phenomenon's stable functioning, for example, the solving of the teacher's or some students' *problems* or the fulfilling of a teacher's *role*.

To study this kind of selected data is like studying an arbitrarily chosen cubic inch of the left ventricle of the heart as if that cubic inch were an entity unto itself. One *could* gather data on that chunk of tissue, no doubt with high reliability; one *could* do experiments to see how it reacted, and could create theories of its action—all independent of its relation to the ventricle, the heart, or the heart's function in the circulatory system. But to do so would be simply to ignore part–whole relations and functioning, that is, to miss how the part contributed to the whole and how the whole set constraints on the operation of the part.

MK's class: The revoking of senior privileges. Here we have clear evidence, from the intensity and content of students' participations, of students' problems being dealt with in the very content of discussion. Some seniors who do not smoke are bothered by the revoking of senior privileges on account of the misbehavior of some seniors who did smoke in a prohibited area. Other seniors who do smoke are bothered by the prohibition of smoking. Other students, juniors or others, synthesized still other problems. In each case, the precipitating event was an administrative edict known to all.

The teacher appears to be capitalizing on this event, and on his evidently correct surmise that it had precipitated problems in the students. He exploits the inner frustrations and the manifest conflict between the administration and the miscreants for an educational end. What educational end, exactly? Well, once again we do not have either observational or interview data about the teacher. But we can speculate that MK wants to exploit this conflict for what it can reveal, upon classroom examination, about the citizen's relationship to other citizens who are violating rules, and about the role and possible responsible domain of action of the citizen in confronting his or her peers' rule violation. Part way through the exchange, the focus shifts from the citizen's to the Christian's responsibility, but that merely shifts the domain of values, not the fact of values being implicated.

MK's discussion of seniors' smoking is far livelier than HK's on Washington's army precisely because, I would argue, MK is dealing with problems already operating in his students. But the data still do not go much beyond the manifest level and they do not follow the problem solving to its conclusion, where either the whole matter is dropped as no longer important or it leads to some new actions on the part of either the administration or the students. We are left mid-stream, with the teacher saying, "With that in mind . . ." That's *precisely* where education becomes more than merely academic, when bearing something in mind leads to or implies something else of importance.

Commenting on the other three segments of classroom discussion is unnecessary; I have made my point, I think. These 10-minute segments, first, capture manifest action, not latent—excluding both operating realities and part–whole relations; and second, exclude data about sequential dependencies necessary to determine effects, effectiveness, or function. Like the cubic inch of tissue of the left ventricle, it is always *possible* to study such arbitrarily defined segments to understand physiological functioning. But it is not likely to be fruitful. Such research is not likely to be fruitful, in these 10-minute (or otherwise arbitrary) segments, because it excludes powerfully constraining forces at higher levels of complexity as well as events after these brief segments which reveal the effects, effectiveness, and functions of the actions sampled in these focal 10 minutes.

THE PROBLEM OF UNITS: WHEN DOES A DATA SEGMENT CAPTURE A STABLE UNIT OF BEHAVIOR?

A difficulty arises with what I have called functional dependence. Let me elaborate and correct that idea a bit. The concept of functional dependence, and the associated principle of indeterminacy, asserts that some segment of action at time t is indeterminate regarding its effects, its effectiveness, or its function until some later time when effects, effectiveness, and function are determinate. The difficulty lies in specifying that later time. This is equivalent to specifying the concluding boundary of a unit of data. If arbitrary time limits of action at time t are ruled out as excluding later, ongoing action that effectively or functionionally "goes with" or is an integral part of the action segment at t, what time limit takes its place without being equally arbitrary? When *does* the effect or effectiveness or function of an action segment become determinate?

If the nature of all action is continuously ongoing, of course, then any segmentation at all violates that continuous reality. But is human action, individually or collectively, merely smoothly continuous, without breaking points or lulls in the action, without any stable beginnings or endings? Observations and analysis of organizational action persuade me otherwise. What sorts of whole units of action might be identified that minimize arbitrariness of action segmentation?

Three general sources of stable units of data seem available: (1) a social psychological unit of action, the problem-solving episode; (2) a cultural unit of action, the ritual or ceremony or legal procedure (e.g., trial); and (3) a cultural unit of time, e.g., class period, fiscal year.

I can think of only one social psychological unit that is not arbitrary, i.e., takes its termini not from units of my convenience but from the local realities of the participant. I refer to the "problem"—a state of operating reality or, if you like, state of minding, dominated by incompatible relations among or between (consciously or unconsciously) cognized elements. I consider such states to be universal, not culturally limited, and to have universally attention-directing and motivating effects in directing the actor's action. A person synthesizes a problem out of confusion. This leads to psychological responses to the problem—thinking, feeling—and sometimes to overt action. All of this eventuates, sooner or later, in a transformed condition of that person's operating reality where one or more of those earlier incompatible elements are now sufficiently changed to reduce that incompatibility very much below the intensity of other incompatibilities. At that point, these other incompatibilities (problems) take over as the objects of thought, feeling, and action. The problem solving episode (problem plus the solving), thus, has a beginning, a middle (sometimes very long) and an end.[8]

The second kind of stable unit of data is the culturally prescribed procedure or ritual. It is a unit that is thought of as a unit by the actor him- or herself. That is, it is a culturally provided category which happens to refer prominently to a segmenting of prescribed operations. A wedding ceremony, for example, has a beginning, a middle, and an end, with a minimum of confusion over the moments of beginning and the moments of ending.

The third source of stable units of data is the cultural segmenting

---

[8] The idea of seleting such a unit of study as the problem-solving episode is parallel in content and purpose to the ideas of George Herbert Mead and of Robert W. White. The "social act" was Mead's (1938) basic unit of action, possessing a beginning in troubled, unsettled conditions, a middle of perception and manipulation, and an end of consummatory action. White's (1959) "transaction," argued by White to be the basic, *coherent* unit of observation, consisted of a cycle of activities involving sensation, perception, action upon the environment, and affective response to activity and to the results of activity. Each of these scholars saw the basic unit as exercising influential constraint upon each of its parts and construed the parts as contributing particular functions to the underlying purpose of the "act" or the "transaction." For Mead the underlying purpose was survival through adaptation; for White it was the pleasure of experiencing one's power to have a controlled impact on the environment. Mead's act and White's transaction both seek to incorporate complexities of purpose, perception, motivation, and action in a single unit rather than consider the separate parts—purpose, perception, motivation, thought, behavior—as separate domains of study. The problem-solving episode is an attempt to bring psychological *and social-organizational* processes into a single unit of data. Unlike Mead's and White's units, however, the problem-solving episode is not a unit of only individual action, but of collective action within an organization to which an individual, the problem originator, is linked. It is, in short, a social psychological unit of data.

of time—hour, day, year, and variants. These units possess a stability provided by culture far beyond any arbitrary segmenting of time, a stability derived from their widespread operation and committed roots. More to our purpose, the cultural world of education offers the school class period, the school day, the course, the quarter or semester, the school year, and the degree—to name a few. In law, a parallel is the sentence; in medicine, the periodicity of medication; in finance, the fiscal year or quarter; in the legislative sphere, the legislative session, the elected term of office—and so on.

In each sphere of life, culture develops and passes on units of time which order people's expectations, evaluations, and actions and, being shared, order social commitments and collective definitions of what is legitimate and illegitimate regarding sequence and timing. Since these units operate so as to constrain action within them, to substitute for them arbitrary units of time is not only to reify nonentities as entities; it is also to exclude powerful forces which constrain the *integral connectedness* of actions being studied.

It may be objected that I am killing sparrows with cannons here, and that no such complicated argument is necessary against arbitrary segmentations of actions since few social scientists simply take time samples. I am not referring only to arbitrary time segments, however, but to other segmentations as well: The command and obedience interchanges studied by Milgram (1974); the conformity pressure and response studied by Asch (1955); the attributions studied by Kelley (1973), Jones and Davis (1978), and many others—all fix on action segments for which unitariness is claimed but never examined in ongoing action. When one finds such "phenomena" in ongoing organizational action, however, they turn out to be highly unstable, conditional *parts* of action whose effects, effectiveness, and function depend on other, following action.

Each of these arbitrarily segmented actions, defined or assumed to be unitary phenomena, is held to have important, reality-distorting or socially disrupting consequences. The scientist's attribution of reality distortion or social disruption to such "phenomena" as "yielding" (Asch, 1955) or "attributions" (Kelley, 1973) is largely the basis in the first place for isolating and focusing on the action in question (i.e., yielding or attributing cause). But social or organizational life has rich resources for reversing or for sustaining the immediate effects of conformity or obedience or misattributions. Actions which in short segments look like blind obedience or conformity or erroneous attributions often become, in somewhat longer segments, *moments* of blind obedience, *brief instances* of conformity, and *temporary errors* of attribution.

In this regard, each of these supposed entities—obedience, conformity, erroneous attribution, or, to come closer to home, a "silly" answer to a question—is like the error of the individual child in spelling or reading or learning to walk. The error itself is not important. In most endeavors one cannot learn without errors. Important, rather, is whether subsequent events do or do not sustain the error and its effects.

If normal organizational processes, like normal processes of learning, correct the defects immediately apparent in blind obedience or conformity or misattributions, or "silly" answers, the supposed defects recede in significance and lose their claim to unitariness. They also lose their claim to be isolated and studied as phenomena. They become, like errors, just *part of a larger process*. It so happens that organizational life offers commonplace reversals of these and many other short-term actions—not guarantees against them, but nonetheless commonplace reversals and mitigations.

The principle of indeterminacy, then, that the function and effects of action at time t are indeterminate at time t, is answered by a principle of cultural and intentional determinancy. This principle states that effects, effectiveness, and function are not only culturally defined and relative, but also, within cultures, are intention-bound; that actions are generated out of, and are properly evaluated in terms of, both culturally shared segmentings of time and actors' intentions.

Return to Billy's teacher's action of rejecting Billy's answer. The effects, effectiveness, and function of that action are to be determined, says this principle of cultural and intentional determinacy, not in reference to Jones' sampling of time, but in terms of the segments of time provided by the teacher's own subculture—say, the unit of study or the marking period. It is these locally stable, culturally provided units of time that enter into the teacher's planning and corrective action. Educationally it is not Billy's immediate response to her "silly" comment that counts, his interpretation, for example, that it is "too late," that he cried wolf once too often. Rather, the function and effects that count have to do with the educational resources actually available to the teacher and student. Most prominent among these resources are the units of time available for teacher and students to interact with each other—time in which the effects at time t can be reversed or built upon.

What does this all imply for our interdisciplinary project? It all comes down to something quickly and easily said, but not quickly or easily done: The principles of indeterminacy and determinacy imply that we move away from two old habits and develop two new ones. First, the principles suggest that we move away from our habits of attending only to manifest behavior to a new habit of examining the manifest always in relation to its latent intended effects, effectiveness, and function within the actor's culturally supplied units of time. Second, the principles suggest that we move away from our habit of selecting our units of data on the basis of short-term convenience of the investigator to a new habit of developing our units from the intentions of the actors we are observing as they relate to culturally provided time segments assumed or planned for by the actors themselves. Data would be gathered which answered the question, for example, "What do the actors intend to do in what units of time and by what sequence of implied deadlines or phases in the units of time available to them?" This second implies a habit of following effects over sufficient spans of the local culture's time segments to examine the cumulativity or non-cumulativity of effects recognizable by actors in that culture or subculture.

Imagine some next steps for an interdisciplinary project. Imagine a focus on two corpuses of data, each containing not only manifest classroom interchanges with some topical (i.e., cultural) unity, but also interview data from several of the participants, both active and silent ones, both teacher and student, promoting discussions about what they intended to accomplish, what they believed or perceived to have happened, and about what one from that subculture ought to expect to accomplish within time segments relevant to the subculture of schooling. Imagine that each interviewee had listened to or read a transcript of taped segments of action they had witnessed or participated in. Imagine further that such observations and interviews were conducted across a three-week instructional unit, like the American revolution, from the beginning to end, sampling one early and one late segment on the same topic, a sampling taken against descriptions of topics discussed in each of the classes devoted to the unit. Imagine, finally, that the two corpuses were chosen as representing contrasts in educative effectiveness as judged by explicit criteria applied to that unit's instruction *as a whole*. Would such an enterprise not bring us closer to comparative educational processes than our project's first, arbitrary sampling? Would we not be studying segments of education more stable, more pervasively present in schools, and more widely understood and expected by both educators and students (in our culture) than the 10-minute segments we have now cut our teeth on?

REFERENCES

Abelson, R.P., Aronson, E., McGuire, W.J., Newcomb, T.M., Rosenberg, M.J., and Tannenbaum, P.H. (Eds.) (1968). *Theories of Cognitive Consistency: A Sourcebook.* Chicago: Rand McNally.

Asch, S.E. (1955). Effects of group pressure upon the modification and distortion of judgment. *Scientific American,* November, 31–34.

Blumer, H. (1969). *Symbolic Interactionism.* Englewood Cliffs, N.J.: Prentice-Hall.

Festinger, L. (1957). *A Theory of Cognitive Dissonance.* Stanford: Stanford University Press.

Jones, E.E. and Davis, K.E. (1978). From acts to dispositions. In L. Berkowitz, (Ed.), *Cognitive Theories in Social Psychology,* 283–330. New York: Academic Press.

Jones, R.M. (1968). *Fantasy and Feeling in Education.* New York: New York University Press.

Kelley, H.H. (1973). The processes of causal attribution. *American Psychologist, 28,* 107–128.

March, J.G. and Olsen, J.P. (1979). *Ambiguity and Choice in Organizations. Second Edition.* Bergen, Norway: Universitetsforlaget.

Mead, G.H. (1934). *The Philosophy of the Act.* Chicago: University of Chicago Press.

Milgram, S. (1974). *Obedience to Authority.* New York: Harper and Row.

Petrie, H.G. (1976). Do you see what I see? The epistemology of interdisciplinary inquiry. *Journal of Aesthetic Education, 10,* 29–43.

White, R.W. (1959). Motivation reconsidered: The concept of competence. *Psychological Review, 66,* 297–333.

CHAPTER 8

Review of Disciplinary Perspectives

William Knitter

Educational Studies
Concordia University
Montreal, Canada H3G 1M8

The six studies reviewed here are different disciplinary analyses of a common set of data, five high school discussion classes. The studies illuminate the discussions in a variety of ways while revealing much as well about the perspectives of the authors.

LOGIC

C.J.B. Macmillan elucidates and applies to the discussions an "erotetic" concept of teaching. An erotetic analysis (derived from the Greek work for questioning) focuses on the logic of the questions put during a whole lesson. Its guiding presumption is that, when a teacher is teaching, he is attempting to answer the students' questions about the subject matter. Not the questions that the students have actually asked, but rather those that the teacher thinks or assumes that they *should* ask, given their present state of knowledge about the subject matter under consideration.

Just as the game is the essential aspect of a bridge party, Macmillan asserts, the core of the student–teacher relationship in an educational discussion will be ordered by the logic of questions inherent in a particular lesson about a subject matter. Thus, from that logic one can draw criteria for assessing when a teacher's questioning is on the mark, when the order of questions is helpful, when opportunities have been missed, and so on.

Applied to the discussion data, Macmillan's model brings to light interesting aspects of the discussions. In particular, the analysis of a U.S. History class on George Washington's military strategy reveals an underlying order or logic of questions which gives unity to a lesson that other authors in the project found to be a mere recitation.

One strong point of Macmillan's analysis, then, is the honoring of the place of the subject matter of discussion. Another strong point, likely to be appreciated by teachers, is that the erotetic approach conceives of teaching in the intentional and literal terms which teachers themselves use.

COGNITIVE PSYCHOLOGY

Irving Sigel takes as his starting point a Piagetian cognitive-developmental perspective. The central assumption is that since "cognitive growth proceeds through assimilative-accommodative processes activated by discrepancies arising from internal and/or external violation of expectation," one can foster cognitive growth through the appropriate use of distancing strategies to generate cognitive discrepancies.

Following this assumption, Sigel discusses linguistic types of questions and statements in terms of their demand characteristics. His claim is that initiators of open-ended discussion are more demanding and thus potentially more facilitative of cognitive growth. In any Piagetian scheme, of course, respondent characteristics such as developmental and intellectual level and verbal sophistication must, as Sigel declares, also be considered.

In addition, Sigel offers a sensitive discussion, from a psychodynamic point of view, of contextual factors that affect students' affective states, which in turn interact with cognitive demands. The effect of a child–adult power differential on the child's potential moves is a central topic here.

Drawing on this background and on an explicitly formulated set of rules for inquiry, Sigel examines the Dillon tapes in terms of their potential for promoting cognitive growth. His conclusion is that generally, though not uniformly, the students were not intellectually challenged by the questions put. "Few contradictions were posed, few questions sought evidence, and few questions were linked to previous aspects of the discussion to build a case." He concludes with a statement of confidence in the power of appropriate distancing strategies to promote students' representational and problem-solving skills.

SOCIOLINGUISTICS

Mary Thomas Farrar's analysis is the most fine-grained and detailed of the 6 reviewed here. Applying qualitative and quantitative methods to the discussion data, she attempts to discern and explicate the teachers' underlying or tacit conceptions of teaching.

The qualitative analyses are comprised of (1) speech act, (2) conversational, and (3) interactional analyses that reveal the complexity and convey the flavor of the interaction in these discussions. In the quantitative analyses, she tabulates such conversational features as exchange patterns, use of evaluation, and topic control.

By way of conclusion, she finds 3 implicit conceptions of teaching in the discussion interactions: discussion as course covering, as expressing, and as integrating. The solid contribution of this paper, though, consists in something more and other than giving us some labels to stick on teaching styles. Associated with the labels are correlated patterns of differences in topic control and verbal interaction; thus, we understand more of what such pattern labels mean in the flesh.

Moreover, having brought to light the complexity of interaction that a sociolinguistic analysis can reveal, she draws implications for research and practice in a penetrating series of points. In light of the demonstrated complexity of interaction, one must be careful of (1) imposing on a discussion unresponsive coding schemes and hard and fast distinctions (e.g., of higher–lower level questions); and (2) of reifying categories of analysis and overgeneralizing the effects of strategies or patterns of discussion. While we might like to make normative judgments about what discussion strategies and patterns to recommend, Farrar maintains that we cannot do so until we have a more informed idea of what constitutes the various complex patterns of interaction during discussion.

ORGANIZATIONAL PSYCHOLOGY

Lighthall's paper inclines me to repeat my opening remark that the papers reveal as much about the authors' disciplinary commitments as they do about the discussion data. In all of these papers, these commitments are revealed in deliberate explications of theory in the paper's introduction as well as in the subsequent differential modes of treatment of the common data. The commitments that Lighthall places center stage are, however, decidedly methodological. From an "organization watcher's" view, he sets out and applies some fundamental methodological principles that he thinks crucial to the understanding of discussion.

In the intrepretation of human action, Lighthall urges us to keep in mind four related principles, in the light of which he discusses the adequacy of the common data set analyzed by all the authors in this project.

1. The first is a distinction between manifest and latent function.
2. A related distinction is between objective and subjective reality. Lighthall enjoins us not to confuse some one objective reality with the one to which people might be responding.
3. The part–whole or subordinate–superordinate principle cautions us that wholes constrain parts more so than vice versa.
4. The principle of indeterminacy is that the effect of a segment of action at a certain time is indeterminate at that time. One of the difficulties Lighthall explores under this heading is that of backward sequential dependency: that which actions good and bad in themselves may come to, depends in part on what we do later; for instance, to consolidate good beginnings or to learn from mistakes.

From Lighthall's point of view, these four points suggest that the data base analyzed in this multidisciplinary project (segments of discussion classes) is limited. Without further knowledge of teachers' and students' mind states and of larger contexts, it is difficult to see through to the latent functions of the discussion activity. And, without knowledge of the eventualities of action in the classroom episodes, the effect and import of the discussion activity is indeterminate.

The general issue of what constitutes an appropriate unit of data is treated skillfully by Lighthall. Whether or not other researchers on questioning and discussion agree with Lighthall's conclusions, his essay should help us to be more reflective about the connections between various data units and the research questions that we can use them to address.

SOCIAL PSYCHOLOGY

Brian Mullen's "self-attention" perspective focuses on the relations between class composition and participation in discussion. In self-attention theory, awareness of aspects of oneself is related to self-regulation processes; and group composition, described in terms of the ratio of *others* (teachers, where students are the primary subjects) to the *total group* (teachers plus students), is thought to predict individuals' levels of self-attention. The explanation is that where "others" form the majority of a group, individuals pay more attention to gaps between their own behavior and group standards. Thus, in discussion settings Mullen expects that self-attention and levels of participation will vary with differences in group composition (the other–total ratios).

Because he uses statistical regression procedures, Mullen applies his analysis here to a set of 27 classroom discussions, including the five in common (which derive from that larger set). He operationalizes the general notion of self-attention theory into six precise variables, in three groupings. *Self-reference* is the use of first person pronouns; *discussion performance* comprises number of student turns per student, and number of student words per student, and seconds of student talk per student; *teacher behavior* comprises number of teacher questions and number of teacher encouragements.

The first four outcome variables are regressed both on the other–total ratios for the different discussion groups and on the teacher bahavior variables. The latter are included to control for the alternative hypothesis that differences in participation would be due to teacher behaviors.

The results can be summarized in three propositions:

1. There is a statistically significant tendency for other–total ratios to predict levels of self-attention and participation.
2. There is a statistically significant, though weak, tendency for teachers' encouragements to lower students' levels of self-attention and participation.
3. There is a marginally significant, weak tendency for teacher questions to lower the student's levels of self-attention and participation.

Also of interest is Mullen's discounting of two relevant alternative hypotheses. Sheer size is not found to account for as much variability as other–total ratios; and, while there are differences due to interest in topic, the results cannot be reduced to this dimension.

Size, then, through its effect on group composition, makes a difference for discussion participation. Mindful of budgets, we should do what we can to create in classrooms other–total ratios that are more productive of discussion.

PHILOSOPHY

David Bridges' framework for analyzing the discussion transcripts is functional in form. After locating the rationale or purpose of discussion, he attempts to discern and describe the "qualities, principles, or conditions of discussion" requisite to the purpose.

The central function of purpose of discussion is "the improvement of the understanding of its participants on the matter under discussion." Thus, Bridges puts epistemological considerations center stage, relegating to supporting roles other functions which discussions may serve. Two classes of improvements in understanding are distinguished under the headings of enrichment and refinement. Enrichment involves elaboration of thought, reflective awareness, and the articulation of thought to others. Refinement involves the notions of precision, clarity, appreciation of reasons, and so on.

Having specified the functions of discussion, Bridges is able to do two important tasks in his analysis of the five discussion transcripts. He uses the functional terms as criteria for discriminating quality (or its lack) in discussions; and, he can say something of the characteristics of appropriately functioning discussion groups. In particular, he examines the discussion transcripts for evidence of concern in the groups for six specified qualities: reflectiveness, responsiveness, diversity, clarity, evidence, and consistency.

The analyses of the transcripts themselves are illuminating, although too detailed to report here. Suffice it to say that—with appropriate cautions about the limitations imposed by these data— Bridges finds little concern by teachers or students for the qualities which allow discussion to serve its central function.

CONCLUSION

The papers reviewed here provide a stimulating and kaleidoscopic view of classroom questioning and discussion. Taken separately, each constitutes a legitimate way into the life of classroom discussion. The explications of the approaches are informative and substantial, and the applications are well executed and revealing of the nature of discussion. Taken together they reveal that the phrase "classroom questioning and discussion" comprehends a rich and complex subject matter for inquiry.

In bringing to light and contrasting the approaches to, and faces of, classroom discussion, these studies remind us that no one approach comprehends the full set of realities. This is surely a subject matter for which coordinated multidisciplinary analysis is in order.

PART II

PEDAGOGICAL PERSPECTIVES

CHAPTER 9

Models of Discussion

Thomas W. Roby

City Colleges of Chicago

How do the common components of classroom questioning function educationally? We can begin to answer this question through inquiry into the commonplaces, questions, and models of group classroom conversations.

The commonplaces mentioned above are the broad and general notions of student, teacher, subject matter, and (social, cultural) milieu (Schwab, 1973; Roby, 1985). For any given problematical educational situation we must specify commonplace generalities by reference to particular students, teachers, subject matters, milieux, and their interactions. The commonplaces provide the axes for the functional set of questions and models.

The nine functional types of questions and five models of classroom conversations are defined in summary fashion in the Tables at the end of the chapter. Although certain kinds of questions tend to generate different types of discussions, I have made the models the unit of analysis in order to coordinate them with the transcripts (see the Appendix).

MODELS OF GROUP CLASSROOM CONVERSATIONS

Group classroom conversations become an option when a teacher is involved with the class as a whole rather than with one-on-one instruction. They concern more or less formal verbal exchanges, between either teacher and students or among students. I have used the generic term, conversations, because two of my five models must be distinguished from discussions proper. These are the QUASI-DISCUSSIONS: *Quiz Shows* and *Bull Sessions*. They are often confused with DISCUSSIONS, among which I have discriminated three main types: *Problematical, Dialectical,* and *Informational.*

These five models can be set on a scale whose axes are specifications of the four commonplaces of education. I have specified students and teachers as the agents of conversations, while subject matters and milieux function as content. Each model gives different answers for two questions based on the above division: (1) "Who leads the conversation?" and (2) "What is the conversation about?". Conversational leadership can be by either of the active agents— teacher or students. Conversational content is generally about terms in the students' milieu or those in the teachers' subject matter.

In practice these logical possibilities, which I shall elaborate later, are limited or enhanced by the location, status, or transformation of the "right answers". Location concerns who has control of the right answers, whether teacher or students or both. Status involves the degrees of deference (resistance or acceptance) by either agent of the right answers of the other. Transformation entails the refinement of initially proferred right answers into better or worse answers as tested by the discussion.

Quasi-discussions are so-called because, while often mistaken for discussions, they lack the fruitful, reflective interactions which arise from the discussions proper. They carry the flavor of discussion by encouraging student participation; they negate the essence of discussion by failing to generate either self criticism by students on their own positions or reflection on the various processes and outcomes of each type of group conversation.

Discussions modify the meanings of the right answers to become the best available answers worked toward and discovered in its context. Whereas in Quasi-Discussions the right answers are both the alpha and omega of the conversation, i.e., its beginning and (unaltered) end points, in Discussions they supply grist for the mills of examination. While either agent can lead a discussion, progress depends upon a developing sense of mutual enterprise. This involves discovery of unrealized capacities in oneself and others, and exploration of unsuspected richness in the content. Teaching and learning are created by discussion, not imposed upon it. The conclusions of one discussion are understood to become the starting points for the next one, with an eye for improvements in comprehension and exchange.

Figure 1 shows the five models on a scale of Group Classroom Conversations with the two Quasi-Discussions at either extreme and the three Discussions in the mean. Quiz Shows, which tend to be dominated by the teacher's version of the subject matter, lie at one extreme; Bull Sessions, controlled by the students and their milieux, occupy the other. Problematical discussions tend toward the Quiz Show end of the scale; Dialectical and Informational ones are closer to Bull Sessions. In practice each kind of discussion slips most readily into its indicated extreme. The capital letters in parentheses refer to the five Dillon transcripts used for this multidisciplinary study (Appendix).

I have specified the axes for any conversation by means of the commonplaces of education. The end points of the scale concern dominance by the indicated agents or content, with the subordination or assimilation, but not the disappearance, of the others. The proportions shift to a relative balance in the middle. However, just as some Problematical Discussions can be oriented to problems in the students' lives (as well as those in the subject matter), so some Dialectical Discussions are subject matter based.

ANALYSES OF THE DATA

Any given group classroom conversation depends upon a number of factors. One set involves the interaction of terms present in or (from my "observer's" standpoint) omitted from the conversation. These are locatable at each of the four commonplaces, i.e., the terms of the students, teachers, subject matter or milieu. The overall *topics* of the conversation arise out of this interaction. For my analyses I shall characterize the representative transcript of each model by specifying each of the four commonplaces through a question:

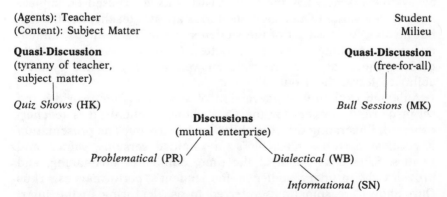

Figure 1. Scale of group classroom conversations.

"What happens to the subject matter?"
"What is the influence or relation to the milieu?"
"What, implicitly as well as explicitly, are the teachers teaching and
  the students learning?"
"What would I tell them about each episode?"

Another set of crucial components are the questions used or ignored
by either of the agents. Questions can be directed by teacher to
student (typically), by student to teacher (less frequently), or by one
student to another (rarely). Therefore we have the questions:

"What is the role of questioning in the conversation?"
"What is the status of the (right) answers?"

A detailed description of each model will precede the analysis of
each transcript. Since we are limited to the 10 minute episodes,
crucial dimensions of the conversations are omitted from our pur-
view. We do not know how these episodes mesh with those that
preceded or followed. We lack access to the overall sequence of
class lessons. Further, there is no way of checking as to whether
the meanings that I have assigned to the terms of teachers and
students are exactly their meanings. Even with these restrictions,
however, I believe that one can say some useful things about the
episodes.

QUASI-DISCUSSIONS: QUIZ SHOWS

At one extreme on the scale we have Quiz Shows. One party, almost
always the teacher, has the right answers usually based on subject
matter. In a variant Quiz Show the terms are still teacher-controlled,
but involve some aspect of the students' lives. The students' milieu,
as it were, becomes the subject matter. In either case the students
defer to the location of the right answers and gain status by their
ability to ferret them out.

Although explicitly some version of subject matter provides the
script of right answers for the Quiz Show, implicitly it is teacher-
centered, illustrating the vice of the led discussion. The presentation
is permeated with the teacher's unexamined versions, values, and
verities. S/he talks much of the time, dominates turn-taking, and
provides the primary audience for student's performances. Thus
Quiz Shows are sometimes referred to as "lecturing in the interrogatory mood."

As in the radio or television parallel, the students compete to show off their "knowledge." Those who develop the knack of hitting on the teacher's correct formulations are rewarded with approval. The others are put down with more or less grace, or ignored. Unless the teacher uses a class list for the order of participant, a Quiz Show conversation has a narrow base in the closed shop of a few, generally no more than a half a dozen "discussion leaders." Some of these students even consciously study "what the teacher wants." In this way the students learn to defer to and follow authority. On a more positive note the Quiz Show is one way to run a recitation or give a test, provided that students and teacher are clear on the differences between these functions and those of discussions.

The basic question for the Quiz Show tends to be the Fact Finder, supplemented by the Prompter with an occasional Prober. Properly employed, the Fact Finder is a useful kind of question. One of our goals is to enable the students to inform themselves about the details of a story, experiment, or case study. Information is necessary in order to proceed with other kinds of questions. Quiz Shows, however, tend to employ the Fact Finder in a comprehensive manner which reduces content to recitable bits of information—the "right answers." Principles are identified instead of argued; arguments are parroted rather than understood; methods are named but not applied. Often biographical or historical facts are substituted for principles, arguments, or methods. Here the Fact Finder usurps the functions of other questions like the Puzzler or Stretcher.

Frequently used Fact Finders atomize teacher as well as student thinking into immediately recitable bits of information—the facts or fact-like principles and methods, preset from textbook or lecture. There is no time for silent reflection in which to wrestle with puzzlements or chew on ideas. Questions codable as higher cognitive types actually function to reduce student answers to lower levels.

Emotionally, the feeling of the Quiz Show is one of suppressed tension and anxiety. Sometimes students attempt to break out of this hot box with two possible escapes. One occurs when a student takes over the teacher's role, often with the teacher's implicit approval, and quizzes another student. More commonly, students attempt to reverse the Quiz Show by asking the teacher straight out for the right answer rather than just guessing at it. Often the Reverse Quiz Show is generated out of real student puzzlement: they want the teacher to make sense of some aspect of the topic for them.

For the Quiz Show Mr. HK (see Appendix) provides a relatively straightforward example. In light of my above comment about meaning, let us note that although both teacher and students characterized every transcript as a discussion, HK waffled a bit in a side remark to Dillon before the start. ("It's more of a question-answer approach"). None of our five episodes, in fact, are set up in the circle or horseshoe seating format which facilitates the face to face encounters most desirable for discussion.

HK'S QUIZ SHOW

The topic of conversation is composed almost exclusively of the terms of the subject matter. These turn on the question of how the colonials won the American revolution. The right answers concern Washington's successful strategy (he never allowed his army to be destroyed, he didn't fight by British rules) and aid from allies (money, supplies, military genius). HK's control of these terms consists in two maneuvers: (1) he tries to insist on his preset order of right answers (terms introduced by the students at 1b must wait until HK is ready at 46a; likewise 35b must wait until 40b); (2) he rejects discussion of terms which are a problem for the students (the draft at 21b; the war debt at 37b).

HK typically operates by series of rapid-fire questions. There are hardly any silences and no reflective silences. His one statement at 21a is a distinct surprise, but it seems that even he needed a rest. The questions are mostly Fact Finders on the subject matter axis (2a, 13a, etc.), with an occasional foray on the student axis (15a). He often repeats information from the students in querulous inquiries, or repeats his questions in a prompting or demanding manner. The students very soon tire of this (16b, 18b), retreating from time to time into Reverse Quiz Shows (21b–22a; 37b–40a). These seem motivated by a genuine student puzzlement, to which the teacher fails to respond.

Overall I sense a high level of frustration among the students. This is sad since HK has a coherent vision of the topic. Macmillan (this volume) points out this characteristic in MK's underlying structure. Sigel, on the other hand, notes how the way this structure engages the students in the conversation is inconsistent and confusing. This is because HK is stuck with the responses he gets, a probable cause of his own frustration and consequent querulousness. Any responsiveness to students in the classroom can constitute a delay in "getting over the material." Note the contrast with "Professor Kingsfield," the imposing law professor in John Osborn's 1971 novel *The Paper Chase:*

It was very special that months after they'd started, Kingsfield would end on the last page in the book. How many other professors could so exactly delineate the subject, and so completely dominate the class, that no small measure of the students' independent interest would vary the progress? (pp. 173–4)

Well, not HK! I would suggest that HK work up his set of right answers as a lecture which develop ideas and arguments that supplement the textual information referred to in the transcript. Then he can take time during and after for student questions. The lecture would communicate the higher cognitive character of his explanations more adequately than the Quiz Show format. The questions would enable him to delineate the subject matter inquiry in an interactive way congruent with Macmillan's erotetic analysis.

Alternatively, if HK wants to run a recitation or give a test, then he should tell the students as well as Dillon. The thrust of this point, which I shall elaborate later, is to involve the students as much as possible in understanding what pedagogy they are undergoing.

QUASI-DISCUSSIONS: BULL SESSIONS

At the opposite extreme of the scale are Bull Sessions, the mirror image of Quiz Shows. Here both agents have the right answers on which they may agree or disagree. These right answers are the unexamined "right opinions" (which should be obvious to everyone!) of students and teacher. The topics of conversation, however, are dominated by the terms of the students and their milieu. The script is improvised from their impulsive cliches, uncritical stereotypes, empty generalizations, or idiosyncratic sallies. The students need not defer to one another, or even to the teacher, since no standards are developed for judging opinions.

Location and status of the right answers, therefore, are equally distributed, although the teacher always has the option of reasserting (not always successfully) the authority of her/his right answers through a return to a Quiz Show or lecture. The basic question, expressed or implied, is the Inviter, which sets the permissive atmosphere. Beyond this, Bull Sessions are generally lacking in questions motivated by inquiry. Instead Prompters tend to state positions or control the stage. Blind assertiveness is the key to participation in a Bull Session, whose terms are improvised by the impulses of those who feel the strongest about the topic at hand. Thus the status of those who participate shifts from opinion to opinion in an open-ended manner—the opposite to the closed shop of the Quiz Show.

There are irenic or eristic variations within the Bull Session, depending upon whether it takes a Controversial Turn or not. The first is what many persons would think of as a Bull Session—a rambling, uncoordinated conversation in which the participants ventilate their implicitly agreed upon right opinions with a certain passion but with little purpose and no reflection. The alternative to this *Rambling Bull Session* is the *Wrangling Bull Session* in which students have differing opinions from one another and/or the teacher. Participants then argue over whose opinions constitute the right answers. People may tend to ramble more in dorms or pubs and wrangle more in classrooms. Either the teacher or the students can initiate the Controversial Turn which introduces the vexed topic.

Not only are Bull Sessions run by students; their primary audience also becomes the students. In deference to them the teacher moves to the sidelines or, seeking to persuade them, becomes just another participant. Inside the student audience, however, a certain competition remains as each vies for on-stage time to voice opinions. The forum becomes an empty one since the students fail to listen to one another. Each is full of what to say next and, while there may be rhetorical winners and losers, ultimately no one convinces anyone. Each becomes an audience of one, giving him/herself high marks ("I won that one!") or low ("I made a fool of myself.").

Predictably, teacher dominance of class time and frequency of turn-taking go down in a Bull Session, while those of the students go up. Higher cognitive turns may go up or down, depending upon what scheme one is using, but learning is unenhanced or accidental, since conditions for understanding and reflection are absent.

If the feeling of the Quiz Show is that of suppressed tension, that of the Bull Session tends towards euphoria. Released from the disciplines of a discussion or restraints of a Quiz Show, it moves through peaks and valleys of excitement. Ultimately, like a riot, it ends in exhaustion and frustration. Everyone tires of the aimlessness in a Rambling Bull Session, or gives up on the endless haggling in a Wrangling one (each feeling unfairly attacked or misunderstood), since no one has learned anything. Often the bell rings before a given Bull Session reaches its natural terminus. Particular Bull Sessions may be more or less energetic, depending upon the degree of controversy and how often the students and teacher are in agreement or disagreement.

Bull Sessions are predictable when tackling controversial issues. Teachers fearful of the Controversial Turn should note the quasi-therapeutic factor suggested by the above paragraph. As an outlet for pentup student emotions, a Bull Session can help identify issues of high student interest and clear the air for subsequent discussion.

MK'S BULL SESSION

MK presents us with an archetypal Wrangling Bull Session (see Appendix). He kicks it off with an Inviter on the students' feelings about the burning issue of the moment in the school milieu—the revocation of students' smoking privileges. The students angrily seize the Controversial Turn. The first page is illustrative of the whole. There is a resentful right opinion at 1c, an irrelevant sally reflecting junior versus senior student sub-milieu at 1d, and a wrangle between students from 1e–1n (cf 13b–13j). This makes a great contrast to the students' theorizing in PR's Problematic Discussion, where there is room to entertain the validity of more than one idea.

Note how MK jumps in at 2a, becoming just another participant responding to the student's query at 1n. From time to time he tries to use questions or statements to control the conversation and redirect it to some fundamental issues (6a, 7a, 12a, 13a, 14a). Like HW he puts forth his viewpoint, but unlike him doesn't insist upon it. MK tries hard, but he's locked himself into defending the school's policy and discipline. This effectively closes off any real discussion of the problems and leaves the students angrier than ever. The rhetorical questions by students and teacher (17c, 19a, 19b) are indicative of the dead end for learning here. All agents have reached the ultimate point in defense of their right answers by setting Dilemma Producers for their opponents.

I believe that the frequency of "higher" cognitive turns here is deceptive and indicates a pressing need for revision of our conceptions of classroom talk. Certainly we expect that the participants in a Wrangling Bull Session will do more explaining, opining, and justifying, but it doesn't follow that they are becoming more thoughtful about the issues. Instead they become more argumentative, generating more heat than light. The absence of reflection is mirrored in the short wait times recorded by the Swifts and Gooding (this volume). What the students are really learning is how to debate and win points. Despite the great differences in ratios of student turn-taking and talk-time, the students are not learning to think any better in either HK's or MK's classes. These ratios do indicate, however, at which extreme each conversation lies.

This division of the topic of conversation between teacher insistence on enforcing rules and student resentment about lost priv-

ileges is crucial to my interpretation of MK's episode. Given the
student passions involved, perhaps he does as well as anyone could.
What might rescue this Wrangle for Discussion is some later reflective episode in which the teacher detaches the students from
their positions by means of the Devil's Advocate. This would provide
opportunities, as Russell puts it (this volume), for the students to
examine the "Backing" for the variety of "Warrants" in the Conversation. The teacher could provide a model for this move by
considering possible changes in the rules. Then our present episode
would have cleared the air by permitting the students to let off
steam.

DIALECTICAL DISCUSSIONS

Dialectical Discussions are next to Bull Sessions on the scale of
conversations, because the student commonplace in both tends to
be central. The dialectical aspect concentrates on articulating, comparing, and refining student (and teacher) opinions. Here teacher
and students attempt to resolve opposing narrow opinions by broader
understandings. Such understandings involve acknowledgement of
the element of truth in, or related to, the competing opinions.
Resolution comes through the compromise of competing interests,
the synthesis of opposed tendencies, or the approximation to a higher
reality. Sometimes these are not possible in the context of the
convictions on each side, and the wider understanding must become
the "agreement to disagree." This level of insight at least acknowledges the existence of the opposition's position, if not its rightness.
    A teacher can open a dialectical discussion in a nonthreatening
kind of way with the Inviter, e.g., "Would you tell us about it?",
spoken as the teacher's gaze wanders randomly around the room.
The indefinite reference of "it" allows the students to select the
specific topic of conversation. The random gaze permits any student
with strong enough convictions about any term of the conversation
to participate.
    With three or four positions on the table the teacher develops
the discussion by rationalization of the opinions expressed. This
concerns examination of their assumptions, arguments, and consequences (Russell might add warrants and backing). Such a course
inevitably involves Controversial Turns, as we shall see later. Successful negotiation of these leads to the development of common
understandings and a sense of community in the classroom.
    Evidence for such appears when the students develop sympathetic

sensitivity towards opposing viewpoints, discriminate assumptions from opinions, become flexible in meeting objections, and set conditions of agreement or dissent. Opposing views become alternatives to be explored rather than competitors to be eliminated. Consensus on a large scale is not too much to hope for. The initial sense of rightness about one's own answers merges into a sense of rightness about the process which scrutinizes all answers.

Dialectical Discussions operate on a set of variations which depend upon students' recognition, articulation, and examination of parallels between their own viewpoints and those of others. Alternative views can be those expressed either by other students or through authors of the subject matter. Classification by parallels gives us three key kinds of Dialectical Discussions. We can develop parallels (1) between positions in the text, (2) between those in the subject matter and those of the students, or (3) between the students' own positions. These give us *Subject Matter, Subject-Life,* and *Existential* types of *Dialectical Discussions* respectively. Another key to these variations is the degree (as well as kind) of involvement of the students. The greatest degree of personal involvement is generally, though not invariably, at the student end of the scale rather than at the subject matter end.

Let us look more closely at the meaning of parallels which creates these distinctions in Dialectical Discussions. Parallels consist of similarities and differences. They develop from the tried and true techniques of English teachers who have over the years assigned many a paper with instructions to "compare and contrast" (Tom Jones with Huckleberry Finn, Antigone with Ismene, Faust with Don Juan). The Subject Matter Dialectical Discussion develops from such *Subject Matter Parallels.*

We can adapt the widely used comparison and contrast method by showing the students how to incorporate the subject matter into their experience in a way that illuminates both. These are *Subject-Life Parallels* which can be either general (referring to others) or personal (referring to oneself). *General Life Parallels* enable students to see similarities and differences between the setting in a short story, for instance, and some circumstance of their own lives. *Personal Life Parallels* involve a student in criticism of his/her own character in relation to that of an agent in the story. One use of the personal parallel places the student inside the circumstances of the story, e.g., "What strategy would you have followed had you been General Washington?" The other places the story into the student's life, e.g., "What would George Washington have to say about your opinion that we should have tried to win the Viet Nam

War?" Personal parallels can be extremely effective in making students think more deeply about what could otherwise be merely academic problems.

The third main kind of parallel which relates student to student are *Existential Parallels*. They also divide into personal and general, this time in comparisons and contrasts between the lives and positions of the students. *Personal Existential Parallels* examine the question of what student *A* would do in student *B's* shoes and vice-versa. *General Existential Parallels* examine the relationships between their differing life experiences and their varying interpretations of common experiences.

We can see the dialectical potential in discussions using such parallels for "integrating" racially, socially, or religiously heterogenous classrooms. There are also possibilities for Wrangling Bull Sessions! Thus Existential Dialectical Discussions vary according to degrees of students' involvement as they make comparisons, promote contrasts, and encourage felt understandings of alternative positions in students' lives.

Besides the Inviter, the questions which are most highlighted by the Dialectical Discussion are the Stretcher and the Devil's Advocate. The Stretcher is the "answer improving" question which insists that the students clarify the terms of their opinions by illustrating their empty generalizations, generalizing their strings of instances, refining their gross stereotypes, and tightening their rambling arguments. The most crucial question for dodging the wrangling dangers of such discussions is the Devil's Advocate, which forces the students to face the "other side of the question."

CONVERSATIONAL TURNS

Conversational turns are the critical moments in instruction when teachers and students passionately or reflectively seem to agree on a shift from one model to another—e.g.: Quiz Show to Bull Session; Bull Session to Informational to Dialectical Discussion; Problematical Discussion to Quiz Show to Informational to Problematical, again to . . . There can also be turns from discussion to an alternative to discussion, such as lecture or one-on-one.

Sometimes such turns are determined by teacher choices, e.g., in following a set of text questions, the critical moments are set by a teacher's determination to get through the sequence. Sometimes they involve a felt, unreflective move to change the flow of conversation. In addition to turns to Quiz Shows and Bull Sessions, there are Informational, Dialectical and Problematical Turns. Two others require further explanation here—Controversial and Reflective Turns.

THE CONTROVERSIAL TURN

Dialectic (and Problematical) Discussions can proceed in an ironic manner with a minimum of disputation. Generally these are subject matter based discussions which have failed to touch a nerve. To the extent that the introduction of alternative conceptions arouses student or teacher passions, however, the conversation can take a Controversial Turn and become eristic. The Controversial Turn often leads to a Wrangling Bull Session, full of argumentative responses over opposing positions among the students or between students and teacher.

Sometimes students themselves will seize the Controversial Turn and begin arguing. Many Controversial Turns also involve Inviters in which the teacher solicits students' opinions, then further invites other students to disagree. Or the teacher takes an opposing position her/himself by using a provocative question or statement, e.g., the Stinger. For instance, a teacher responds to students' assertions that the right of revolution no longer exists with the comment that they are less patriotic than Jefferson. When the conversation gets out of hand, teachers tend to put a clamp on the resultant Bull Sessions by switching them to Quiz Shows in which only responses with the right answers are recognized.

Teacher-selected Controversial Turns are best illustrated in Dialectical Discussions. Teachers can argue against what they perceive as the students' prejudiced positions on a given issue. Mr. PR (11a–17a) offers his "knock two of 'em out" solution to the problem of Eve's "three faces" in opposition to the students' efforts to combine them. Such leaning against students' positions is often mistaken for Devil's Advocacy.

THE DEVIL'S ADVOCATE

The Controversial Turn signals the need for students and teachers to work through the alternatives in a different way. This way is by use of the Devil's Advocate and the Reflective Turn. Other questions put students inside the discussion by developing their involvement with its perspectives and problems. The Devil's Advocate puts the discussion inside the students by forcing them to reconsider rejected alternatives as their own. Thus teachers need to go beyond disagreeing with John and Jane or asking George to disagree with Janis. They also must ask John and Jane to disagree with themselves, and require Janis and George to switch positions.

As Devil's Advocacy proceeds, the teacher's questions should shift from expository Fact Finders ("Can you explain Jane's position precisely before we discuss it?") to Probers for reasons behind the divergent viewpoints. The teacher asks the opponents for the best arguments, perhaps omitted by the advocates of each position. S/he encourages proponents to look for the evidence of weakness in their own viewpoints.

In such ways students can be brought to the experience of Devil's Advocacy. The experience is crucial, since it entails a transformation of the conversation's atmosphere from eristic debates (Wrangling Bull Sessions) to irenic forms of Discussion (Dialectical or Problematical). Joseph Schwab (1969) describes the transformation as discovering the value in diverse habits of mind and instituting the collaborative community where:

> . . . differing views will still be voiced by partisans, but the examination, the debate of them will not be partisan. Rather, once a number of views have been laid before the group, they will be treated as inperfect opinions, raw material for conjoint scrutiny aimed at discovery and repair of their errors and omissions, and formulation of a better or best opinion by the group as a whole and not as contestants in a sparring match. (p. 61)

THE REFLECTIVE TURN

Development of this irenic atmosphere provides the essential environment for the desirable transformations. These concern possible strengthening, abandonment, or modification of one's own position. Such results tend to arise as a natural consequence from integration of the Devil's Advocate into the discussion at the Controversial Turn. We have not yet reached reflective responses. To gain these the teacher needs to give the discussion a Reflective Turn by asking the students to articulate the ways their participation has changed them, perhaps using a Prober like "How has your view shifted from the opinion you gave earlier?".

Strengthened or modified viewpoints are easiest to obtain. One can strengthen a position by informed consideration of the alternatives, thus changing it from blind opinion to enlighted choice. One can modify a position by the achievement of consensus. Abandonment is the most difficult change for students, as admission of retreat from an untenable position seems to be for most people.

Yet, given the elements of truth in any position, total abandonment of its every aspect is rarely required. Ultimately students can be brought to see the advantages in taking account of a variety of opinions, not as mere opinions, but as involvements with and refinements of a community of viewpoints. The collaborative community of ideas thus becomes internalized in the formerly exclusive and precious thinking of the individual student. Instead of resisting change, students start to articulate how they can improve their ideas. This constitutes the self critical episode in the Reflective Turn.

In its reflexive form the Reflective Turn takes into review the whole pattern of Conversational Turns. This makes Devil's Advocacy plus the pattern of commonplaces, questions, and models available to the students as an educational resource. Moreover, the Reflective Turn is crucial for a further move—turning the discussion over to the students. Student-led discussions are the most neglected phase of this kind of pedagogy. The real test is how well they learn to do it on their own. Dillon's 27 episodes are virtually all teacher-led. In addition there is scant evidence for Reflective Turns and only one Devil's Advocate (hit upon by a novice teacher in an inventive moment without any follow-up).

Compared to Problematical Discussions, Dialectical ones appear to be less well defined, more difficult to conduct, and less frequently undertaken. This may be partly because they undertake the ambitious goal of working changes in students, i.e., enabling them to reflect upon and alter their opinions. Moreover, any discussion which confronts volatile and unpredictable student responses is on difficult ground, especially at its start. Dialectical Discussions are likely to slide over into Bull Sessions, raising teacher fears of losing control of the class.

WB'S DIALECTICAL DISCUSSION

WB's Subject–Life Discussion (Appendix) has a dialectical character, but gives us only a beginning. A very nice reflective summary of the terms of the discussion thus far opens the episode at 1a. The individual's need to respond to social influences beyond the family milieu provide the sociological content. This gets transformed by students' general life parallels into what becomes the topic of discussion, i.e., the relationship of parental respect to children's questions. The teacher accepts these student concerns, later taking them as illustrative of the sociological content that he first introduced. The relationships in the parallel, however, are not spelled out. The productiveness of working with student interpretations is seen both here and when Mr. PR (17a) accepts the students' theory which he earlier opposed.

The teacher's Reflective Turn at 1b sets the dialectical tone of the discussion. He attempts to reconcile the "two different ways of looking. . . ." He includes in his statement three distinct Inviters (OK?; You Know?; Does that fit, do you think?). Regina picks up on this Dialectical Turn in her long response at 1b. The dialectical character continues as the students comment on the general existential parallels between their various positions and, encouraged by WB (7a), attempt to reconcile them. By contrast the students in MK's episode exhibit no felt need for reconciliation of their *right* answers. The students also express a need to understand the differing historical milieux of parents vs children which inform the reasons for and acceptance of questioning.

This is the start of a thoughtful discussion. The high mean of time per turn at talk supports this. Although quantity of talk doesn't invariably correlate with quality, here they go together. This is supported by Bridges and Russell (this volume) in their cogent analyses of the argument and its presuppositions. In MK's episode, by contrast, student turns and time at talk is also high, but the mean time is much lower than for WB. In MK the rapid-fire sallies of the participants allow too little time to develop the arguments.

The Inviter is featured at the start of the discussion (1a and 4a). Also note how the teacher helps build it with a Dilemma Producer (8a) and Prober (9a). An especially striking feature of this transcript is the apparently quite powerful combination of statement and question for promoting the discussion. I would urge the participants to continue in this vein and further develop the subject matter side of the parallels by a Reflective Turn.

The teacher neglects to employ the Devil's Advocate, however. For instance, he could have Steve (5b) and Regina (5c) switch positions. Or he could use the personal life parallel to put students into the position of their parents.

INFORMATIONAL DISCUSSIONS

Sometimes the Inviter (or even the Stinger) is insufficient to energize a conversation. This can occur when the terms informing the students' responses are vexed. Fear of controversy with possible loss of face, may be high among the students. They avoid articulating their concerns and ideas. Perhaps they don't want to face these themselves, much less expose them to others. Such vexed topics include the sexual attitudes of SN's high school students. Another example at the graduate level are the pedagogical difficulties of curriculum students who avoid the perplexities of their problematical situations by escaping into algorithms and formulae (Pereira, 1981).

The teacher employs the Inviter and Fact Finder with a light touch, permissive stance, and noncontroversial promise. The discussion proceeds in a low-key and tentative tone. These Informational Discussions are closest in style and content to Rambling Bull Sessions, only more focused. The teacher draws the students out, builds their faith in expressing themselves through the discussion, and allays their fears with assurances that their answers will not be marked down as wrong. Assured that their responses will be honored by the teacher, the students can be encouraged later through Dialectical or Problematical Discussions to search for better ones.

Informational Discussions stand at the threshold of Dialectical ones to the extent that they enable students to look at alternative opinions to their own. Dialectical Discussions proper develop much further. They can probe and switch student opinions. They can relate these by parallels to the subject matter. They can treat the subject matter itself dialectically.

SN'S INFORMATIONAL DISCUSSION

SN (Appendix) creates the topic of discussion by enabling the students to talk comfortably without being wrong about their experiences with the troubling terms of the subject matter—nudity, talk about sex, and physical affection (7a). The vexing character of these terms for the students is indicated by the long early silence at 5b, and the nervous laughter which punctuates the discussion at 13a, 17a–b, 22a, 24a, 24b, 26b–c, and 28c.

The discussion moves almost entirely on Fact Finders (4a, 15a, 23a) with a few Inviters (1a, 12a) on the students' experiences and family milieu. The Klinzings (this volume) point out how the self referencing of student responses reflects success of various teacher moves in exploring the emotional experiences of the students. At 13a the teacher makes some statement of his own experience to encourage the students. The conversation develops along a set of subject-life personal parallels.

Student talk and time goes up appropriately, while teacher–student turns remain high as he keeps the discussion jogging along. Teacher power, however, as measured by the Woods (this volume) is quite low. Given the informational cast and purpose of this discussion, it is not surprising to find "lower" levels of cognition. Not all instruction aims at higher level cognition, or should. It is, of course, much more difficult to measure levels of anxiety.

The importance of this kind of discussion lies in what teacher and students can do with it. Perhaps SN might try a Problematic Turn with a Particular Puzzler: "Why do you think your families avoid sex as a subject in their conversations with their children?" This might be combined with a Fact Finder on the Personal Parallel: "How would you conduct sex talks with your (projected) family?" and a Prober: "Why would you do it in the way that you just described?" Dialectical Turns, much less Controversial ones, would not be indicated until the students are much more confident in the discussion.

PROBLEMATICAL DISCUSSIONS

I have differentiated three varieties of problematical discussion whose variations depend upon the size, focus, and solvability of the problem undertaken. The largest size problem concerns the mysteries of life. Human beings must tackle these problems by either spending a lifetime exploring them, arbitrarily adopting a dogmatic response, or turning their backs because "there are no final answers to these questions." The basic type of question here is the Perennial Puzzler.

More delimited problematical situations require specific posings of problems and working out of solutions. Here there may be better or worse answers, if not ideal ones. I refer to educational writers like Dewey (1922) and Schwab (1973), as well as to the "problem solving" literature generally. The generating question is the Particular Puzzler.

Finally there are problematical situations whose solution is found, not in the situation to which the question points, but in the terms by which the question is put. The task set by the Cryptic Puzzler is to discover the meaning of the question itself. Once mastered, the terms of the Cryptic Puzzler become working distinctions previously inaccessible to the user.

Let us look more closely at Perennial and Particular Problematical Discussions.

PERENNIAL PROBLEMATICAL DISCUSSIONS

Perennial Puzzlers are the basic questions which underly all subject matter and generate the academic disciplines. They are more or less visible in catalogues of college courses and surface with more or less energy in scholarly articles or classroom teaching. From the viewpoint of such questions, scholarship and teaching have the same root—a phenomenon often referred to by scholars who teach and teachers who pursue scholarship.

The following examples give the range and flavor of the Perennial Puzzler: "What is art? or music? or poetry?"; "Why are we here?" (religious studies); "How does society function?" (sociology); "Where are we in relation to the rest of the universe?" (astronomy); "What is man that thou art mindful of him?" (anthropology, humanities); "Who was Jesus? or Socrates? or the Buddha?" (history, theology). "What is time?" (indefinitely multidisciplinary).

The examples show that the Perennial Puzzler is ambiguous, open-ended, and complex. It is ambiguous because different questioners can interpret it in diverse ways leading to a variety of complementary or even contradictory answers. It is open-ended, since it is never completely solved. Not only are the answers inadequate and subject to further questions, but rising generations tend to re-raise the fundamental question. Perennial Puzzlers are aimed at fundamental recalcitrant human problems which "bug" us. Finally, each one is complex and can be broken down into subsets of subordinate questions which themselves need solving in order to clarify a piece of the main Puzzler.

PARTICULAR PROBLEMATICAL DISCUSSIONS

The Particular Puzzler specifies a problematical situation which involves a narrowing of the group for which it is a puzzler. The global character of Perennial Discussions becomes delimited and specified by the pressing troublesome particulars of a given situation. This makes the problems themselves more focused and manageable, if not easier to formulate. The problems to be posed and solved can be found in either the subject matter or the students' lives. Solutions may concern either a proposed action to deliberation or a confirmed hypothesis for inquiry. These are the relatively right answers to particular puzzling questions. Neither action nor hypothesis, however, has any prior claim to rightness. They cannot be preset by text or lecture. Rather they are defensible decisions or warranted assertions chosen from considered alternatives and subject to review and revision.

Management of particular problematic discussions involves a pattern which has been variously described in general terms by a number of writers in education (Roby, 1985). It features (1) the search for meaningful details in a problematical situation, (2) the formulation of these details into discrete problems, (3) the setting of solutions to the posed problems, (4) the rehearsal of consequences or predictions for each solution, (5) the concomitant revising, weighing, and deciding among problem-posings and solution-settings, (6) leading to termination and action(s) or conclusions, and (7) the monitoring of these to identify their effects in explaining or mitigating formulated problems or creating new ones. A conversation which includes all these elements is obviously a complex one! It doesn't become simpler when we factor in the four commonplaces of education.

Experience shows that simplified versions of deliberation seriously underestimate the interplay of the elements in problematical situations. Take curriculum deliberation. By posing at least one problem for the students, teachers, subject matters, and milieu we have a minimum of four formulations, avoiding the "either . . . or" thinking which vitiates so much deliberation. By formulating three solutions for every problem we avoid a "rush to *the* solution"—another impoverishment of the process.

The Reflective Turn becomes a crucial tool for reflexive criticism upon the biases through which we assign some meanings and ignore others, on how adequately we have managed the process, and for resolving the essentially interminable character of any given discussion. Thus we have the Informer: "What do we need to know in order to pose this problem properly?" The Prober: "What preconceptions have kept us from seeing this situation fully (i.e., in terms of all four commonplaces)?" And the Stretcher: "How will our solutions coordinate with further deliberations on the situation?"

Examples of Particular Puzzlers tend to be situated in a range of particular problematical discussions. There are subject matter questions like those generating Mr. PR's discussion (below). Likewise the kindly old dissertation advisor inquires: "What is the problem of your thesis?". Alternatively there are problems in the lives of students, e.g., how to resolve the controversial smoking situation which MK's Wrangling Bull Session failed even to define.

Particular Problematical Discussions can also develop in the context of a Perennial Problematical Discussion. The building of the Atomic bomb, for instance, involved Particular Puzzlers such as where to get the scientists and fissionable materials together, or how to organize the laboratories. These took place in relation to the Perennial Puzzler: "How can an open society secure itself against its enemies, and remain an *open* society?" This question mirrors a tension between the needs simultaneously to restrict and enhance the flow of information among scientists. This tension recently resurfaced in President Reagan's seizures of academic papers deemed useful to the Soviets.

PR'S PROBLEMATICAL DISCUSSION

Mr. PR (Appendix) provides a good example of a quasi-deliberative Problematical Discussion with a subject matter orientation, in this case the psychopathology concerning the famous case of the "three faces of Eve." It is quasi-deliberative since no concrete action is contemplated. 1a–9b concentrates on formulating the problems of dominance presented by the factual relationships among Eve's personalities. 10a–17b focuses on solutions. The remaining transcript, 18a–END returns to the problem posing area by examining the possible causes of Eve's personality split.

The greater time expended on problem formulations is interesting, because it is atypical. As Getzels and his students (1982) have repeatedly pointed out, everybody prefers a solution, but nobody loves a problem. Often alternative problem-posings are ignored altogether, or the problem for which solutions are proposed is indefinite. Thus we may distinguish partial problematical discussions from those which exhibit the complete process.

Farrar's incisive analysis (this volume) indicates that PR's episode is too brief to illustrate more than a part of the process we outlined above. It is weak on solution-settings, and there are no Reflective Turns. What we have, however, is remarkable. Two key moves by the teacher make most of it possible. At 11a he takes a Controversial Turn, using his Prompter to advocate the "knock-em-out theory of treatment as opposed to the students' "combine-em" theory. But at 17a he relinquishes the Controversial Turn (perhaps in a very honest moment—he really doesn't know!). At 18a he takes the discussion back into the problem posing stage. This makes possible significant inventions from 20b–END as the students cast the discussion in terms of the idol and conflict models.

The animating question of the discussion overall is the Particular Puzzler on the Personal Parallel (1a and 10a), "How can we help Eve unify her three personalities?" What really gets it cooking are a series of Stretchers (21a, 22a, 23a, 27a) combined with a few Probers (18a, 19a)—a good mix. Another striking point about this transcript is the crucial role of student questions (15c and 16c—a pair of Stretchers *for* the teacher) to which he listens, then takes up with the class. Compare this to HK's suppression of his Reverse Quiz Shows.

The feeling of this discussion is the inverse of HK's. There is excitement and interest. A lecture clearly would not have the same effect, since some of the students' terms are not even in the book! Here I tend to disagree with Sigel's assertion (this volume) that the structure is predetermined; however, I do agree with his observation that the students are encouraged to think through the problem in a structured and distanced manner. More than the other four episodes, this one raises the possibility of a student-led discussion, and points up the need for pedagogical training for the students.

COORDINATING THE RESEARCH LOOP AND SPREADING THE WORD—WHAT TO TELL TEACHERS AND STUDENTS

Reflexive examination of the topics of discussion brings to light a dimension of discussion worth elaborating. Concentration upon the terms of the question itself through the Cryptic Puzzler can be extended to scrutiny of the other terms which have structured the discussion. For instance, PR might take a Reflective Turn by using an Informer ("In what terms have we been examining Eve's problems?") followed by a Stretcher ("In what other ways might we connect our conceptions of problem and solution?").

The terms of teaching and learning are not only the explicit ones. The Reflective Turn can bring out the hidden curricular learning which involves the pedagogical models of instruction and educational roles of teacher and student. MK, for example, might attempt to short circuit his Wrangling Bull Session through a Cryptic Puzzler on what the students have been *learning* in the discussion. Such a diversion from the heat of debate into consideration of its underlying principles—rules (law), and fairness (justice)—would be welcome relief.

By "model" in the above paragraph I do not refer only to my own tools for sorting out practices (Discussions and Quasi-discussions). I also refer to the example of the teacher in the conduct of instruction. These examples provide a powerful but narrow source for the early education of prospective teachers. The often authoritarian character of these examples is attested to by the limitations of our transcripts with their virtual absence of Devil's Advocates and Reflective Turns. Similar problems beset discussions in the larger society where devices such as "quality circles" and "nominal group techniques" become necessary for equalizing participation among unequals.

The resources described in this essay provide one way to improve these "exemplary" teacher behaviors. A Discussion need not be confused with a Quiz Show, or limited to a Problematical one. Teachers can vary the episodes in patterns according to the needs of students and requirements of the subject matter. A Discussion could begin Problematically, degenerate through a Controversial Turn into a Bull Session over whose solution is best, and pull back through an Informational Turn into an episode which brings out the vexed terms of controversy. It then might take a Dialectical Turn with the Devil's Advocate in which the terms of the interfering passions are examined and resolved, return to complete the Problematical session, and conclude with a Reflective Turn on the vicissitudes, omissions, and qualifications of the Discussion overall. Thus the combination of models, questions, and commonplaces is quite variable.

The pattern for my present treatment is a coordinated loop in which research grows out of teaching and feeds back into it on a continuous track. This ideal has been only partly realizable here, since (adapting Heraclitus) "the upward and downward ways are not the same" in research, and the teachers and students studied here (adapting again) "are from a time long ago in classrooms far away."

Variability on the downward track includes the modification of the models by teachers and students. The models and questions set forth here are meant to be useful, but should not be considered either authoritarian or complete. Evidence is strong that behind the classroom door teachers are pragmatic and eclectic, altering the curricular packages and doctrines handed to them from above in terms of what works. Teachers who use discussion may be especially inventive in this regard. Moreover, discussion itself is best studied reflexively through discussion. This helps explain why it has been a traditional vehicle for invention (e.g., "brain storming"). Therefore I would welcome as worthy additions to curricular lore, communication of the inventive alterations and elaborations of these models which work for teachers.

Even more important is the need for teachers and students to challenge the presupposition (best articulated by Francis) underlying these transcripts that in order to be effective a discussion must be teacher-led. If we really believe in the educative powers of discussion to explore issues and exercise abilities in a way not available to other methods, then we should allow the students to develop its virtues for themselves. Instruction in the pedagogy of discussion entails two steps for teachers: (1) providing models for the students and (2) turning the discussion over to them. Involved here is a shift of authority from the fixed roles of teacher and student to flexible teachings and learnings presupposed in the discussion process. Here students can learn to become their own teachers, and teachers can benefit from the learning process implicit in all teaching.

MULTIDISCIPLINARY IMPLICATIONS

This section is a difficult one. Some colleagues in the group were charged with this specific task. The rest are presenting recommendations at the end of each essay. Readers, of course, will draw their own multidisciplinary conclusions. Given the complexity of our endeavor and the variety of reader purposes, this latter result is to be encouraged. So I will try to be brief.

First, I have put in a small sample of cross references to the others' work—sometimes agreeing, sometimes disagreeing with their analyses. But in either case I could hardly catalogue here the tremendous impetus given to my own work by consideration of theirs. For instance, there is the Woods' contrast between teacher and parental models in providing a proper context for children's inquiries. The establishment of discourse space by relatively long contributions from the teacher helps to explain why WB seems more successful than HK, despite correspondingly short wait times. Students, of course, have more time to think through the problems while the teacher is setting things up.

Overall, the most promising development in the fluid give-and-take of exchanges in our group—by mail, at Wingspread, and in the AERA—has been this emergence of context as crucial for analysis and practice of classroom discussion and questioning. The need to attend to such problems has been most extensively argued in Bridges' philosophical presuppositions, Farrar's linguistic coding ambiguities, and Lighthall's call for stimulated recall from longer data units. It also appears throughout other essays: in Mullen's sensible recommendations on class size; in complaints and caveats involving limitations of the data (which, on the other hand, proved so stimulating in beginning and sustaining our endeavors); and in calls for more varied investigations.

A salient consequence of this development is the questioning of rules and algorithms as descriptive or prescriptive absolutes for the classroom. In addition to Farrar's useful discussion we also have the summary remarks of the Klinzings and Sigel, as well as Russell's shrewd disclaimer. I believe that this is a *multidisciplinary* consequence of this project because isolated researchers tend to establish rules on a narrow empirical or conceptual base in one or another of the disciplines, then broadly apply them across the diversity of classroom contexts.

An example of one such longstanding rule: "Always ask more and higher level questions," has only recently been questioned by the work of Dillon (1982) who discovered that the seminal studies failed to distinguish between statements and questions. In addition the Swifts and Gooding point out that without sufficient wait time, a steady stream of higher cognitive questions necessarily drives exchanges to lower cognitive levels than intended. Opposing rules, e.g., "Only employ alternatives to questioning," may improve some discussions while undermining others depending on a variety of other factors in the context.

This is because the diversity of discussions depends upon a variability mirrored by the commonplaces of education in teacher style, student readiness, social values, and subject matter requirements, etc. Thus I have striven for maximum flexibility in my models in order to include as many possibilities for productive discussion as the evidence indicates. This means providing room for Macmillan's subject centered problematical erotetic inquiries as well as Francis' student centered dialectical group processes. Rules for effective discussion are generally "rules of thumb," resources to be practically exploited and empirically validated in each discussion.

APPENDIX

Table 1. A Functional Typology of Questions

The Puzzler (PZ), Perennial (PN). The basic questions concerning the enigmas of life. These underly subject matters and generate the academic disciplines, e.g., "What is virtue? or art? or God?". Ambiguous, complex, and open-ended. Not all PZ-PNs are of interest to every kind of student, though their global character makes each potentially engaging.

The Puzzler, Particular (PT). Involves specific student groups in formulating and solving problems in either the subject matter or the students' lives. Solutions may concern either a proposed action (deliberation) or a confirmed hypothesis (inquiry). Found problems and their working solutions are of a more manageable kind than possible with the PZ-PN. (PR: 1a, 10a).

The Puzzler, Cryptic (CP). Presents students with unfamiliar but potentially useful distinctions: e.g., "What is the author *doing?*" (rather than *saying*); or "What do you *think* about _____?" (not *feel*); or "What is the author's *starting point?*" (not always at the beginning, (Dunkel, 1960). Discussion centers on the meaning of the unfamiliar terms (Schwab, 1958).

The Inviter (IV). Solicits student responses broadly and permissively, with degrees of freedom. At its most indefinite, "Tell us about it?". Can be narrowed down to specific terms of various content (viz., questions on particular subject matters, students, milieux, parallels, discussions, or questions themselves), i.e., "Tell us about _____?" (MK: 1a, 4a).

The Stinger (SG). The "Agent Provocateur." Directs students' attention to terms of the text or their lives that are controversial for them. Often used by teachers seizing the Controversial Turn. For withdrawn students. Runs the risk of Wrangling Bull Session, but DA (see below) can keep the discussion cooler and on the track.

The Fact Finder (FF). The "Sergeant Friday" question. Aims at establishing the facts of the text (HK: 12a, 13a, 14a, etc.) or students' lives (SN: 4a, 10a).

The Prompter (PM). The "Grant's Tomb" question. The answer is contained within or strongly suggested by the question as in the nickname. Or the answer will be obvious within the context. (Who *was* buried in Grant's Tomb, anyhow?). (Many examples in HK: 3a, 4a, 19a & MK: 1f, 1h, 1n, 17c, 19a).

The Prober (PB). Attempts to discover and develop the meanings of the terms in the discussion, e.g., the principle organizing the facts of the text (HK: 1a) or the reasoning behind students' opinions (PR: 18a). Works closely with the "what" established by the FF to focus on the "why."

The Stretcher (SR). The "Answer Improver." Extends student thought or imagination to consider terms omitted in the original response. If a student gives us the facts, we ask for their organizing principle (PR: 22a); if the student has the principle we inquire for the details that prevent it from remaining an empty generalization (HK: 78); if the student puts forward a theory we ask for the alternatives (PR: 27a).

The Devil's Advocate (DA). Persuades students to argue against their own position. Generates alternatives by having students consider contraries (which are better than the "either . . . or" thinking encouraged by contradictories) to his/her chosen position. Breaks up student debates by forcing opposing students to take up, improve, and learn from one another's arguments. Develops a Controversial Turn into a Reflective Turn.

The Dilemma Producer (DP). Presents students with contradictions (real or apparent) in the text, in their own positions (WB: 8a; HK: 9a; MK: 19a), or between their positions and the text. Closely related to the PZ, since some dilemmas are perennial, e.g., "How can a good God make an evil world?"

Table 2. A Functional Typology of Group Classroom Conversations

Group Classroom Conversations. Involve the class as a whole in the more or less formal and verbal exchanges between teachers and students or among students concerning the subject matter and/or their milieux. Includes Discussions and Quasi-discussions that are defined by the status and location of "right answers."

Quasi-Discussions. Encourage student participation, but fail to generate Reflective Turns involving student self criticism or reflexive scrutiny of the Conversation.

Quasi-Discussions: Quiz Show (HK). Students attempt to ferret out the teacher's right answers. At its most efficient it is "lecturing in the interrogatory mood." More positively it is one way to run a recitation. Students can quiz the teacher (Reverse Quiz Show) or one another (Student Quiz Show).

Quasi-Discussions: Bull Session (MK). Both students and teacher have the right answers about which they may aimlessly converse (Rambling Bull Session) or endlessly argue (Wrangling Bull Session).

Discussions. Modify the meanings of the right answers to become the starting points for the best available answers worked toward and discovered in their context.

Discussions: Problematical. May be *Perennial, Particular,* or *Cryptic* depending upon which kind of PZ generates and sustains it. Generally, teachers and students pursue questions for which neither has the ideal answer. Perennial Problematical Discussions are based on global questions which have no absolute right answers. Questions in Particular Problematical Discussions (PR) delimit the situation to pose problems with working solutions for answers. Cryptic Problematical Discussions focus on the terms of the question which then become the working terms of the conversation.

Discussions: Dialectical (WB). Students and teachers attempt to resolve opposing opinions by searching out and synthesizing the elements of truth in each. The right answers can be strengthened, modified, or abandoned. Often focus on parallels between positions within the subject matter, between the subject matter and the students', lives, or between the student' own positions.

Discussions: Informational (SN). Bring to light difficult or taboo terms in a permissive, or non-judgmental atmosphere. CONVERSATIONAL TURNS. Concern the "critical moments" in Conversations when the direction, content, or leadership of a given episode change.

Quizzy, Bully, Problematical, Dialectical, And Informational Turns. These can lead to episodes as defined above in the overall Conversation.

Controversial Turn. A point in the conversation when the topic touches terms of passionate conviction in teacher (PR: 11a) or students (MK: 1c, 1d), leading to opinionated arguments. Can issue in a Wrangling Bull Session (MK) or take a Dialectical Turn with deployment of the DA.

Reflective Turn. Functions variously in a Conversation. In a Dialectical Discussion it can involve reflective student responses. These concern students strengthening, abandoning, or modifying prior positions. It also can involve reflexive scrutiny of the terms, questions, or episodes for any Conversation (WB: 1a), as well as its future prospects.

Student Or Teacher Turn. This refers to Conversational leadership. Dillon's Data Format provides clues to this possibly major turn, but does not completely define it. The Reverse Quiz Show (HK: 21b-22b) is one kind of Student Turn. Also see the longish student dialogues in MK (1b-1n; 13b-13j). Dillon's data overall is marked by few Student Turns of any kind.

REFERENCES

Dewey, John. *Human Nature and Conduct.* New York, Henry Holt, 1922.
Dillon, James. "Cognitive Correspondence Between Question/Statement and Response." *American Educational Association Research Journal,* Winter 1982, Vol. 19, No. 4: 540–551.

Dunkel, Harold. Mimeographed Notes for Education 300 (Education as a Field of Study). University of Chicago, 1960.

Getzels, Jacob W. "The Problem of the Problem." In Hogarth, R. (ed.) *New Directions for Methodology of Social and Behavioral Science: Question Framing and Response Consistency*, No. 11 (San Francisco: Jossey-Bass, March, 1982: 37–49.

Roby, Thomas W. "Habits Impeding Deliberation." *Journal of Curriculum Studies*, 1985, vol. 17, No. 1, 17–35. Reprinted in Taylor, Phillip H., *Recent Developments in Curriculum Studies*. Philadelphia, Nfer Nelson, 1986, pp. 41–69.

Schwab, Joseph J. *College Curriculum and Student Protest*. Chicago: University of Chicago, 1969.

Schwab, Joseph J. "The Practical 3: Translation into Curriculum." *School Review*. 81 (1973): 501–522. Reprinted in Westbury, I. and Wilkof, N. (eds), *Science, Curriculum, and Liberal Education: Selected Essays of Joseph J. Schwab*, Chicago, University of Chicago Press, 1978, pp. 365–383.

Schwab, Joseph J. "Enquiry and the Reading Process." *The Journal of General Education* 11 (1958): 72–82. In *Westbury and Wilkof*, pp. 149–163.

CHAPTER 10

Questions and Wait Time

J. Nathan Swift, C. Thomas Gooding, and Patricia R. Swift

State University of New York
Oswego, N.Y. 13126

There are many approaches to understanding the attributes of a segment of classroom dialogue. In the following, we have chosen to identify certain quantifiable variables that other research workers have linked to teaching quality. The fact that the variables can be counted permits statistical comparisons to be made. If an intervention program is utilized, with the goal of improving some aspect of classroom instruction, then inferences can be drawn concerning the effectiveness of the intervention.

The Classroom Interaction Laboratory of the State University of New York at Oswego is an interdisciplinary research group consisting of educators, psychologists, content area specialists, and statisticians. This group is interested in the analysis of classroom dialogue for the purpose of developing a clearer understanding of the effects of interaction patterns on the teaching and learning process. Specifically, we measure the content levels of teacher questions and the pauses or wait times in dialogue between teachers and students. We also assess teacher and student perceptions of both the cognitive and affective aspects of the classroom environment. Through this analysis we attempt to paint a portrait of the interactive patterns of classrooms.

Although the five classroom tapes analyzed in this chapter are too small in number to permit valid statistical treatment, and should be considered only in an ethnographic sense, this chapter is illustrative of the thick data base that may be generated from brief interactive segments. As can be seen, if one assumes that the dialogue segments are typical performances of the teachers, then intriguing, albeit tentative, conclusions can be drawn.

CONCEPTIONS AND THEORETICAL FRAMEWORK

Pauses in classroom dialogue, particularly those pauses between questions and responses, have been studied intensively for more than a decade, since Rowe (1974) observed that these key pauses (termed *wait time*) could influence the quality as well as the quantity of teacher–student interaction.

Rowe (1974, 1978) noted that the first wait time occurs after teachers ask questions (and before students respond). The second wait time occurs after students pause momentarily in their replies, often before teachers have ascertained that the students have completed their replies. Rowe has labeled the pauses *wait time 1 (WT1)* and *wait time 2 (WT2)*, respectively. The relationship between the two is illustrated in Figure 1. In some studies (Tobin & Capie, 1981) wait time 1 has been called "student wait time," because it is controlled by student responses. In a similar manner wait time 2 has been called "teacher wait time." We have identified an additional wait time category, *wait time 3*. This is the pause that occurs between student-to-student dialogue.

Usually wait times are found to be exceedingly short. When the pauses of 40 middle school science teachers were measured (Swift & Gooding, 1983), the mean wait time 1 was determined to be 1.26 seconds; the wait time 2 mean was only 0.55 seconds. These pause durations have been found to be too brief to allow for thoughtful responses by students or teachers.

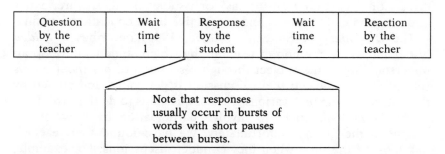

Figure 1.   Wait Time 1 and Wait Time 2.

Rowe (1978) has characterized typical fast-paced classrooms as resembling inquisitions. Roby (this volume) used the term "quiz show" as a descriptor. Dillon (1983) has designated these classes as recitation sessions and contrasted them with discussions that facilitate higher cognitive thinking in classrooms. By increasing wait time and permitting teachers and students to take advantage of the increased time to reflect on issues and compose responses, classrooms become more pleasant and discussions more meaningful. Some of the changes observed by researchers include increases in the length of student responses, higher cognitive level questions asked by teachers (Rowe, 1974; Swift & Gooding, 1983), and improved student achievement (Tobin & Capie, 1981; Wise & Okey, 1983).

Wait time has been characterized by Berliner (1985) as a crucial factor in effective teaching. He has stated, "If we were medical researchers, we would say these are miracle findings. We can cure classroom ills with no contraindications." Our research indicates that teachers can learn to use longer wait times if they are provided with electronic devices that offer immediate feedback concerning the duration of their pauses.

DEFINITIONS

Many educators start their teaching sessions with the statement, "Today we are going to discuss . . ." Based on our examination of transcriptions of classroom data, the term "discuss" seems to be misused. Often, that which follows the introductory statement bears little resemblance to a discussion. Typically, the class activity turns into a lecture, drill, or an inquisition. This confusion emphasizes the need for clear definitions of key terms. Three basic models that have been identified are guided discussion, recitation, and permissive discussion. Depending on the task or issue at hand, all three types of discussion can be useful and productive in an educational setting.

The *Dictionary of Education* (Good, 1983) describes a *guided discussion* as, "a method of teaching by which students develop an understanding of the subject through discussion of pertinent points related to that subject; their discussion is generated and guided by the instructor who uses various types of questions to do this" (p. 187). A true discussion ought to involve participation by most of the people in the group. Unfortunately, we have found that teachers talk most of the time when they conduct discussions. For example, the middle school science teachers in a semester-long study who were assigned to the comparison group talked 87.8% of the time when they were recording lessons that they believed to be discussions (Swift & Gooding, 1983). Their discussions tended to be lectures with questions frequently interspersed. Our research also found that classroom dialogue in middle school science classrooms functions at the lowest memory level as delineated in Bloom's taxonomy of learning (Bloom, 1956). When we asked teachers to tape record "discussions" in their science classrooms, 85.9% of the questions that they posed were at the memory level unless they had special training. Therefore, these classes more commonly resembled recitations than guided discussions.

Recitations appear to be the form of interaction most often used by teachers. A *recitation* is defined as: "a traditional learning exercise and teaching procedure in which students repeat orally or explain material learned by individual study or previously presented by the teacher and in response to questions raised by the teachers" (Good, 1983, p. 478). Thus, Rowe's (1978) "inquisition," Roby's (this volume) "quiz show," Swift and Gooding's (1983) "drill" all appear to be similar to Dillon's (1981) descriptive term "recitation". This type of discussion does not require extended pauses, since higher level cognitive interactions are seldom sought.

If the teacher is not operating in a lecture mode (which the teacher often terms a discussion) or in a recitation (which the teacher may also call a discussion) but is still engaged in an interaction with students, a form of discussion that may be used is that of a *permissive discussion*. This type of interaction is described as "a group discussion that moves freely and adjusts to the expressed interests and participation of the members" (Good, 1983, p. 187). Such discussions are typically not focused on a particular content, but usually are based on a sharing of opinions or points of view. Thus, these discussions usually do not meet the criterion of a guided discussion whereby students relate to a subject by exploring key points organized and directed by the instructor.

QUESTIONS STUDIED IN THIS PROJECT

Our research team analyzed five tape recordings of classroom dialogue provided by Dillon using methods tested in previous studies by a team at SUNY, Oswego (see Swift & Gooding, 1983). They provide a basis for the comparison of interactions from a history class, a class on smoking rules, a marriage preparation class, a psychology class, and a human relationships class with the science classes that our research team has studied.

The questions addressed were:

1. What were the cognitive levels of questions asked by the classroom teacher?
2. How did the teachers reply to student answers?
3. What alternatives did teachers use to stimulate discussion when they did not use questions?
4. How often did teachers use chain questions (two or more questions asked without time to provide for answers)?
5. How often did teachers use disciplinary or derogatory remarks?
6. How often do teachers and students interrupt each other in a discussion?
7. How long were the wait times in these classes?
8. What was the percentage of teacher talk versus student talk in these classes?

PROCEDURE

Tape recordings and transcriptions of the recorded classes were supplied to this research team in the fall of 1983. Logging sheets were prepared that enabled the coding of many aspects of classroom interaction.

The cognitive levels of the questions were approached using a modified version (Swift & Gooding, 1983; Swift & Alves, 1984) of The Question Category System for Science, developed by Blosser (1973). The category system was refined by dividing convergent thinking questions into classification B-1, denoting simple transformations (see Table 1). Convergent category B-2 was used to identify more complex operations encompassing application and higher cognitive levels.

Managerial questions were subdivided into ordinary classroom management questions (M) such as "Do you have a pencil?", and management plus (M+) "Do you want to add anything, Tom?". The M+ questions are those posed to facilitate the flow of discussion. The suggestion by Dillon (1983) to use alternatives to questions to stimulate discussions prompted the investigation and categorization of the alternative remarks made by teachers in this sample. Several distinctive alternatives were identified and are listed in Table 2. The list illustrates the limited variety used by those teachers. Further development in this area is suggested.

Questions and their alternatives are used to stimulate further

Table 1.   The Question Category System for Science (Revised)

Level I	Level II	Level III	This Study
	A. Cognitive–memory	1. Recall	
		2. Identify, name, or observe	A
I. Closed Question	B. Convergent thinking	1. Associate, discriminate, or classify	B-1
		2. Reformulate	
		3. Apply	
		4. Synthesize	B-2
		5. Closed prediction	
		6. Make "critical" judgment	
II. Open Questions	C. Divergent thinking	1. Give opinion	
		2. Open prediction	C
		3. Infer or imply	
	D. Evaluative thinking	1. Justify	
		2. Design	
		3. Affective judgment	
		4. Cognitive Judgment	D
III. Rhetorical Questions	(not subdivided)		R
	E. Management		M
IV. Managerial Questions	F. Management plus		M+

Table 2.   Alternatives to questions used by teachers.

Definition of Terms

Lecture or summary
AL—Active listening or reflection of feelings and thoughts
E —Explanation or elaboration of material
R —Repetition of a student reply
AR—Argumentation
FS—Finishing a student's sentence

discussion by students. The nature of the teacher's reply to a student is also of interest. The relationship of teachers' remarks to students is described in Figure 2. Teacher replies, illustrated in Table 3, refer to the previous remarks by students; questions (Table 1) or alternatives (Table 2) encourage subsequent comments.

Student response ⟶ Teacher replies to the response ⟶ Teacher uses a question or alternative ⟶ Student response

Figure 2.   One paradigm for teacher–student interaction.

It is believed (Rowe, 1978) that neutral comments stimulate further discussion, whereas approval or disapproval serves to squelch further interaction. Initial analysis of our research data on middle school science discussions by Gwinn (1984) indicates that this might be true, but only if neutral comments are defined as either encouraging or bland remarks (see Table 3).

For this study, replies by teachers were categorized using these definitions:

The occurrence of chain questions was recorded. Most chain questions consisted of two questions in rapid succession, such as the two that appeared in the tape of the lesson by HK (31a): "Where? When?". The same teacher used four consecutive questions without pausing for a response later in the lesson.

Other significant actions were noted: questions without responses (NRQ's), disciplinary remarks, interruptions, and managerial actions. Word counts for both teachers and students were made from the transcripts. Pause fillers, such as "uh" and "you know", were ignored. These counts gave a value for the percentage of talk by teachers and students.

The ratio of teacher-to-student talk was also estimated using a computer program developed by T.W. Mustico (personal communication, January, 1981). In this procedure, a key on the a microcomputer is depressed if a voice is heard talking on a tape recording. Another key is depressed if a different pitch voice is heard (indicating the difference between a student and a teacher), and a third key is depressed when other sounds occur (confusion). No key is depressed when there is silence, but that time is recorded also. Readings are taken every 0.4 seconds. The outcome of this procedure is the relative percentage of teacher and student talk.

Wait time durations and means were measured using computer driven apparatus described in a report by Gooding, Gooding, and

Table 3.   Teachers' replies to students' responses.

Type of Reply
N—No Reply: teacher ignores a student remark
A—Approval: teacher gives positive reinforcement such as "good" or "correct".
E—Encouraging: teacher supports student response without indicating correctness.
B—Bland: teacher gives an indifferent response without indicating correctness.
D—Disapproval: teacher gives an indication of an incorrect response such as "wrong", "no", or "try again".

Swift (1982). The system is based on a microcomputer and employs analog and digital hardware and digital software. The apparatus enables the measurement of pause times in human speech, precise to better than .01 seconds. The pause duration in seconds and other information to identify transcript and line location is indexed by operator interaction as the apparatus processes the audiotape recording. This is accomplished by following the dialogue on the transcript as the apparatus measures the pauses. Valid pauses can then be separated from invalid pauses, noise, or other inappropriate input. A printout is prepared at the completion of the tape recording. It provides a permanent record of the measurements on a line-by-line basis and prints the frequency and mean pause durations of wait times.

Each of the five tape recordings and their accompanying transcripts were evaluated using the above procedures. The output of the analyses was compared with the data base generated by the research team in studies of middle school science classrooms. Sample data sheets are in the Appendix to this chapter.

FINDINGS

Table 4 summarizes the data gathered from the five classes studied. The tabulated data provide tape lengths, summaries of the cognitive levels of teacher questions, summaries of alternatives to questions, types of teacher replies to students, and the occurrence of non-response questions. In addition, disciplinary comments and derogatory remarks are tabulated, as are chain questions, interruptions by teachers and by students, and classroom management moves by teachers.

Complete wait time analyses are provided for each class. These analyses contain means, standard deviations, and frequency counts of wait time 1 (student wait time after teacher questions), wait time 2 (teacher wait time after student responses), and wait time 3 (student-to-student wait time). Timing cycle measurement is usually discontinued after an adequate sample (20 measurements) has been made. Also included are computerized classroom interaction analyses that indicate the percentages of class time consumed by teacher talk and student talk. This evaluation may be compared to the summaries of actual word counts that are provided.

Initially it should be pointed out that these tapes are somewhat atypical in that student participation is considerably higher than that generally noted in class discussions. Flanders (1970) found that

Table 4.   Summary Analysis of The Five Classroom Dialogues

	History HK		Smoking MK		Psychology PR		Marriage SN		Relation-ships WB	
Duration of Analysis										
(seconds)	569		593		580		576		630	
Cognitive Level										
of Questions										
T = Teacher, S = Student	**T**	**S**	**T**	**S**	**T**	**S**	**T**	**S**	**T**	**S**
Category A Memory	33	2	2	3	4	1	3	2	0	0
Category B-1 Convergent	8	0	1	0	2	0	7	0	0	0
Category B-2 Convergent	10	0	0	0	5	2	2	0	0	0
Category C Divergent	0	0	6	4	4	1	0	0	2	0
Category D Evaluative	2	1	1	3	6	0	0	0	2	0
Total	53	3	10	10	21	4	12	2	4	0
Chain Questions										
Chain of 2	7		2		5		4		2	
Chain of 3	1		1		0		0		0	
Chain of 4	1		0		0		0		0	
Alternatives to										
Teacher Questions										
L—Lecture-Summary	1		3		4		1		0	
AL—Active Listening	0		0		0		13		2	
E—Explanation	9		4		0		1		1	
R—Repetition	4		0		3		0		0	
AR—Argumentation	1		1		1		0		0	
FS—Finish Statement	0		0		0		2		0	
Type of Reply										
N—Nothing	7		2		0		0		0	
A—Approval	4		1		3		2		8	
E—Encouraging	7		3		8		7		1	
B—Bland	30		11		12		5		3	
D—Disapproval	8		0		2		0		1	
Non-Response Questions	5		1		1		0		0	
Disciplinary Remarks	0		1		1		1		0	
Derogatory Comments	0		1		0		0		0	
Interruptions	*		**							
By Teacher	1		4		3		2		0	
By Students	0		21		8		2		1	
Classroom Management										
M : General Management	3		5		4		9		3	
M+: Discussion Management	14		2		5		9		4	

Table 4. Summary Analysis of the Five Classroom Dialogues (Continued)

	History HK	Smoking MK	Psychology PR	Marriage SN	Relation-ships WB
Wait Time 1 (sec): T to S	*	**			
Mean	1.152	.511	1.891	.977	1.002
SD	1.049	.635	2.034	.963	.705
f	24	25	22	25	12
Wait Time 2 (sec): S to T	*	**			
Mean	.532	.381	.752	.868	.653
SD	.275	.029	.873	.607	.024
f	20	23	21	26	11
Wait Time 3 (sec): S to S	*	**			
Mean	.540	.306	.247	.521	-
SD	-	.444	.383	-	-
f	1	28	6	1	-
Percentage of Talk					
Teacher	64.95	38.77	38.40	35.40	36.85
Students	35.05	61.23	61.60	64.60	63.15
Word Count Data					
By Teacher (total)	1009	655	582	370	555
No. of Comments	69	37	34	39	18
Mean Length	14.623	17.703	34.229	19.475	30.833
SD	22.583	24.035	95.590	57.417	38.812
Percentage of Total	65.56	37.39	41.31	32.17	34.73
By Student (total)	530	1097	827	780	1043
No. of Comments	65	67	38	39	13
Mean Length	8.154	16.373	43.385	39.975	80.231
SD	8.401	17.614	129.813	120.138	45.924
Percentage of Total	34.44	62.61	58.69	67.83	65.27

* Evaluated for the first 300 seconds only
** Evaluated for the first 365 seconds only

teachers typically talk in excess of 75% of the time. His findings have been replicated by a number of researchers. Our research showed that science teachers speak in excess of 85% of the time in class settings they have identified as discussion-oriented.

The History Lesson (HK)

An analysis of the questions asked by the teacher and the students in this classroom using the question category system revealed that the teacher utilized 33 memory questions. Convergent questions were also common (18 were asked) but only two requests were noted at the evaluative level; those were for justification. The teacher posed a large number of questions (53 in 9.5 minutes) while allowing the students to ask but three. More than the usual number of multiple or chain questions (nine) were recorded. There were 17 instances of management actions on the teacher's part. Three were of a general management nature; 14 were discussion management.

Most of the teacher's replies were neutral. They were occasionally encouraging, but more often they were bland. Four times he agreed with correct responses, and disagreed eight times with incorrect or undesired responses. About 10% of his questions went unanswered.

This teacher relied largely on questions in order to conduct his discussion. He used some alternatives, mainly explanations of the material or repetitions of students' answers.

Teacher HK dominated the situation, talking 65% of the time, leaving 35% for the many students in his class. The teacher controlled all communications throughout the lesson. Every student comment was directed to the teacher rather than to the class as a whole. His rush to cover the material was shown by his short wait times, averaging .53 seconds. This fast pace was reflected by the students' quick responses.

The history lesson is most like the typical science lesson. It is characterized by the rapid-fire drill or quiz show format as defined by the term recitation. The lesson is a review type of exercise. The content is primarily of memory level and the wait times are typically short. There is little evidence of divergent or evaluative level thinking in the teacher questions and in the subsequent responses of the students. Wait times are too short to permit the reflective thinking necessary for higher cognitive level processing.

The Rules of Smoking Lesson (MK)

The cognitive interaction levels were the highest for both the teacher and the students of the classes included in this series of audiotape recordings. Both teachers and students questioned each other rather frequently (20 questions in 10 minutes), using a high proportion of divergent and evaluative questions. Opinions were solicited with several requests made for justification of positions. A very limited factual and conceptual background was all that was required by any student to participate in this conversation. We feel that the question category system did not account differentially for the conversation in this non-content-based discussion. Cognitive skills of analysis and synthesis were not used.

The teacher's replies, mostly neutral, tended to encourage the students, although on several occasions the teacher utilized the lecture option to expand on his own views rather than allowing the students further expression. As an alternative to questions, teacher MK used explanatory statements and lecture–summary comments. Chain questions were used on three occasions during this session. One disciplinary remark and one derogatory comment were noted.

The most prominent feature of this tape was the frantic nature of the class. The noise level was high. The teacher interrupted the students, and the students interrupted the teacher and each other. Many individual comments were lost in the high background noise. This general rudeness prompted one student to insult another. Wait times were short. Because the wait times for interruptions are recorded as .0 seconds, the wait time means on this tape were extremely short, approximately .3 to .5 seconds.

This tape is of a different character than the others. We would classify it as a permissive discussion. The students are permitted to express their opinions. This topic engendered considerable interest and produced more student–student interaction than in any of the other four classes. However, there is no assessment of progress or synthesis of the material discussed. Generally, few teachers permit students to express their own opinions. Since MK appeared to value the students' opinions, this is a positive factor in this lesson, hence an important point in favor of such a discussion.

The Psychology Lesson (PR)

This teacher utilized a balanced mixture of all cognitive levels, with the teacher asking most of the questions (21 in about 10 minutes), while allowing the students to ask four. Four of his questions were for classroom management purposes and five were to promote the flow of discussion. The teacher and the students interrupted each other frequently.

Although half of this teacher's remarks to students were neutral or bland, he did use a number of approving and encouraging remarks. He expressed disapproval on two occasions. The teacher made use of the technique of lecture or summary on some occasions, and also repeated student remarks. Once he was required to use a disciplinary comment. The students seemed to be frustrated by the instructor's seeming lack of knowledge of psychology.

Even though wait times were considerably shorter than the criterion suggested by Rowe (1974, 1978), a small increase above the baseline of 1.26 seconds for wait time 1 and .55 seconds for wait time 2 has been found to make a significant difference in the quality of classroom interaction (Swift & Gooding, 1983). Such is the case

with this lesson. This class observed wait times of 1.89 (WT1) and
.75 seconds (WT2). That small but important difference is sufficient
to allow adequate thinking time and interaction at higher cognitive
levels.

This is an example of the guided discussion type of class. The
discussion follows a plan set by the objectives of the teacher. The
interaction is guided by the instructor, who uses various types of
questions to elicit student responses. Divergent and evaluative questions are posed in addition to the memory level and convergent
thinking items found more frequently in the previously analyzed
classes.

As noted above, wait times were slightly longer than typical
baseline pauses of teachers who have not had special wait time
training. These slightly longer pauses probably facilitated the teacher's use of higher level questions. Extended wait times were accompanied by increased length of student responses. As a result there
was significantly more student talk in this class than is usually found
in discussions. In fact, the student talk in this class actually exceeded
the teacher talk; a rare occurrence in any class.

We would hypothesize that this teacher would have even greater
success with divergent and evaluative levels of dialogue if wait times
were increased to the 3-second criterion suggested by our research.

The Marriage Lesson (SN)

The questions that were posed by the teacher and the students
during this class were all on lower (observational) levels. There
were 12 teacher questions and two student questions, mostly convergent and memory level, but no high level questions. Four of the
questions were chained. All of the teacher's questions were answered,
but there were four interruptions, two by the teacher and two by
students. There were nine instances of general classroom management and nine more for the management of the discussion. An
unusual aspect of this class is the use of active listening as a means
of encouraging students to participate or elaborate. The teacher
replied to the students using a good mixture of neutral, encouraging,
and approving comments. He expressed no disapproval to any student.

The wait times of the students (WT1) were very short. They often
burst forth with their own experiences. The teacher wait times (WT2)
were the longest of the five classrooms. This patience was mirrored
by the longer contributions by the class members.

The family life lesson approaches being a permissive discussion.

We found few such discussions in the classrooms we previously studied. Such classes are primarily the sharing of unsubstantiated, personal opinions. There may be some structure to the discussion and some evaluation of the ideas, but the teacher had no particular plan for systematic assessment, analysis, and synthesis of the material discussed. There seemed to be no discernible objectives for this lesson.

The content analysis of this class revealed that the cognitive levels of teacher questions were no higher than is usually the case when wait times are brief. The teacher is asking for observations, but whether the observations are informed or uninformed is not probed. Since the discussion is based primarily on unassessed information, there may be less need for extended pauses in order to process this information at higher cognitive levels. However, our research indicates that longer wait times would have made higher levels of interaction more likely. We were astounded to find that the teacher confined this discussion to the convergent level. Opportunities to enter into a discussion of feelings and values were not taken.

Permissive discussions can have utility in arousing interest in a topic that is focused on something other than on content mastery. They also can permit a larger proportion of students to participate more fully. This is often a less productive type of discussion than a guided one.

Family Relationships (WB)

Few questions were posed in this tape recording. Students were permitted to talk at length without being interrupted either by their teacher or by other students. Two of the four questions asked for opinions, two asked for justifications. These served to focus and guide the discussion. The teacher retained control through frequent approving comments, and the discussion alternated between the teacher and students. Comments were always addressed to the teacher. No disciplinary comments were needed and no derogatory inserts were made, possibly contributing to a free and open discussion.

It is unusual to hear responses as long as the ones on this tape with wait times that are so short. This might have occurred because the conversation called only for opinions and justifications that were not necessarily based on informed judgment.

This discussion has both the elements of a permissive discussion and a recitation. The funnelling of all comments through the teacher, usually earning approval, resemble characteristics of recitations. Yet, ideas were allowed to flow in the direction of the students, an element of a permissive discussion. WB permitted the students to recite their anecdotes concerning their relationships with their parents. The ultimate aim of this lesson was unclear.

CONCLUSIONS AND RECOMMENDATIONS

(1) Discussions in all classes appear to have much in common. Regardless of the nature of the topic or the grade level, these classes are characterized by clear interaction patterns. The verbal techniques that teachers use to promote interaction include the use of encouraging replies, thought-provoking questions, and a small number of question alternatives. Their skillful use, accompanied by adequate wait times, promotes interaction that enhances both the cognitive and affective climate of classrooms.

(2) Listening to a class discussion, either live or recorded, and forming a subjective opinion concerning its quality, is often misleading. Quantitative analysis produces much greater detail and, sometimes, quite different conclusions. For example, in the marriage lesson conducted by SN, it is easy to become captivated by the enthusiastic interaction, and not realize that little cognitive depth was present.

(3) The question category system for science, as modified, appears to be as appropriate for the humanities and social sciences as it is for the natural sciences when there is a content base for the discussion. It is sufficiently descriptive to yield adequately detailed explanations of teachers' questions, yet the five categories (A, B-1, B-2, C, and D) are broad enough to minimize confusion. Grouping A and B-1 together and B-2, C, and D together permits comparisons to be made of lower level with higher level cognitive questions. We recommend greater use of the modified system for the analysis of discussions that are content-centered.

(4) The classification of alternatives to questions should be expanded. Although Dillon (1983) has encouraged the use of alternatives, including wait time, the range of options that are available has not been adequately investigated. Knowledge of options can increase the repertoire of discussion-enhancing skills of teachers. Controlled investigations can then yield data on the effectiveness of these alternatives.

(5) In a like manner, additional study should be made of teachers' replies to students' responses. Indications are that encouraging replies are related to improved discussions; the remainder, including

praise, seem to inhibit interaction. The relationship of these replies to questions and alternatives is not understood at present.

(6) It is our view that all of these classrooms would benefit from the extension of wait time. Our studies show that an effective means for achievement of such increases is through the use of a feedback device called a *Wait Timer* (TM) invented by Swift and tested to date in more than 100 classrooms. It is currently available from the authors or from Thought Technologies, Ltd., Montreal, Canada. Rowe (1974) and other researchers (Tobin & Capie, 1981) have found that training teachers to pause effectively is a difficult task. DeTure (1979) has found that teachers who have been taught to pause in questioning have difficulty maintaining their wait times over an extended period without review and practice. The Wait Timer provides for immediate feedback and confirmation of appropriate pause times for both teachers and students. In addition, it enables the teacher to review and check maintenance of appropriate pausing from time to time. If the teachers in the five classrooms examined in this paper practiced effective use of pausing by using a Wait Timer, higher cognitive levels might have been obtained.

(7) As indicated, these five lessons, although very different, do have much in common with each other and with the middle school science discussions that we have investigated. Among other similarities, they exhibit the need for greater understanding of the discussion process. The lack of discussion skills of both teachers and students is obvious. Improvement of these skills is needed by all.

THOUGHTS ON THE MULTIDISCIPLINARY STUDY

As we have indicated our research team has approached the analysis of classroom interaction patterns using a behavioral orientation leading to a descriptive definition of classroom interaction styles emerging from the measurement and classification of specified variables. When we compare our approach with those of our multidisciplinary colleagues in this study, we find that certain of them (most notably the applied researchers) have made use of strategies and analysis schemes that are related to ours. Other colleagues in fields such as logic and analytic philosophy take very different approaches to the assessment of transactions in classroom dialogue. Interestingly, we find that we have become so highly specialized in our own disciplines and subfields of research that we have considerable difficulty in communicating across our technical vocabularies. The development of a glossary of terms has facilitated our communication to some extent, and we continue the process of seeking increasing interdisciplinary understanding.

As we examine the results of the symposium experience, we find that the project has reemphasized the value of taking the holistic perspective advocated by Francis (this volume). It is through a synthesis of the components of discussions, tempered by thoughtful reflection on the totality of the experience, that the true value of discussions can be assessed.

Of the researchers taking the pedagogical perspective in this study, we find the work of Klinzing and Klinzing–Eurich most congruent with our own. Therefore, even though they were communicating in a second language (their native language is German), the ideas were easily shared and the behavioral approaches to the study of question–answer dialogue took us along similar paths.

An exciting, though quite different approach from our own, was revealed to us in the work of Roby. His models of discussion provide ways to conceptualize the diversity of questions and responses in dialogue. It appears to us that Roby's work could evolve to become an effective way to explain the importance of learning how to conduct a discussion to practitioners in the schools. Thus, what began as a research tool, may become part of training in pedagogy.

The cognitive developmental approach taken by Sigel has served to illustrate for us the important phenomenological differences between posing an open question in contrast to a closed one. As Sigel notes, simple declarative statements require only passive listening and associative responses. However, open-ended inquiry demands active engagement. The discrepancies created by inquiry propel the person to change and create the potential for motivation. This also merges effectively with the thesis proposed by Bridges, who states that a true discussion must serve to enrich an individual's understanding, to refine that understanding, or transactionally to enhance both.

Discussions and dialogues are the essences of education. If you ask college graduates to evaluate their courses, many will tell you that their most memorable courses are those that have given them the opportunity to share their readings and knowledge through discussions. Recently one of us, Patricia Swift, had a chance to talk to two "average" seniors from a public high school. She asked them, "How would you like your school life to be different?". Neither hesitated. They both answered, with enthusiasm, "More discussions about what life is really like, and more talking about how to manage after we leave school." Educators since Socrates have known that students crave this need to participate verbally in the daily search for knowledge, yet discussion seems to be the most elusive component of the classroom.

Roby's clear delineation of the continuum that exists with classroom interaction is particularly helpful in explaining the rarity of true discussions. It is easy for an intended discussion to lose all structure and slip into an unfocused mode. It is equally easy for the teacher to feel the need of greater structure and to impose the regimen of the recitation. Even when teachers think they are having discussions they still talk approximately 85% of the allotted class time. When teachers talk this much, the students tend to daydream. We know that achievement is raised when students are allowed to contribute their thoughts and concerns, but teachers seem to suppress the very outcome that would allow the product they wish to produce—achievement.

Finally, it comes as a shock that it is difficult to communicate effectively with fellow researchers and theoreticians from related disciplines when considering a common data set from our various perspectives. For the opportunity to experience a concerted drive to understand a data set through these various perspectives, however, the effort required to do so has been well spent. Our gratitude goes to Dillon for the foresight and vision to organize this venture. We have been impressed with the importance of taking the broad view from time to time in order that we might not lose sight of the holistic experience of education.

REFERENCES

Berliner, D.C. (Speaker) (1985). *Research in teacher education: What are the questions?* (Cassette Recording No. 85RA-52.01). Chicago, IL: Teach'Em, Inc.

Bloom, B.S. (Ed.) (1956). *Taxonomy of Educational Objectives: Handbook I. The Cognitive Domain.* New York: David McKay.

Blosser, P.E. (1973). *Handbook of Effective Questioning Techniques.* Worthington, OH: Education Associates.

DeTure, L.R. (1979). Relative effects of modeling on the acquisition of wait time by preservice elementary teachers and concomitant changes in dialogue patterns. *Journal of Research in Science Teaching. 16.* 553–562.

Dillon, J.T. (1981). To question or not to question during discussions. II. Non-questioning techniques. *Journal of Teacher Education, 32,* 15–20.

Dillon, J.T. (1983). *Teaching and the Art of Questioning,* Fastback #194. Bloomington, IN: Phi Delta Kappa.

Flanders, N.E. (1970). *Analyzing Teaching Behavior,* Reading, MA: Addison-Wesley.

Gwinn, B.A. (1986). *The relationship between wait time and interaction in the classroom.* Unpublished master's thesis, State University of New York, College at Oswego, Oswego, NY.

Good, C.V. (Ed.) (1983). *Dictionary of Education,* New York: McGraw-Hill.

Gooding, S.T., Gooding, C.T., & Swift, J.N. (1982). A microcomputer based pause analysis apparatus. *Behavior Research Methods and Instrumentation, 14,* 121–123.

Gooding, C.T., Swift, P.R., & Swift, J.N. (1983, November). *Wait time and classroom learning.* Paper presented at the meeting of the Eastern Educational Research Association, Baltimore, MD.

Rowe, M.B. (1974). Wait-time and rewards as instructional variables, their influence on language, logic and fate control. I. Wait-time. *Journal of Research in Science Teaching, 11,* 81–94.

Rowe, M.B. (1978). *Teaching Science as Continuous Inquiry: A Basic* (2nd ed.). New York: McGraw-Hill.

Swift, J.N. & Gooding, C.T. (1983). Interaction of wait time feedback and questioning instruction on middle school science teaching. *Journal of Research in Science Teaching, 20,* 721–730.

Swift, P.R. & Alves, T.A. (1984, April). *Using question analysis to improve discussions: a comparison of schemes.* Paper presented at the annual meeting of the National Science Teachers Association, Boston.

Tobin, K.E. & Capie, (1981). *Wait-time and learning in science.* Burlington, NC: Carolina Biological Supply Company.

Wise, K.C. & Okey, J.R. (1983). A meta-analysis of the various science teaching strategies on achievement. *Journal of Research in Science Teaching, 20,* 419–437.

APPENDIX A

A Sample of a Data Recording Sheet

Line No.:   line number on the transcript
   Dil: numbered by Dillon
   Osw: numbered consecutively at Oswego
T or S: dialogue by a teacher (T) or a student (S)
Question Type: see Table 1 for definitions
Alternative: see Table 2 for definitions
No. of Words: number of actual words spoken by a teacher or a student
Type of Reply: see Table 3 for definitions; time is in seconds
   X = an unmeasurable pause due to background noises
Other: CH2 means that the teacher asked two questions consec-

utively without pausing for a reply, **CH3** = three consecutive questions posed without a pause for reply, etc.
M.: see explanation accompanying Table 1

Tape #805

Line #	Wait Times Type 1 Ratio	Type 2	Sec.	Classroom Interaction	
10	1		.732	Tape Length 630	
11	1		1.846		
21		2	.311	**Number**	
22	1		.33	Total	1475
29		2	.713	Teacher	534
36	1		.751	Student	915
46		2	.579	Confusion	6
49	1		.000	Silence	20
50		2	.484		
51	1		.368	**Percent**	
57		2	.865	Teacher	36.2034
58	1		.3	Student	62.0339
64		2	1.056	Confusion	.4068
65	1		1.444	Silence	
71		2	1.3559		
78	1		2.093	**Observation**	
85		2	.465	**Rate**	.427119
91	1		1.405		
96		2	.846		
98	1		.904		
117		2	.827		
118	1		1.846		
136		2	.732		

No. of Type 1 = 12
Type 1 Mean = 1.00158333

No. of Type 2 = 11
Type 2 Mean = .6533636

CHAPTER 11

Questions, Responses, and Reactions

Hans Gerhard Klinzing and Gisela Klinzing–Eurich

Center for New Learning Methods
University of Tuebingen
Muenzgasse 11
D-7400 Tuebingen 1, West Germany

BACKGROUND AND POINT OF VIEW: SYSTEMATIC TEACHER TRAINING

For the last two decades, the major concern of one of the teams at the Center for New Learning Methods,[1] an institute for educational technology, has been the development of a model for teacher pre- and inservice training, taking into consideration Israeli and American research and development efforts particularly in the area of Micro-teaching (Allen & Ryan, 1969; Perlberg, Bar-On, Levin, Bar-Yam, Lewy, & Etrog, 1976; Borg, Kelley, Langer, & Gall, 1970; Zifreund, 1966, 1968, 1983; Klinzing, 1982). As this research suggests, changes in the competency of teaching personnel can be expected when the focus of the respective teacher training program is on the teaching process itself. Thus, there are good reasons for using classroom

---

[1] The "Zentrum fuer Neue Lernverfahren" emphasizes areas like the use of pro-grammed learning, computers, TV, and language laboratories in educational settings on the one hand, and the development of new methods and materials for training educational personnel (microteaching, sensitivity training, creativity training, etc.) on the other. So the word technology is not used in its narrow sense referring to tools in the form of hardware but as an application of science to practice.

observation systems, particularly low inference systems, in teacher education: teachers are provided with the opportunity of receiving precise data-based information on their behavior. This specific information may be used by the teachers to think about their teaching, and enables them to work at changing their behavior where necessary and/or to expand their teaching repertory by experimenting with new behavior presumed or suggested by research, to be helpful for promoting student growth (Peck & Tucker, 1973; Simon & Boyer, 1974; Klinzing, 1982).

CLASSROOM DISCUSSION

The basis for selecting, describing, and assessing the behaviors suggested to teachers or teacher trainees for clasoom discussions was the philosophical and pedagogical literature. It identifies the goals and purposes of discussion in classroom and other settings, differentiates this method from others (e.g., recitation), and describes the tasks and behaviors of a (democratic) discussion moderator and of the participants.

According to Gall and Gall (1976) and Potter and Anderson (1963), "discussion" can be defined as a purposeful, (intentionally) systematic, mutual, oral exchange of facts, ideas, opinions, points of view, feelings, and beliefs by a group of persons (usually in the roles of moderator/leader and participants) assembled in order to achieve cognitive or affective objectives, or joint action. Discussions can be classified according to their objectives: initiating of higher cognitive processes in subject matter mastery discussions; problem solving and getting ready for joint action in problem-solving discussions; increasing of awareness and understanding of one's own and of other participants' points of view, ideas, beliefs, feelings, and actions, as well as facilitating their critical analysis and eventual subsequent changes in attitude in issue-oriented discussions.

All of these types of discussion may occur in classrooms, but there is a specific difference between classroom discussions and discussions in general. This difference refers to the objectives classroom interaction has in addition to everyday interaction, and to the specific role of the teacher as a discussion moderator and the students as participants: one additional purpose of the discussion method when used in classrooms is to motivate the students toward learning and participating, to foster or maintain a positive attitude towards instruction and to assist them in using their discussion skills effectively and appropriately (like increasing the ability to give reasons, awareness of the quality of responses etc.; cf. Gall & Gall, 1976; Gall, Weathersby, Elder, & Lai, 1975; Gage & Berliner, 1984). These latter purposes are particularly important when the emphasis of education is on preparing students for a democratic society (Bridges, 1979). This requires an increased responsibility on the side of the teacher, a thoroughly planned and evaluated teacher guidance.

TASKS OF THE DISCUSSION MODERATOR AND OF THE PARTICIPANTS

The specific tasks of a discussion moderator/teacher in a particular situation may vary with the different goals or participants, etc. but the main functions (as summarized, for instance, by McKeachie, 1965; Maier & Solem, 1952; Gall & Gall, 1976; Gage & Berliner, 1984; Gall et al. 1975) appear to be similar throughout the different discussions. More concretely, they can be described as follows.

In the *beginning* of a discussion, the teacher/moderator introduces the topic of the discussion as precisely and concretely as possible, and clarifies its goals. In the course of the discussion, he *stimulates it* (if necessary), *encourages the participation* of all group members, and distributes the participation appropriately (e.g., by asking silent group members for their opinion or personal experience), facilitates interaction among the participants (e.g., by redirecting), tries to decrease tendencies to monopolize the discussion, and helps the group move toward the goals of the discussion focusing on higher cognitive processes (using higher cognitive questions, self-reference questions, and opinion questions) while altogether limiting the stating of his opinion, his own comments, and his control. Furthermore, he *maintains* a good flow of discussion, using supportive, conciliatory, friendly statements, decreasing hostility, establishing an openness for exchanging ideas in the group and for enhancing effective interpersonal processes. To keep the discussion focused and to increase its depth, the moderator (if necessary) provides *guidance,* especially so in classrooms. Sometimes it may be necessary to remind the participants of the initial task by restating the issue or again clarifying the goals of the discussion, and to *relate* ideas of the participants to these goals or to each other. With the latter, at the same time he helps to *upgrade* the group's thinking. This can be reached also by skills like asking for reasons, clarification, and relationships (probing), furthermore by identifying, stating, or clarifying differences in opinion and areas of agreement, and making them explicit, or by mediating or contrasting contradictory statements, and accepting or acknowledging them without valuing. At the *end*, the moderator should give (or ask for) a brief review or evaluation of the discussion and suggest, or ask for, the next steps in the discussion or in the following action.

The tasks and behaviors of the discussion *participants* can be described accordingly. The participants should interact with each other frequently without monopolizing the discussion. This interaction should be on a high cognitive level, should be thoughtful and of high quality, support, and originality, without engaging in personal attacks, and in a supportive and conciliatory manner (e.g., acknowledging, restating other's ideas). Their contribution should be stimulating and focused on the topic, and should maintain, guide, and upgrade the discussion process.

While the *general* categories of the behavior used in discussions may be basically the same because the functions of discussion moderators and participants are basically the same, the different kinds of discussion vary to some degree in specific behaviors and in the frequency of their use, depending upon the specific objectives and the related tasks and functions of discussion moderators and participants. So a system for observing discussion has to be designed to flexibly allow for modifications in the framework of the basic categories with respect to the different purposes of the respective discussion. In light of the problems outlined above, the procedure of developing the observation instrument was a follows: Concepts of behavior of a discussion moderator/teacher and of participants/ students were collected from the literature about classroom discussion. These concepts of behavior were related to descriptions of behavior, the effectiveness or appropriateness of which are suggested by classroom interaction research, i.e., which are validated against criteria like desired directly observable student classroom behavior or measures of student outcome. In cases where the behaviors were derived from research on teaching methods other than discussion (e.g., recitation), the intention was that the criteria against which they were validated could be related, or would at least not contradict, to the goals of the discussion method. These definitions, then, can provide a basis for the development of an observation system for teacher training and feedback.

PREVIOUS RESEARCH ON TEACHER QUESTIONS, STUDENT REACTIONS AND INITIATIONS, AND TEACHER REACTIONS

Teacher Questions in Classroom Discussion

There is not enough space here for discussing the importance of teacher questioning in general and the different opinions about the role of questioning in classroom interaction. Also, the research on the relationship of the frequency of questions (Rosenshine, 1971; Dunkin & Biddle, 1974), of different cognitive levels of questions, or of different levels of difficulty of questions, with different outcome measures cannot be discussed here in detail (Gall, 1970, 1984; Rosenshine, 1976; Tausch & Tausch, 1978; Redfield & Rousseau, 1981; Klinzing, 1982). Though the results of this research apply mostly to the context of recitation, it is possible to point out a few tentative conclusions of the research on higher cognitive questions because they appear to be relevant for classroom and other discussions.

First, in normal classroom settings teachers ask many questions (Dunkin & Biddle, 1974; Klinzing, 1982) but higher cognitive questions occur infrequently. The repeated findings show that up to 80% of the questions asked by teachers require mere recall of knowledge while only about 20–30% call for higher mental processes. This has been documented for more than half a century in the USA (Hoetker & Ahlbrand, 1969; Gall, 1970; Arnold, Atwood, & Rogers, 1973; Atwood & Stevens, 1976; Barnes, 1980; Dunkin & Biddle, 1974), in Australia (Tisher, 1970; Tisher & Power, 1978), in New Zealand (Nuthall & Lawrence, 1965), and in West Germany (Klinzing–Eurich & Klinzing, 1981). This means that in schools the recitation method is very popular while classroom discussions in the above sense do not occur very frequently.

Second, teachers can be trained to increase the frequency of higher cognitive questions in classroom discussions (e.g., Gall, Dunning, Galassi, & Banks, 1970; Klinzing–Eurich & Klinzing, 1981; Willson, 1973). Several studies show that teachers maintain these newly acquired higher cognitive questioning skills for several months up to three years (Borg, 1972; 1975; Perrott, 1977; Boeck & Hillenmeyer, 1973; Rector & Bicknell, 1972; Klinzing–Eurich & Klinzing, 1981).

Third, the predominant use of higher cognitive questions has a positive effect on student achievement, especially in higher grade levels and with students of average and high ability (Redfield & Rousseau, 1981; Klinzing, 1982)[2].

Fourth, higher cognitive questions tend to elicit more and longer student answers, more student–student interaction (and more student talk), and more student behavior at higher or more complex levels (Gall, 1973; Borg, 1975; Dillon, 1982; Klinzing–Eurich & Klinzing, 1981).

Fifth, the correspondence between the cognitive levels of teacher questions and student responses is low. In naturalistic studies of Australian (Tisher, 1970) and New Zealand (Nuthall & Lawrence, 1965) junior high classes, for instance, it was found that about 40% of student responses to questions demanding explanations were couched at *lower* cognitive levels such as factual description than as completed causal statements. This was not the case in some North American junior–senior level classes where Dillon (1982) found that only 16% of student responses to questions demanding explanations were at lower cognitive levels. On the other hand, he also noted that there was not as high a correspondence between the levels of responses and questions requiring students to give reasons for or against arguments ("justifying") or to evaluate ideas ("opining"): 54% of student responses were at cognitive levels lower than the teacher questions. Other studies on correspondences between cognitive levels of questions and responses only add to the mixed results with some (e.g., Bellack, Kliebard, Hyman, & Smith, 1966) reporting high proportions of correspondence, some (e.g., Barnes, 1980) low proportions, and others (e.g., Mills, Rice, Berliner, & Rousseau, 1980) a 50–50 chance that student responses will be at the same cognitive level as the teacher questions. Dillon (1982) suggests that given this mixture of findings, albeit from a very small research base, the common educational presumption "ask a higher level question, get a higher level answer" should be replaced by "ask a higher level question, get any level answer". But it was also shown

---

[2] This result of a meta-analysis of 18 experiments seems to contradict results from correlational studies, where narrow questions were found to be more effective for student learning than higher cognitive questions. According to Gall (1984), the contradiction can be resolved by analyzing the populations represented in the studies: "Taking this difference into account, I would conclude that (1) emphasis on fact questions is more effective for promoting young disadvantaged children's achievement, which primarily involves mastery of basic skills; and (2) emphasis on higher cognitive questions is more effective for students of average and high ability, especially as they enter high school, where more independent thinking is required. While emphasizing fact questions, teachers of young disadvantaged children should take care to include some higher cognitive questions to stimulate development of their thinking skills." (Gall, 1984, p. 41)

that correspondence can be increased through systematic training (Klinzing & Klinzing–Eurich, 1981). Be that as it may, the weight of the evidence is such that ". . . asking higher level questions "works" in the sense of making students behave at relatively higher levels of cognitive processing" (Gage & Berliner, 1984, p. 636). It seems justifiable that asking predominantly higher level questions be recommended for classroom discussions.

Student Talk

Active participation of students is essential for classroom discussions. In early studies of process–outcome relationships this was often assessed with gross measures such as the amount of student talk (Rosenshine, 1971; Dunkin & Biddle, 1974; Klinzing, 1982). Research on classroom processes shows that student talk comprises only 20% to 33% of all classroom interaction time. Of that proportion, only 20% is attributed to student responses and less than 10% to student initiation and/or higher level utterances (Dunkin & Biddle, 1974; Klinzing, 1982). Again, these data show that classroom discussion is not the predominant method used in schools, though in textbooks it is generally considered as desirable. As stated above, the amount and cognitive level of student talk can be influenced by higher cognitive teacher questions in the immediate classroom context, and the degree of student participation is positively related to the total number of thought units uttered by pupils (Taba, 1966; Taba, Levine, & Elzey, 1964). However, only a positive non-significant trend is found for the relationship of aspects of student verbal participation and achievement, with the exception of the seldomly occuring student questions (Klinzing, 1982).

Apart from the research on the amount of student verbal participation and of student response and initiative utterances on a higher cognitive level, other specific student behaviors possibly desirable for discussions are unstudied. Especially relevant to this topic may be the effects of student–student interaction and the quality of student utterances. Here, the length of student utterances may be a rough index of quality (see Gall et al., 1970; Borg, 1975), but more direct measures are needed (like clarity, accuracy, appropriateness, specificity, support), as M.D. Gall (1973) proposed. Such indices may be used by discussion moderators as a base for their decisions when guiding and increasing the depth of a discussion.

Teacher Reactions

Student utterances in classroom discussions can serve as an occasion for the discussion moderator or student to react and thereby keep the discussion focused, maintain and guide the flow of the discussion, and increase its depth using more of an "indirect" influence which seems appropriate for democratic discussion leaders, as described above (Gall & Gall, 1976). The moderator's reaction may be classified as follows: (1) *reflecting* behaviors: acknowledgement or repetition of an utterance, indicating understanding of an utterance or idea for enhancing quality, relating to preceding utterances or to topic, lifting of level of utterance, (2) *sustaining:* repetition of original question or probing, and (3) *judging:* praise, criticism. When used appropriately, i.e., only where necessary for the flow and quality of the discussion, the "indirect" interventions seem to be the heart of a "democratic" moderator's role. As meta-analyses show (Glass, Coulter, Hartley, Hearold, Kalk, & Sherrez, 1977; Gage, 1978), process–process and process–product research of discrete behaviors which are related mostly to "indirect teaching" (e.g., Flanders, 1970) suggests that such behaviors (generally used less frequently than behaviors of direct teaching) are positively related to more student talk, more student initiation, more student questions, and a higher level of classroom discourse (Dunkin & Biddle, 1974; Klinzing, 1982). And last but not least, they are positively related to student attitudes and achievement, although achievement (as assessed in the studies) may be not a good index, because in discussions the major purpose is not predominantly to encourage the conveying of facts but rather the independence of thought, etc. Behaviors which are classified by Flanders (1970) as accepting and using student ideas and as probing, elicit more student utterances, student initiation, higher level responses, and achievement (Dunkin & Biddle, 1974; Gage, 1978; Gage & Berliner, 1984; Klinzing, 1982). And finally, behaviors of indirect influence can be shaped successfully (Flanders, 1970; Klinzing–Eurich & Klinzing, 1981; Klinzing, 1982).

Judgements like praise and disapproval seem to be inappropriate as a reacting behavior of a discussion moderator. They are inconsistently or negatively related to desired behaviors or outcomes (Rosenshine, 1971; Dunkin & Biddle, 1974; Wilkinson, 1980). Exceptions to this are the use of positive reinforcement, which has a positive influence on the amount of student participation (McDonald & Allen, 1967) and on student attitudes (Gage, 1978).

Another result which should be interesting for teacher training is that the way teachers react to a student response is unrelated to whether or not the student response is congruent or incongruent to the preceding solicitation (Tisher, 1970; Bellack, Kliebard, Hyman, & Smith, 1966; Zahorik, 1968; Medley, Impellitteri, & Smith 1966).

In summary, from the literature about discussions and classroom research it seems possible to derive descriptions of behaviors validated against desired student behaviors and attitudes, or—less appropriately—against indicators of student achievement.

A CONCEPTUAL FRAMEWORK FOR THE DEVELOPMENT OF CATEGORIES FOR THE ANALYSIS OF CLASSROOM DISCUSSIONS[3]

As briefly outlined above, a number of concepts and definitions from classroom interaction research could be found relevant to the analysis of classroom discussion. Since they are taken from very different sources and therefore mostly have different definitions, an attempt was made to screen them in light of a general conceptual framework based in part on the observation systems of Bellack, Kliebard, Hyman, and Smith (1966), Taba (1966), Flanders (1970), Gall (1973), Brophy and Evertson (1974), and Stallings (1977).

It was intended to arrive at categories symmetrical for the observation of teacher *and* student behavior *and* also symmetrical for initiating and reacting behavior. Any of these behaviors can be differentiated also by subcategories. Table 1 shows this conceptual framework for the selection and development of classroom behavior observation categories.

CATEGORIES FOR THE ANALYSIS OF CLASSROOM DISCUSSION

For developing an observation instrument for analyzing the five transcripts of this multidisciplinary project, various facets of the conceptual framework were selected and combined with types of behavior in order to obtain categories relevant to the goals of discussion and complementary skills for teachers as well as for students. The categories are listed in Table 2.

---

[3] We would like to thank W. Zifreund for his valuable critique and comments in developing this conceptual framework.

Table 1. Conceptual Framework for the Development of Categories for Classroom Observation

Type of Behavior Initiation	Reaction	Source A	Direction B	Mode C	Material D	Domain E	Level F	Quality G		Relation H	Tone I
Providing information	Responding (fulfilling expectation of demand, answering a question)	(1) teacher (T) (moderator) (2) other adult (OA) (3) student (S) (partner)	(1) to T (2) to OA (3) to S (4) to SG (5) to WhC (6) to E	(1) verbal (2) non-verbal	(1) content (2) self-reference (personal) (3) procedure/ organization/ management	(1) cognitive (2) affective (3) psychomotoric	(1) low (2) higher	originality	1-2-3	(1) repetition (2) combination (3) comparison (stating of identity/difference)	(1) positive (2) neutral (3) negative
Providing structure	Restructuring, reflecting	(4) small group (SG)						completeness	1-2-3	(4) elaboration	
Demanding	Sustaining, probing	(5) whole class (WhC)						relevance/appropriateness	1-2-3	(5) conclusion	
Valuing	Judging	(6) physical environment (material, media, etc.) (E)						clarity	1-2-3		
								correctness	1-2-3		

ANALYSIS OF THE FIVE TRANSCRIPTS OF
CLASSROOM DISCUSSIONS

Five transcripts of classroom conversations, representing a randomly selected 10-minute period from different high school classrooms which were provided for this project by J.T. Dillon, were analyzed according to the categories listed in Table 2.

Two observers coded each transcript twice. Disagreements in coding were discussed among the coders until an agreement was reached. Such disagreements were not infrequent, particularly regarding the cognitive level and quality of the utterances. They resulted mainly from the fact that the curriculum material that the teacher questions and student utterances were based upon as well as the classroom climate and routines, were not known to the coders (cf. Gall, 1970).

The final observer agreement seemed to be high enough (about 75%) for the analysis to result in recommendations to the teachers for improving their classroom behavior. There are some differences between the ground rules for coding used in this study and the rules commonly used for coding classroom behavior, especially teacher questions. In our study, behavior generally is classified from the point of view of its meaning to the participants (not the estimated intention of the teacher). Also, every change in behavior is intended to be recorded.

Furthermore, student or teacher utterances are coded as questions whenever an answer is expected, regardless of their syntactical structure, tone of voice, or question marks. Finally, there is a distinction made between initiated and reactive questions (follow-up questions, like sustaining feedback questions, or questions asking for the use of other students' ideas). Table 2 summarizes the results.

First, we will outline our analysis and results of each transcript. Then, we relate this to the conclusions of other participants in the project. And finally, we give recommendations to the respective teacher for improving his or her discussion behavior. (Time line displays of all transcripts may be obtained from the first author.)

HK's Transcript

The discussion may be classified as a subject matter mastery discussion calling for higher cognitive processes (finding explanations why the American Revolutionary War was won), based on previously heard or read information. The rough discussion characteristic, as provided by Dillon (e.g., teacher talk: 59%), indicates that the discussion is highly teacher-centered and focused on reaching an un-

Table 2. Categories of Teacher and Student Verbal Behavior in Discussions

Categories	HK		WB		MK		SN		PR	
	T	S	T	S	T	S	T	S	T	S
I. Initiations, verbal, teacher, students, others (T, S, O)										
1. Giving information/structuring, T, S, O	7	2	2	10	3	10	6	17	7	3
1.1 Giving information, content, cognitive	4	2	-	-	-	-	-	-	4	2
1.2 Giving information, content, affective	-	-	-	-	-	-	1	1	-	-
1.3 Giving opinion	1	-	2	5	1	5	1	1	1	-
1.4 Giving information, self-reference	-	-	-	4	2	-	1	15	1	-
1.5 Giving information, procedural	2	-	-	-	-	5	3	-	1	1
1.6 Unclassifiable	-	-	-	1	-	-	-	-	-	-
2. Demands (questions/directions) (T, S, O)	26(42)	4	2(9)	-	9(14)	7	20	2	14(28)	5
2.1.1 Questions/directions, content, cognitive, low level, total (fact questions)	14	3	-	-	-	1	-	2	3	1
2.1.2 Questions/directions, content, cognitive, higher level, total (higher cognitive questions)	12	1	1	-	5	4	1	-	7	4
2.2 Questions/directions, content, affective	-	-	-	-	1	-	1	-	-	-
2.3 Questions/directions, content, opinion (opinion questions)	-	-	-	-	1	1	-	-	-	-
2.4 Questions/directions, self-reference	-	-	1	-	2	1	8	-	1	-
2.5 Questions/directions, procedural (e.g. calling on students)	16	-	7	-	5	-	11	-	14(17)	-
2.6 Unclassifiable	-	-	-	-	-	-	-	-	-	-
II. Reactions, verbal, teacher, students, others (T, S, O)										
3. Reactions, responses to demands	3	56	1	3(5)	5	36	2	15	2	28
3.1.1.1 Responses, content, cognitive, low level, low quality	-	13	-	-	-	4	-	-	-	4
3.1.1.2 Responses, content, cognitive, low level, medium quality	3	9	-	-	1	-	-	-	-	1

(continued)

Table 2. Categories of Teacher and Student Verbal Behavior in Discussions (Continued)

Categories	Results for Teachers (T) and Students (S) Frequencies of behaviors									
	HK		WB		MK		SN		PR	
	T	S	T	S	T	S	T	S	T	S
3.1.1.3 Responses, content, cognitive, low level, high quality	-	-	-	-	-	-	2	-	-	5
3.1.2.1 Responses, content, cognitive, higher level, low quality	-	13	-	-	-	4	-	-	-	8
3.1.2.2. Responses, content, cognitive, higher level, medium quality	-	8	-	1	1	4	-	-	-	8
3.1.2.3 Responses, content, cognitive, higher level, high quality	-	-	-	1	-	1	-	-	-	-
3.2 Responses, content, affective	-	-	-	-	-	-	-	-	-	-
3.3 Responses, content, opinion	-	-	-	-	2	13	-	-	-	1
3.4 Responses, self-reference	-	-	-	1	1	5	-	13	-	1
3.5 Responses, procedural	-	-	1	-	-	-	-	-	-	-
3.6 Responses, indifferent, "I don't know" responses, no responses, incorrect responses	-	4	-	-	-	1	2	2	2	3
3.7 Responses, partly correct	-	5	-	-	-	-	-	-	-	-
3.8 Responses, irrelevant	-	2	-	-	-	2	-	-	-	5
3.9 Responses, unclassifiable	-	2	-	2	-	2	-	-	-	2
4. Reactions, restructuring, reflecting	26(31)	4	8(16)	4	19	7	20	1	13	1
4.1 Simple acknowledgement, repetition of preceding utterance	18	1	8	-	15	2	6	1	9	1
Rephrasing (quality): clarification, emphasis, correction, appropriateness, completeness	2	-	1	-	2	-	11	-	1	-
4.2 Relating to preceding utterances, topic, issue, problem, or other resources (summarizing/combining, comparing/contrasting, elaborating/expanding, concluding	6	3	6	4	1	5	3	-	1	1
4.3 Lifting: abstraction/complexity	-	-	1	-	-	-	1	-	2	1
4.4 Redirection, asking other student	5	-	-	-	1	-	2	-	-	-
4.5 Unclassifiable	-	-	-	-	-	-	-	-	-	-

No.	Category									
5.	Sustaining, probing, helping reactions	39	1	5	1	9	5	3	15	-
5.1	Repetition of question	11	-	-	-	4	1	-	2	-
5.2	Giving clues	3	-	-	-	-	-	-	-	-
5.3	Probing for clarification or emphasis, correctness, appropriateness, completeness	5	-	1	1	4	1	3	2	-
5.4	Probing for relating (to topic, issue, problem, prior statements, or other resources): summarization/combination, comparison/challenging comment, elaboration/expansion, conclusion	17	1	2	-	1	1	-	7	-
5.5	Probing for lifting (abstraction, complexity)	3	-	1	-	-	2	-	4	-
5.6	Challenging comment	-	-	1	-	-	2	-	-	-
5.7	Unclassifiable	-	-	-	-	-	-	-	-	-
6.	Judging feedback	6	1	4	1	3	7	2	3	1
6.1	(Simple) agreement, confirmation	3	1	-	-	2	5	2	1	-
6.2	(Simple) disagreement, giving correct answer	1	-	1	1	-	5	-	-	1
6.3	Praise, approval	1	-	3	-	1	1	-	2	-
6.4	Criticism, disapproval	1	-	-	-	1	1	-	-	-
6.5	Unclassifiable	-	-	-	-	-	-	-	-	-
	Student utterances directed to the teacher	63	5	5	1	40	-	36	29	-
	Student utterances directed to other students	1	3	3	-	26	-	-	4	-
	Student utterances, direction not classifiable	2	6	6	-	-	1	1	4	-

teacher-initiated questions (26 questions, 46% higher order and 54% lower order, all cognitive and content-related), and through 39 questions trying to obtain more relevant and improved quality responses and higher level responses. Only very little structuring and informing occurs (seven utterances). Student utterances for the most part consist of very quick and short responses (only six student utterances can be classified as student-initiated). Student to student interaction occurs only twice. All other student utterances are directed towards the teacher, almost without any reflecting, acknowledging, or relating to other students' ideas (five utterances only).

Almost all student utterances are relevant to the preceding questions. Of these, 17% are indifferent, incorrect, partly correct, or "I don't know" responses. From the relevant and correct responses, 51% are on a low cognitive level and 49% on a higher cognitive level. Only a few student responses are incongruent to the teacher-initiated questions and repetition of questions. But more than half of the responses (60%) are low in quality (62% of the higher cognitive level responses, 59% of the lower cognitive level responses). This result may explain the emphasis of the teacher on improving the students' utterances by using sustaining feedback in order to help the students to get to the desired explanation of why the war was won, or to find more facts to support the (implicit) explanation. Most of the inappropriate student responses are probed—not very successfully, though. Almost every student utterance is followed by a teacher utterance, mostly by reflective and/or sustaining feedback (as mentioned above), only once by praise, but 18 times by simple acknowledgement, three times by simple agreement, and twice by stating disagreement or criticism. This leads to the situation that the discussion is continuously moving back to the teacher, with very little chance for student–student interaction to develop.

This subject matter mastery discussion is characterized by frequent question–answer-sustaining feedback patterns—resembling very much the "recitation" pattern (Hoetker & Ahlbrand, 1969). The alternating use of higher and lower cognitive questions seems to have puzzled the students. They are uncertain whether they are to rehearse facts or think about them. As a consequence, there is neither a real recitation nor a real discussion.

Although the other participants in this project analyzed the transcripts from different perspectives, there is a high agreement between their analyses and conclusions and ours. For teacher HK, this should be discussed here briefly with emphasis on his style of leadership, his students' behavior, and the quality of the discussion. Almost all authors in this volume agree that the tight control and the dominant style the teacher revealed by using a very high amount of questions and sustaining feedback (probing), is inappropriate when the lesson is to stimulate what is commonly seen as a classroom *discussion*. Although not all authors consider this lesson as "bad" teaching (like Macmillan), there seems to be a general agreement in the way they classify the instructional method used. It is characterized as a quasi-discussion or quiz show (Roby), recitation lesson (Swift, Gooding, & Swift; Farrar), or testing approach (Wood & Wood). Also, others' and our own analyses reveal that the requests for "warrants" and the discussion of "data" (Russell), or the mixing of closed and open questions (Sigel) or of lower and higher cognitive questions are not a successful approach to teaching and to conducting a classroom discussion. This can obscure the objectives of the lesson. The frequent use of sustaining feedback (repetition of questions and probing) seems to indicate the concern of HK for improving the quality of student utterances and the quality of the "discussion" (this resulted from Bridges' and our own evaluation). But since the teacher continuously moved the discussion back to his own ideas, there was the danger that the students were kept from developing an understanding of the topic and merely had to guess what the teacher expected (Bridges; Francis).

Recommendations for the Teacher

In light of the observation system used for coding this classroom discussion, the following tentative recommendations for improvement can be given to the teacher (assuming the behavior revealed in the transcript is representative for this teacher):

- Clarify the goals of the discussion in the beginning and during the discussion (finding reasons why the Revolutionary War was won).
- Use predominantly higher cognitive questions instead of using higher *and* lower cognitive level questions alternatively.
- Limit the classroom control by avoiding frequent questions, repetition of questions, sustaining feedback, and acknowledgements which tend to draw the attention back to the teacher.
- In order to stimulate thoughtful student initiation and student–student interaction, use more supportive silence, ask students to listen to, and acknowledge, other students' utterances, to relate their ideas to each other, and to question or probe each other; and use questions that relate utterances to each other.

• Enhance the depth of the discussion by elaborating on student utterances, relating student utterances to each other, and lifting, improving, and clarifying student utterances (instead of just repeating the question).

WB's Transcript

Noticeably different from the history lesson of HK, the lesson of teacher WB may be classified as an issue-oriented discussion. The teacher talks only 33% of the time. Teacher-initiated statements (only two times: giving his opinion) as well as teacher-initiated questions are rare (one higher cognitive question, one self-reference question). The teacher controls the discussion by relating student statements to other utterances, by rephrasing and improving the utterances (eight times), by sustaining feedback (five times), praise (three times), stating disagreement (once), and simple acknowledgement (eight times). The teacher is highly reactive. Every student utterance is followed by a teacher utterance through which he moves the discussion forward. The dialogue is highly controlled by often calling on students to speak next (seven times).

Student utterances (like teacher utterances) are relatively long (mean length: 31 sec.). Only five utterances can be classified as responses to teacher questions (two higher cognitive level responses, one self-reference response, two unclassifiable); 10 statements are student initiations (half stating opinion, half self-reference). Seven times the students talk to the teacher and six times to other students or to the class in general. In their comparatively long and thoughtful statements or questions, at least four times the students relate to other preceding student statements and comment on them.

Clearly, this discussion is different from "recitation"—as should be the case with issue-oriented discussions.

Most of the other participants in this multidisciplinary project came to the same conclusion that WB's classroom discussion was of high quality and thoughtfulness; at least quite different from HK's recitation lesson (Russell; Bridges; Wood & Wood; Swift, Gooding, & Swift). All authors emphasized the long student turns. Though this lesson was considered as one in which the teacher used a style of indirect influence, our results supported the conclusions of Swift, Gooding, and Swift, Francis, Wood and Wood, and partly of Farrar that the teacher was retaining his control by reacting to any student utterance (by approving them, relating previous turns to each other, reflecting on them, seeking for clarification, and pressing for reason or argument) in order to improve the quality of the conversation

(Farrar; Francis; Wood & Wood; Swift, Gooding, & Swift; Bridges; partly Russell). So the students' comments were mainly addressed to the teacher and only little student–student interaction occurred.

Recommendations for the Teacher

• Limit your control of the discussion by not reacting to every student utterance, and react only at key points. For the same reason, do not call on students to speak next too often to prevent the discussion from moving back too frequently to you as the teacher.

• Increase the depth and quality of the discussion by using probing questions (probing to lift or improve the level or quality of preceding utterances), or ask the students to do so.

MK's Transcript

In this discussion, which may be classified as a problem-solving or issue oriented discussion, the teacher limits his initiation and direct control. He talks only about one third of the time (37%), three times he gives self-reference information, or gives his opinion, and he asks teacher-initiated questions only nine times (he calls on students only five times). When he intervenes he does it by questions based on preceding student utterances (sustaining feedback: nine times; repeating of questions: four times; redirecting: once; probing: five times). Only three times does he make statements of agreement or disagreement, but 15 times there is simple acknowledgement. In conclusion, the teacher uses considerably more behaviors of indirect than of direct influence, thereby minimizing his authority as a teacher. There is no direct teaching, rather the teacher intends to clarify statements of students so that the students are better able to deal with this information in the subsequent course of interaction.

The students ask nearly as many student-initiated questions as the teacher: four higher cognitive, one low cognitive, one self-reference, one opinion question. Also, they use sustaining feedback five times. Student responses to teacher questions and to other students' questions (36), often more than one response to each question, are mostly on a higher level (nine times), and only seven are on a low level, indifferent, or irrelevant. They also state their opinion (13), use self-reference responses, and two could not be classified. The students acknowledge once and relate their comments to each others' statements seven times. They give sustaining feedback five times and express their agreement five times or their disagreement and criticism twice. In summary, the teacher and students participate in the discussion showing a similar behavior and giving the impression of having an equal status, a situation which seems to be very appropriate for problem solving discussions.

Again, there is a certain agreement among the participants in analyzing this classroom discussion. The analyses of Farrar, Roby, Swift, Gooding and Swift, Bridges, Wood and Wood, and ourselves agree that teacher MK did not really guide this lively discussion. He took the role of facilitating an open discussion, he acted much more like the other participants than like a discussion leader. Only from time to time, he controlled the flow of the discussion by questions, reflecting behaviors, and sustaining feedback. There were more student-initiated questions and comments, and there was more student–student interaction than in the other lessons presented in the project. Student utterances were often based on each others' contributions.

Some disagreement occurred about the quality of this discussion. Sigel and Russell interpreted the lesson as a high quality discussion which proceeded in an orderly sequence. On the other hand, Roby, Lighthall, Macmillan and Swift, Gooding, and Swift, though they agree that there is a relatively high frequency of higher cognitive turns, did not find much indication of thoughtfulness or progress in this conversation. Bridges found at least some kind of concern of the teacher to develop the quality of the discussion and an understanding in his class. Our own analysis of teacher questions and especially of teacher reactions to student utterances supports the latter view. There were many more situations where the teacher could have improved the level and quality of student contribution.

Recommendations for the Teacher

- Increase the depth of the discussion by asking the students to compare and relate their statements to each other, and to use probing questions to lift or improve the cognitive level or complexity of student utterances.
- State the areas of agreement or disagreement in order to move the discussion forward at key points.
- Reduce the use of unnecessary simple acknowledgement in order to avoid interrupting the flow of the discussion. Instead, use more complex reflective behaviors at key points.

SN's Transcript

This issue-oriented discussion is remarkably different from the other discussions described above, in that it is almost exclusively concerned with the emotional experience of the students. There are 17 student-initiated statements and 15 responses. These are self-referenced 28 times, affective once, and opinion-giving once. The teacher talks 22% of the time. His initiated comments are in the affective domain once, self-reference domain once, and opinion giving once, as are the nine teacher-initiated questions. He does not give suggestions or cognitive information. Most of the time he is using reflective statements (rephrasing for clarification, 11 times; relating, three times; accepting or non-valuing acknowledgements, six times). This indicates that he accepts the student statement, encourages the students to express themselves, and creates an openness to talk about their intimate experiences. Where he uses sustaining feedback at all (only three times), he does so cautiously and only in a simple form by asking for clarification. He does not use sustaining feedback to increase the depth or quality of the discussion, for example asking for the elevation of the level of student statements or responses (which were almost exclusively factual information) or relating to previous utterances or other resources. In connection with these acknowledging, summarizing, or rephrasing reactions, the teacher tries to find out if he reflects the student contributions correctly, which is confirmed by the students in most cases (five times).

The discussion is controlled by calling on students to speak next (11 times), giving procedural information (three times), by self-reference questions (invitations to the students to talk about their experiences), and by the reflective statements, as mentioned above. Almost every student utterance is followed by a teacher utterance. The result is that the discussion tends to permanently move back to the teacher (almost all student utterances are directed towards the teacher) thereby inhibiting student–student interaction. This pattern is observed frequently in classroom discussions.

As mentioned above, the student utterances contain merely factual information about their experience and are relatively long contributions. According to Dillon, these statements averaged 12 seconds in length. This illustrates that the length of an utterance is not always a reliable indicator for its level or quality.

Given the intimate nature of the content, the selected teaching strategy (commonly used in client-centered counseling) may be appropriate for certain stages of the discussion, such as the beginning. The danger is that the discussion stays with the exchange of personal–affective experiences without moving beyond this point. With encouragement, this discussion could have moved toward development of new insights into one's own and other peoples' feelings and experiences.

While Bridges (this volume) found at least some kind of teacher concern for the development of thoughts in MK's lesson, he did not find any evidence of this concern in the transcript of SN's classroom discussion. All participants of the project who analyzed this discussion agreed with Bridges' conclusion: In the 10-minute excerpt, the focus was merely on the exchange of personal experiences without moving beyond this point, e.g., to explanation, analysis, or synthesis of the material discussed (Francis; Russell; Sigel; Swift, Gooding, & Swift; Roby; Farrar; Wood & Wood). Teacher SN used an enabling style which was very accepting.

He did so by using active listening and reflecting back what the students said as a means of encouraging students to participate (Francis; Swift, Gooding, & Swift; Farrar; Wood & Wood; partly Bridges; and our analysis). But, as mentioned above, almost every student utterance was followed by a teacher utterance, the discussion moved always back to the teacher and prevented student–student interaction. Bridges, Roby, Wood and Wood, and ourselves noted that—given the intimate nature of the topic—the teaching strategy used by teacher SN may be appropriate at the beginning of a discussion of this kind. The improvement of the quality of the discussion is to follow as a next step.

Recommendations for the Teacher

- Ask higher cognitive questions or use reflective reactions and probing questions to help the students make their own experiences accessible to analysis, evaluation, and new insights.
- Limit reactions that move the discussion back to the teacher; facilitate student–student interaction by relating to utterances other than the preceding ones and ask the students to do so.

PR's Transcript

Teacher PR's subject matter mastery discussion is highly controlled, though the teacher talks only 36% of the time. This is done by 11 teacher-initiated questions (three lower cognitive questions, one self-reference question at the factual level, and seven higher cognitive questions). Other controlling moves consist of directions (three), reflecting reactions (four), praise (two), acknowledgement (nine), sustaining feedback (15), and calling on students to speak next (14). Therefore, most of the student utterances are responses (28 times), mostly on a higher cognitive level (nine low, nine medium quality), while only eight are initiations (five student-initiated questions, three student-initiated comments). The student utterances are almost exclusively directed to the teacher. There are very few reflective behaviors of students (one acknowledgement, one relating utterance, and one disagreement). The predominant use of higher cognitive questions and the frequent use of sustaining feedback following unsatisfactory student responses indicate the teacher's concern for fostering thought processes and analysis in the discussion. He probes for elaboration or improvement 11 times, repeats the question twice, and probes for clarification twice.

All in all, this lesson looks more like a recitation lesson than a discussion-type interaction.

Not quite as much as in teacher HK's subject mastery discussion but in a similar way, teacher PR in his "guided discussion" retained a tight control of the topic by using questions, directions, and sustaining feedback (Wood & Wood; Farrar; Swift, Gooding, & Swift; and partly Sigel came to the same conclusion). Therefore, most of the student utterances were responses and directed to the teacher. Very little student–student interaction could be observed. The predominant use of higher cognitive questions (Swift, Gooding, & Swift; Sigel; Bridges; and Russell)—in contrast to HK's history lesson— led to long student utterances, which were probed when unsatisfactory. This suggests that PR had a concern to develop the quality of thoughts (Bridges; Wood & Wood; Swift, Gooding, & Swift; Sigel; Russell; and Roby).

Recommendations for the Teacher

- Facilitate more student–student interaction and limit the control of the discussion
  - by asking questions (initiative or reactive) only at key points,
  - by asking more than only one student to respond to the question and by using redirection,
  - by not reacting to every student utterance in order to prevent the discussion from moving back to the teacher, and
  - by asking the students to relate their ideas to prior statements and asking them to give reasons for their ideas.
- Use more comparing, contrasting, and relating to previous statements or other resources to increase the depth of the discussion.

CONCLUDING COMMENTS

Research in the field of teacher education suggests that, in order to develop effective and appropriate teaching behavior, it is essential that meaningful and well-defined components of the teaching process be provided. It is essential that these concepts can be taught to the teachers who will then experiment with the competencies and go through a subsequent self-evaluation. In keeping with these principles, an attempt was made to analyze five transcripts of classroom discussion and to give tentative recommendations for improving the discussions. Analyses are based on the assumption that the behavior shown by the teachers is representative of normal behavior.

The approach of having analyzed five selected transcripts of classroom discussions in American schools turned out to be interesting and worthwhile. For foreigners the task was not easy. Much effort had to be taken to merely understand what was going on in the classroom and to describe it appropriately. This was particularly so since the transcript materials could not give sufficient information on context, prior knowledge, or routines in the classroom. A number of interactions could be understood only on the sociocultural background of the class. Furthermore, transcripts of this kind rarely provide information about the curriculum material upon which the discussion is based. In a number of cases it was not easy to estimate whether a response of a student had required independent thinking or was merely the reproduction of previously heard or read information. Also, since the coding was based on excerpts there were cases where it was difficult to differentiate between initiation and reaction.

In analyzing the transcripts we felt that in some instances our observation instrument was not sufficient for classifying particular behaviors. This was especially true where the dialogue gradually moved toward a genuine exchange and development of ideas. The reason may be that the observation instrument developed for this study was too much based on typical classroom interaction (or recitation). It turned out that a facet should be included which may be called "type of rational argument" like Russell used in his analysis, instead of level of abstraction or complexity. Also, the concept of dealing with single behaviors need to be reconceptualized.

Although the discussions represented in the five transcripts varied greatly in many respects, they have a number of characteristics in common. These characteristics are also found in classroom discussions observed in West Germany.

1. Teachers seem to know much more about how to stimulate thought processes and to control the flow of the discussion, about asking questions and in particular higher cognitive questions, than they do about how to guide a discussion and to improve its quality in a more indirect way by reacting to preceding utterances.

2. Teachers tend to be more concerned with acting like teachers are expected to act, than with being moderators of discussions. Probably not consciously, but more than seems necessary, they tend to move the discussion back to themselves by reacting to almost every student response, question, or comment, rather than intervening only at key points of the discussion. Very seldom do teachers facilitate or ask for student–student interaction, encourage students to listen to each other, acknowledge others' ideas, relate them to their own, direct questions to each other about each others' ideas, feelings, or opinions, or ask the students to clarify or give reasons for their opinions in order to help them enhance the depth of their own discussion.

3. On the other hand, teachers rarely use reflective or sustaining feedback as they should. Methods for increasing the depth or quality of the discussion include feedback behaviors like contrasting student utterances, relating student utterances to each other or to other resources, lifting or improving the level or quality of the response, or asking students to do so. There is a remarkably small variation in reacting behaviors on the side of the teachers and almost none on the side of the students (except with teacher MK).

4. In a similar vein, there seems to be little help for the students to improve their own discussion skills, e.g., to use the bahaviors mentioned above.

5. Reactive judgements are observed infrequently. This holds in spite of the fact that textbooks in teacher education commonly recommend the more frequent use of genuine praise.

6. Incongruences in the cognitive level between teacher questions and student responses rarely occur. If they occur at all, teachers react appropriately. We found this to be the case in our previous research, as well (Klinzing–Eurich & Klinzing, 1981). This contradicts the research in the US, Australia, and New Zealand. The difference may be due to differences in the coding of the behavior. Teachers frequently accept student utterances in spite of the fact that they are of a low quality. Therefore, it seems necessary to develop indices for the quality of utterances for use in research and teacher training.

Much needs to be done to help teachers and students develop and improve their discussion skills. This means that we need to improve our instruments for observing classroom discussions and to intensify our research about what is effective and appropriate in classroom discussions. We must determine which behaviors and strategies are to be recommended for teacher training, and which models for training teachers are most effective.

REFERENCES

Allen, D.W. & Ryan, K.A. (1969). *Microteaching*. Reading, Mass.: Addison-Wesley.

Arnold, D.C., Atwood, R.K., & Rogers, V.M. (1973). An investigation of relationships among question level, response level and lapse time. *School Science and Mathematics, 73*, 591-594.

Atwood, R.K. & Stevens, J.T. (1976). Relationships among question level, rsponse level, and lapse time: Secondary science. *School Science and Mathematics, 76*, 249-254.

Barnes, C. (1980). Questioning: The untapped resource. Paper presented at the annual meeting of the American Educational Research Association, Boston. (ERIC, Document Reproduction Service No. ED 188-555)

Bellack, A., Kliebard, H., Human, R., & Smith, F. (1966). The language of the classroom. Final report, USOE Cooperative Research Project, No. 2023. New York: Teachers College, Columbia University.

Boeck, M.A. & Hillenmeyer, G.P. (1973). Classroom interaction patterns during microteaching: Wait-time as an instructional variable. Paper presented at the annual meeting of the American Educational Research Association, New Orleans, Louisiana.

Borg, W.R. (1972). Minicourses: Individualized learning packages for teacher education. *Educational Technology, 12*, 52-69.

Borg, W.R. (1975). *Moving Toward Effective Teacher Education. One Man's Perspective*. Utah State University, Logan.

Borg, W.R., Kelley, M.L., Langer, P., & Gall, M. (1970). *The Minicourse: A Microteaching Approach to Teacher Education*. Beverly Hills: Macmillan Educational Services.

Bridges, D. (1979). *Education, Democracy and Discussion*. Windsor, Berks.: NFER Publishing Company.

Brophy, J.E. & Evertson, C. (1974). *Process-Product Correlation in the Texas Teacher Effectiveness Study: Final Report* (Report No. 74-4) Austin, Texas: University of Texas.

Dillon, J. (1982). Cognitive correspondence between question/statement and response. *American Educational Research Journal, 19*, 540-551.

Dunkin, M.J. & Biddle, B.J. (1974). *The Study of Teaching*. New York: Holt, Rinehart, and Winston.

Flanders, N.A. (1970). *Analyzing Teaching Behavior*. Reading, Mass.: Addison-Wesley.

Gage, N.L. (1978). *The Scientific Basis of the Art of Teaching*. New York: Teachers College Press, Columbia University.

Gage, N.L. & Berliner, D.C. (1984). *Educational Psychology*. (3rd ed.). Chicago: Rand McNally.

Gall, M.D. (1970). The use of questions in teaching. *Review of Educational Research, 40*, 707–721.

Gall, M.D. (1973). What effect do teachers' questions have on students? Paper presented at the annual meeting of the American Educational Research Association, New Orleans.

Gall, M.D. (1984). Synthesis of research on questioning. *Educational Leadership, 42*, 40–47.

Gall, M.D., Dunning, B., Galassi, J., & Banks, H. (1970). *Main Field Test Report: Minicourse 9. Thought Questions in the Intermediate Grades* (Report A 70–19) Berkeley, Calif.: Far West Laboratory for Educational Research and Development.

Gall, M.D., Weathersby, R., Elder, R.A., & Lai, M.K. (1975). *Discussing Controversial Issues*. San Francisco: Far West Laboratory for Educational Research and Development.

Gall, M.D. & Gall, J.D., (1976). The discussion method. In N.L. Gage (ed.): *The Psychology of Teaching Methods*. The seventy-fifth yearbook of the NNSE, part I. Chicago: University of Chicago Press, 166–216.

Glass, G.V., Coulter, D., Hartley, S., Hearold, S., Kalk, J., & Sherrez, L. (1977). *Teacher "indirectness" and pupil achievement: An integration of findings*. Boulder: University of Colorado, Laboratory of Educational Research.

Hoetker, J. & Ahlbrand, W.P. (1969). The persistence of the recitation. *American Educational Research Journal, 6*, 145–167.

Joyce, B.R. & Showers, B. (1981). Teacher training research: Working hypotheses for program design and directions for further studies. Paper presented at the annual meeting of the American Educational Research Association, Los Angeles.

Klinzing, H.G. (1982). *Training Kommunikativer Fertigkeiten zur Gesprächsführung und für Unterricht*. (The Training of Communication Skills for Discussion Moderators and Classroom Teaching). Weil der Stadt: Lexika.

Klinzing–Eurich, G. & Klinzing, H.G. (1981). *Lehrfertigkeiten und ihr Training. Untersuchungen zum Training von Fragen höherer Ordnung und Sondierungsfragen mit Selbststudienmaterialien*. (Teaching Skills and Their Training. Studies of the Effects of Training of Higher Cognitive Questions and Probing Questions with Independent Study Materials.) Weil der Stadt: Lexika.

Maier, N.R.F., & Solem, A.R. (1952). The contribution of a discussion leader to the quality of group thinking: The effective use of minority opinions. *Human Relations, 5*, 277–288.

McDonald, F.J. & Allen, D.W. (1967). *Training Effects of Feedback and Modeling Procedures on Teacher Performance*. (Final report on USOE project DE-6-10-0178) Stanford, Calif.: Stanford University.

McKeachie, W.J. (1965). *Teaching tips: A Guide Book for the Beginning College Teacher* (5th ed.) Ann Arbor, Mich.: George Wahr.

Medley, D.M., Impellitteri, J.T., & Smith, L.H. (1966). *Coding Teachers' Verbal Behavior in the Classroom: A Manual for Users of OScAR 4V.* New York: City University of New York, Division of Teacher Education.

Mills, S.R., Rice, C.T., Berliner, D.C., & Rousseau, E.W. (1980). The correspondence between teacher questions and student answers in classroom discourse. *Journal of Experimental Education, 48,* 194–204.

Nuthall, G.A. & Lawrence, P.J. (1965). *Thinking in the Classroom.* Wellington: New Zealand Council for Educational Research.

Peck, R.F. & Tucker, J.A. (1973). Research on Teacher Education. In R.M.W. Travers (ed.) *Second Handbook of Research on Teaching.* Chicago: Rand McNally, 926–978.

Perlberg, A., Bar-On, E., Levin, R., Bar-Yam, M., Lewy, A., & Etrog, A. (1976). Modifikation des Lehrverhaltens durch die kombinierte Anwendung von Microteaching-Techniken und dem Technion Diagnostic-Systems TDS. (Modification of teaching behavior through the combined use of microteaching techniques with the Technion Diagnostic System). In W. Zifreund (ed.) *Training des Lehrverhaltens und Interaktionsanalyse.* (Training of Teaching Behavior and Interaction Analysis). Weinheim: Beltz, 83–110.

Perrott, E. (1977). *Microteaching in Higher Education: Research, Development, and Practice.* Guildford, Surrey.

Potter, D. & Andersen, M.P. (1963). *Discussion: A Guide to Effective Practice.* Belmont, Calif.: Wadsworth.

Rector, D. & Bicknell, J.E. (1972). *The Usefulness of Minicourse 1 in the Inservice Training of Elementary Teachers.* (Report A 72–6) Far West Laboratory for Educational Research and Development, San Francisco.

Redfield, D.L. & Rousseau, E.W. (1981). A meta-analysis of experimental research on teacher questioning behavior. *Review of Educational Research, 51,* 237–245.

Rosenshine, B. (1971). *Teaching Behaviours and Student Achievement,* London: National Foundation for Educational Research.

Rosenshine, B. (1976). Classroom instruction. In N.L. Gage (ed.): *The Psychology of Teaching Methods. The Seventy-fifth Yearbook of the National Society for the Study of Education,* Part I. Chicago: University of Chicago Press, 335–371.

Simon, A. & Boyer, E.G. (eds.) (1974). *Mirrors for Behavior III. An Anthology of Observation Instruments.* Wyncote, Penn.: Communication Materials Center.

Stallings, J.A. (1977). *Learning to Look. A Handbook on Observation and Teaching Models.* Belmont, Calif.: Wadsworth.

Stallings, J. & Kaskowitz, D. (1974). *Follow Through Classroom Observations Evaluation 1972–1973.* Menlo Park, Calif.: Stanford Research Institute.

Taba, H. (1966). *Teaching Strategies and Cognitive Functioning in Elementary*

School Children. (USOE Cooperative Research Project No. 2404) San Francisco: San Francisco State College.

Taba, H., Levine, S., & Elzey, F.F. (1964). Thinking in Elementary School Children. (USOE Cooperative Research Project No. 1574) San Francisco: San Francisco State College.

Tausch, R. & Tausch, A. (1978). Erziehungspsychologie (Educational Psychology) (8th ed.) Göttingen: Hogrefe.

Tisher, R.P. (1970). The nature of verbal discourse in classrooms. In W.J. Campbell (ed.): Scholars in Context. Sydney: Wiley.

Tisher, R.P. & Power, C.N. (1978). The learning environment associated with an Australian curriculum innovation. Journal of Curriculum Studies, 10, 169–184.

Wilkinson, S.S. (1980). The relationship of teacher praise and student achievement: A meta-analysis of selected research. Unpublished doctoral dissertation, University of Florida.

Willson, I.A. (1973). Changes in mean levels of thinking in grades 1–8 through use of an interaction analysis system based on Bloom's taxonomy. Journal of Educational Research, 66, 423–429.

Winne, P.H. (1979). Experiments relating teachers' use of higher cognitive questions to student achievement. Review of Educational Research, 49, 13–50.

Zahorik, J.A. (1968). Classroom feedback behaviors on teachers. Journal of Educational Research, 62, 147–158.

Zifreund, W. (1966). Konzept für ein Training des Lehrverhaltens mit Fernseh-Aufzeichnungen in Kleingruppen-Seminaren. (The Training of Teacher Behavior in Small Groups Aided by TV) Berlin: Cornelsen.

Zifreund, W. (1968). Training des Lehrverhaltens und Micro-Teaching: individualisierende Verwendungsmöglichkeiten des Fernsehens in Kleingruppen. (The training of teacher behavior and microteaching: Individualized use of TV in small groups) In W. Zifreund (ed.) Schulmodelle, Programmierte Instruktion und Technische Medien. (Models of Schools, Programmed Instruction and Technical Media) München: Ehrenwirth.

Zifreund, W. (1983). Training des Lehrverhaltens (Microteaching) als mögliches Instrument der Lehrerausbildung (Lehrerfort- und -weiterbildung) im Dienst der Prävention sozialauffälligen Verhaltens in der Schule. (Training of teaching behaviors (microteaching) as an approach of teacher education (inservice training) as a mean of prevention of deviant student behavior in schools). In R. Fricke, & H. Kury (eds.): Erzieherverhaltenstraining, Braunschweig.

CHAPTER 12

Questions and Arguments

Thomas L. Russell

Faculty of Education
Queen's University at Kingston
Kingston, Ontario

An invitation to participate in the multidisciplinary study of questions and discussion came as a result of Dillon's interest in my study of the potential influence of teachers' questions on the nature of scientific authority suggested to students in science classes (Russell, 1983). This chapter begins with an account of the theoretical perspective developed in the earlier study and an illustration of the application of that perspective to an excerpt from one of the five transcripts. Then the use of the same perspective to analyze Dillon's five transcripts (Appendix) is discussed, first on a transcript-by-transcript basis and then across all five transcripts.

TEACHERS' QUESTIONS AND THE AUTHORITY FOR ARGUMENTS

The first section of the chapter presents a philosophical perspective on the nature of authority in teaching, with particular reference to the relationship of a teacher's authority to the discipline that underlies the subject matter presented. Then an analytical scheme is developed, drawing on additional philosophical analysis of the nature of argument, to permit assessment to be made of the attitude toward authority suggested in classroom dialogue. Of particular interest is the role of teachers' questions in determining how arguments are developed and discussed.

Rational and Traditional Attitudes Toward Authority

Peters (1967) draws a fundamental distinction between a rational attitude toward authority and a traditional attitude. He compares the distinction to the difference between "having good reasons" and "taking someone else's word" (pp. 13–24). The relevance to Western education is obvious, for we have come to regard the development of reasoning as a central purpose of schooling. Green (1971) argues that "instruction" strives to establish beliefs on the basis of reasons and evidence, while "indoctrination" is concerned only with the content of beliefs transmitted, not with the basis of beliefs. In Peters' view, the teacher's manner is crucial. He sees the authority of the teacher as having two distinct senses: a teacher is *an* authority in some aspect of our culture and *in* authority to accomplish the task of teaching (Peters, 1966; p. 240). A teacher is an authority by virtue of certain knowledge, and in authority by virtue of appointment to the position of teacher.

Most concisely, then, a teacher is *an* authority *in* authority. A teacher's authority of knowledge appears to be fundamental, the basis upon which an individual is appointed to the position of teacher. A teacher is *an* authority by virtue of knowledge that enables the teacher to give reasons and evidence, to demonstrate rational authority for arguments presented to students.

The distinction between traditional and rational authority provides a basis for analysis of classroom dialogue when we note that a teacher's authority of position makes it possible to present knowledge claims without reasons, an event that would suggest a traditional attitude toward authority rather than a rational one. By virtue of the authority of position conferred to enable a teacher to maintain the classroom learning setting, a teacher acquired the *potential* to present knowledge claims on either of two types of authority— rational or traditional. This is not to imply that a teacher would intentionally present claims on authority of position, only to recognize the possibility of doing so inadvertently. A teacher has many elements to attend to during instruction, and the authority for an argument is neither familiar nor prominent in a list that includes discipline, pace, student attention, group dynamics, room conditions, distribution of opportunities to speak, and so on.

The Pattern of Rational Arguments

We need more detailed criteria for examining classroom dialogue if we are to recognize a distinction as broad as that between traditional and rational authority, between authority of position and authority of knowledge. Toulmin (1958) provides a useful set of distinctions in *The Uses of Argument*, in which he argues that there is a single pattern common to all types of rational argument. Toulmin's argument pattern specifies six elements and the relationships among them. Four elements are of central importance: Data, Warrant, Conclusion, and Backing. Capitalization of these terms throughout the paper serves to indicate that they are being used in the sense specified by Toulmin.

In introducing a scheme such as Toulmin's, I am forced to make a choice between using "everyday" language that is familiar but imprecise and using "specialized" terminology that is unfamiliar but precise. The use of specialized terms requires extra effort by the reader to gain access to the analysis that follows. I believe the extra effort is rewarded by the more precise distinctions that can be made in the detailed analysis of teachers' use of questions in the five transcripts that form the data for this study. The detailed analysis of each transcript is available to the reader in the material appended to this paper. The demonstration that the scheme *can* be applied across five quite different transcripts is one useful result of this study.

Of the four terms from Toulmin that I will use extensively in the analyses that follow, two are unfamiliar (Warrant and Backing) and two are familiar (Data and Conclusion). The two familiar terms may require more effort initially, because they are used in restricted ways. An outline of the terms follows, with a diagram to help illustrate their relationships in a rational argument.

A Warrant is a rule that permits one to move from Data to Conclusion. Warrants are given different names in different disciplines; explanations in history, theorems in mathematics, laws in science. Backing expresses the conditions and assumptions that support a Warrant, the "facts" that give authority to the Warrant. Historians are well aware that the two sides in a war give different explanations for the events of the war, depending in part on the differing positions about who "won the war." Different explanations for "the same" events proceed from different Backing. Similarly in science, progressively "better" laws are developed, often bringing a broader range of events under the same Warrant. Toulmin explains that Backing often remains implicit until an argument is challenged. He also notes that different disciplines use different *kinds* of Backing for their Warrants (pp. 103–106). Backing is particularly significant when alternative explanations (Warrants) are being considered. Familiar examples of new Backing being developed in science would include Darwin's analysis of the origin of biological species and Einstein's theory of relativity that reinterpreted Newton's Laws. Backing may be particularly significant for students coming to know a subject, because features distinctive to a discipline are revealed at the level of Backing.

We often use the term "data" to refer to all that is known at the outset of an argument, but that sense is not intended by Toulmin when he speaks of Data. Data refers to information that is to be interpreted by the argument; Conclusion expresses the resulting interpretation. A special sense of Data is required because, as Toulmin notes, we make arguments in two quite different ways—to *use* a Warrant to reach a Conclusion, and to *establish* a Warrant based on a Conclusion. In a Warrant-establishing argument, the Conclusion must be available at the outset. Once a Warrant has been established, it can be used in subsequent arguments—to interpret other historical events, to make predictions in science, to calculate unknowns in mathematics, to decide other cases in a court of law.

The remaining two elements in Toulmin's pattern of an argument are Qualifier and conditions of Rebuttal. A Qualifier indicates the extent to which the Data fully support the Conclusion; conditions of Rebuttal are special circumstances in which a Warrant may not apply (pp. 101–103). These two elements play minor roles in the pattern, and frequently are not required for the analysis of classroom dialogue. The pattern itself is shown in Figure 1. (The same argument pattern is used in Toulmin, Reike, & Janik, 1979; the names of some elements have been changed and the pattern has been rearranged without changing the relationships.)

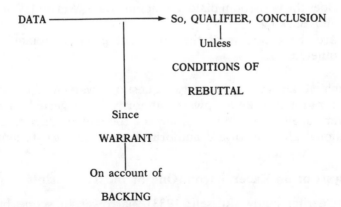

Figure 1. Toulmin's argument pattern (adapted from Toulmin, 1958, p. 104).

To summarize, then, Toulmin's special terms that appear frequently in the analysis that follows may be given these brief descriptions.

Data: The facts to be interpreted in the argument
Backing: The assumed perspective, taken for granted unless challenged, and characteristic of the discipline in which the argument is made
Warrant: The rule or law that permits a Conclusion in a Warrant-using argument
Conclusion: The end point of a Warrant-using argument, or the known result in a Warrant-establishing argument

An Analytical Scheme

Toulmin's argument pattern gives sufficient detail to the concept of a rational argument to suggest criteria for recognizing when a teacher establishes a Conclusion or a Warrant on the basis of rational authority. I make the assumption that suggesting to students a rational attitude toward authority requires providing all necessary elements of an argument, properly related to each other. This seems plausible because students would have no basis for accepting an incomplete argument, were it not for a teacher's alternate source of authority, that of position. Authority of position can bridge gaps in rational arguments, but a teacher then risks suggesting a traditional attitude toward authority. The following analytical scheme is used.

1. Does the classroom dialogue include Data, Warrant, Conclusion, and Backing?
2. Are the elements of the argument properly related to each other?

Affirmative answers to these two questions warrant the conclusion that a rational attitude toward authority is suggested. A negative answer to either or both questions produces a judgement that a traditional attitude toward authority is suggested to students.

Analysis of an Excerpt from One of the Transcripts

In an earlier study (Russell, 1983), narrower in scope but more detailed than this discussion, I demonstrated the application of the analytical scheme to excerpts from three science lessons. In this chapter, the same scheme is applied to the five transcripts of the multidisciplinary study of classroom questioning and discussion. Analysis of one excerpt helps to introduce the reader to the application of Toulmin's argument-pattern terminology to transcribed classroom conversation.

The selected excerpt is from HK's history lesson on "why we won the Revolutionary War." The 10-minute transcription contains 64 speeches by the teacher; only the portion containing the first 21 teacher speeches is used here. The purpose of the discussion here is to illustrate the application of Toulmin's argument-pattern terminology. In the right-hand column, brief statements indicate what each speaker is doing in terms of elements of an argument. The teacher's questions are capitalized for easier recognition. The symbol T is used to identify the teacher, whose speeches are numbered to permit quick reference. Three symbols are used to indicate student speeches: G-girl; B-boy; S-student.

HK: "Why We Won the Revolutionary War"

Transcription	Analysis
T1: What—I want to go into another question about his military capabilities. WHAT WAS IT THAT MADE HIM MILITARILY SUCCESSFUL? WHAT WAS IT ABOUT HIS STRATEGY THAT ENABLED HIM TO BE SUCCESSFUL? (Howard)	*T* requests Warrant to "explain" Washington's military success (the Known Conclusion).
B: He didn't fight straight out like the British. He fought behind brick walls, trees, and stuff like that.	*S* provides Data related to "tactics" (see T46 and following).
T2: DID YOU READ ANYWHERE IN THE BOOK WHERE HIS ARMY WAS DESTROYED?	*T* requests Data; first use of "destroyed" (see T3 and T7).
S: No.	
T3: That his army was destroyed— DID YOU SEE THAT ANYWHERE? THAT WASHINGTON'S ARMY WAS DESTROYED?	*T* requests Data again.
S: Not completely.	
T4: NOT COMPLETELY? (Tony)	
B: They were outsmarted, but not destroyed.	*S* speaks of "outsmarted"

T5: Well, IS THERE A DIFFER-
ENCE BETWEEN THOSE TWO
STATEMENTS?

B: Yeah, there is.

T6: Well, WHAT IS THAT DIFFER-
ENCE?

B: To be outsmarted (-) out of the
larger army.

B: Other than that, if you're destroyed, you're destroyed,
you're dead.

T7: IF THEY'RE DESTROYED,
THEY'RE DEAD? AND WHAT
IF THEY ARE OUTSMARTED?

B: That means they could get by
or move into better territory.

T8: SO, WHAT DO YOU THINK
WASHINGTON'S SUCCESS
WAS AS A MILITARY
LEADER?—taking into con-
text, you know, tactics and so
on. (Tony)

B: He was always taking it step
by step, he never wanted to be
outsmarted.

T9: But you said he was, at times.

B: Right, yeah but then you asked
what about his success.

T10: Well, WHY IS IT THAT HE—
(ah Jim).

B: He was able to go back and
fight harder; even after he was
outsmarted, he was able to get
'em back on the rebound.

T11: Ah, BECAUSE WHY? (Chris)

G: Maybe he had to learn by the
mistakes that happened, to
learn by them and realize what
it was that had gone wrong.

T12: Well, DID THE COLONIES
HAVE A LARGE ARMY?

G: No, they—I don't know.

T13: Those of you who worked on
that question about the

T5 through T7 deals
with possible differ-
ences between "de-
stroyed"
and "outsmarted"
(see student in 6, 8,
10).
Note emphasis on "tac-
tics."

T repeats request for a
Warrant; see T1.

S offers Data related to
tactics.

Rebuttal
Rebuttal

More Data on tactics

T requests Warrant.
S offers Warrant, on the
tactics theme.

T requests Data on the
"size of army" theme
that continues to T21,
with attention to the
volunteer nature of
Washington's army.

army, and some of the problems of wartime govern-
ment—WHAT DID YOU FIND
OUT ABOUT THE ARMY IT-
SELF? (Howard)

B: Well, the colonial army was
really outnumbered by the
British. Some of the people—
the lack of interest by some of
the colonies and stuff like
that—most of the colonies had
to fight it by themselves, so
they were outnumbered.

S provides Data.

T14: Well, OK, HOW DID ONE GET
TO BE A MEMBER OF THE
ARMY? BY WAY OF THE
DRAFT?

T requests Data.

B: No, more or less by volunteering.

S provides Data.

T15: By volunteering. COULD CON-
GRESS, COULD CONGRESS
TELL THE STATES TO FUR-
NISH MORE MEN?

T requests Data.

B: No, I don't think so.

S provides Data.

T16: WHAT DID CONGRESS HAVE
TO DO?

T requests Data.

X: (no response)

T17: Now, you're on the right track.
WHAT DID CONGRESS HAVE
TO DO IN ORDER TO GET
MORE MEN INTO THE
ARMY?

T requests more spe-
cific Data.

B: I guess make it worth their
while.

T18: Well, let's get away from pay.
Let's assume that wages are not
a factor at the moment. If the
army is a volunteer army, as
such, WHERE DID PEOPLE
VOLUNTEER TO?

T again clarifies the request for Data.

X: In other words, WERE THERE
NATIONAL OFFICES ESTAB-
LISHED BY CONGRESS TO
WHICH A PERSON WENT
THAT WANTED TO VOLUN-
TEER?

T requests Data.

B: You'd just go find where the
army was, and join it.

S provides Data.

T20: Not exactly. THEY WENT BY WAY OF WHAT VEHICLE, DO YOU KNOW?

T disagrees and repeats request.

G: (-) their colonies back home.

T21: That's right, they went by way of each colony. So, what we're saying, then, is that Congress could not merely order a colony to furnish more men. It had to ask a colony for more men. And if people did not volunteer into that colonial army—the Virginia army, for instance, the South Carolina army—if people didn't then they just didn't. So, Washington commanded an all-volunteer army. And another problem with that army—in addition to just sheer numbers, it's not professional as such, it's all volunteer, and people come and go as they want to. Now, when you have a person leading that type of a military group, you certainly are not leading a professional army, and something that he does with it is very important. It's not that large—probably the most they ever had at one time was maybe 5,000 people. He never permits what little army they had to be destroyed. But that's not to say he never lost.

T summarizes the Data that is required to establish the Warrant, given the Conclusion that Washington won the war.

T closes the sub-themes on the nature of the army and the fact that Washington never permitted his army to be destroyed.

(T24 indicates that the teacher sees the Warrant as one that is summarized under the term of "leadership.")

Analysis of the argument in this portion of HK's transcript begins with an attempt to identify requests for and statements of Data, Warrant, and Conclusion. It is also necessary to identify points at which one argument is concluded and another begun; T1–T21 is the first argument in the transcript. In the above excerpt, T1 indicates the teacher's interest in Data about Washington's strategy that would build an explanation of his military success. This signals that we are examining a Warrant-establishing argument with a known Conclusion—that Washington was militarily successful. As HK moves through the next 20 questions, he requests and discusses Data.

Between T2 and T7, the discussion seems sidetracked on the difference between "destroyed" (HK's term) and "outsmarted" (student's term). Students' use of the term "outsmarted" continues after T8 and T10; HK's efforts to use the term "destroyed" are finally explained in T21. In T8 and T11, the teacher appears to be requesting a Warrant, but in most of the other speeches, he requests Data. Students respond with Data, but it is an explanation that HK seems to be looking for.

Many would characterize HK's questioning strategies as an illustration of a "recitation," not of a discussion. As noted in the complete analysis of this excerpt, when students do not provide the explanation (Warrant) that the teacher seems to have in mind, HK asks questions about Data that are related to the desired Warrant. This excerpt provides no illustrations of the argument element of Backing; the teacher does not step back from the argument to indicate the particular perspective being followed, or to explain what is being taken for granted. There is no reference to alternative explanations, such as the British perspective on Washington's military success. The process of applying argument-pattern elements to speeches in classroom dialogue is by no means as straightforward as the "finished analysis" above might suggest. It is very much a "trial and error" process, frustrating when a "good fit" is hard to obtain, yet also exciting for what it achieves in terms of perspective on the teacher's use of questions.

In this excerpt from HK's lesson, there do not appear to be any errors in the relationship of argument elements to each other, but as noted, there is no discussion of Backing that would be appropriate in any Warrant-establishing argument, to suggest a rational attitude toward authority. I see considerable evidence in the excerpt to suggest that the students are having difficulty "tuning in" to what the teacher is looking for. It seems to be inappropriate for the teacher to step out of the dialogue long enough to indicate that he seeks a particular explanation (Warrant) that brings the Data about tactics to the Conclusion of military success.

This approach to analysis of classroom dialogue should not be read as suggesting that rationality of a teacher's argument should be a major criterion of good teaching, though for some teachers it might be. Teaching has many dimensions, and that may be one reason why good teaching is such a challenge and why all teaching is so easily criticized. Each teacher must decide which dimensions take priority, personally and in light of students' backgrounds, abilities, and goals. The analytical scheme presented here may suggest to teachers a cluster of issues not previously considered. Teachers' questions can play a major role in determining how fully the parts of an argument are developed, individually and in relation to each other.

ANALYSIS OF THE FIVE TRANSCRIPTS

The opportunity to extend my study (Russell, 1983) of questions within arguments to lessons in subjects other than science was particularly welcome. The analyses of authority in teaching and of the form of rational arguments seemed in no way specific to science. It is interesting to compare teachers' use of questions across subject boundaries. Several adaptations were required in extending the analytic scheme to the transcripts provided by Dillon. First, I accepted the transcripts as they were sent to me, and I declined the opportunity to listen to the tape recordings of the entire lessons, thereby avoiding the temptation to make reference to information that I could not make available in a written format. Second, my own analysis of science lessons was based not on random selection of excerpts but on selection of all the dialogue for a particular point, subdivided into segments containing individual arguments. Adaptation to a new selection procedure shifts the use of the analytical scheme away from the issue of authority for arguments and toward the issue of how a teacher's questions move students through various elements of rational argument.

Each of the five transcripts was analyzed in the manner illustrated above in the partial transcript of the history lesson by HK. Space does not permit presentation of the complete analyses of the transcripts. Descriptive summaries of the five analyses are presented here as background for subsequent discussion of similarities and differences across the five transcripts, in terms of teachers' use of questions to develop elements of rational argument.

HK on the American Revolution

This history lesson is interpreted as an attempt to construct Warrants that permit one to move *from* known Data about what the colonials and the British did in the Revolutionary War *to* the known Conclusion that the colonials did win the war. The teacher alternates between requests for Warrants and discussion of Data, to which both teacher and students contribute Data with the teacher as the judge of Data accuracy. Three Warrants are relatively explicit in the teacher's statements, on the themes of Washington's leadership

(T1–T21/T24), foreign aid—interpreted as money (T25–T37/T40), and colonial tactics (T46–T64). The 10-minute excerpt ends without a summarizing statement for the third Warrant.

Categorization of HK's 55 questions reflect the observation that the teacher alternates between requests for a Warrant and requests for Data. Questions that request a Warrant are T1/8, 10/11, 23, 24/25, 37/40, 44 through 47, and 48 through 64. Questions that request Data appear in T2 through 7, 12/13, 14 through 20, and 26 through 36. Here we see several instances of teaching behaviors that seem to occur frequently in "recitations." When the students do not produce the Warrant the teacher seems to have in mind, the teacher asks questions about Data that lead in the direction of the desired Warrant. The teacher's questions in T41 and 43 do not fall into the same categories; they occur in what seems to be a transition period in which students continue to speak about the topic of aid while the teacher seems to be trying to move on to the area of colonial tactics (T46).

This transcript suggests that Warrants in history are explanations for the occurrence of events. At no point in this excerpt do we find in the teacher's statements any references to what might be construed as Backing for arguments in history, statements that indicate how we organize and interpret historical data to construct explanations. The teacher serves as the arbiter of Data accuracy, without commentary on how Data are known to be accurate.

There is an interesting pattern in student behavior following each of the summaries by the teacher of discussion relating to the Warrants of leadership and aid. After the teacher's lengthy summary in T21, a student seeks further Data about the draft, an element in the preceding discussion; at T24, the teacher explicitly requests that the topic shift. After the teacher's summary on aid, in T37, students seek further Data on the aid topic, even though the teacher has asked for "other reasons why we won;" at T46, the teacher indicates the next topic to be discussed.

MK on Seniors' Smoking Privileges

This excerpt from a lesson in a course on Christian relationships is interpreted as an effort by the teacher to have the students relate principles developed in the course to a "dilemma of relationships" being faced by the senior class in the school. The shift from "ordinary" arguments to ones with Backing in Christian principles is introduced by the teacher at T14. (No spontaneous references to this Backing occurred before T14). T14 through T17 pose the same questions four times, but only after T17 does a student respond as the teacher requests and the discussion then continues to refer to Christianity. It is interesting to note that the teacher does not indicate to the students in T15 through T17 that their responses have not included reference to the type of Backing he wishes to work with.

The first four of MK's 15 questions seek Data (T1, 3, 4/5) about the event being discussed. In the middle of the excerpt, the teacher's questions request Conclusions (T7, 8, 10, 11, 12), sometimes in response to hypothetical Data that he presents (T7, 8, 12). Near the end of the excerpt, the teacher's questions request a Warrant that may resolve the situation (T13, 14/15, 16/17) and from T14 on the Warrant is to be one that takes Backing from principles of Christianity.

Prior to T14, many of the significant argumentative moves are made by the students. The teacher poses questions, accepts some answers, contributes data, and invites other contributions, but students seem to share in the development of arguments, shifting among a variety of Warrants to obtain different Conclusions to the dilemma over rules about smoking in the school. It is apparent, after an analysis of the type of move made by each speaker, that the skill of referring to elements of an argument could have contributed clarification to the discussion. In the rather free flow of events prior to T14, there are opportunities to "make sense of" the relationship of one speech to another. The interpretation that the dilemma is so difficult to resolve because there are so many different Backings available and because it is so difficult to develop the commitment of everyone involved to a single Backing is not presented in this excerpt.

PR on Multiple Personality

This excerpt from a course in psychology is directed at the single goal of developing ways to reduce the number of personalities in an individual who is displaying three personalities. From the perspective of argument, the desired Conclusion will be a reduction in the number of personalities. The discussion focuses on developing a Warrant that permits the desired Conclusion, given the known Data.

Initially, PR's questions focus on the known Data (T2, 4, 6, 7, 9) after setting the topic by requesting a Warrant in T1. That request is restated in T10, and the remainder of the excerpt is more concerned with possible Warrants, which the teacher eventually characterizes as "models." When Gabriella introduces the idea of combining personalities, the teacher focuses on the idea of "knocking out" personalities (T11, 12, 13, 14), shifting in T15/16 more toward whether there is Backing for that Warrant. When Yvonne suggests gathering more Data, the teacher first asks what Data are expected (T18/19), then asks how the Data could be used (T21/22), and finally challenges the students to explain why multiple personalities develop in a few people when they don't develop in most (T23). Students then shift to childhood idols, the teacher indicates that trauma must be involved, and when the teacher asks if other "models" are possible, the ideas of conflict and overprotection are suggested. In two instances (T24/29), the teacher seeks information about student background in the area under discussion.

The teacher's 20 questions in this excerpt are seen to move the discussion from clarifying Data to seeking a Warrant. Several Warrants are introduced and discussed, and referred to as "models," but it is difficult to detect the presence of disciplined knowledge from psychology. The discussion between T11 and T17 is interesting because the teacher seems to be pushing students into the area of Backing for a Warrant, yet the students seem unclear about the intent; the discussion moves on without closing the matter of "knocking out" personalities. The discussion of models (Warrants) has moved in several directions in quick succession.

SN on Sex in Homelife

In this excerpt from a lesson in a course on marriage, we never learn whether arguments are developed in the course. Virtually every speech involves Data on the topics of talking about sex, nudity, and physical affection. Data is provided, requested, or clarified. Many of the teacher's speeches involve checking whether he has understood correctly the Data a student has provided; this is true in six of seven instances (T3, 10, 15, 18, 21, 27, 28) when the teacher uses the phrase "you're saying." This phrase appears in all four of the teacher's questions (T10, 15, 21, 27) that check his understanding of what a student has said.

The most common purpose of SN's questions is a simple request for Data on a specific topic (T1, 4, 12, 23, 24, 25, 26). The two remaining questions seek clarification (T8) and check if a student is indicating agreement (T21). All of the teacher's 13 questions focus on bringing Data into the discussion, on specific points and with clarity. The teacher's questions do not move into the area of analyzing the Data, and the discussion does not move into that area spontaneously. With no other argument elements present, there are no clues about how Warrants are used or established in this course.

WB on Parent–Child Relations

The content of this lesson excerpt (from a course in Society and Christian Lifestyle) is intriguing because it approaches so closely the content of the analytical scheme being applied to all five transcripts. The discussion compares two Backings: doing what parents say because of their *position* as parents, and doing what they say because one understands their *reasons.* The discussion considers which Backing students prefer, which parents use, how these preferences seem to have changed over time, and to what extent respect for parents is challenged by questioning (or seeking reasons for) their requests and decisions.

Only six of WB's eleven speeches are questions, and it is informative to summarize the purpose of each of the six:

> *T1:* Is my argument (about two ways of looking) a plausible one?
> *T2:* What Warrant supports the Conclusion that children should voice their own opinions?
> *T3:* What are parents' reactions to being questioned? (Data)
> *T6:* (seeks clarification)
> *T8:* How can you seek reasons and also indicate respect for parents?
> *T9:* Do students agree that respect is shown by accepting parents' position regardless of whether they have offered the authority of reasons? (Backing)

This teacher has used questions to draw out the students on key elements in the discussion, in which the students show themselves capable of covering significant ground on their own. Although the teacher does not speak in terms of elements of arguments, he does deal directly with the analysis of parent–child differences in terms of different Backings about the relationship among reasons, position, and respect for parents' position. As the discussion of the basis for the analytical scheme indicated, there are two quite different sources of authority in our culture, and individuals obviously differ in the extent to which they assign respect to either authority of reasons or authority of position.

QUESTIONS AND THE DEVELOPMENT
OF ARGUMENTS

Interesting patterns emerge when these five transcripts, each of 10-minute duration, are compared in terms of how teachers use questions to develop arguments. As comparisons are drawn across the five transcripts, bear in mind that I have not been asked to assess the potential appropriateness of applying a "development of rational arguments" perspective to each teacher's use of questions, nor have I been given access to information on which such an assessment would be based.

HK, teaching history, asks questions in 55 of 64 speeches, and moves rapidly through three separate arguments. His basic strategy is to request a Warrant and then request Data related to and leading toward the Warrant that eventually completes an argument. MK, teaching a course in Christian relationships, asks questions in 15 of 20 speeches. He asks first for Data and then a Conclusion for the problem of school rules about smoking, and continues by requesting first any Warrant and then a Warrant with Backing in Christian principles. The excerpt from PR's psychology lesson on multiple personalities contains questions in 20 of 29 teacher speeches. From a perspective of argument, the questions move in many directions, seeking a Warrant, discussing Data and a Warrant, exploring the nature and use of possible additional Data, and ending with requests for other plausible Warrants. Data, Warrants, and Conclusions are all in evidence, and the teacher's questions move the discussion along through the arguments. Backing for Warrants is not prominent; in MK's excerpt, the request for a Warrant with specific Backing was repeated several times before its effect appeared in student responses.

The last two transcripts differ significantly from each other and from the other three. The excerpt from SN's lesson in a course on marriage contains questions in 13 of 20 teacher speeches. More than half of the questions request Data, which students provide. Most of the remaining questions seem to check the teacher's understanding of student replies; the phrase "you're saying" appears frequently in SN's speeches. Argumentatively, this excerpt involves Data only, and it provides no information about how Warrants are used or established in this course. In sharp contrast, WB, who is teaching a course in society and Christian lifestyle, speaks only 11 times, with questions in only six of his speeches, yet the discussion moves from a request for a Warrant through requests for Data and clarification to questions at the level of Backing for Warrants of behavior. Backing is more explicit here than in any of the other transcripts. The content of that Backing happens to be closely related to that used in this chapter to indicate why it may be important to attend to the completeness of teachers' arguments, in order to suggest a rational attitude toward authority.

As noted earlier, the lesson excerpts that appear in these five transcripts were selected at random, not on criteria related to arguments. It is inappropriate to attempt to judge whether each transcript suggests a rational attitude toward authority. Nevertheless, it is possible to comment on the appearance of various argument-pattern elements in the transcripts, and from this perspective, WB would be at one end of a continuum and SN at the other. The argument in WB's excerpt deals directly with Backing as well as other elements; there is no argument at all in SN's excerpt. The other three transcripts fall somewhere in between. Arguments are being made, but with little or no reference to Backing for Warrants. HK's questions in the history excerpt appear to focus on finding the right Warrants; other Warrants attempted by students appear to be "inconvenient." In the excerpts from lessons by MK and PR, the problems posed are not ones that lend themselves to single correct Warrants. MK eventually seeks Warrants with particular Backing, appropriate to the course, but students seem slow to pick up on this shift. PR seems to be encouraging students to explore psychology by attempting various Warrants; at one point he insists that "trauma" must be part of a student's Warrant, but he does not provide Backing for this move. Table 1 summarizes this analysis of the five transcripts into four general patterns with respect to the use of questions to develop arguments.

Distinctive characteristics of a discipline appear at the level of Backing for Warrants used in arguments within the discipline. It is interesting to note the relationship between course titles and the Warrants teachers seek. In history, a Warrant is an explanation for an event; in psychology, a Warrant is a model for interpreting behavior. In the two courses that concern Christian living, the Warrants are rules to guide personal behavior. Is it coincidental that the excerpt from a course on marriage, a title that suggests no particular discipline, is the excerpt that shows no features of argument at all?

The history excerpt (HK) is the only example here of a "traditional" high school subject clearly based in non-religious disciplines. My earlier analysis of science lessons (Russell, 1983) revealed questioning patterns similar to those in HK's history lesson. Warrants are treated more as "facts" to be covered than as significant rules

Table 1. Teachers' Ways of Using Questions to Develop Arguments in Five High School Transcripts

WB	HK	MK	SN
Parent-child relations	American Resolution	Seniors' smoking privileges and **PR** Multiple personality	Sex in homelife
Backing explicit in argument	Arguments treat "correct" Warrants as "facts;" no reference to Backing	No single Warrant is "correct;" no clear indication of importance of Backing	Only Data appear in the discussion; no argument is developed

to be understood in terms of their associated Backing. There is no simple explanation for the acceptance by teachers, students, and society of this familiar style of teaching. My own participation in the development of case studies of science teaching (Olson & Russell, 1984), based in observation and interviews of teachers, suggests that Warrants are treated as facts within the context of a system of testing and grading that values most highly maintaining each student's opportunity to gain access to the next grade or level of schooling.

Although there is a close relationship between the element of Backing for arguments and the characteristics of a particular discipline's arguments, only one of the five transcripts shows a teacher posing questions at the level of Backing. My conclusion is not that this is unfortunate or undesirable. A few of my colleagues in this multidisciplinary project have wondered why I do not conclude with a recommendation that teachers attend to the completeness of the arguments they present as they teach. I find such a recommendation inappropriate because I have focused exclusively on but one of many criteria that could be applied to instances of classroom teaching. Away from the immediacy of the practical pressures and dilemmas of the classroom, it may be easy to call for complete arguments that would suggest a rational attitude toward authority. But those who wonder why schools do not accomplish everything they value and espouse must consider the constant series of compromises that a teacher makes. Values compete constantly in moments of practice. As Schön (1983) has pointed out, the prevailing view of the relationship of "theory" to practice is one that ignores and masks the problem-framing features of practice. The findings in this analysis of the role of questions in arguments are consistent with the hypotheses that most teachers are not familiar with the analysis of arguments in their teaching discourse and that our schools do not *in fact* demonstrate to students the basis for a rational attitude toward authority.

REFERENCES

Green, Thomas F. (1971). *The Activities of Teaching*. New York: McGraw-Hill.

Olson, J. & Russell, T. (1984). *Case studies of science teaching*. Volume III of *Science education in Canadian schools*. Background Study 52. Ottawa: Science Council of Canada.

Peters, R.S. (1967). *Authority, Responsibility, and Education*. New York: Atherton Press.

Peters, R.S. (1966). *Ethics and Education*. London: George Allen & Unwin.

Russell, T.L. (1983). Analyzing arguments in science classroom discourse: Can teachers' questions distort scientific authority? *Journal of Research in Science Teaching, 20*, 27–45.

Schön, D.A. (1983). *The Reflective Practitioner*. New York: Basic Books.

Toulmin, S.E. (1958). *The Uses of Argument*. Cambridge: Cambridge University Press.

Toulmin, S.E., Rieke, R., & Janik, A. (1979). *An Introduction to Reasoning*. New York: Macmillan.

CHAPTER 13

Group Processes

Eileen Francis

Moray House College of Education
Holyrood Road, Edinburgh, Scotland
United Kingdom EH8 8AQ

This contribution to the multidisciplinary study is in three sections. The first describes the context of the study, with reference to methodological issues relevant to a Scottish project and to the multidisciplinary study. The second applies the principles of analysis on which the Scottish project is based to the analysis of five transcripts of teacher/student interaction from classrooms in the United States. The third sets the findings of this analysis in the context of our conversations and comments on participation in this multidisciplinary venture.

THE SCOTTISH CONTEXT

Since 1977 educationists in Scotland have been engaged in a curriculum development program which will transform the future education of 14–16 year olds (Kirk 1981). The role of the teacher as primary information-giver and initiator of classroom events is to evolve into the role of teacher as resource person and enabler. Strategies such as "learning through discussion" and small group work are to be used as frequently as more directive teaching methods.

The Discussion Development Project

A Discussion Skills Project sponsored by the Scottish Education Department in 1981, as one of a series of multidisciplinary projects funded in connection with the Government's Development Program, established a Discussion Development Group (D.D.G.) at Moray House College of Education to respond to the need for research on process innovation in relation to the new curriculum. The research project is examining the development and function of the D.D.G. resource unit in training teachers to become associates of the D.D.G. through an inservice training program which focuses on the observation and analysis of discussion group processes. The aims of the associates are to promote the effective management of classroom discussion by teachers and to enable the development of discussion skills in students.

The work of the D.D.G. is based on the premise that it is necessary to scrutinize the strategy of teaching and learning which is described as "learning through discussion." Bullock (1975) states that far too many classroom discussions are in reality no more than a series of "disconnected endeavours to read the teacher's mind" and could be more appropriately described as synchronized rituals of teacher/student talk. Furthermore, when the perceptions of teachers and students on what constitutes discussion are examined, a weakness in the conceptual understanding of the nature of discussion can be identified. It is the task of the D.D.G. to illuminate the process of discussion and to disseminate its findings throughout educational institutions in Scotland (Francis, 1986).

The D.D.G. encourages teachers to become engaged in small-scale action research projects which promote a model of classroom discussion derived from Bridges (1979), which emphasises

1. More than one point of view being put forward.
2. Participants being responsive to different points of view.
3. Participants being willing to understand or being affected by opinions other than their own.
4. Participants feeling an obligation to offer opinions and to examine the opinions of others.
5. Participants realizing that while listening and observing are important, being a silent member of the group fulfills only half the contract in discussion.

The teachers are supported by two consultants who collate and disseminate the findings of the projects to other teachers with the aim of producing a multiplier effect.

The Multidisciplinary Study

Participation in the multidisciplinary study reported in this book was seen as an opportunity to focus this network of teachers around a common project. It was hoped that the multidisciplinary project would be a factor in reinforcing the group cohesiveness generated by contact with the D.D.G. The project offered an opportunity to express a view of the transcripts (Appendix) based on a previously negotiated understanding of the nature of classroom discussion.

Dillon's extensive literature on questioning is regarded as a major resource by the D.D.G. and it was with this respect for Dillon's work that the associates addressed his questions about the transcripts:

How shall we conceive of these conversations?
How do we describe them?
What might we learn from them about educative exchanges?

The Methodological Basis of the Study

The Discussion Development Project's primary characteristics are those of action research: a case study approach which addresses itself to a learning milieu (ie. the network of cultural, social, institutional, and psychological variables which influence the context), as much as to the components of the study itself.

MacDonald and Walker (1977) describe the case study as the examination of an instance in action—the objectives of the research being to reveal the properties of the class to which the instance belongs.

The case study model raises questions concerning the relationships between the evaluator and the various interest groups that he/she serves. McDonald maintains that these relationships commit the evaluator to a stance which has consequences for the selection of techniques of information gathering and analysis. He offers a classification which distinguishes between three differing types of evaluation study: the bureaucratic, the autocratic, and the democratic. The D.D.G. has approached the evaluation of the transcripts in this study as it approaches its other reflective activities, within a framework of democratic evaluation which has as its key concepts "confidentiality," "negotiation", and "accessibility."

Embedded in the D.D.G.'s understanding of democratic evaluation is another contributory strand, that of the "human relations" style of research which focuses on institutions undergoing change as social systems and studies the participants' response to innovatory schemes. Rippey (1973) describes this as 'transactional evaluation' which is "concerned with the system undergoing change rather than the outcomes of the system's activity."

The D.D.G. aims to analyze the system of group events in a sample of classrooms, schools, and regions, the effects of innovation and change on those systems, and the forces and role relationships which can be enhanced to overcome resistance to change.

Of prime significance is the finding of a methodology for describing the quality of the interpersonal relationships within these social systems, holding to Adelman's (1981) definition of collaboration between the researchers' and the practitioners' group: "collaboration within a mutually agreed ethical framework, deriving from practitioner's theory."

Our approach is based on the premise that what each individual learns in a consultancy contact is unique and that this learning is best described as the building of a responsive, reflective system rather than the structuring of a replicable model. The system is geared to the definition of appropriate questions rather than the giving of definitive answers; and the fact that the consultants come from a background of particular experiences and disciplines which cannot be reproduced for others, may be a positive rather than a negative attribute of the multidisciplinary effort.

One of the issues which has emerged from the work of the D.D.G. is an interest in describing the nature and quality of the networks initiated by the project in school and college settings, and at regional and national level.

The opportunity to develop these ideas internationally and to observe the networking skills of Dillon with his regular dissemination of information, his generation of feelings of value and reciprocity across the network, and his capacity to shift the network into associated areas of study, has contributed to the D.D.G.'s development.

THE MULTIDISCIPLINARY TASK

Introduction

It will be understood from this description of the methodological basis of the Discussion Development Project's work that analysis of the transcripts provided for the multidisciplinary study would prove difficult. The qualitative information required about the network of cultural, social, institutional, and psychological variables was felt to be absent, and associates' comments such as "I become aware of the impossibility of judging the discussion by the transcripts alone." and "There is a risk of objectifying structural features of the transcripts and losing contact with the process dynamics." express the reservations the D.D.G. had about the value of the contribution it might make to this multidisciplinary study. Concern was also felt about the practitioners who had provided data for the study without participating in its evaluation, as this challenged our notions of democratic and transactional evaluation. Effective analysis in our view is dependent on nonvocal, nonverbal features as much as on linguistic features, and knowledge of the context from which the transcripts come is crucial. However, as all the participants in this study appeared to have similar reservations about the database and were agreed that what might be achieved could only be a partial view of a classroom situation, the D.D.G. overcame its initial misgivings and looked for the learning that could be achieved from reflection on the transcripts.

It must also be said that the *process of participation* in the multidisciplinary study was of more importance to us than its outcome, as we felt that this was of great significance to the development of our insight about networking, consultancy, and dissemination.

A Framework for Analysis

The analysis the D.D.G. offers is based on the belief, articulated by Lawrence (1979), that "we can work more effectively and with greater satisfaction if we come to understand in a direct and personal way the dynamics of groups and inter-group processes within social systems."

The "open-system" approach as it is called, emphasizes:

1. Reflecting on the "here and now" experience.
2. Providing a framework for self-analysis.
3. Learning which is unique to each group member.

The aim of the open-system approach is to heighten process thinking. The group leader's role is to communicate to each group member that he/she is in possession of perceptions which can illuminate the whole group process and that the group as a social system is poorer if it does not take advantage of contributions from all its members rather than depending on a few of its members. Indeed the term "leading" is unhelpful as it carries too many connotations of the didactic teaching role. "Conducting" may describe more accurately the sensitive listening and appropriate responding fundamental to the enabling role to which the group worker aspires.

The work of Lawrence (1979) at the Tavistock Institute of Human Relations, that of Bramley (1979) of the Institute of Group Analysis, and Salzberger-Wittenberg, Henry, and Osborne (1983) provide insights into the open-system approach.

These insights contrast with what might be regarded as the "closed" systems which tend to operate in many of our educational institutions. These institutions are organized hierarchically and are based on leadership models which may at times appear authoritarian rather than authoritative. Response to the need for change in a closed system is often partial, the members of the system "structuring a system of defense against anxiety" as Menzies (1960) described it, to avoid coping with the difficult choices which would have to be made if the whole system was opened up to scrutiny.

The Analysis of Classroom Discussion as a Group Event

Associates of the D.D.G. have applied insights relating to the open-system approach to classroom discussion, to develop a concept of applied group analysis. A shift in perception is necessary before the teacher views the classroom situation as a group event. Observation of classroom discussion from an open-system perspective places the teacher within the group system rather than separating the leadership system of the teacher from the membership system of the student. As one Associate said, "I've been made aware of . . . what's happening in a group of pupils that includes myself."

Singer, Astrachan, Gould & Klein (1979) categorize group events in terms of two basic parameters,

1. The task of the group event.
2. The psychological levels or systems involved in the task.

The Task System

They describe tasks on a continuum extending from cognitive/perceptual learning to psychological change. Some tasks can be multidimensional, providing opportunities for both learning and change, incorporating elements of cognitive/perceptual development with developments in awareness, insight and skill.

The strategy of classroom discussion might be described as the interface of cognitive/perceptual learning and elements of psychological change. Its effectiveness lies in the awareness of the participants of the implicit and explicit assumptions which determine the management of the task. Ineffective classroom discussion is often the result of the teacher's lack of clarity in communicating the aims and objectives of the discussion task to the class members.

The Psychological Levels Involved in the Task

Group events can be further analyzed at the levels of (1) group process (2) interpersonal process and (3) intrapersonal process. For analysis of this kind, both verbal and nonverbal information is required. Mehrabian (1972), reporting a series of research studies on non-verbal communication, concludes that the analysis of individual communication behaviour is dependent on non-verbal data (7% verbal, 38% vocal, 55% facial is the finding of one experiment). Analysis of interpersonal communication and group communication is even more dependent on non-vocal elements, as the proxemics of the situations become more significant.

Application to the Multidisciplinary Study

When reviewing the transcripts and audio recordings in this study we asked ourselves: is the teacher pursuing a learning goal or a learning/change goal? How are the primary tasks of these group events perceived by student and teacher? Are the objectives content-oriented or process-oriented? How will the teacher evaluate the effectiveness of these group events? Are the students expected to demonstrate learning through cognitive/perceptual change and/or psychological change?

The phrase "learning through discussion" is seen in all its ambiguity when the group event is explored using the task system model. The learning possibilities of the discussion strategy might be permutated in a variety of ways, e.g.,

1. The content of the discussion can be oriented toward the achievement of cognitive/perceptual learning goals.
2. The content of the discussion can be oriented toward the psychological end of the continuum to achieve learning/change goals.

The task system of (1) and (2) might be described as discussion in which the student will demonstrate understanding and/or insight in relation to the content of the curriculum.

Other options open to the teacher might relate to process aims and objectives:

3. The process of the discussion will be oriented toward the achievement of cognitive/perceptual learning goals.
4. The process of the discussion will be oriented toward the achievement of psychological learning goals.

The task system of (3) and (4) might be summarized as discussion which gives the student opportunity to demonstrate awareness and insight in relation to the discussion process and an increased capacity in discussion skill.

Analysis of the task system from the data of the transcripts (Appendix) can only be based on partial evidence. The transcripts can be located in the task system referred to as (1) and (2). None of the group events are located in the process task system of (3) and (4). The aims of HK and PR appeared to be to test the student's understanding of reading they have completed on the topic of the American Revolution and multiple personality, therefore cognitive/perceptual gains appeared to be the goal of these group events. MK, SN, and WB appeared to value gains in the development of awareness and insight about the topics of smoking and human relationships, a learning/change task.

The aims of the five teachers could not be said to have been achieved, as contributions were made only by certain class members in all groups. The teachers would be unable to monitor whether the silent members had understanding which they did not demonstrate, or avoided making a contribution because they did not understand. HK and PR must have wondered whether they might have tested their students understanding more effectively using a different strategy. The fact that the teachers were participants in the group event rather than observers of it, would also have an effect on the monitoring function.

None of the teachers made the process dynamics of the discussion an explicit task. Statements which would heighten perception concerning the nature of the discussion in relation to the content themes, or comments which might enable the students to reflect on their management of the discussion task, do not appear in these extracts.

Examination of the transcripts demonstrates how little we know about the participants, particularly those who are classified as listening/observing members of the group. Were they closely engaged in the listening/observing task or were they expressing quite a different message from the one we can hear? The transcripts do not reassure us that *all* the students have *learned to discuss,* nor that the teacher has awareness and insight about the effects factors such as physical setting, group composition, and style of leadership have on discussion.

The transcripts present us with samples of classroom discussion from which it can be argued that the implicit assumptions of the teacher about the nature of the task are not shared by the students, where appropriate interaction is experienced by a few students with no reference to the understanding and feelings of the majority of students.

The views of the Associates of the D.D.G. reinforce this description of the discussion. A content analysis of a questionnaire completed by 10 associates following discussions about the transcripts, described the physical settings as "unsuitable," "normal class arrangement," "appropriate for teacher/student questioning *not* for discussion," and "were some of the students looking at one another's heads?"

The associates were equally dismissive of the group size: "Too large. What many teachers euphemistically call discussion," "Impossibly large for meaningful discussion to take place," "All too big—student does not know classmate's name!," and "Far too large—voices had to be raised—side conversations going on."

With regard to group composition one of the associates was particularly concerned that in HK, "seven exchanges out of 63 are from girls *but* nearly *half* the group of 30 are girls."

On the theme of leadership the comments described the discussions as "teacher-dominated," "traditional teacher role of organiser and initiator—the teacher has to be dominant and directive because of numbers," "active controlling style," and "teachers clearly in control—students have no opportunity to lead."

Those teachers who completed the questionnaire and those who conversed about the transcripts were agreed that the interactions did not reflect their perception of effective classroom discussion.

The Transcripts as Case Studies

Would the five teachers agree with the assumptions of their D.D.G. colleagues that the transcripts provide examples of classroom interaction which could be more effective? Would HK regard his discussion task and his management of it as qualitatively different from that of WB?

Approaching the transcripts as case studies—instances in action—we would wish to suggest themes which influence all group events

implicitly or explicitly, processes of which participants are aware
or unaware and which the five teachers might deny or be willing
to explore. The processes described shape the group event whether
or not they become the task of that event. Interpretative comments
on the transcripts are presented with the view that they would
require reciprocal validation by the five teachers before full understanding of the group events could be achieved.

Process Shapers in Classroom Discussion

Teachers and students must work typically with the following six
process shapers in classroom discussion, three of which can be
under conscious control and can readily be made explicit:

1. Physical setting
2. Group composition
3. Leadership style

and three which may be unconscious process shapers and will remain
implicit, or can be made explicit, depending on the task of the
group:

4. The boundary system
5. The resistance/resonance dynamic
6. Personal background
    (a) its influence on perception of the group event
    (b) its effect on teacher/student functioning

Physical Setting

Discussion is an activity which requires concentrative listening. It
is enhanced if the participants are in close, physical proximity so
that the quietest voice can be attended to without strain and eye
contact can be maintained with every participant. The physical
setting needs to communicate that discussion is a peer relationship
which aims to reduce the impact of authority relationships to encourage a view that each participant's contribution is of value. The
organization of the physical setting prior to the discussion taking
place will communicate nonverbally to the members of the group,
the perception the teacher has of the discussion task. Associates of
the D.D.G. frequently comment on the contrast between the physical
setting of the D.D.G. and the environment which is provided for
discussion in school. Components such as low level, comfortable

seating arranged is a circle, in a quiet room without visual or auditory distractions, become an explicit part of our discussion as teachers realize the effect this has on the quality of discussion.

> "We had a staff meeting today. I realized that one of the reasons for us not having a good discussion was because I had to turn round to talk to the people behind me."

> "As I left the school I saw a departmental meeting going on in one of the classrooms. The staff were seated in rows, just as the children had been, and one of them had his hand up to make a point. . . . I wouldn't have noticed that before coming to the group."

It is interesting to speculate what effect an 'eye-glance' group and the placement of the teacher within the group, with equal proximity between himself and the members of the group, would have on the educative exchanges of the transcripts.

Group Composition

We know that high cohesive groups are more effective than low cohesive groups in achieving their respective goals and that members of high cohesive groups are generally better satisfied than members of low cohesive groups. We also know that group cohesiveness is reduced the larger the group becomes, so that groups of 2–6 members can achieve group cohesiveness more quickly than groups of 12–15 members. Groups of more than 15 members will find that the difficulties they have in achieving group cohesiveness for reasons of group size will interfere with the management of the discussion task.

Other elements related to group composition, which will affect the discussion task, include the differences in performance of mixed-sex groups and same-sex groups, the differences in groups composed of members having diverse, relevant abilities and those having similar abilities.

We would suggest that there was little evidence that these issues had been addressed by the five teachers in the sample group, and that development of the communication potential of each class situation was limited by this lack of attention.

Leadership Style

If we assume that discussion as a classroom strategy is aimed at developing the student's ability to contribute, to listen and to respond effectively within a discussion context, efforts by the teacher to maximize student interaction will be regarded as beneficial.

The teacher needs to recognize that student interaction will be facilitated if he recognizes the difference between 'conducting' a group of students and 'leading' a group. The conductor does not necessarily participate verbally in discussion, he may arrange the physical setting, organize appropriate group composition, present a structured task to the group members, and act as observer during the actual discussion process. If he does participate, his contributions will be recognized by his use of statements which either summarize content or comment on process, and he will be aware of the effect his verbal and nonverbal interventions might have in initiating content or validating the authenticity of the discussion. The conductor aims for a style of leadership which will be seen as authoritative rather than authoritarian.

HK represents the antithesis of the conductor, offering us an example of classroom interaction which has few characteristics of discussion. He asks 50 questions and makes three statements in a 10-minute sample (Appendix). In response the students are passive receivers of his controlling style, many of their contributions reduced to one- or two-word utterances, with few examples of extended utterances or linguistically complex utterances. HK not only controls the questions but authenticates the answers:

> HK   17a   "Now you're on the right track"
> 18a   "Well, let's get away from pay"
> 20a   "Not exactly . . ."
> 21a   "That's right . . ."
> 26a   "Very good"

HK as the result of this analysis might decide to consciously reduce his number of questions, to elicit responses through statements or through silence and to include positive reinforcers only for process feedback rather than content feedback. Would such a change in leadership style greatly improve the quality of student interaction? We suggest that it would not unless HK also took account of the issues surrounding the boundary system of the group event. Aspects of the boundary system are not under conscious control and it is this unconscious shaping of process which will now provide material for analysis and reflection of the group events of the transcripts.

The Boundary System

Every group event is limited by boundary constraints, and perceptions about the limits or rules of the task may differ between student and teacher. The most effective discussions demonstrate a clear understanding of the boundary system by leader and members. The group members have contracted in to an event which they assume has certain goals and are satisfied if these expectations are met. Problems may arise if a group having contracted in to fulfill one set of goals perceives itself being directed to work on a task with different goals.

MK, SN, and WB (Appendix) are working on tasks which may have caused students to reassess their expectations of the contract. The titles of the courses are "Christian Relationships", "Marriage" and "Society and Christian Lifestyle" (Table 1 in Appendix). These courses could be addressed on a cognitive/perceptual basis—at a "knowing about", "understanding" level—or a psychological change basis—at a "getting in touch with feelings" or "reflecting on personal experience" level. The educative exchanges on these topics would only be seen to be of value if the dimensions the teacher thought appropriate to include in the task were in synchrony with the students' perceptions of the task. If, as Egan (1970) states, explicit contracts facilitate desirable behavior such as self-disclosure, we might conjecture that members of MK, SN and WB's groups who fail to participate may have concerns about the boundary of the task.

The students have also contracted into a group event in which they have certain expectations of the teacher's role. Previous experience may have demonstrated to them that their teacher adopts a "closed" rather than an "open" system approach to classroom interaction, i.e. the teacher has a clear idea of his intentions but the student is less clear about his purpose. The expectations of HK's controlling style will differ from that of SN's more enabling style and to some extent HK has conditioned an interactive response from his students which would be inappropriate in SN's class. HK's students would need time to learn the style of response appropriate to SN and would require some sensitivity to shift from a period of History to a period of Social Education during a school day. It would not be surprising if some students were more able to achieve the transition than others. The fact that we do not know how long HK and SN's students have been working together makes it difficult to interpret the important contribution that group stability and group permanence have had on the development of discussion.

The Dependency Dynamic

Our interpretation of the evidence of the transcripts indicates that there tends to be an impermeable boundary between the leadership and the membership region of the groups. The impermeable boundary is sustained by the teachers' questioning and responding behaviour. MK (12a) and SN (13a) choose to move into the membership region on two occasions by disclosing their own personal material, but students tend not to take on the leadership of the group. A dependency dynamic is created, shown in its strongest form in HK and in a weaker form by SN and WB, where students learn unconsciously through experience of the impermeable boundary between leadership and membership tasks that they may not feel their own authority in initiating the task, or shift the work of the group in a direction which may not be sanctioned by the teacher.

It is appropriate to be dependent in some learning situations when the teacher is demonstrating skills which the student has not achieved. It is not appropriate to be dependent when the learning strategy is discussion as the dependency dynamic interferes with the outcome of the discussion task. The dependency dynamic promotes feelings of powerlessness in the students and leads them to express these feelings either in dependence on the teachers' actions or in alienation from interaction.

The D.D.G. hypothesizes that the more inappropriately dependent the student group has been encouraged to become through past experience of a "closed" system, the more resistant it is to taking opportunities to acquire new skills when the occasion offers itself.

The Resistance/Resonance Dynamic

The success of every group event can be assessed by noting the "resonance" experienced by the leader and the members of the group in their management of self and the task during discussion. The opposite of resonance is resistance, which emerges as a result of inaccurate assumptions, inappropriate role allocations, prejudices, and differences in the value systems of the group. Resistance may be used deliberately or unconsciously and has much to do with the "luggage" of our own personal backgrounds which we carry into each group event. (Bramley, 1979).

If we examine MK (13a–15a) we can observe the teacher coping with resistance among his students in their discussion on smoking. The teacher's leadership style has created a benign, closed system which has provided the students with reassurance that they do not have to take responsibility for the discussion task. The task is located midway on the learning/change continuum—the learning element includes understanding of a Christian lifestyle and the change element includes developing awareness and insight of the differences in the psychological stance of the student group on social issues. The topic of smoking is a contentious issue in school at the time of the discussion, issues external to the here and now of the group event are having a powerful effect and are tending to contaminate the primary task of the group, i.e., learning about Christian relationships. We sense a certain ambivalence on the teacher's part. The group is talking, there is much interesting material being presented, but he begins to demonstrate concern about what is actually being achieved. What will the students take away from this discussion as a learning outcome? MK counteracts the resistance to work in the group by asserting his authority as leader and shifting the discussion from one topic to another, which he understands to be the implicit task of the course. The lack of synchrony in the turn-taking of the group at this point reminds us that the management of resistance in closed systems gives inappropriate power and influence to the opinions of the teacher. The teacher in this extract has displayed his "luggage" but he is not able to dispel the students' resistance as the final exchange indicates:

MK   19a   "Does that mean if you don't smoke, you're a better Christian then?"
        19b   "It doesn't mean you're a worse one."
        19b   SILENCE (3 secs.)

The Effect of Personal Background on the Group Event

This exchange and the subsequent silence reminds us of the part the expectations and personal histories of both students and teachers play in the life of each group. As a result of these expectations and individual histories it might be anticipated that a number of 'fantasies' or perceptions that have no basis in reality might be influencing the groups' work. The presence of fantasy has much to do with our own personal experiences which have been shaped by the variety of social and institutional groups to which we have belonged in the past. The "luggage" we bring to groups on issues such as power, authority, cooperation, and rivalry will affect the interpersonal process. Teachers carry with them their own learning experiences from the classroom. They may have learned to censor the feelings they bring to the group believing that they can maintain discussion at a rational level. They may deny the value of the irrational in exploring and developing the quality of discussion. Students may gain the impression that how one *feels* about the class is less valuable than what one *thinks* about it. Student perception may be shaped in the direction of the academic, rational approach which denies the ability to respond spontaneously and sensitively.

The Gatekeepers of Insight

The effect of unspoken personal issues will be highlighted on courses which appear to be discussing feelings, attitudes and values but resist exploration of the feelings of the here and now situation. In MK, SN, and WB we might interpret that the personal issues surrounding the group have the effect of putting the boundary system of the group event in conflict with the task system. In WB's session, for example, the talk revolves around the theme of parents and children being open with each other. How open are the students able to be in questioning the role of the teacher? Will the fact that WB uses his authority to validate contributions or to question the validity of contributions have an effect on this group's long-term use of the discussion strategy? WB's role in this extract might be interpreted as the gatekeeper of insight—his benign power filters the gold out of the dross of the students' discursiveness creating an appreciative dependency.

> WB 1a ". . . I think that's what he's saying . . ."
> 2a "I would presume that you think . . ."
> 5a "O.K. good. That's a really good illustration there . . ."
> 7a "I think it's probably good."

The Imagery of the Group Event

Foulkes (quoted in Bramley, 1979) described the group as a "hall of mirrors in which parts of ourselves are reflected and counter-reflected. We see ourselves in others and others see themselves in us. We like some of what we see and identify it as part of our better selves. We decide to get angry with or deny parts of other people because they remind us of bits of ourselves we prefer to leave hidden".

Associates of the D.D.G. have produced their own imagery:

"I see the group as a tapestry. The threads seemed randomly placed at first but now I'm beginning to see blocks of colour emerging—the shapes are taking on a meaning, just as our discussion is".

"We seem to be digging a hole, a pit. It's dark, there's a lot of mud . . ."

"We're digging a mine. We're finding gold."

Is there evidence of this rich material in the transcripts or are group discussions which focus on process very different from those that focus on content? The D.D.G. would suggest that this material exists in all groups whatever their task, but it is not generally made explicit. When the transcripts are examined for themes which might be explored in process-oriented terms we find the following:

HK	3a–7a	
	63a–End	Themes of violence?
MK	le–lj	Themes of power and authority?
SN	1a–3b	Themes of envy? rivalry?
PR	23a	Themes of group realities and fantasies?

The essential dilemma of this interpretation is that these themes cannot be addressed in content-oriented courses. If, however, they are not addressed, the themes which emerge as the unspoken work of the group will have an effect on the relationships within a school and on the educational task it intends to fulfill.

We have found that the mechanism of displacement is one of the typically unaddressed themes of group discussion in educational settings. Difficult feelings which emerge in discussion as a result of teacher intervention or student attitude, but which are not regarded as the work of the group, will often be displaced onto something or someone else—the head of department, the headteacher, the school, the school next door, the regional authority, etc.

MK lj "Cause like a Loyola, all right, and *Loyola is just as strict as this school*, and seniors smoke there".

lk "Yeah, but they probably got a whole lounge".

The D.D.G. considers that there is a need for teachers to be reflective about such group processes checking out the realities of their individual perceptions of the class group. It may not be the task of the discussion group to illuminate process in this way, but the teacher's effective management of the task may be dependent on recognition of the processes which are shaping the functioning of the group in discussion.

REFLECTIONS ON THE MULTIDISCIPLINARY TASK

At the outset the D.D.G. was convinced that the description and analysis of the educative exchanges of the transcripts would be most effectively served by a holistic, person-centered approach. Having worked alongside our multidisciplinary colleagues during this study and concluded our analysis, we must now reflect on the nature of the findings that have been achieved by the team and relate them to the work of the Discussion Development Group.

It is rare for researchers who have communicated extensively in writing to find themselves, as they did in this study, in face-to-face interaction with the task of negotiating the process of each individual's perspective. Participants who on paper appeared remote from one's own perspective emerged as having common ground. Others, who appeared to use a common language were found to have fundamental differences in the interpretation of that language, so that shared meaning became elusive. This appeared particularly true of the philosophers and the psychologists, the behaviorally oriented practitioners and the holistically oriented practitioners.

Members of the multidisciplinary group in this study showed differing strengths in relation to analyzing the "what" and the "how" of the transcripts. We suggest that future analysis of discussion requires us to reflect on the relationships between the following elements in discussion:

Practitioners have the opportunity to be eclectic, or as O'Brien described, 'meta-disciplinary'. The D.D.G. is resourced by researchers with a background in the applied behavioural science of speech pathology and therapeutics. It was suggested by Gooding that we approached the transcripts 'therapeutically', searching for the point of disablement in the communication between teachers and students.

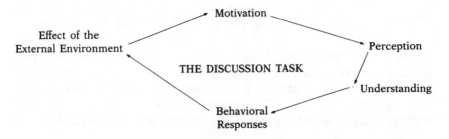

We suggest that there was already evidence in our analysis of the application of the disciplinary perspectives represented by Farrar and Mullen and the pedagogical perspectives represented by the Klinzings, Gooding, and the Swifts. Indeed one of the tasks of the D.D.G. is to preserve the balance of the behavioural/psychodynamic interface in communication analysis.

There is also echoes of themes developed in the contributions of Lighthall, Russell, and the Woods and these themes of context, system, and authority as in a figure-ground configuration already seem to us more dominant as we approach the analysis of Scottish transcripts.

Sigel illuminated for us a strand of our work which was implicit but lacked conceptualization. His contribution on distancing behaviour together with Gooding and Swifts' work on wait time enabled us to analyze the process of our consultancy, particularly in relation to group work.

Group analysts typically do not ask questions but formulate statements which are intended to summarize the major themes or process-shapers emerging from group discussion. The use of such statements has the effect of creating longer 'wait-time' as group members reflect on the apparent lack of synchrony between their turns in the interaction and those of the group leader. The statements may in fact be perceived as questions by the group membership and the effect of this interpretation appears to be that the subsequent turns of the group members are at a higher cognitive level than previous turns.

We have observed two recent examples, the first in a discussion by an adult group on the leadership role. Group members commented that they were unsure of the content to be discussed, that they had never experienced discussion where the content had not been specified explicitly before the interaction began. The intervention of the group leader suggesting that the group may be concerned about leadership responsibility in the group focused the group members around a discussion on the concept of group leadership.

A second example was demonstrated on a video recording by one of our teacher associates. A student group (average age, 11 years) is discussing a topic. After each turn students reflect on whether (s)he asked a question, made a statement and whether the utterance indicated agreement or disagreement with the previous speaker. By explicitly embedding this process of reflection into the group event, the students created longer wait time, showing a corresponding increase in higher cognitive level responses as predicted by the Swift and Gooding team.

The process of this interaction satisfied the need of the D.D.G.

for a skills orientation which emanates from individual motivation and perception rather than the external stimuli described by the Klinzings, Gooding, and the Swifts.

The publications of our teacher associates Hunter and Pratt (1984) and Johnson (1985) together with the early work for this multidisciplinary project indicate the deepening interest of the D.D.G. in language, authority, and reflection in relation to the process of learning to discuss.

The multidisciplinary symposium has demonstrated the need for a shift of focus in our project onto issues concerning the value and meaning of classroom discussion. Teachers will value Bridges' analysis of what might be achieved in classroom discussion but will be aware of the difficulty of fulfilling such goals in the present school system. There will be a need for inservice training on discussion and consultancy support if teachers are to achieve the qualitative goals he defines.

Many teachers will disagree with O'Brien that discussion is more appropriate to developing understanding in aesthetic and humanistic studies as this reinforces the current confusion surrounding the validity of the concept of "scientific" thinking and "scientific" values (Munby, 1985) on which many educationists feel the need to reflect. Discussion research can challenge the reductionist attitudes and the devaluing of subjective reality which has in the past permeated much educational development.

In conclusion we contend that it may not be possible for participants in this project to conduct a multidisciplinary study of discussion, nor to encode multidisciplinary findings. It may be that "multidisciplinary" research exists only in an applied form, its multidisciplinary nature being perceived when a receiver decodes and integrates the findings of the research venture in the context of a specific educational setting.

REFERENCES

Adelman, C. (1981). *Uttering, Muttering*. London, U.K.: Grant McIntyre.

Bramley, W. (1979). *Group Tutoring: Concepts and Case Studies*. London: Kogan Page.

Bridges, D. (1979). *Education, Democracy and Discussion*. Oxford, U.K.: NFER.

Bullock (1975). *A Language for Life: The Bullock Report*. London: HMSO.

Egan, G. (1970). *Encounter: Group Processes for Interpersonal Growth*. Belmont, CA: Brooks/Cole.

Francis, E. (1986). *Learning to Discuss*. Edinburgh: Moray House College.

Hunter, R. & Pratt, L. (1984). Putting in a word for discussion skills. *Teaching English*, Scottish Curriculum Development Service, Edinburgh: Moray House College.

Johnson, Thomas (1985). *The Changing Face of Education* 14–16. Munn, P. & Brown, S. (Eds.), Oxford, U.K.: NFER.

Kirk, G. (1981). *Curriculum and Assessment in the Scottish Secondary School: A Study of the Munn and Dunning Reports*. London, UK: Ward Lock.

Lawrence, W. Gordon (Ed.) (1979). *Exploring Individual and Organisational Boundaries*, Chichester, U.K.: John Wiley.

MacDonald, B. & Walker, R. (1978). *Changing the Curriculum*, London, U.K.: Open Books.

Mehrabian (1972). *Non-verbal Communication*. Chicago: Aldine-Atherton.

Menzies, I. (1960). A case study in the functioning of social systems as a defence against anxiety. *Human Relations 13*, 95–121.

Munby, H. (1985). *Exposing the Myth of Scientific Thinking in Teacher Education Programmes*. Chicago: AERA.

Rippey, R. (1973). *Studies in Transactional Evaluation*. Berkeley: McCutch.

Salzberger-Wittenberg, Henry, & Osborne (1983). *The Emotional Experience of Learning and Teaching*. Routledge, Kegan Paul, London, U.K.

Singer, Astrachan, Grould & Klein (1975). Boundary management in psychological work with groups. *Applied Behavioural Science 11*, no. 2.

ACKNOWLEDGEMENT

I wish to acknowledge the contribution to this project of Associates of the Discussion Development Group in the Lothian and Central regions of Scotland, and of my research associate, Jane Davidson.

CHAPTER 14

Questioning Versus Student Initiative

David Wood and Heather Wood

Department of Psychology
University of Nottingham
University Park, Nottingham
England NG7 2RD

INTRODUCTION

The focus for much of our work over the past decade has been on the way in which teachers and their young pupils (hearing and deaf) talk to each other. For teachers of the deaf, encouraging children to use their voices and helping them to learn how to make themselves understood is one of their main responsibilities. Similarly, many trained teachers who work in British nursery schools (and volunteers who help to run local, non-state-maintained playgroups), also believe that encouraging children to talk and to share ideas is important for social, linguistic and intellectual development. In both these situations, however, we have been struck by the very different approaches taken by teachers in attempting to fulfill such objectives. Furthermore, in some classrooms the children seemed active, interested, involved, and loquacious. In others, the children were more reticent, passive, and even monosyllabic. Were such differences due simply to factors located 'in' the children, or were they heavily influenced by the social relationships established by the teachers and manifest in the ways they talked to children? Were there any common factors involved in the interactions with the deaf and hearing children which acted to encourage or inhibit children from displaying linguistic initiative? The answer to this last question, we have found, is 'yes'. Interactions with both deaf and hearing children in conversations with their teachers are governed by similar principles.

We were intrigued, and a little apprehensive, to receive Jim Dillon's invitation to analyze discussion sessions with much older children. Our research, as we have just said, has been concerned with the analysis of 'conversations' and with the evaluation of different teacher styles in terms of their success in encouraging children to talk, show initiative, ask questions and generally contribute actively to the discourse (Wood, McMahon, & Cranstoun, 1980; Wood, Wood, Griffiths, Howarth, & Howarth, 1982). Should we expect to find any similarities between the effects of different styles of teacher talk in conversations with English deaf children on the one hand and discussions between American teachers with their 16–18 year old students on the other?

In considering this question, we have been led to think about the nature of conversation, discussion, and teaching as categories of verbal interaction, and about some of the factors which serve to differentiate these three broad types of exchange. We suggest that the key differences reside in the relative status of each participant's knowledge. In conversations, each contributor's thoughts about or interest in the topic at hand has equal status (in theory, at least!). In everyday discussion too, what each person has to say about the topic has equal weight, but the "rules" of relevance in discussion are more stringent than they are in conversation. The participants all have some responsibility (perhaps unequally shared, as in classroom discussions) for editing what they have to say to keep on topic. Such editing functions may be formalized if someone takes on a "chairing" role, along with the right to judge that which is relevant or irrelevant. In a teaching–learning encounter, unlike spontaneous conversations and discussions, relevant knowledge is assumed *a priori* to be asymmetrically distributed, and the teacher's task is to impart aspects of their more advanced or superior knowledge to the learner.

It may be argued, then, that the aims and objectives involved in conversations, discussions and lessons are different as are the "rules" governing them and the demands made on the participants. If so, is it sensible to undertake the task of analyzing classroom discussion or teaching sessions with coding systems based on the analysis of less formal conversations?

We suggest that it is. Despite the differences in aims and procedures in conversation and teaching there are some important similarities both in function and structure. The dynamics which dictate whether or not pupils will show initiative and display their ideas are *common*. Before moving on to our analysis of the Dillon transcripts, however, we must define and illustrate the main terms that we use in analysing discourse. First: *control* and *teacher power;* and second: *repair* in teacher talk.

POWER AND CONTROL

The inspiration for these concepts came not from reading the literature nor from conceptual analysis. Their origins were much more mundane. One day, I (David) spent a morning in a lively playgroup for hearing children and the afternoon in a rather depressing classroom for deaf children. Whilst standing outside this classroom and constructing a brave face before entering, I was struck by the fact that I didn't really need to go in to find out what was going on. Even though what the children were trying to say was largely unintelligible without seeing what they were doing, it was not difficult to work out what they were trying to say. The reason, of course, was that the teacher was exerting so much control over what the children were saying that they had little part to play in deciding what they would contribute. This led to the notion of "control" in conversations. Subsequently, of course, we were to find that many other students of classroom discourse (many of them introduced to us through Dillon's writings) had formulated similar ideas.

In Table 1, we outline our very simple and admittedly crude system for coding conversational control.

Consider the first level, 'enforced repetitions'. These moves are rare in speech addressed to young hearing children but employed frequently by some (though by no means all) teachers of the deaf. If the person to whom this move is addressed honors its force and is compliant, then their next move in the conversation is fully prescribed. Two-choice questions leave only one degree of freedom for a compliant listener, while Wh-questions specify the semantic focus of his next move. Each of these types of utterance, then, imposes a different degree of control over what will happen next (again, assuming a compliant listener). Added together (along with requested repetitions—"Pardon?") and expressed as a percentage of total teacher turns, these moves constitute our "power" measure.

In contrast, contributions (i.e., comments, statements, etc.) leave a number of options open to the next speaker, who might simply acknowledge the move, ask a question arising from it, or make a contribution of his own. Phatic moves (usually used to express interest or at least acknowledge another's move) offer even less

Table 1. Levels of Teacher Control and Child Response

Five Main Levels

1.	Enforced repetition:	"Say—I went to the park."
2.	Two-choice questions: (require only yes/no or one of two given alternatives)	"Did you have a good time?" "Did you go on the swings or the roundabout?"
3.	Wh-type questions: (All 'Wh' questions plus How, 'Tell me about')	"Where did you go over the weekend?" "What happened?" "What colour is your dress?"
4.	Personal contributions: (Comments and statements)	"I like going to the park too." "That must have been awful!"
5.	Phatics: ('Conversational oil')	"Oh the park, lovely/super/good!" "I see.", "Hmm" (nodding) (or repeating what child just said).

Mixtures of the Five Levels Commonly Found in Preschool Settings

5.1	Requests for repetition:	"Pardon?", "What?"
5.2	Tag Phatics*:	"Did you?", "It was green, was it?"
4.2	Tag Contributions*:	"That's green, isn't it?"

Other Moves

ch	Chairing: (directs who is to speak when)	"OK, Sharon.", "Tell us more."
m	Management of behaviour:	"Turn round so we can hear you"

Responsive Moves

√   Appropriate answer to a question (even if factually wrong).
√4 Appropriate answer plus elaborating contribution.
x   Clear misunderstanding of what required in question.
x4 Clear misunderstanding but child goes on to add a contribution.
nr No response.
?   Unintelligible and/or not codable.
Other: Any move not covered above, e.g., teacher pointing to picture.

* Tag questions—where a statement or phatic is 'tagged' with a two-choice question—occur only rarely in the Dillon transcripts, and so will not be discussed at any length. We do not include them as 'questions' unless specifically stated.

Note: Teacher and child turns are coded, then entered into a matrix where child turns are distributed according to the preceding teacher turn.

"director" as to what is to be said next, leaving the floor open to anyone with something to say. Recently we have added "chairing" to our list of move types. When we came to analyze sessions with older deaf children, we clearly needed a category for those moves where the teacher stood "outside" the conversation, directing it rather like a chairperson of a meeting. These moves resembled phatics, but kept overall "control" of the floor without controlling what was to be said next. All these moves, then, do not prespecify what a compliant listener is to say—they are all "low control" moves, or, as Dillon calls them, "alternatives to questioning."

But listeners need not be compliant, of course. We may and do respond to questions, on occasion, with questions—for example "Do you want a lift?"—"What time?" Such question–question sequences are, we suggest, one mark of relative equality in discourse. They often signal that the person questioned is negotiating the conditions under which he is prepared to respond; calculating the implications of a given response; assessing the questioner's need and right to know, and so on. We have almost never encountered question–question sequences in teacher–child interactions where the child asks the second question. When we were working mainly with deaf and preschool children, we thought this might be due to their limited linguistic or cognitive resources. For instance, do they know when other people know what they know? Gordon Wells (in preparation) on the basis of his observations, largely rules out the possibility that the children's responses are due to their own verbal inadequacies. In addition we have performed small experimental studies to show that four-year-olds *do* show some awareness of other people's knowledge about an event and, furthermore, when an adult's questions continually interrogate a body of information that *is* already shared and should be presupposed, the child becomes relatively inactive and terse in his verbal responses (Wood & Cooper, 1980).

An alternative explanation is that children do not ask questions because they are inhibited from taking *control* of the teacher. After all, he who questions dictates how his listener will spend his next few cognitive moments as well as what they will say. Perhaps children appreciate that they are not allowed to dictate what the teacher should think about?

So, we suggest, the reason why children will usually answer teacher questions, but seldom ask questions themselves, lies not in the limited linguistic resources of the child but in the asymmetry of the teacher–child power relationships. In fact, as we shall see, children (young ones at least) are very predictable in how they respond to their teachers' moves; they behave almost exactly like the imaginary compliant listener described above. But teachers do not. One of the main reasons for this is that while teachers often make several linguistic 'moves' during their speaking turn, children seldom do. For example, it is not unusual for a teacher, without pause, to acknowledge what a child has just said, make a contribution to the topic and then ask a question (e.g., "Oh, that's nice. I went shopping too. What did you buy?"). And teachers vary widely in how often they terminate their turns with a controlling move. But children make more than one move only rarely and, as we shall see, under rather specific circumstances. Generally speaking, children answer questions but do not often go on to elaborate on their answers by giving additional, unsolicited contributions. They usually follow teacher contributions by making one of their own or, much more rarely, by asking a question. But they almost never *both* contribute and then question, for example.

One obvious implication of this pattern in children's responses is that teachers tend to get only what they "ask" for. If the intention is, for example, to encourage questions from children by asking them questions, this will not happen. This simply is not part of their matrix of responses. Questions usually solicit answers but little more, and the teachers we have worked with have been concerned that children should not only fill the gaps left to them after questions, but should also "participate," be "forthcoming," telling things about themselves that the teachers do not already know. In an attempt to quantify such behaviour, we have focused on measures of child "initiative."

CHILD INITIATIVE

Following *any* move from the teacher a child may put forward an idea (or question) which has not been specifically requested. It may be something as simple as a shake of the head and "green" to the question "Is that blue?" So, any occurrence of a child offering more than he has to as a compliant listener is counted as an instance of initiative. To give us a measure of how often children actually do so in any given session, we simply add up all turns which contain contributions or questions and express this as a percentage of all child turns (measure A in tables 3 and 4). Because in previous studies children have tended to be compliant listeners most of the time, giving only one move per turn, this measure has always correlated strongly, and negatively, with teacher power (see Table 4). But this general measure can be broken down into a series of components. If children are always compliant listeners, then teacher power and overall child initiative are complementary. As one goes up, the other comes down. But the "tenor" of a session can affect children's behaviour in a different way—in terms of how children react to individual move types. We therefore go on to look at how often children elaborate on answers to two-choice questions and tags, as against how often they merely answer yes or no. As this measure (B in the tables) is expressed as a percentage of how many two-choice questions and tags are *asked* in a session, we can look directly at question-answering behaviour. Measure 'C' then looks at how children react to teacher contributions and phatics. Finally, measure 'D' merely looks at the proportion of time that children give elaborated answers to all questions and tags—expressed as a percentage of *all* answers. What we are doing, then, when we correlate teacher power with, say, measure D, is to ask: in which sessions do children most frequently give elaborated answers—when there are many questions to be answered, or when there are relatively few? By taking different angles on the question of initiative, we can examine more precisely the effects of teacher control.

MEAN LENGTH OF TURN (MLT)

In previous studies, where children are still gaining mastery of their language, their *mean length of turn* in sessions has been of obvious interest (measured in words, not time—cf. Dillon). Like child initiative, how many words a child will use in responding to his teacher has varied systematically with both what move type the teacher uses at any one point in time, and also with how many questions have already been asked—i.e., teacher power.

REPAIR

This analysis is less relevant to our current concerns than those we have just explored. Briefly, we analyze each teacher into a second series of categories designed to reveal the general function or purpose it serves in the discourse. Very briefly, most of what we would call "normal discourse" consists of moves which either take the topic forward ("substantive" moves) or allow the other to do so unhindered ("continuity" moves). Repair, however, consists of all instances of the teacher going *backward* in the conversation—to clarify, to repeat questions inadequately answered, or to simply ask the child to "Say that again" or "Pardon?" He/she might also offer the same question to another child, or return to a question or a statement offered earlier. The main reason for developing this classification was to highlight marked differences in the conversational experiences of deaf and hearing children. Some teachers of the deaf make frequent attempts to 'repair' their children's utterances. Others are less likely to. What we have found, using this analysis, is that teachers who repair more are drawn into an increasing "spiral of control" (Wood, 1983). We have found, for example, that frequent repair is associated with more teacher questions, greater misunderstanding on the child's part, less initiative, and shorter utterances from children. The pedagogical implications of these findings will not, however, be explored here.

THE DILLON TRANSCRIPTS

Does it make sense to extend a system of analysis based on very pragmatic questions about how we get preschool children and deaf children talking? Implicit in our system is the assumption that one of the major goals of the interaction is dedicated towards increasing children's initiative and loquacity. If we find, then, that the teachers in Dillon's transcripts do not encourage such things in their students, we clearly must allow for the fact that this may not have been their *intention*. Thus, our analyses are only likely to prove useful to them if they address the objectives teachers are seeking. But we do not know the teachers and cannot ask such questions, so we apologize now if what we do to *their* recordings does scant justice to their objectives. But although we cannot make judgements about how "successful" these sessions have been, they did happen—during the 10-minute segments teachers did ask questions, etc.; students did respond. Thus although we may have many reservations on the enterprise, we shall carry out our analysis in the usual way. Indeed one of the purposes of a multidisciplinary approach is to take deliberately different "slices" through the data presented to us. *Our* concern will be to focus on power and initiative, in the hope that others will be looking at the *content* of the interactions. Then, if the same dynamics apply in formal discussion sessions as they do in "conversations," we can at least provide evidence that if and when teachers really want their students to offer their own ideas on a topic, there are certain simple ploys for encouraging them to do so.

But there is another issue that we *can* address directly. Dillon's teachers are several thousand miles away from those upon whom our analyses were based. They live in a different culture, have undergone different training and, perhaps, have quite different views about the nature of education. Their students are much older than those involved in most of our earlier work and, hence, for reasons of both maturity and culture, might differ markedly in their responses to teachers. Indeed these students are young adults who in a few years' time, may be teachers, mothers, preschool workers themselves. By now they might be expected to be *capable* of taking a large part of the responsibility for how discussions proceed. Then again, the whole situation is very different. There is now a curriculum to be pursued, and teachers will be at least as concerned with keeping most students *quiet* most of the time, as they will be to encourage them to be forthcoming individually.

RESULTS

In Table 2 we present the percentages of teacher moves in each major category, derived from the Dillon transcripts as well as from our own studies. In Table 3 we summarize the measures of teacher power, repair, and MLT and child measures of initiative and MLT. In order to examine common features of teaching talk across very different settings we have, in fact, included not only the five initial transcripts sent by Dillon (listed individually and then averaged over the five sessions) but 11 additional ones that he kindly let us have (we did not have time to analyze yet another 11 he sent, only the first 11 in alphabetical order). We return to the five later. The English teachers in Tables 2 and 3 include 16 working with deaf pupils from six to 11 years of age and 16 working with preschool children in playgroups and nursery schools. Cathy Murphy has also used this system to analyze conversations about television programs between mothers and their two to three year olds (Murphy, 1983, referred to in the tables as "30 TV watchers").

If we look at the five Dillon classes listed individually, it is obvious that there is a very great deal of individual variation in how far different teachers use the different levels of control—and thus great differences in terms of their power measures. HK asks questions in four out of every five moves, SN in only one out of five. This range in "power" scores mirrors previous studies of "conversation," but what is interesting is that when we *average* the scores for very different groups of children, these averages are very similar indeed. There are some obvious developmental changes revealed in Table 3—in terms of increased MLT and initiative being displayed by the Dillon students, but even so, students will contribute their own ideas more often after low control moves (measure C) than after questions

Table 2.   % Teacher Moves in All Categories

5 Dillon	High Control 5.1	2	3	Low Control 4	5	ch	other
HK	2	27	49	8	3	2	11
MK	13	15	23	13	13	15	8
PR	3	11	43	14	3	11	15
SN	0	5	15	22	20	17	20
WB	0	13	13	19	0	38	18

Group Averages

	High Control 5.1	2	3	Low Control 4	5	ch	other
5 Dillon	4	14	29	15	8	17	14
16 Dillon	3	18	26	17	9	16	10
16 Deaf	2	20	26	14	18	2	16
16 Preschool	2	23	24	14	12	?	23
30 TV watchers	3	22	28	11	6	?	23

% Child Moves in All Categories (where child follows teacher)

5 Dillon	High Control 5.1	2	3	Low Control 4	5	✓	✓4	other	(cc)
HK	0	2	3	9	0	56	24	7	
MK	0	8	5	37	0	16	24	10	(42)
PR	0	6	6	29	0	29	24	6	(11)
SN	0	5	3	60	3	15	13	3	(5)
WB	0	7	0	60	0	0	27	(7)	(0)

Group Averages

	High Control 5.1	2	3	Low Control 4	5	✓	✓4	other	(cc)
5 Dillon	0	6	3	39	1	23	22	6	(12)
16 Dillon	1	5	3	38	2	26	19	6	(20)
16 Deaf	1	0	1	25	9	42	9	11	?
16 Preschool	1	1	3	19	6	42	14	13	?
30 TV watchers	1	3	4	15	6	44	9	17	—

1 = enforced repetitions
2 = two-choice questions
3 = 'wh-type' questions
4 = comments and contributions
5 = phatics

ch = chairing
✓ = appropriate answer
✓4 = ✓ plus elaboration
(cc) = % of all child turns
where 1 child speaks
after another child.

(measure D). And in no way do the students' profiles resemble their teachers'. Teachers ask questions, students do not. It seems to us, therefore, that there *is* a powerful common underlying structure in the "language of the classroom." But does teacher power correlate with measures of child initiative?

Table 3.   Measures Used

	Teacher			Child				MLT
	Power	Repair	MLT	Initiative				
				A	B	C	D	
5 Dillon								
HK	78	28	15	39	57	100	30	8
MK	51	21	16	79	83	100	60	16
PR	57	6	17	65	43	100	44	21
SN	20	0	9	80	80	88	45	17
WB	25	0	35	93	100	100	100	75
Group Averages								
5 Dillon	46	11	18	71	73	98	56	27
16 Dillon	47	11	22	67	66	91	45	26
16 Deaf	53	24	8	37	30	66	18	3
16 Preschool	50	?	?	38	31	76	25	?
30 TV watchers	53	13	?	34	29	67	16	?

Adult power moves: 5.1 + 1 + 1 + 2 + 3 (%)
Adult repair: Going backwards to repeat or clarify position (%).
Child initiative: (%)
   A: Overall: $\checkmark4 + 2 + 3 + 4 + 4.2 + 5.2 + \times4$
   B: as A but only after two-choice questions and tags.
   C: as A but only after contributions and phatics.
   D: $\checkmark4$ elaborating on answers to all questions.
     $\checkmark+\checkmark4$
MLT: Mean length of turn in words.

TABLE 4.   Correlations Between Teacher Power and Child Measures

	Child Measures of Initiative				MLT
	A	B	C	D	
5 Dillon:	−.89*	−.71	.61[#]	−.62	−.57
16 Dillon:	−.79***	−.57**	.17[#]	−.41	−.52*
16 Deaf:	−.87***	−.64**	−.44	−.55*	−.59**
16 Preschool:	−.76***	−.57**	−.31	−.81***	?
30 TV watchers:	−.48**	−.06	−.16	−.05	?

   * Significant at .05 level (over .43 for 16 subjects)
  ** Significant at .01 level (over .57 for 16 subjects)
 *** Significant at .001 level (over .74 for 16 subjects)

Pearson Product Moment Correlations: One-tailed tests, with the exception of measure C.
Note: the same conventions used in parentheses in text.

[#] These correlations are neither significant nor meaningful since there is a ceiling effect in children's responses (Table 3). They almost always take up this opportunity to take initiative.

These results, though not all significant, are in the same direction as in previous studies and the relationship between the general initiative measure A and teacher power is remarkably similar. To some extent, then, American students would seem to be "compliant listeners," just as are English preschoolers—and also university (psychology) undergraduates (Kingdon, 1983). The correlation with students' MLT is also very similar to that found (and since replicated) with English deaf children, even though, as one might have expected, the American teenagers say much more overall.

What has not been replicated with this older sample, however, is the different MLT's with which the younger children responded to the various move types. Deaf children tend to give very short answers to two-choice questions, then increasingly longer ones to wh-type questions, contributions, and finally, phatics. One problem in the current study was the sheer paucity of data from the 10-minute sessions; there being too few of each move type in each session to average with any confidence. Using these averages the results showed no significant differences between most teacher moves, the exception being that chairing moves proved to promote significantly longer student MLT's than anything else. Just in case we were missing anything by our averaging procedures, we also entered every single response (from 16 classrooms) to two-choice questions, wh-type questions, and contributions—to no avail. The grand, overall averages were 15, 18, and 18 words, respectively. These teacher moves per se, then, do not engender differential lengths of turn (a finding which replicates Dillon's use of "duration" measures). And yet MLT over sessions was negatively correlated with proportion of questioning (-.52*). One possibility immediately springs to mind. Chairing moves are not counted as "high control" and yet engender long responses. Almost by definition they are least frequent in high power sessions (-.51*) and if we correlate proportion of chairing moves with students' MLT, there is a very strong relationship between them (.72**). Thus although phatics and contributions engender more initiative than do questions, it may well be the number of chairing moves which is responsible for higher MLT's in low power sessions.

One very small point before we leave MLT; it is rather intriguing that of the very few times that teachers answer student questions (4% over the 16 sessions), students in five out of six classrooms responded at greater length to non-elaborated teacher answers than when teachers added a contribution, even though, of course, the latter tended to be longer.

PACE AND PATTER

Who says more overall, teacher or student? What are the "tempi" of lessons like and how does this relate, if at all, to the degree of participation of the pupils? Again using measures based on number of words rather than time, we can replicate Dillon's finding that in sessions where teachers take long turns, students tend to do so too (.66**). We agree with him that there are some important implications associated with this seemingly trivial connection. Our impression is that teachers who take long turns *prior* to asking a question, get more elaborate responses from the students. Some statistical support for this notion is the finding that teachers who take longer turns overall, tend to receive longer replies to wh-type questions from their students (0.72**). But again *average* MLT measures hide some confounding factors. Chairing moves are very short, but get longest responses, so we cannot say that long teacher turns *per se* engender long student turns. To investigate this point further we decided to take the length of each and every turn made by teachers and note the length of the student response to it. There was no significant overall correlation between them. If, however, we looked at each of the common move types in turn, then for wh-type questions and statements the teachers' length of turn was significantly related to how many words their students used in response (.29** and .30** respectively). This was not the case for two-choice questions (.12ns).

One explanation for this finding might be that the teacher who 'sets the scene' more fully before asking questions or making comments, provides students with much more to work out from when they come to reply. This again raises important issues about the relationships between the "declarative" and "interrogative" voices in teaching.

Another aspect to this question is that of pace (simply how many turns get taken in the 10 minutes) and the number of words that get spoken in sessions (the overall total does not vary very much). Over the 16 transcripts teachers and students spoke similar numbers of words (averaged across transcripts: 656 and 877, respectively). Thus, although the teacher usually gets to speak more than any other single person, he or she shares the floor with the students (but note that Dillon analyzed only those transcripts where student talk accounted for at least 40% of total talk). We also found that as pace increased the teachers' share of words spoken went up and that of their students down. So having found that teacher MLT's are *positively* correlated with student MLT's, it is fascinating to find that the total *number* of teacher words is *negatively* correlated with number of student words (-.54*). We must therefore distinguish between teachers who "talk a lot" in terms of taking *longer* turns and those who do so by taking *shorter but more rapid* turns at the expense of student participation. There is also a suggestion, though no more than that, that a fast pace goes hand in hand with more teacher questions (.45) and less student initiative (-.46). Thus, teachers who do *not* tend to preface their short interrogatives with long declaratives have students who say relatively little and show low initiative. A very simple measure of pace, it would seem, might be a useful general guide to how much initiative and talk students are likely to display and, interestingly, to how expansive their answers to the teacher's questions are likely to be.

REPAIR

We did not really expect to find much of interest in our repair analysis since, as we have said, this was devised specifically to look at interactions with children with severe communication problems. However, in our studies with deaf children, we found that teacher repair went hand in hand with child misunderstanding (of the teacher) and we discovered the same phenomenon in the Dillon transcripts (.43*). Why? We will speculate.

Repair covers a variety of activities that need not concern us here. Teachers who are highest in repair on the Dillon transcripts, however, are so, generally speaking, because they keep going back over a question, presumably to obtain a better, fuller or more appropriate answer to it. This is reflected in the finding that, as with deaf children, repair and control are positively correlated (.62**). Teachers high in repair, then, are often repeating their questions. In so doing, they maintain high control in the face of "failure" from the students (it seems reasonable to propose that when a teacher repeats a question it serves as a signal to the students that previous answers were less than exhaustive or compelling).

Such tactics, in our view, are non-contingent. If an intervention fails to get a satisfactory response it should *not* be repeated in the same form. The teacher, ideally, should offer more help. Here, that would involve the teacher making a relevant contribution (perhaps before rephrasing the question) or soliciting one from another pupil (perhaps by a chairing move, for example).

Another feature of teachers high in repair is that they tend to get through more "turns" in the 10-minute sessions (.50*), and their students are low in initiative (-.55*). It seems, then, that if teachers repeat their questions, turns tend to be short, repetitive (by definition) and frequent, with students playing a relatively passive and non-participatory role in the interaction. Perhaps it might be worth discussing the nature of repair after all.

DISCUSSION

We felt it would only be sensible to extend our analysis of teacher control, child initiative and talkativeness to the Dillon transcripts if we could be sure that similar principles apply to them as to our previous work. Using the larger sample, we are confident that they do. Note again, however, that it does not follow that the teachers involved were *trying* to achieve the objectives we are measuring. All we can say is that *if* teachers do want to hear their students' thoughts on a topic, then the same rules of the game apply. The more teachers question students, the less initiative they show and the less they say. As we have found in earlier studies, teachers display a very high incidence of questioning; students very little. We must conclude, then *either* that highly controlling teachers do not want students to show initiative and give loquacious responses, or that they adopt strategies that defeat their own objectives.

But why should teachers "want" their children to air their own views? Let us speculate on some possible reasons for and against. On the "against" side must come a whole range of necessities defined by the job itself. Teachers are paid to educate the young, transmitting knowledge, preparing students both personally and professionally for their future. In the classroom it is the teachers who are aware of the curriculum to be covered, and the aims implicit in that curriculum. They are also responsible for orderly, task-related behavior in lessons, and we would agree that being "in control" of the classroom is a *sine qua non* of education. If students felt free to chip in with their own long-winded opinions on everything, or to offer comments in an *undisciplined* way, this would not be likely to be acceptable in many teaching situations. Take, for example, a math lesson where a complex line of argument must be "got through" quickly and efficiently, with occasional questions to obtain feedback on whether the students are following. By asking questions teachers control the next turn taken, and frequent questioning ensures that children are unlikely to diverge from the teacher's line of thought. But what about in discussions? Again, teachers may feel that *they* know all the points worth discussing, and a planned set of questions will take students through them. Such a plan will be effective— students *do* try to answer questions, but what students actually get out of such an exercise will depend totally on how well the teacher's plan fits in with their existing knowledge and with their abilities to grasp what it is that the teacher is trying to either put across or draw out of them. The trouble with questions is not that they do not "work" but that they work too well. And, after all, it takes up time for students to contribute their own ideas, perhaps at the expense of the number of points a teacher wants to cover.

What is open to question, however, is how far "discussion" is the most efficient situation for these kinds of objectives. And what *is* a discussion anyway? A precise definition which we can all agree upon seems to be extremely elusive. Teachers, dissatisfied with the incessant "talk and chalk" routine, have turned to more interactive modes of teaching for at least some of the day. If we could specify exactly what teachers hope to achieve in these sessions, then we might be able to devise evaluation procedures to measure how far these aims had in fact been fulfilled. How and why do teachers choose a discussion as opposed to paper and pencil tests, essays, lectures, or set reading, etc.?

Unfortunately we do not have much experience with children of this age group. Our views on "discussion" are coloured by our experiences of "conversation" with much younger children who are just beginning to master skills of self-expression, of putting more and more complex ideas into words. But with 16-year-old students, we would expect teachers to be more concerned with relevance and thoughtfulness than with initiative or loquacity per se. On the other hand, there may be occasions when teachers actually wish or need to know what experience or knowledge students already possess on a theme in order to build a lesson which starts from where students "are at" and which then stretches them into higher order activity. There may even be a time and place for encouraging discussion skills per se. Children's school experiences will have given them practise in the responsive role of formal lessons, but they may never have had to take responsibility for actively leading in a rational debate or discussion.

Reasons "for" encouraging initiative thus seem to be of a different order from those "against". Many on the "against" side are practical considerations, those on the "for" side pertain more to vague notions like "active learning," "student participation," or "involvement" in a "relevant" curriculum. The problem is, of course, that teachers probably want to pursue many aims at one and the same time. Some aims will be compatible, others—like questioning and encouraging initiative—are not. Fortunately for us, we need take no responsibility for taking decisions as to when or how often teachers should encourage students to talk *around* a topic (bringing their own experiences and knowledge to bear on it) as against leading them straight through it. Nor have we touched on what is perhaps the major factor in such decisions—the subject matter under discussion. On some topics students' personal experiences will be relevant, even the focus for discussion. On others they will be irrelevant and time-wasting. It struck us that if we were to list the teachers in the transcripts according to their power measures, then subject matter covered would be in the order: history; psychology; Christian relationships and smokers; family relationships; marriage and sex—an ordering which seems to us to move from formal academic topics to more "personal development" ones.

CASE STUDIES

We turn now to a consideration of individual transcripts (Appendix). Having established the general pattern of results, we can use it as a framework for exploring and discussing similarities between, and differences across, recordings. Here we must rely on our intuitions as much as on empirical findings. Not knowing the aims or context of the lesson, or what these students and teachers are normally capable of, we cannot predict how things may have gone if handled differently; we can merely comment on how the students reacted to different aspects within each session.

High Teacher Power Session (78%): HK

This session focussed on possible reasons for Washington's successes (viewed, of course, from an American historical perspective!). It was the session highest in both teacher power and frequency of repair.

The recording illustrates graphically what we have been saying about "conversations" with these characteristics. For example, the teacher's mean length of turn was far below average in comparison with the other teachers in the 16 lessons analyzed; his students were the least loquacious of any group and displayed very low levels of initiative, especially so as the session proceeded, and a high level of questioning had been sustained.

This is without doubt a "lesson" designed to test the students' listening/reading about Washington's military capabilities and it is perhaps unfair to judge it by standards based on analyses of conversations—or is it? In the first 20 rounds (i.e., T + student turns) the pace is fast, turns are very short, and questions seem to be independent of (or non-contingent on) what students have to say. They try to guess at what exactly the teacher is asking for, but, after virtually all pupil responses, he seems to change tack to ask questions from other angles. Finally, at 21a he reveals what it was he was trying to draw out of the students—in the longest turn he makes.

Following this contribution, one student immediately comes back with a question about the draft and, when the teacher *answers* the question the student responds with another contribution, hypothesising that generals could not be as "strict" with a voluntary army (making one of the longest student contributions in this session— 37 words).

But the teacher then takes back control, deflecting the topic to *why* people left the army. Control is reestablished and the fast pace of questioning resumes. Then comes another rare but brief contribution when the teacher tells the class of the French loan of two million dollars. Again, the contribution leads to a question from one of the pupils and the teacher responds—but ends with a question. Then a pupil (the same one?) ignores the teacher's question going back to pursue the implications of the teacher's previous contribution, asking *who* would be repaying the huge debt. HK answers but immediately returns to his initial line of questioning about "why we won." The students settle back to the task of trying to find not only "a" correct answer, but "the" correct answer.

Overall, such a "testing" approach seems to be incompatible with any attempt to stimulate discussion, but then maybe this teacher never intended to. On the rare occasions on which he revealed information and a point of view, students responded by asking questions and trying to reason about implications and so forth. But the teacher quickly terminated such possible points of discussion to pursue answers to a question that had been asked several times before.

It could be argued that HK worked in this way to make the pupils keep on the track, giving an example of how to analyze an issue in a systematic and directed way and testing specific aspects of their knowledge. But is the strategy adopted really the most efficient way to achieve such goals (assuming that this is an appropriate interpretation of what the teacher was trying to do)? The questions themselves seem to us to be general, provocative ones asking for reasons for Washington's success. But little by way of background is given to cue students into profitable areas for discussion. There seemed to us no obvious, single right answer to the questions (perhaps American readers know better?) but the style operates as though there is such an answer. The pace and rate of questioning, the fact that questions are repeated frequently, (indicating dissatisfaction with the answers), suggests that the teacher actually wants only short answers. And this, generally speaking, is what he got.

Average Teacher Power Session (57%): PR

Next in order of "power" are PR and MK, whose profiles on our measures are very similar, with one exception. Whereas PR's session is specifically aimed at answering the question "How could we help Eve?" MK's direction is much less clear and nearly half of the students' turns actually follow on from what another student has just said.

PR tries very hard to keep up a spirit of enquiry as to the problem of Eve's three personalities. Again it seems as if there must be a "right" answer in there somewhere, only it doesn't emerge in the 10 minutes at our disposal. We wondered if we could gain some purchase on the question of whether PR's search for reasons and possible solutions might be betrayed in the number of instances of words like "why," "how," "if," "then," and "because". As one thing our computer can do easily is to pick out such key words, we quickly found that although HK and PR used twice as many "hows" and "whys" than anyone else, it was MK's and WB's students who used twice as many "ifs," "thens," and "becauses." We do hope that other colleagues will have a better stab at this question, but we remain skeptical of direct, high-power attempts to elicit reasons and hypotheses.

Average Teacher Power Session (51%): MK

As we just mentioned, MK's session is exceptional in the frequency of what we usually call child–child moves. In our studies of deaf children such moves were infrequent, and found mainly in low-control sessions. But in the absence of videotape, we may be missing many nods and nonverbal chairing moves, which, if they happened, would bring down MK's power ratio. However, by whatever means, MK certainly did get the students discussing—or rather arguing about—the obviously very topical issue of what to do about all of the seniors being penalized because of the actions of a few. They cover both the justice of the situation, and possible solutions—hence the larger number of "ifs," "thens," and "becauses." The role of the teacher, however, is rather obscure to us. Near the end of the 10 minutes he tries rather unsuccessfully to drag Christian attitudes into it, but we, like the students do not really see what he is getting at.

Lower Teacher Power/Chairing Session (25%): WB

At the other end of the continuum of power lie WB and SN. Although both are low in control, their approaches to the discussion task are quite different. WB spends a good deal of time in a "chairing" role, SN in an "accepting" one. WB makes very long turns himself, with students then contributing at every turn (only one student's turn was unintelligible) and speaking on average at twice the length he did! The cost of course, in such a short session, is in terms of the number of students who get to *take* a turn—only 15 as against SN's 43 and HK's 69.

WB's session starts off with an immediate reference to how his students' previous turns relate to each other, adding his own views on what went on. He then intersperses such moves with short "chairing" moves, such that overall his role is one of chairman/co-discussant. His restraint from asking questions still leaves him "in control"—his students react at length to his and others' ideas and this is the only session where students are given both opportunity and stimulus to give their own experiences, reflect on them, *and* relate their views to those of others.

Low Teacher Power/Phatic Session (20%): SN

SN was lowest in power, and the pupils in his session contributed at a fairly high rate overall. However, their initiative following questions (ie. going on to elaborate on their answers) was only at the normal rate, and their MLT was slightly below the norm.

If "low power" were synonymous with "good" discussion, all measures of student initiative and MLT should be very high. Why are they not? For a start the subject is potentially a very delicate one—how families discuss sex. The students appear to be rather hesitant, and although the teacher is very accepting—reflecting back what they say in a very positive way, his short phatics and chairing moves do not give the students much to go on in terms of the dimensions *he* considers worthwhile or acceptable. He gives few clues within the 10 minutes of whether he approves or disapproves of what they say on this very private topic being given a public airing. Note, in Table 2, how frequent the incidence of phatic responses are in this teacher's responses to students. WB, also relatively low in control, makes no such moves and this leads to two very different episodes. If this was a session for getting several students to contribute on a topic, for *learning about* students as opposed to *teaching* them (in the "traditional" sense) then this has been very successful. It reads, in part, rather like a Rogerian, client-centred therapy session, designed to get students to open up on what is a sensitive topic for group discussion. What it does not do is to follow any clearly definable route. Offerings are not drawn together to be discussed at a higher level. The 10 minutes—as they stand—reveal this teacher as a very sensitive listener but we would like to have seen what he *makes* of the information he so skillfully elicited.

What happened in this "naturally occurring" session is very similar to what we found when we asked teachers of deaf children to adopt a phatic strategy in talking to their children. Children respond to such sessions by talking a lot and making contributions, but seem unwilling (or unable) to comment upon, synthesize, or evaluate the various offerings of different participants.

CAUSE AND EFFECT

In exploring the teacher's role in these sessions, we have made no reference to any differences between individual students. Naturally, we do not deny that students differ in their readiness to show initiative and to talk. Nor do we wish to minimize the importance of the topic under discussion. As we have already said, we also realize that teachers might be pursuing quite different objectives to those implicit in our coding systems. Indeed, in some ways, we find the task of taking apart a teacher's professional activities, without an opportunity to *discuss* with them what we are doing and to negotiate about the nature of the descriptions we offer, somewhat distasteful. However, we obviously could not get our debate off the ground without something "concrete" to discuss and we are delighted that Jim Dillon has taken this initiative. Nonetheless, implicit in our disquiet is a fundamental conceptual issue to do with the value and legitimacy of Olympian pronouncements offered by "outsiders" about interactions between others that take no account of the participants' views, ideas, and criticisms.

There are many factors, then, that might be involved in determining the patterns or correlations we have been discussing between teaching style and pupil response. However, in the past, when we have asked teachers to vary the way in which they maintain classroom conversations with the same children, we have invariably found that the children will respond systematically to changing power in teacher speech. Thus, how forthcoming and loquacious a child appears is determined, in part at least, by the structure and tenor of the interactions in which he is involved. We hope that we have highlighted some of the specific factors that help determine such structures. In so doing, we have not attempted to prescribe how teachers should go about the task of imparting knowledge, helping students to understand, or encouraging them to think and communicate. It is not that we hold no views on such matters. Rather, our existing knowledge is simply not robust enough to make firm pronouncements legitimate.

Notwithstanding these questions and uncertainties, we argue that the dynamics underlying the discussion sessions we have just been considering are governed by similar principles to those at work in less formal conversations with much younger children. In both types of encounter, styles of teacher talk influence the nature and extent of learner participation in similar ways. Our analyses offer teachers an opportunity to orchestrate verbal interactions with their students with a greater degree of confidence than may have been the case previously.

In responses to our earlier draft manuscript, it has been pointed out that there is a body of literature which suggests that the nature or form of questions addressed to learners influences what they learn and remember. Furthermore, we have provided no evidence that increasing pupil participation has any effect on how and what they learn. We shall not attempt to review this large and somewhat equivocal literature here, but we would like to discuss our current findings in the light of some of the more relevant studies. Various intervention studies have shown that helping teachers to change their questioning style away from relatively specific questions demanding factual, "correct" answers, towards more open ones which invite reflection, abstraction, and reasoning may affect what and how children learn. Also relevant are studies which have explored relationships between the way in which parents talk to their children and features of children's development. Sigel and his colleagues, for example, (e.g., Sigel & McGillicuddy-Delisi, in press) have used the concept of "distancing strategies" (as we have mentioned, other theorists talk of "decontextualisation," "decentration," or "disembedding") to study relationships between parent–child discourse and the development of abstract thinking in children. They have provided some evidence to show that parental talk which impels children to think, consider and puzzle about their experiences is positively correlated with aspects of children's problem solving abilities. Parent talk which does not encourage the child to reflect and think about what is happening in the world, on the other hand, does not correlate with and, by implication, does not engender effective reasoning and problem solving skills. While different forms of questions help to differentiate high level parental distancing behavior from lower levels, it is interesting that Sigel et al. conclude that the *forms* of talk (e.g., inquiry, imperative, telling) are probably less important than their *content*. Put another way, statements to children which express uncertainty, speculation, or contradiction may be as effective as questions in helping a child to "distance" himself from his immediate concerns.

Along somewhat similar lines, Robinson and Rackstraw (1975), after a series of studies of the relationships between questioning, social class, and educational performance in the U.K., concluded that:

> Mothers who were providing clear structuring, making materials relevant, assimilable and challenging, had children who were curious and proficient in the verbal expression of their curiosity as well as knowledgeable. . . . Interestingly enough, direct maternal attempts to focus attention or to arouse curiosity through posing questions bore no relationship to the children's behaviour. Children would feed on food provided, but appeared to be uninfluenced by the chef's recommendations.

Our own view is that the high incidence of teacher questioning in schools serves no special intellectual or linguistic purpose *per se*. Rather, it fulfills the function of group control (see also French & MacLure, 1979). Before concluding this argument, however, we would like to offer some views about where we might direct our attentions in exploring such issues further.

SOME QUESTIONS FOR FURTHER THOUGHT

The first issue we would raise for discussion involves a brief comparison of aspects of questioning in the home and at school. The second concerns the need to look more analytically at the nature and consequences of the declarative voice in influencing learning and understanding while the third focuses on the potential rewards of looking beyond the kinds of "move–move" sequence in interactions (e.g., question–answer exchanges) which characterize our own analyses and are typical of many others. First, questions at home and school.

There is evidence showing that the topics, themes, or ideas that are involved in parent–child exchanges in the preschool years are most likely to arise out of initiatives or overtures made by the child (Wells, 1979). At home, in comparison to school, young children are more likely to display "epistemic" behaviour; asking questions, participating in relatively long discussions, and considering why, how, when, and where things happen, for example (Tizard & Hughes, 1984). Interactions in school are usually initiated by teachers, and, as we have seen, likely to be introduced and sustained with frequent questions.

Given such differences in the balance of initiative at home and school it seems likely to us that parental questions (and other utterances) are more likely to arise in response to topics, issues or themes that are initiated by children whereas, in school, they are often teacher-initiated. Further, we suggest that the home context is more likely to create conditions in which what adults do, ask, say, and suggest to children is contingent upon what children themselves are trying to understand, and that such contingency is important in promoting learning and understanding (Wood, 1986). In school, questions are less likely to be contingent upon a child's line of thought (in fact, the child's usually has to be contingent upon the teacher's). The differences in patterns of contingency coupled with the inhibiting effects of frequent questions on initiative and loquacity help to explain why children often appear more curious, involved, and loquacious at home than at school.

In our present analyses, we noted how questions that came after relatively long contributions from the teacher seemed likely to meet with lengthy answers from pupils. It may be that by setting up a discourse space prior to asking questions (setting the scene with contributions) teachers can establish better conditions for contingent demands. We have noted elsewhere (Wood et al, 1986), that teacher questions which come "out of the blue" are less likely to meet with an elaborate response from a child than those which relate to what has just been said (particularly if said by the child). Although speculative and not properly formalized, such observations imply that detailed, analytic examinations of sequences of discourse could help us to understand what constitutes an effective and timely question. It may also shed some light onto the effects of different contexts, such as home and school, on the epistemic activity of children.

Sigel, as we have already said, has suggested that the content of instructional language may be more important than its form. In our small scale study of the effects of different styles of teacher talk on the language of young children, we found that the statements or contributions made by children as young as four years of age parallel those of the teacher. Where the teacher, for example, was involved in speculating, reasoning, and wondering, children tended to adopt a similar "register" or stance.

So far as we are aware, intervention studies designed to examine the effects of different types of questions on pupil performance have failed to explore any potential differences occasioned by the use of different forms of the declarative voice. If the results of our small-scale study generalize, then it will turn out to be the case that the skillful use of more challenging statements might not only encourage children to reciprocate in kind but also to become more active, loquacious, and involved as well. Such hypotheses remain untested but seem amenable to inquiry. Thus, we join Dillon in his quest to tie down some of the alternatives to questioning. Perhaps the people who can so ably describe "intelligent questions" might also be persuaded to try their hand at "intelligent comments." Perhaps, if and when they do, questions can be discussed rather than asked!

REFERENCES

French, P. & MacLure, M. (1979). Getting the right answer and getting the answer right. *Research in Education, 22*, 1–23.

French, P. & MacLure, M. (1981). Teachers' questions: pupils' answers. An investigation of questions and answers in the infant classroom. *First Language, 2*, 31.

Kingdon, J. (1983). *Face-to-Face Instruction in Relation to Teaching-Strategies and Children's Perceived Ability* M. Phil. Thesis, Nottingham University.

Murphy, C. (1983). *Talking about Television: Opportunities for Language Development in Young Children.* Report on IBA Research Fellowship. London: Independent Broadcasting Authority.

Robinson, P. & Rackstraw, S.J. (1975). *Questioning and Answering.* Sydney, Macquarie University: Joseph Rowntree Memorial Trust Project (Now at Bristol University).

Sigel, I.E. & McGillicuddy-Delisi (in press). Parents as teachers to their children: a distancing behaviour model. To appear in A.D. Pellegrini and T.D. Yawkey (eds) *The Development of Oral and Written Language: Readings in Developmental and Applied Linguistics.* Norwood, NJ: Ablex.

Tizard, B. & Hughes, M. (1984). *Young Children Learning. Talking and Thinking at Home and School.* London: Fontana.

Wells, G. (1979). Variation in child language. In P. Fletcher and H. Garman (eds) *Language Acquisition.* Cambridge: Cambridge University Press.

Wells, G. (in preparation). The language experience of five-year-old children at home and at school. (Draft only)

Wood, D.J. (1980). Models of Childhood. In A.J. Chapman and D.M. Jones (eds) *Models of Man.* Leicester: British Psychological Society.

Wood, D.J. (1986). Aspects of teaching and learning. In M.P.M. Richards and P.L. Light (eds) *Children of Social Worlds*. London: Blackwell.

Wood, D.J., Bruner, J.S., & Ross, G. (1976). The role of tutoring in problem solving. *Journal of Child Psychology and Psychiatry, 17,* 89–100.

Wood, D.J. & Cooper, P.J. (1980). An experimental study of Maternal Facilitation for 4 to 5 year-old children's memory for recent events. Paper presented to XXIInd International Congress of Psychology, Leipzig, East Germany.

Wood, D.J., Wood, H.A., Griffiths, A.J., & Howarth, C.I. (1986). *Teaching and Talking with Deaf Children*. London & New York: Wiley.

Wood, D.J., MacMahon, L., and Cranstoun, Y. (1980). *Working with Under-fives*. London: Basil Blackwell.

Wood, D.J., and Middleton, D.J. (1975). A study of assisted problem solving. *British Journal of Psychology, 66,* 181–191.

Wood, D.J., Wood, H.A., Griffiths, A.J., Howarth, S.P., & Howarth, C.I. (1982). The structure of conversations with 6- to 10-year-old deaf children. *Journal of Child Psychology and Psychiatry, 23,* 295–308.

Wood, D.J., Wood, H.A., & Middleton, D.J. (1978). An experimental evaluation of four face-to-face teaching strategies. *International Journal of Behaviour Development, 1,* (1), 131–147.

Wood, H.A. & Wood, D.J. (1984). An experimental evaluation of five styles of teacher conversation on the language of hearing-impaired children. *Journal of Child Psychology and Psychiatry, 25,* (1), 45–62.

Wood, H.A. and Wood. D.J. (1983). Questioning the preschool child. *Educational Review, 35,* 149–162.

CHAPTER 15

Review of Pedagogical Perspectives

William W. Wilen

Teacher Development and Curriculum Studies
Kent State University
Kent, OH. 44242

Those associated with the field of education have long recognized the influential role a teacher's questions play in the classroom. Since the first systematic research study on questioning was conducted during the early 1900's, considerable data have been collected on the nature of teachers' questions and the impact they have on students and learning. While this research continues to grow in the 1980's, the trend of investigating questions and questioning from a multidisciplinary view appears to be developing. The realization is that researchers from a variety of disciplines and perspectives can make significant contributions to the information on questioning. The six studies reviewed here reflect this trend by representing the areas of affective education, educational psychology, philosophy, preschool and deaf education, curriculum, teacher training, and speech communication.

INTERACTION PATTERNS

The purpose of the Swift, Gooding and Swift study (Chapter 10) was to objectively describe and analyze the teachers' questioning behaviors in the taped episodes. Although the focus was on the use of wait time because of the authors' long-time interest in this questioning skill, other aspects of the interaction patterns were analyzed. These included cognitive levels of questions, how teachers replied to student answers, alternatives teachers used to stimulate discussion, and the extent of teacher and student talk.

Three forms of wait time were investigated: (1) *wait time 1*—the pause after teachers ask questions and before students respond, (2) *wait time 2*—the pause after students respond before the teacher reacts, and (3) *wait time 3*—the pause between student–student dialogue. Wait time data were gathered using an innovative computer-driven apparatus that measured wait time accurate to .01 seconds.

The authors found the interaction patterns in the transcripts were generally similar to the science classrooms they have investigated. Three of the interaction patterns were classified as discussions (guided and permissive), one was labelled a recitation during which the teacher asked 53 questions in 9.5 minutes, and the last contained elements of a recitation and permissive discussion. Students spoke on the average of 57% of the time and teachers, 43%. This was the most unusual finding because research has generally revealed that teachers speak 75–85% of the time.

The wait time teachers used during the recitations and discussions was found to be short, typical of most discussions. Wait time 1 was found to be 1.1 seconds, wait time 2 was .6 seconds and wait time 3, .3 seconds. For the most part the cognitive levels of teachers' questions were at the memory and convergent levels. Students asked few questions except in one class where teachers and students each asked ten questions, mostly at the higher divergent and evaluative levels. Teachers replied to students' responses by primarily using bland or encouraging remarks, and when the teachers used alternatives to questions, they were primarily in the form of explanations.

The authors concluded that the teachers and students in all the lessons lacked an understanding of the discussion process and therefore, displayed few discussion skills. The classes would have benefited particulary from increases in wait time because higher cognitive levels of thinking would have been attained. They further recommended that more research needs to be conducted on teachers' replies to students' responses and the use of alternatives to teachers' questions as a means to stimulate discussion.

The Swift, Gooding, and Swift analysis convincingly documents teachers' lack of those discussion skills that contribute to effective interaction. Teacher education programs need to intensively train their preservice and inservice teachers in the application of discussion skills to increase the probability that discussion-related objectives will be reached.

DISCUSSION METHODS

The purpose of Roby's analysis of the taped episodes was to categorize the types of discussions conducted and describe how the kinds of questions asked by the teachers contributed toward the development of the discussions. The author devised an elaborate typology of group classroom conversations and questions based on his study of a wide range of sources from his interest in Socrates to analyzing experiences in his own classroom. The types of discussions (group conversations) can be placed on a continuum with quasi-discussions at the extremes. The primary reason for the location of the discussion models depends on whether the teacher or students, or both, have control of the right answers. The quasi-discussions are the Quiz Show and the Bull Session and the discussions are Problematical, Dialectical, and Informational, located around the center of the continuum:

Quiz Show—students try to discover the right answers to subject matter oriented teacher questions. The basic question is the Fact Finder often supplemented with the Prompter and occasionally the Prober.

Bull Session—both teacher and students have the right answers which they share, generally without the need for support, within a permissive atmosphere. The primary question is the Inviter.

Dialectical Discussion—focus is on expressing, comparing and refining student (and teacher) opinions using broader understandings. The basic question is the Inviter with support from the Stretcher and the Devil's Advocate.

Informational Discussion—focus is on discussing controversial issues within a permissive atmosphere. The primary questions are the Inviter and Fact Finder.

Problematical Discussion—there are three varieties: Perennial, Particular, and Cryptic. A Perennial Problem Discussion focuses on broad and complex issues of society for which there are no absolute answers; a Particular Problem Discussion focuses on specific problematic situations that are solvable; a Cryptic Problem Discussion focuses on the meaning of words. The primary question is the Puzzler with support from a variety of others depending on the kind and focus of the particular discussion.

The author found each transcript discussion represented one of his discussion models. In analyzing the use of questions, and directional turns within the discussions, the author concluded that the discussions were narrow with teachers not realizing the flexibility they have to move discussions in different directions depending on the goals. Another conclusion is that all discussions do not need to be teacher-led. Teachers need to demonstrate more flexibility by shifting authority to their students during discussions so that, ". . . students can learn to become their own teachers."

Roby provides an insightful and practical approach to categorizing and analyzing the varieties of discussions and the types of questions teachers ask in the classroom. Teachers will be able to perceive a greater variety of purposes for conducting discussions in their class-rooms. In addition, planning will be facilitated with information on the kinds of questions appropriate for particular discussions.

POWER AND INITIATIVE

The purpose of the Woods' study was to analyze the taped episodes in terms of the control teachers exerted through their questioning behaviors and the initiative students took in class discussions. A secondary purpose was to compare the data from the transcripts, which involved high school students, with the data they have gathered from their own research on hearing and deaf preschool children.

In their research in England, the authors have found that teachers control discourse in the classroom through their verbalizations by limiting students' freedom to participate, sometimes by the kinds of questions they ask. For example, teachers use of "two-choice questions," from their systematic observation instrument, requires students to answer only yes/no or to choose one of two alternatives. The basis for the authors' system of analysis is five main conversational moves arranged in descending order from high degree of control to low control. A statistical analysis of the data collected yielded a "power" score.

The student displays initiative by asking a question or making a comment other than that which was specifically requested by the teacher. The authors have found that while children readily answer teachers' questions, they rarely ask questions. The reason lies in the teacher–child power relationship and the inhibition of children to challenge the control of the teacher. Another area related to student initiative is "repair." It is the attempt by the teacher to go "backward" in the conversation by asking students for clarification, or repeating or redirecting questions, for example. The authors' research has found that repair is closely associated with control because as teachers ask more questions to repair a response, students show less initiative.

Findings related to the analysis of the taped teachers' questioning behaviors were similar to those in the authors' research with deaf and hearing children. Teacher control ranged from high power, exhibited by a teacher conducting a recitation in which students displayed very low initiative, to low power in a discussion during which students displayed only average initiative. This was probably due to the topic (sex in marriage). Data supported the positive relationship of teacher power to student initiative. It was also found that control and repair were positively correlated. Repair was highest for the teacher conducting the recitation and lowest for two low power teachers conducting discussions.

The authors concluded that teachers' questions can stifle students' initiative and serve more the purpose of group control than stimulating thinking. Students also adjust and change according to the extent of control being displayed. The authors point out, though, that their system is based on the assumption that one of the teachers' major goals in a discussion is to increase students' initiative and loquacity. The transcript teachers' lessons may not have had this objective in mind and therefore, it may not be fair to judge their performances with the criteria inherent in the Woods' system.

The Woods have provided an important beginning understanding of the role and influence that teachers' verbal structuring behaviors have on classroom interaction. Teachers will be able to systematically gather and analyze information about their behaviors to determine the extent they encourage or inhibit student involvement in classroom interaction.

QUESTIONS AND ARGUMENTS

The purpose of Russell's study was to examine the attitude the taped episodes' teachers had toward authority and the role of questions in determining how arguments are developed and discussed. Teachers can possess a traditional or rational attitude toward authority with the difference being how knowledge claims are presented. The presentation or request for support, or evidence, for a knowledge claim would be an indication of a rational approach. As the author stated, the teacher is an authority, because of his or her position, and in authority as a result of possessing certain knowledge. In order to determine the attitudes teachers had towards the authority of knowledge, criteria were selected to serve as the basis for analysis and judgment. Four elements of rational argument were identified such that if they were being developed through questions in a class discussion and properly related to one another, the teacher would be judged as possessing a rational attitude toward authority. The elements are:

1. *Warrant*—rule, theory or reason.
2. *Backing*—assumptions and fundamental perspective supporting a Warrant.
3. *Data*—known facts and information.
4. *Conclusion*—resulting interpretation.

The discussions analyzed from the taped episodes were found to range from one lesson in which Backing was explicit in the argument to another in which only Data appeared in the discussion and no argument had been developed. The other three lessons fell in between with questions being used to develop arguments but very little or no request for Backing to support Warrants. Although it is tempting to conclude that the teachers do not possess a rational attitude toward authority, the author cautions that the transcripts were only excerpts of classes and were not selected based on the criteria related to arguments.

It was concluded that the transcript teachers were not familiar with the analysis of arguments. Data collected by the author related to his research with science teachers supports this. A final caution by the author is that rationality of a teacher's argument should not necessarily be a major criterion on judging effective teaching. Teaching is too complex an act by virtue of the diverse variables involved, such that it would be inappropriate to single out only one dimension to evaluate teaching.

Russell showed that questions can serve a variety of functions in the classroom, one of which is to encourage students to develop rational arguments. Teachers now have available an analytical scheme to evaluate the extent the kinds of questions they ask in the classroom facilitate achieving lesson goals.

QUESTIONS, RESPONSES AND REACTIONS

The purpose of the Klinzings' study was to describe and analyze the taped episodes in terms of the teachers' questioning and student reaction behaviors. A conceptual framework for the development of categories was devised based on a review of the research and their experience as teacher trainers. The resulting systematic observation instrument was then applied in the analysis of the tapes. Implications for the improvement of instruction were provided for each of the teachers in the form of recommendations.

Based on the data collected, the authors characterized the conversations as subject matter, problem-solving, or issue-oriented discussions. A variety of cognitive levels of questions were used as appropriate for the perceived purposes of the discussions. Data were reported on the extent teachers used direct and indirect behaviors to guide the discussions. Frequencies of teacher and student talk were reported with specific focus on student questions and statements, and teacher reactions to student responses.

Several of the recommendations offered were common to the performances of most of the teachers. More interaction needed to be stimulated by working with the students' responses. Probing initial student responses for the purpose of seeking clarification and extending thinking would have added depth to the discussions. Another recommendation was to facilitate more student–student interaction. This could have been accomplished by having more students respond to individual questions, asking students to relate their ideas and probe each others' responses, and using redirection. The final major suggestion was to reduce control of the discussion by stimulating more student involvement. This could have been facilitated by asking only key questions, as opposed to frequent questions, and avoiding reacting to every student response. These approaches will help keep the discussion from moving back to the teacher.

Although the discussions varied greatly, the authors discovered there were many characteristics in common with classroom discussions in West Germany. Teachers know how to directly stimulate a variety of levels of thinking through their questions but not how to use more indirect techniques to guide a discussion. The authors thought teachers unconsciously tend to be more concerned about how they are expected to act than as moderators of discussions. This is obvious in their control of discussions and their unwillingness (or inability) to encourage more student involvement. They concluded that much more needs to be accomplished to assist teachers and students to develop and improve their discussion skills.

The Klinzings provided a comprehensive and sophisticated conceptual framework and method of systematic observation to gather information and analyze teachers' questions and the reactive verbalizations of students. Teacher education programs need to provide preservice and inservice teacher training in working with students' responses to stimulate more depth in thinking and participation.

GROUP PROCESSES

The purpose of Francis' study was to analyze the group dynamics of the classroom discussions represented by the taped episodes. For this purpose the author involved a resource group of inservice teachers, with whom she has been involved as the project director, who have been trained in the observation and analysis of group processes.

The analysis of the discussions was based on the task systems involved. According to the author, the possible task systems range from the achievement of cognitive/perceptual learning goals to psychological change goals. Students involved in discussions with these goals are expected to demonstrate understanding and insight in connection with the content being taught. Another task system available to the teacher relates to process goals which focus on providing students opportunities to demonstrate awareness and insight related to the discussion process and skills. The psychological levels involved in a task normally could also be analyzed but, because of the nature of audiotapes, the necessary nonverbal information was not available.

Analysis of the transcripts revealed that the goal of three of the five teachers was to assist students to achieve awareness and insight about the topics involved, a psychological learning/change task. The goal of the other two teachers was to test students' understanding of the reading they had completed, a cognitive/perceptual task. None of the teachers made learning and practicing the discussion process a task.

The resource group was particularly critical of the lack of discussion skills displayed by the teacher and students. Disappointing were the traditionally arranged physical settings ("appropriate for teacher/student questioning, not for discussion"), large group sizes characteristic of typical secondary classrooms, and leadership style which was judged to be teacher-dominated ("students have no opportunity to lead"). They concluded that the taped episodes were not illustrations of effective classroom discussions.

Francis shows that teachers need to prepare their students with discussion skills in order to effectively interact. Teachers also need to monitor the display of these skills in discussion situations. Teacher education programs need to train teachers in specific discussion skills and they, in turn, need to train their students how to participate in group interaction more effectively.

CONCLUSION

Although the analyses of the taped episodes were quite diverse in the perspectives taken by the researchers, several generalizations about discussions and teachers' questioning behaviors can be offered based on the findings presented.

The first is that classroom interaction patterns are generally similar across grade levels, subject areas, and cultures. This seems particularly evident in terms of the range of types of discussions in which teachers involve students, variety of questions asked, and use of a narrow range of traditional questioning techniques applied to conduct discussions.

Another generalization is that teachers tend to excessively control discussions. Discussions are traditionally teacher-led with teachers asking questions, students responding, and teachers providing feedback. Within this familiar format, little opportunity is provided for students to interact with other students, ask questions, or initiate comments.

A final generalization that relates to the others is that teachers need to learn more about conducting discussions. Some of the skills considered essential to effective discussions that were not displayed consistently by the teachers in the taped episodes were: arranging the physical setting of the classroom to be conducive for communication; stimulating students to assume more control and responsibility for discussions; using questions to encourage students to rationally support knowledge claims; working more with student responses by, for example, probing for clarification and extension of thinking; encouraging students to ask questions; and using a variety of alternatives to asking questions when appropriate.

The major implication for the improvement of instruction is that preservice and inservice teachers need to be trained in, and have an opportunity to apply, those skills that contribute toward conducting effective discussions.

The research studies have provided pertinent information on the role questions and questioning play in conducting effective discussions. Although the findings were based on only five excerpts of longer classroom discussions, the data gathered and analyzed supported and confirmed, for the most part, previous studies conducted by the researchers. The multidisciplinary studies reported here make a positive contribution toward answering the more complex questions about questioning in the classroom setting.

APPENDIX

Classrooms Analyzed in This Study

Table A1. **Classroom Characteristics**

	HK	MK	PR	SN	WB
Teacher					
Sex	male	male	male	male	male
Experience	9 yrs	4 yrs	12 yrs	5 yrs	2 yrs
School	D.	L.	W.	M.	D.
Course					
Title	U.S. History	Christian Relationships	Psychology	Marriage	Society and Christian Lifestyle
Level*	jr.	jr.–sr.	sr.	sr.	jr.
Topic	American Revolution	senior privileges, smoking	multiple personality	sex in homelife	changing parent–child relations
Time					
Date	Nov. 8	Oct. 21	Oct. 26	Oct. 13	Nov. 8
Day	Tues	Fri	Weds	Thurs	Tues
Hour	8:15	10:35	11:30	2:00	10:40
Class length	40 mins.	40 mins.	57 mins.	45 mins.	40 mins.
Tape excerpt	10′ 5″	10′ 14″	10′ 16″	9′ 54″	10′ 48″
Seating	Rect.	Rect.	Rect.	Rect.	Rect.
Students					
Number present	30	28	27	24	41
% Male	60	43	48	58	56
% White	83	100	11	13	93

* jr. = 11th grade (16–17 yrs old); sr. = 12th, final grade (17–18 yrs. old)
** 100%-White = Black + Latino + Oriental, etc.

A1. HK ON THE AMERICAN REVOLUTION

1a. What—I want to go into another question about his military capabilities. What was it that made him militarily successful? What was it about his strategy that enabled him to be successful? (Howard) (t-11) (t-11) [teacher-11 secs]

1b. He didn't fight straight out like the British. He fought behind brick walls, trees, and stuff like that. (b-6) [boy-6 secs]

2a. Did you read anywhere in the book where his army was destroyed? (t-6)

2b. No. (s-1)

3a. That his army was destroyed—did you see that anywhere? That Washington's army was destroyed? (t-6)

3b. Not completely. (s-1)

4a. Not completely? (Tony) (t-1)

4b. They were outsmarted, but not destroyed. (b-3)

5a. Well, is there a difference between those two statements? (t-3)

5b. Yeah, there is. (b-1)

6a. Well, what is that difference? (t-1)

6b. To be outsmarted (-) out of the larger army. (b-4)

6c. Other than that, if you're destroyed, you're destroyed, you're dead. (b-2)

7a. If they're destroyed, they're dead? And what if they are outsmarted? (t-5)

7b. That means they could get by or move into better territory. (b-5)

8a. So, what do you think Washington's success was as a military leader?—taking into context, you know, tactics and so on. (Tony) (t-9)

8b. He was always taking it step by step, he never wanted to be outsmarted. (b-4)

9a. But you said he was, at times. (t-2)

9b. Right, yeah, but then you asked what about his success. (b-3)

10a. Well, why is it that he—(ah, Jim) (t-2)

10b. He was able to go back and fight harder; even after he was outsmarted, he was able to get 'em back on the rebound. (b-7)

11a. Ah, because why? (Chris) (t-2)

11b. Maybe he had to learn by the mistakes that happened, to learn by them and realize what it was that had gone wrong. (g-11)

12a. Well, did the colonies have a large army? (t-2)

12b. No, they—I don't know. (g-4)

13a. Those of you who worked on that question about the army, and some of the problems of wartime government—what did you find out about the army itself? (Howard) (t-8)

13b. Well, the colonial army was really outnumbered by the British. Some of the people—the lack of interest by some of the colonies and stuff like that—most of the colonies had to fight it by themselves, so they were outnumbered. (b-16)

14a. Well, OK, how did one get to be a member of the army? By way of the draft? (t-5)

14b. No, more or less by volunteering. (b-2)

15a. By volunteering. Could Congress, could Congress tell the states to furnish more men? (t-9)

15b. No, I don't think so. (b-1)

16a. What did Congress have to do? (t-2)

16b. NO RESPONSE (4 secs) (x-4)

17a. Now, you're on the right track. What did Congress have to do in order to get more men into the army? (t-4)

17b. I guess make it worth their while. (b-2)

18a. Well, let's get away from pay. Let's assume that wages are not a factor at the moment. If the army is a volunteer army, as such, where did people volunteer to? (t-11)

18b. NO RESPONSE (5 secs) (x-5)

19a. In other words, were there national offices established by Congress to which a person went that wanted to volunteer? (t-10)

19b. You'd just go find where the army was, and join it. (b-2)

20a. Not exactly. They went by way of what vehicle, do you know? (t-6)

20b. (-) their colonies back home. (g-6)

21a. That's right, they went by way of each colony. So, what we're saying, then, is that Congress could not merely order a colony to furnish more men. It had to ask a colony for more men. And if people did not volunteer into that colonial army—the Virginia army, for instance, the South Carolina army—if people didn't then they just didn't. So, Washington commanded an all-volunteer army. And another problem with that army—in addition to just sheer numbers, it's not professional as such, it's all volunteer, and people come and go as they want to. Now, when you have a person leading that type of a military group, you certainly are not leading a professional army, and something that he does with it is very important. It's not that large—probably the most they ever had at one time was maybe 5000 people. He never permits what little army they had to be destroyed. But that's not to say he never lost. (t-59)

21b. When did the draft come about? Or when was it, you know, where it was not a come and go situation? (b-6)

22a. It would—Tony, it's strictly a guess on my part, but I think that the Civil War was the first time that there was a wartime draft. (t-7)

22b. Because at this time leaders, like Washington, they couldn't give orders and be mean, 'bcause it was a come and go thing, and they'd just leave, so as you (-) and come out, you get more strict generals. (b-11)

23a. That's right. Do you know why people left, by the way? Why, we say, they come and go? Do you know why they left? (t-5)

23b. To do the harvest. (b-1)

24a. They went home and farmed. When it was time to harvest the crops—stop fighting, go home and take care of the home front, and when you come back, you fight again. That was even true to some extent in the Civil War; that was not terribly uncommon. OK, so we've kind of covered leadership and some of the things that Washington brought with it. Why else did they win? Leadership is important, that's one. (t-19)

24b. France gave 'em help. (b-3)

25a. OK, so France giving aid is an example of what? France is an example of it, obviously. (t-7)

25b. Aid from allies. (b-1)

26a. Aid from allies, very good. Were there any other allies who gave aid to us? (t-5)

26b. Spain. (b-1)

27a. Spain. Now, when you say aid, you can define that? How can we define aid? (Greg) (t-7)

27b. Help. (b-1)

28a. Define "help." Spell it out for me. (t-3)

28b. Assistance. (b-1)

29a. Spell it out for me. (Joe) (t-1)

29b. They taught the men how to fight the right way. (b-5)

30a. Who taught? (t-1)

30b. The allies. (b-1)

31a. Where? When? (t-1)

31b. In the battlefield. (g-1)

32a. In the battlefield? (t-1)

32b. The allies would help if they would gain something after their help, a reward or something. (b-7)

33a. Well, Greg has said that we received aid from France. I've merely indicated what do you mean by aid? What do you mean by help? What do you by assistance? Those are general words. Can you spell out concretely, exactly what that aid was? (t-12)

33b. Food and ammunition and stuff like that. (b-3)

34a. Food, ammunition. (t-2)

34b. Clothes. (b-1)

35a. Was there anything more important than all of those? (t-2)

35b. Men. (b-2)

36a.   Did they send large numbers of men here? (Miss Edwards)
       (t-2)
36b.   Money. (g-1)
37a.   Money. France loaned us $2 million. [Is that all?] That was
       a lot in those days. We also received some from Spain. We
       also received some from Holland, eventually. OK, so we have
       leadership of Washington, we have foreign aid—now, are there
       any other reasons why we won? (t-20)
37b.   I wanted to go back—after this is over, we have to repay
       them, right? (b-3)
38a.   We—yes, we do. (t-2)
38b.   So that might mean that taxes start higher. (b-3)
39a.   No, oddly enough, no. (t-2)
39b.   Who'd pay for it—Congress itself? (b-2)
40a.   Congress would have to pay itself in the form of gold or silver,
       it could pay that debt off. Now, we could have reneged on
       that debt, but that's another chapter. We'll get to that, in fact—
       we do give that money back. Are there any other reasons why
       we won? (Fred) (t-15)
40b.   The French, I think they brought some military genius—Van
       du Peau or something like that. (b-6)
41a.   Well, is that not part of foreign aid? Remember, we asked
       about aid? Those Frenchmen who enlisted or came here on
       their own to fight, would I think be a form of aid, whether
       it was individual or not. (t-16)
41b.   Propaganda. (b-1)
42a.   Propaganda. (t-1)
42b.   Get people thinking the right way. (b-3)
43a.   That's right. Is propaganda important in war? (t-2)
43b.   Control the negative ideas (-). (Chris) (b-5)
43c.   I'd say yes, for getting men. (-) their own way of saying, we'll
       fight for you. (g-10)
44a.   What else? (t-1)
44b.   Yes, (-) organized army or something (-). (g-6)
45a.   From the colonies? (t-1)
45b.   Yes. (g-1)
46a.   Well, you said something a while ago about tactics. Could
       that have played a role in our winning? Could that play a
       role, colonial tactics? (t-10)
46b.   They weren't predictable. [What?] They weren't predictable.
       (g-1)
47a.   What do you mean by "not predictable"? (t-1)

47b. They couldn't be—they couldn't guess at what they were gonna do before they did it. (g-7)

47c. Would it be because they attacked at night? (b-2)

48a. Did they? (t-1)

48b. Sometimes they did. (b-2)

49a. Was that bad? (t-1)

49b. No. (b-1)

50a. No—I don't mean "bad," was that different? (t-3)

50b. Yes. (b-1)

51a. How did Europeans fight? (Joe) (t-1)

51b. Straight out in lines, in the fields. (b-3)

52a. Open in the fields? in lines? (t-2)

52b. In lines, straight. (b-2)

53a. How did the colonials fight? (t-2)

53b. Behind trees. (b-1)

54a. Behind trees? (t-1)

54b. On farms, wherever they could hide. (b-3)

55a. Was that fighting by the rules? (t-2)

55b. No. There was no rules. (b-2)

56a. Is there such a thing as fighting by the rules? (t-2)

56b. That's what war is, though. (b-3)

57a. Is war fought by rules? (t-2)

57b. Heck, no. It's supposed to be. (s-3)

58a. Golombiesky, is it fought by rules? (t-2)

58b. It's supposed to be. It usually isn't, though. (b-3)

59a. Can you give me an example of something that would be unfair in time of war? (t-3)

59b. Fire, and shooting on an ambulance. (b-4)

60a. What's unfair in time of war, Howard? (t-2)

60b. Killing somebody that's surrendering. (b-2)

61a. All right. Can you name me anything else? (t-2)

61b. A paratrooper is falling in flames and you're not supposed to—you shoot him—No! (g-11)

62a. What can't you do during time of war? (Tony) (t-2)

62b. Kill prisoners of war. (b-4)

63a. Kill prisoners of war. Can you torture 'em? (t-2)

63b. Yes/No. (s-6)

63c. You're not supposed to, but they have been known to do it on occasion. (laughter) (b-4)

END. Is there anything else that people would look down upon a nation for, if a nation did it? /END/10 mins., 5 secs

A2. MK ON STUDENTS' SMOKING PRIVILEGES

1a. Does anybody have any strong feelings about that—about what happened—about the seniors having their privileges taken away? [t-8] (teacher-8 secs)

1b. I think (-) [s-5] (student-5 secs)

1c. Seniors should get to do what they want. (OK, John) [b-2] (boy-2 secs)

1d. If the seniors can't handle it, the juniors will handle it. [b-5]

1e. Ah! (-) why can't you smoke? (-) [s-6]

1f. Why can't you just smoke cigarettes at this school? [b-3]

1g. 'Cause it's illegal. [b-1]

1h. Why? [b-1]

1i. 'Cause you're a minor. [b-1]

1j. 'Cause like at Loyola, all right, and Loyola is just as strict as this school, and seniors can smoke there. [b-7]

1k. Yeah, but they probably got a whole lounge. (OK) [b-2]

1l. I don't see why just because of what a few kids did, the rest of us have to suffer—it's not fair. [g-5]

1m. (-) this neighborhood. [s-9]

1n. What if you're 18? [b-1]

2a. Still can't. The reason we say that if you're 18 is because, if we would let people who are going to school here—it'd be kinda two-faced, let people who are 18 smoke in front of prople who are not 18 and they smoke. [t-14]

2b. Then why do they let the teachers smoke? (Personally, what I think—all right) [g-3]

2c. I think the teachers are justified and it's something the seniors have to decide amongst themselves. (Now, say that again). The teachers are justified, and it's something the seniors have to decide amongst themselves. [b-11]

3a. Like what, say? [t-11]

3b. They have to decide amongst themselves the problem, it's not the teachers' problem. We wanted the rights, now we have to decide how to get 'em back. The teachers were justified. [b-18]

3c. In taking them away, you mean? [b-1]

3d. Yeah. [b-1]

3e. Get out of here! [g-1]

3f. I was there, I saw it happen! They're justified. [b-3]

3g. (-) they are so fair! (-) [s-10]

4a. Let me ask you something—was somebody smoking out there? [t-5]

4b. No, they didn't catch anybody. [b-2]

5a. No, I didn't ask that. (It's on tape!) Was somebody smoking out there? [t-8]

5b. No, nobody was smoking out there. Somebody came—(what?) somebody went off campus and they came back in a car, and then they got out of the car, and I guess they reeked of pot. [b-13]

6a. You know, the way I understand the problem is—and correct me if I'm wrong—the way I understand the problem is, out in back, there's been some trouble with smoking, and the seniors have been trying to do something about it, but the people who smoke out there won't listen. [t-17]

6b. Right. Right. [g-1]

6c. Well, maybe it's because they don't care if they have the privileges or not. [g-3]

6d. Right. [b-1]

6e. Maybe it's because they have "nic fits" during the day, and they have to have a cigarette, or they go nuts. (Now, say that again.) [b-6]

6f. I'd like to see if you smoked cigarettes regularly, I'd like to see you put off—what?—8 hours or something like that. [b-6]

6g. From 8:00 in the morning till 3:00 at night—till 3:00. I just—it's very hard to handle. [b-7]

7a. What if they said—what if they said, "I'll tell you what, I don't know how you're going to work this out, we can't make anybody stop smoking, but the rule that they've given us is that we don't smoke out in back"—You don't smoke out in back? [t-12]

7b. You smoke in the john, you get busted, get probation. [b-3]

8a. Well, what if they say, "Well, that's your choice, but at least outside let's don't smoke"—what would happen with that? [t-5]

8b. What's the difference? [b-1]

8c. You know what would happen with that. They'd say, "All right, don't smoke outside, smoke in the johns." The minute they'd say that, OK, all the teachers would be in the john, every mod. [b-11]

8d. You'd see the teachers walking in the johns. [b-2]

9a. OK, I can understand that. [t-2]

9b. So then you go back outside again. [b-2]

10a. What do the people—the rest of the seniors in here who don't smoke—what do you say to Joe? (Shh!). Ingrid, say it, what do you say to Joe? [t-12]

10b. Quit! Smoking. If you're a freshman, sophomore, and junior, you just can't be outside, to go out and smoke, you just smoke in the johns. So why can't you continue to smoke in the johns? I don't smoke. [g-14]

11a. Does anybody else have anything to say to Joe and to Mark about smoking? [t-5]

11b. They should quit smoking cigarettes and only smoke the good stuff. (laughter) (Say that again.) They should quit smoking cigarettes. They're bad for 'em anyway, they'll just kill 'em. They should just smoke what's good for 'em. [g-14]

12a. Well, you know—let me respond to that as somebody who is a smoker. You know, I think you know, last year I smoked like a stuffed hog and I quit in April. (Cigarettes?) Cigarettes. And my wife and kids, my wife and kids got on my tail, and I know what it's like. It was—you know, I could say, "Yeah, sure, I'll quit"—but it was very hard. And finally, to this day, I don't jokingly say, "Well, ah, that's easy." Because I know for a fact that I could pick up a cigarette right now and I could start puffing away. But I personally don't think that that's the question. My question is, is that we have a back out there, and we have a few people who smoke, and we've got other people who don't smoke, and the rules say, "Don't smoke." And I hear a senior class saying, "We don't know what to do—how do we make them stop smoking?" [t-57]

12b. All right, there was an assembly and they said, ah, "The reason that everybody's privilege gets taken away is because you're supposed to be responsible enough to go over to that person and tell him to put it out", right? (Yeah) All right, you go up to Eric and say, "Eric, put out your cigarette." What's he gonna do? He'll pick you up and throw you on the roof. (What, Anne) [b-20]

12c. I did that! I was sitting next to him and he started lighting up a cigarette, and I said, "I wish you wouldn't do that, because we're all going to suffer." And he goes, "Well, I won't get caught." [g-8]

12d. Well, I wanna know why— [b-2]

13a. Well, is the answer then to that struggle—if there's not supposed to be any smoking out there—is the answer to that struggle to say, "Well, we can't do anything"? [t-10]

13b. I think—you can't take away everybody's privileges, because it's awful hard to make everybody stop. Just bust the people who are smoking out there. Just give them quads. (ss- -).

'Cause it's really not fair to take away everybody's privileges. [g-15]

13c. 'Cause if we wanna take the chances, then we should suffer the consequences. (OK, go ahead, Barb) [b-5]

13d. I was going to say, like, they should have that seniors—like, I dunno, who's the senior advisor?—like if I would see a kid out there smoking, I could give him a quad for it. [g-12]

13e. Oh yeah, sure! (-) give him a quad. [s-9]

13f. Because that's how it is, like in band, like if you're an officer, you can give a quad to anybody in band if they're doing something that's not right. (OK) But like, you would give it to them, maybe it wouldn't stick or something. [g-14]

13g. Barb, what do you think of narcs? What do you think of narcs? They're two-faced— [b-8]

13h. No one would want to do that. [g-3]

13i. No one would want to do that, because they tried to get a committee together to watch kids and stuff, and there were no volunteers. You don't want to fink on your best buddy. [g-6]

13j. That would start a lot of fights in the school, though. [b-3]

14a. What if somebody came by to you and said, "Listen, I'll tell you what, it's about time that you started to act Christian about this"—How would you define a Christian behavior in something like this? Can it be defined? [t-15]

14b. Yeah, it could, but you'd have to think about it. [b-2]

15a. OK, let's look at it in terms of the smokers. Is there such a thing as a Christian behavior in terms of the smokers? How would the smokers respond? (Christian behavior?) If you identify—I'm not saying that it can be, but I'm asking a question. [t-14]

15b. Let the smokers go in the john and do it, so if they get caught, it's their responsibility—it's not everybody else'll get in trouble. [g-7]

15c. That's right. We'll take our own—if we get caught, it's our fault, not anyone else's. (OK, Barb) [b-4]

15d. Yeah, do not smoke out there where everybody else in the school (-). You got to have respect for that, you know? [g-8]

16a. What's the Christian response to the people who are out there? Or who are not smokers, who are not smokers? [t-6]

16b. Tell 'em, "Man, get out of here with that." I mean, "You're gonna get us all in trouble." [g-6]

17a. What's the Christian response—if you go up to somebody

who's sitting down there smoking, and you say, "Hey, stop smoking," and they say, "Bug off"—? [t-9]

17b.   (-) wrath of God. (The wrath of God? All right, let me—Barb?) [s-5]

17c.   I was just wondering, like—I dunno, this might be kinda dumb and stuff—but, OK, like, people go up in front of the church— well, I think it's two people—OK, they go up in front of church and they always say how much Christian they are, and stuff like that. And then like, just now you were talking about— the way it sounded to me was—like you said, "What is the Christian attitude to people who smoke?" So, does that mean if you smoke, you're not a Christian? [g-29]

18a.   Well, I—that's a good question. [t-3]

18b.   There's no sin against smoking. (What?) There's no sin against smoking. [b-5]

19a.   Does that mean if you don't smoke, you're a better Christian, then? [t-3]

19b.   It doesn't mean that you're a worse one. [b-2]

19c.   SILENCE (3 secs) [x-3]

19d.   And just like I hear 'em, like I know these two people and they talk about, they go off and get bombed and stuff. And like, I dunno if that's (A good question that we might struggle with—) Christian or not, that's what I'm saying. [g-14]

19e.   I remember something you said, Larry (LARRY-TEACHER), a while ago—I think it was right in the beginning of class where you were explaining Christian relations, OK, to the class. (Yeah.) And you said that you were hitching and you got a ride or something like that. And you were sitting in the back seat of the car. (Yeah.) And you brought out a cigarette, and the lady said, "You're defiling the Holy Temple of God," and she offered you a stick of gum, and you said, "No, it'll rot my teeth." Same thing! [b-24]

END.   That's true. With that in mind—/END/ 10 mins, 14 secs.

A3. PR ON MULTIPLE PERSONALITY

1a.   Look, we've got a woman that we're responsible for at the moment. She has three personalities—good Lord, it's hard enough having one! How are we going to help her deal with three? (Christy, try it) [t-13] (teacher-13 secs)

1b.   Have the two personalities helping the one that was most aware of the other personalities. [g-9] (girl - 9 secs)

2a.   Who knew who? (Anthony) [t-2]

2b.   Eve Black knew Eve White. [b-2]

3a.   Eve Black knew Eve White— [t-2]

3b.   And Jane knew . . . both of them. [b-4]

4a.   Jane knew both of them. Who did Eve White know? [t-3]

4b.   Neither/none of them. [s-1]

5a.   Neither of them. Neither of the other two. (Duane) [t-2]

5b.   Then why couldn't Eve Black come out any time she wanted to? [b-4]

5c.   She did! [g-1]

5d.   (-) [s-4]

6a.   I don't recall that, but it's probably true. She—why do you think that happened?—she could come out any time she wanted to. [t-8]

6b.   Because (-). [s-3]

7a.   Why? [t-1]

7b.   'Cause Eve White was more dominant, I guess. [b-3]

8a.   Eve Black was more dominant. [t-2]

8b.   Uh-uh. Eve White was. (-) (Wait a minute!) [s-7]

8c.   Jane knew Eve Black. It was Eve Black and Jane that knew each other. Eve White didn't know nobody. [g-7]

8d.   But she was still more dominant than the other two. [b-4]

9a.   Was not Eve Black the extrovert, the kind of sleazy, "Hiya, Doc, how ya doin' man?"—kind of person? [t-8]

9b.   (laughter) (-). (OK, now wait a minute. Hold it . . .) (BELL) [s-6]

10a. So, Eve White the quiet introvert, was the most dominant. OK, now we're back to the question. We're trying to solve, with the little bit of psychology that we have—we know it's dysfunctional to have three personalities—we want to help this woman to have one personality. How—what might we do? (Gabriella) [t-21]

10b. I think you could try to, ah, get Eve White to see herself as Eve Black, and ah, once she sees herself like this, then, whatever's causing this, split personality, she might try and deal with both of them, and make both one personality, and change it. Because, I wouldn't knock them out, I would combine them. [g-28]

11a. Do you think there'd be an advantage of knocking them out? [t-3]

11b. Yeah, If you knocked both out. [g-4]

12a. If you knocked Eve White and Eve Black out, and left Jane? [t-4]

12b. Well, aren't Eve White and Eve Black Jane? [b-3]

12c. (-) [s-3]

13a. What would be the danger of that? Why not, as one solution, why not destroy the first two—if you had the psychological tools—and leave Jane? [t-11]

13b. That's what we want to do. [g-5]

14a. That's what you want to do? [t-1]

14b. That's why I'd combine them, you know—Eve Black and Eve White. But you can't do that. [g-6]

15a. Well, supposing you have the tools? In other words, supposing you have the psychological knowhow to knock out two personalities. Now, from what you know, is that a good idea? [t-9]

15b. Yeah, I think so/I don't think so. (Duane) [s-3]

15c. Wouldn't she gain another personality? (Say that again) Wouldn't she gain another personality? [b-9]

16a. How do you know—that's a good question—how do you know she wouldn't gain another personality? You got rid of Black and White; you got Jane left; how do you know she wouldn't get another one? [t-11]

16b. (-) (Mitchell) [s-3]

16c. I said, how do you know that the two that you knocked out, and the one that you left, are suitable?—the one that's left is—the original one? [b-9]

17a. I don't know. (Yvonne) [t-3]

17b. OK, now, first I would—if I was the psychiatrist, I would go all the way back to her childhood. And I'd find out from her how she was—not from her but, you know, through other sources—ask them exactly how was she as a child, even when she was one or two years old, because it did say that, in the book, that her split personality started as far back as a child. I mean, as far back as when she was a child, she used to do, you know—get into different things. Then I would—I wouldn't knock out— [g-42]

18a. Stop there for a moment, Yvonne. Supposing you take this approach—what do you expect to find? If you have a grown woman winding up in your office with three personalities— what do you expect to find back there in her childhood? [t-16]

18b. Something that could have flared up or something. [g-4]

19a. Like what? [t-1]

19b. I don't know! That's what we're looking for! [g-3]

20a. OK, come on, let's find it! (Mike) [t-2]

20b.   You'd probably expect to find problems she had at home, you know—like mistreatment from her parents. [b-7]

21a.   How would that— [t-1]

21b.   'Cause, ah, like it set up, like, insecurity—and she might look for something else inside herself to compensate for that, so she developed a new personality. (OK, Darryl) [b-12]

21c.   OK, like getting back to the childhood thing—like see who her idols were. See where the person had her idols. [b-12]

22a.   OK, but how would that—if you found out who her heroes or her idols were, what would that have to do with splitting off into two personalities? (Terrence) [t-9]

22b.   Wouldn't you want to try and be like your idol? You know, if you were idolized, you know, you were more or less one of the big idols, to a certain point. Then like, ah, she had an auntie that was shot, and you know, she admired her for the way she was—maybe she'd be shot down as long as she's like her auntie. She'll go home and see that her mother is a nice housewife. She'd want to be like that. Or somebody else— her friends—something like that. [b-35]

23a.   We all experience what you just said! How come—so it— don't we? (Yeah.) How come she wound up in such a, such a dump? [t-11]

23b.   Well, wouldn't that be some kind of restrictions in her background that wouldn't allow her to do that, such as her parents not letting her do something, to the point that she had to, like, ah— [g-14]

24a.   Did you see the movie? [t-1]

24b.   No. [g-1]

25a.   No. OK, something like that is suggested in the movie—that the trauma was so great that it caused the creation of a new personality. (Duane) [t-10]

25b.   It could be like—you want to do something like that, (-) go with the stronger personality. (-) a person, you know, like is reading a lot of books and stuff like that. (-) "I want to be just like her." [b-26]

26a.   OK, I think you'd have to put that together with trauma. That kind of idea, that several of you have expressed, put that together with trauma. In other words, if you try to imitate as a little child, your idols, and you were severely punished for it—this is just one general example—then, for whatever reasons, you might be forced to split in two. I think that's the only way I can put it together—it's been a long time since I read that. (Yvonne) [t-33]

26b. OK. Isn't it true that whatever your conscious mind turns out, your subconscious reacts, don't it, right? Now, say she's saying to herself—she's getting it in her mind that she wants to be just like that lady, and her subconscious mind's gonna pick up on that and react on that, and she's gonna start acting like a certain person, doing the same kind of things that certain person do, you know—she's gonna pick up that personality, act that person. [g-37]

27a. You're working—we're working on one model now, aren't we? We're working on the idol model. I wonder if there are others. (Mike) [t-10]

27b. There's got to be others, 'cause you can have a personality that you develop under, you know, constant conflict. Like a child might be exposed to two opposites and it's always rehearsing, it's always going on, over and over and over again. OK? The child might be split into each one of those worlds, in order to deal with it. [b-22]

28a. OK, good. That wasn't in the book, either. If there's so much conflict—if there's so much conflict, you might have to shift gears without even knowing it, just to protect the self—is the model that he's using, the conflict model. (Anthony) [t-15]

28b. What about like, an overprotective parent and stuff? Like, you can be very shy and things like that. And maybe she had parents that told her, you know, that she shouldn't go out with no guys, or nothing like that. (-) that wasn't the kind of person she was. She was a little more outgoing. And maybe when she was young and that, maybe that (-) her parents had a real overpowering effect on her. That could change her. [b-31]

END. OK, how many of you read *I Never Promised You a Rose Garden?*—Hannah Green's book. /END/ 10 mins., 16 secs.

A4. SN ON SEX IN HOMELIFE

1a. Someone else want to address themselves? What were the patterns of behavior in your family in regards to these three things? (Tony) [t-6] (teacher-6 secs)

1b. In my house, they were very strict on the kids, they didn't wanna talk about sex or nothing like that. They did touch each other, express affection. [b-11] (boy-11 secs)

2a. They would do that. [t-1]

2b. Yeah. But they wouldn't talk about it with us. We learned it off the street. [b-6]

3a. So you're saying that your parents never sat you down and talked to you about sex. [t-4]

3b. (-) You know, I learned it off the street. [b-7]

4a. OK, we'll talk about that. That's another question—What did you learn about sex off the street?—What about nudity? [t-6]

4b. That was nothing, like—ah, you know (-) [b-12]

5a. That was sort of natural. [t-1]

5b. NO RESPONSE (7 secs) (Larry) [x-7]

5c. Are you talking about when we were kids? [b-11]

6a. Or even today, though. It's safer to talk about ten years ago, you know. [t-4]

6b. Because—well, what was it? [b-5]

7a. Nudity, talk about sex, and physical affection. [t-7]

7b. Yeah, talking about sex, that was—it was there, but it was controlled. [b-6]

8a. Controlled? [t-1]

8b. I mean, it was kinda, you know, like—it wasn't like now, you know, when you couldn't even mention anything about sex. It wasn't like that. [b-9]

9a. It wasn't that strict. [t-1]

9b. Because my cousin would make jokes and all that. (-) Like I was saying, it was always under control. (-) little kids. [b-13]

10a. It was more open. Is that what you were saying? Were you saying there was more freedom to talk about it the older you got? [t-7]

10b. No, it's just what we talked about. [b-3]

11a. The kinds of things you talked about. [t-2]

11b. Yeah . . . [b-3]

12a. What about affection? [t-1]

12b. Yeah. I mean, it's not like I'd see my folks naked on the couch, no. (laughter) [b-9]

13a. Right. So, quickly, one problem I know I have when I think about this question, I can't ever imagine my parents having sex, or whatever. But the thing is, you know, at least the kids—my parents had 10 kids, so I know they went to bed together at least 10 times. You know. (laughter) You know, but I still have this trouble connecting that—the reality. [t-25]

13b. Yeah, I have that trouble, too. I just couldn't—remember I was saying that they showed signs of affection. But (-) children. (Right. OK, Marilyn.) [b-11]

13c. In our family, you know, we have something like, we sit down and talk about sex. (-) to understand it, the way the oldest ones— [g-12]

14a. You all do this together. [t-1]

14b. Yeah, my mother and father and all the rest of us. And just like he said, "Control." In a way I understand, because you have to specialize what you mean, you can't use slang, like vulgar language (or street language). Yeah, you can't use that. But you can express, "What do you mean? What is this?" [g-21]

15a. So there's a time, you're saying, for questions and answers? [t-3]

15b. Um-hm. [g-1]

16a. I don't know, you seem to feel good about that. [t-2]

16b. In a way, yes, 'cause (-). (Larry) [g-11]

16c. That's—something like that I think is good, too, because it makes for more openness amongst members of the family also, in a sense, you know. (-) [b-10]

17a. Helps to tie it up. . . . (Laughter) (John) [t-1]

17b. My parents talked—(Talk louder). They talked to me about this, you know. They'd discuss about sex and all that. But I feel like—a lot of times I feel uncomfortable talking about sex. I know that (-) takes place. (laughter) [b-23]

18a. You're saying they're willing to talk to you, though. [t-2]

18b. Right. [b-1]

18c. See, and in my case, what they're telling me, I know something that they don't know. Because, they have (-) and you look at them seriously and all that. (-) And I want to get their attention. 'Cause if I try to correct her, she doesn't believe me. [b-20]

19a. She won't listen. [t-1]

19b. Right. So I feel, I get angry with her, you know. [b-5]

20a. So, even though she's willing to talk about it, it still sounds strained, right? (Jackie) [t-4]

20b. (-) talk about sex (-) (Among yourselves.) (-) You know what I mean? (Name) [g-25]

20c. In my family situation, (-) [b-10]

21a. Like you were saying, you learn a lot from your older brothers and sisters. (Alvin, are you agreeing? OK, Shawn) [t-4]

21b. One thing I don't understand, you know, like in my family, even though my mother—I know my father is different—but my mother and my sister are all real close, you know. I mean, talking about sex is nothing in my house— [g-17]

22a. Pardon me, Shawn. (MESSENGER INTERRUPTION) OK, I'm

sorry for that, Shawn. Hey, let's settle down. I'm sorry for that interruption. [t-19]

22b. That's OK. I don't understand why (-) talk about. My mother talked about it like talking about going to a dance or something. (Like the weather.) It's no big deal. (Right.) I mean, I can remember she telling me about sex when I was about 8 years old. [g-16]

23a. How did you react as an 8-year-old? [t-2]

23b. I think I was curious, you know. [g-3]

24a. Did you ask her? [t-1]

24b. I think I used to ask her questions. And my mother, she says, "Look—" she said, she rather for me to ask her than ask somebody off the street. Because she said, now if I come home pregnant, she said, "I told you so." I mean— (laughter) [g-12]

24c. My mother—it's no big deal. I'll go home and talk about it tonight, you know. [g-5]

25a. You talk with her about the class? [t-1]

25b. Oh, yeah, all the time. [g-2]

26a. What did she say? [t-1]

26b. She didn't say nothing. She just say, "Oh, yeah?" (laughter) (Sharee) [g-3]

26c. Like, in my house there's not too much talk about it. Like, if you bring it up, you know, like my father, he'll go back into the (-). You know, and stuff like that. He'd never bring it up. When they did bring it up to me, I didn't hardly know about it, so I just sat there and listened. (laughter) [g-26]

27a. So you're saying that your dad goes off on these tangents, talking—what?—telling stories, or— [t-7]

27b. Yeah, or (-) [g-11]

28a. OK, so you're saying they're not so willing to listen or hear your story. [t-3]

28b. Well, my mother, she like, she's sort of open, she realizes that she can't go back (-) everything. So she's real different from my father. (-). (Shan) [g-17]

28c. It's just like sort of—(Speak up.) Just like, sort of like Shawn (-). When I was young, (-) hospital, OK? (-) so I was pregnant, OK? (-) They told me, "To get circumcized." And I said, "What's circumcized?" (laughter) You know, I was real, awful young, you know? (-) She said, "OK, sit down," so we talked about it, you know? (-) We talk about it. (-) We don't have no certain time. [g-66]

29a. It's not a traumatic event. [t-1]

29b. It becomes a little bit lighter, that's what I want to say. [g-3]
END. Let's go on to the last topic. /END/ 9 mins, 54 secs.
[sn-END]

A5. WB ON PARENT–CHILD RELATIONS

1a. I don't think they're totally incompatable, the things you're
saying. I just think there are two different ways of looking at
them. OK? I mean, I think when you say that you're being
led to really kinda make your own way more, I think that's
a response to that you really are being influenced by a lot of
forces beyond—you have to respond to a lot of things beyond
your family, beyond the small society. You know? And I think
that's what he was saying, that in the past we tended to be
limited in those sorts of situations, whereas now we really do
need to go beyond our family, to be able to deal with those
situations, those influences for growing earlier on, maybe.
Does that fit, do you think? OK, good. (Regina) (t-46) [teacher-
46 secs]

1b. I don't see what Paul and Steve said as two separate ideas. I
think that both of them approve of the way things have happened in the past and the future. And that's why I said that
in the past, you know, I think that our generation was led to
believe that, well, the teen-agers, they were young adults, like.
The parents were very strict on them. At that point, I remember my father telling me that people were never allowed
to contradict their parents, whatever they say, it was accepted,
and you weren't able to ask or even think on your own to
see if it fit. And I think that, well, I do think that they had a
little bit more respect for not only their elders but their peers,
too. You know what I mean? (um-hm) And like today, I feel
as though we've made some improvement, but we still like,
slip back in a slump because, well now our communication
is more open, we are able to question, you know, what our
parents say, and disagree with it, and everything like that. I'm
not saying that it'll work, but you know we can bring it up,
not that we're backed down. And we have—even though we
improved it that way, we still, we don't have as much respect
as for other people or our friends. So I don't look at it as a
separate idea, I think both of them are, you know, a combination. (g-23) [girl-83 secs]

2a. All right, in a way you're taking it in a different element, you know, I think more kinda personal relationships, (-) for one another. But not in the (-) case, because you're saying that there's more—could I ask you why do you think—I mean, I would presume that you think it is good that there is some more opportunity for young people to really voice their own opinion. Why do you think that's important, or necessary, now? (t-32)

2b. I think so because, well, in that way, as being taught something, you understand it. There's a difference in being told to do something, understanding it, and being told to do something and doing it because you're afraid of what might happen if you don't. And I feel as though my parents, they were told to do different things then, certain situations were good for them, because this was their parents talking to them, you know, and they weren't going to defy them. Well, if I have another way of thinking, and my mother or father told me to do something, I'm going to question them. Even if I end up doing it, or if I don't, I still have the priority to question, to think through it. (g-39)

3a. Good, OK, good. I think that's, you know, a really clear analysis. Do you feel that—do your parents themselves even agree that they think maybe it's better that you be able to really question them at times? (t-16)

3b. In my family situation? (g-1)

4a. Well, yeah, our parents in general, if you want. (t-3)

4b. It's kinda difficult, because my mother seems to be more of a liberal, I guess you would say, and she goes along with me more and I learn an awful lot from her. But my father—and I can't blame him for it—is like, he can only do what he's been taught. And from his parents I know some things I can't say to him, a lot of things I can't question him on. He's more a "I said it, you do it." (g-23)

5a. OK, good. That's a really good illustration there. (Steve) (t-4)

5b. I agree with her almost all the way up until the end, where she said it should be partly a responsibility of ours. I think the parent should have—there's not enough respect, is what I was trying to say. I feel it should be back the other way. The other way you don't figure out—you lose respect for the parents, let's see, by—you question them. The other way, if you don't question them, you always have somebody to look up to for one answer. (All right. Anna.) (b-30)

5c. (-) But I wasn't arguing with (father). (laughter). (-) And he said, "No." And I just wanted to know why, you know, what he thought. And he started yelling at me, like, why am I arguing with him? "I'm not arguing with you, father, I really want to know why. (-) (g-50)

6a. How do you mean? (t-1)

6b. I was wondering "why?" (-) It's OK, that's human nature. (g-7)

7a. OK, yeah, I mean I don't think that it necessarily is disrespectful. I think it's probably good. I think some people might be just kinda protective. People do try to get into arguments. But—it's human. But there's sometimes people do this want to egg somebody on, to see how they would answer something. But at the same time I think it's legitimate sometimes to just want to know what they think. But that's not like other people do it, so—(-) apparently with her father there are certain limits. (Tommy) (t-45)

7b. You can have all the respect in the world for your parents, but there's no reason why you shouldn't be able to voice your opinion on what you think is right, if your parents don't agree with you. Or sometimes the only reason for talking like that is you're at the age where you should be able to, like if you don't agree with your parents, ask them why. You're not little kids where you have to snap to do everything that they say. (b-24)

8a. All right, how do you maintain the respect? Steve was—you know, that's another problem. Is there a way to really ask for the reasons and that sort of thing without being disrespectful? And where your parents can really maintain their decision as your parents without having to simply say, "Well, I said so, that's gotta be the way it is"—? (Do you want to talk about that?) (t-26)

8b. You don't really lose no respect for them by questioning them. If they tell you to do something, you could ask them why you want to do it and they'll tell you. But if they still want you to do it, you still gotta do it no matter what. No matter what the reasons, if they tell you to do it, you gotta do it. (b-14)

9a. So in the end, the respect might come from accepting their wisdom, whether you understand it or not, huh? (t-7)

9b. My parents will say (-). (b-12)

10a. OK. And yet, you know, as Regina was saying, in the past it did tend to be more like that, that parents were considered kinda total authorities, and I mean, it seemed like it wasn't a completely impossible situation for people to live like that, for long times. And yet for us, it just doesn't seem quite right if you don't have at least the opportunity to hear the reasons why your parents do what they do, or— (t-32)

10b. (-) (Ok. Chris) (s-4)

10c. (-) our family has respect and all that kind of thing. When my parents ask us to do something, like housework, there's no question, because you know housework has to be done. Well, if it does come to questioning why do they do things they do, you're free (P.A. BELL). Both my parents, they didn't have, when they were children, they didn't have the strict parents, "you have to do this, that's it." My mother was in the hospital all her life, my father was in an orphanage. They never had the strict parents. So when it came to us, we were just like, they treated us as little people (-). I dunno, there was always respect. And yet whenever we wanted it (-), you know, they like to hear what we didn't understand. (OK, good. Tommy). (g-66)

10d. Like, most parents when they say, "Don't question whatever I say," I think that's a cop-out, because there could be fault in what they're saying and they don't want you to find fault because they want the human authority. (OK, Regina) (b-17)

10e. I think he has a point of view or whatever, but I think, taking from what Chris said, that that shows the point of view that parents are human too. And they relate to situations only from what they have been taught. And the way Chris' parents were brought up, it's easy for them to relate to her and understand her feelings, because it sounds like a situation they were in, they probably, you know, had a lot of care and understanding given to them. And just like—I don't know what his name is—but just like he said, some parents are "Listen to what I say, and you have to do what I say," and everything—this is because that's the kind of atmosphere they were brought up when they were children. And if you just keep on harping at your parents, what else they going to do? They've been living like that for—what?—30–40 some odd years. You can't bring them up all over again. So, like it's a situation you have to bear with. You have to try and deal with it on your own. (g-60)

END. All right. I think this is really a good illustration of how the family, let's say, really shows the differences partly just in historical development. /END/ 10 mins, 48 secs.

Author Index

Subject Index